Created and Directed by Hans Höfer

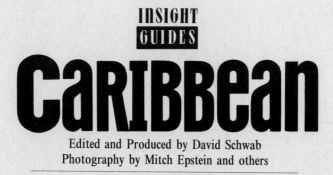

INSIGHT GUIDES

CARIBBEAN

Edited and Produced by David Schwab
Photography by Mitch Epstein and others

HOUGHTON MIFFLIN COMPANY

APA PUBLICATIONS

CARIBBEAN

Second Edition (4th Reprint)
© 1994 APA PUBLICATIONS (HK) LTD
All Rights Reserved
Printed in Singapore by Höfer Press Pte. Ltd

Distributed in the United States by:
Houghton Mifflin Company
222 Berkeley Street
Boston, Massachusetts 02116-3764
ISBN: 0-395-66184-6

Distributed in Canada by:
Thomas Allen & Son
390 Steelcase Road East
Markham, Ontario L3R 1G2
ISBN: 0-395-66184-6

Distributed in the UK & Ireland by:
GeoCenter International UK Ltd
The Viables Center, Harrow Way
Basingstoke, Hampshire RG22 4BJ
ISBN: 9-62421-051-9

Worldwide distribution enquiries:
Höfer Communications Pte Ltd
38 Joo Koon Road
Singapore 2262
ISBN: 9-62421-051-9

ABOUT THIS BOOK

Insight Guide: Caribbean is a detailed, knowledgeable and often lyrical profile of some of the more magical islands of that enchanted sea. Following the tradition of other Insight Guides published by Apa, *Caribbean* brings together precise, journalistic writing, helpful, specific information and colorful illustrations in a new concept of literature for contemporary travelers. This formula was compounded in 1970 by **Hans Höfer**, a German-born exponent of the Bauhaus tradition of design, print and photography. After his first, highly successful *Insight Guide: Bali*, Höfer has supervised the publication of a long series of prize-winning guides that take travelers around the world and into its cities and regions.

As with other Apa books, *Caribbean* is the product of the devotion and hard work of a team of skilled journalists, poets, photographers, novelists and historians.

This project began with Editor **David Schwab**, a free-lance journalist and frequent Caribbean traveler who first moved into the Apa orbit after writing a chapter for the Insight Guide to New York. It was his task to assemble the creative talent for this guide.

The book's principal photographer, **Mitch Epstein**, was born in Mt. Holyoke, Massachusetts, in 1952 and studied at the Rhode Island School of Design and Cooper Union at New York. He has had several one-man shows in New York City and is included in several major photo collections including The Museum of Modern Art and the Biblioteque Nationale in Paris. His most recent book is *In Pursuit of India*.

Also included in this book are the photographs of **Amanda Weil**, who took off a few weeks from her studio to explore every inch of the Virgin Islands. You can also find her work in Apa's *Insight Guide: Greece*. **Edmond Van Hoorick's** contributions in this volume were carefully selected to enhance it from his copious collection of high quality slides.

Gordon Lewis, Professor of Political Science at the University of Puerto Rico, is *the* authority on all things that concern Caribbean history and politics. His books include *The Growth of the Modern West Indies* and *Grenada: The Jewel Despoiled*. In this book, he has composed a masterly account of the history of the Lesser Antilles.

Charles Seibert, the author of the U.S. Virgin Islands chapter is a "have pen will travel" writer. He has written a number of travel pieces for *Esquire* and *Granta* and his poetry has appeared in the *New Yorker*.

Elaine Campbell's doctoral dissertation, *West Indian Fiction: A Literature of Exile*, reflects her interest in West Indian multiculturalism, in Caribbean writing by women, and in the Lesser Antilles. She has published articles on West Indian culture and literature in scholarly journals and is Lecturer in Writing at the Massachusetts Institute for Technology. She resides in Tortola, British Virgin Islands, when not at home in Massachusetts.

Our woman in Anguilla, **Louisa Campbell** is not a stranger to Apa. She was the project editor of *Insight Guide: New York* and her byline is found in just about every medium in New York. She is a respected writer for both print and television, and is also an editor for children's books.

Larry Breiner, professor of English at Boston University, has long been profoundly interested in the Caribbean. He was a resident at the University of West India and has published a book on West Indian poetry.

Schwab   *Alexander*   *Breiner*   *Bissoondath*   *E. Campbell*

Since the early seventies, he has traveled extensively throughout the Caribbean gathering material for his course on West Indian Literature. That passion is evident in his story on St. Martin.

Bob Shacochis, whom *Esquire* called one of the top 100 writers in the United States, is the author of a novel set in the Caribbean, *Easy in the Islands*. He has also written about Grenada and Haiti for the *New York Times Magazine* and *Harpers*. Shacochis, who wrote the St. Barts chapter, has served a few years as a Peace Corps Volunteer in St. Vincent.

Ed Zuckerman is a free-lance writer who has written about Zombies in Haiti, cattle in St. Croix, and killer bees in French Guiana. He is also the author of the critically acclaimed *The Day after World War Three*, a book about the U.S. Government's plans for life in America after a nuclear war. He covered the islands of Saba and St. Eustatius in this book.

The author of the St. Kitts and Nevis piece, **David Yeadon**, has written books on California, New York, Europe and Britain, and travel pieces for the *New York Times*, *National Geographic* and the *Washington Post*.

Our Antigua writer, **Brian Dyde**, is a travel guide writer. After nearly a quarter of a century in the British Navy, he now resides full time in Antigua.

Partly Jamaican in heritage and long interested in West Indian culture, **Elizabeth Alexander** is one of the poets who changed venues for a few weeks for this project. In her story on Montserrat you will find hints of lyricism in her writing as well as a superb insight into the island life.

Maryse Conde, one of the more highly regarded living French writer, poet and novelist, is the author of the chapter on her native Guadeloupe.

Our Dominica author, **Larry Millman**, is a writer of both short stories and novels. His book on the last of the Traditional Irish Storytellers was nominated for a Pulitzer Prize.

With the publication of his book *Digging Under the Mountain*, **Neil Bissoondath** was heralded as one of the major young writers in North America. Raised in Trinidad and Tobago, he is the author of the piece on Martinique.

Rachel Wilder is another Apa editor who picked up a pen again to contribute to this book. Wilder, the project editor of *Insight Guide: Barbados*, wrote, rather appropriately, this book's chapter on Barbados.

Joseph Treaster has been the chief of the New York Times Caribbean bureau since June 1984 and took time off to write two pieces for this book, Grenada and The ABCs. Treaster, who wrote a book on the American hostages held in Iran called *Inside Report on the Hostage Crisis: No Hiding Place,* has won numerous awards for his writing including the Overseas Press Club Award for his coverage of the Columbia volcano disaster.

Liz Saft is another Apa disciple. She was the Editor of the *Insight Guide: Trinidad and Tobago* and wrote the chapter on those two islands for this book.

West Clark served as the troubleshooter for this guide. He wrote the Travel Tips and assisted in the editing.

Much of the book's success must be attributed to Executive Editor **Adam Liptak**. His advice and counsel were vital to the book's completion. A graduate of the Yale Law School and formerly on the staff of *The New York Times*, Liptak worked on the project from its inception through its difficult but successful delivery.

—APA Publications

Dyde

Millman

Treaster

Yeadon

Zuckerman

CONTENTS

History

Places

Maps

TRAVEL TIPS

For detailed Information
See Page 283

WELCOME

Beginning with St. Thomas, The Lesser Antilles extend south in a gentle arc for more than 1,000 miles to their eventual conclusion at the small island of Aruba a few miles off the coast of Venezuela.

What has been written about these islands happens to be true. They comprise some of the most magnificently beautiful acreage on the face of the earth. Within this chain of more than 20 major islands and countless uninhabited cays and islets there seems to be every conceivable shade of blue in the water, every variation of flower, every species of brightly colored bird. The air is balmy and perfumed, the nights are consistently clear, the days inevitably blue. Indeed it seems as if everything, the climate, the waters, the land, is unimaginably perfect.

But in some ways such beauty has been a bit of a curse. The world tends to forget the Lesser Antilles is not one great resort but a collection of small nations, colonies, and territories struggling to forge economic and political identities; that it possesses both a remarkable and often tragic history, and that it has an astonishingly diverse culture.

There is a story told by an English historian about discovering a British school in which there were German nuns teaching native children out of an English textbook which they had to explain in Spanish. A wonderful analogy for a history and culture produced by startling combinations. Begin with two remarkable primitive Indian societies, add the influence of the 16th century gold seeking Spaniards and their European rivals: the French, English, Dutch, even the knights of Malta; add pirates, religious and political refugees, and a huge African slave culture, then stir in Hindus, Jews, and Rastafarians and you have the dizzying recipe that makes up these islands.

It is a land full of surprises. There exits a black society that celebrates St. Patrick's day, a small clan of Huguenots, a reservation of cannibals and a New Bedford like whaling community. You'll find the western hemisphere's second oldest synagogue, voodoo slaves for proud flesh and Hindu cremations. There are chic Parisian villages, English royalty and some of the world's great contemporary writers; V.S. Naipul, Jamaica Kincaid and Derek Walcott.

As the rest of the world becomes less accessible, the Lesser Antilles seems to become more so. In fact because these islands are physically so small, and because their people are, in general, so open, you can easily explore all its realms; political, religious and cultural. What follows will help you map out those explorations.

Preceding pages: outside a photo store, Crocus Hill; Caribbean welcome; end of a race, Anguilla; factory worker takes a lunchbreak, Grenada; dressed for Carnival, Trinidad; a farmer's house, Guadeloupe. <u>Left</u>, Caribbean charm.

INSVLÆ AMERICANÆ
IN OCEANO SEPTENTRIONALI,
cum Terris adiacentibus.

FLORIDA.

GOLFO DE MEXICO.

NOVÆ HISPANIÆ PARS.

YVCATAN.

HONDVRAS.

NICARAGVA.

MAR DEL ZVR.

Ampl.mo Prud.mo Doct.mo Viro
D. ALBERTO CONRADI VANDER BVRCH,
I.C. Resp. Amsterdamensis Senatori, Collegii
Scabinorum Præsidi, Societatis Indiæ, quæ
ad Occidentem militat assessori, et nuper
ad Magnum Moscoviæ Ducem Legato,
Tabulam hanc inscribit Guilielmus Blaeu.

MAR DEL

NORT.

ESPANOLA.

Annllas sive
Camercanæ
vulgo
Caribes
Insulæ

S. MARTHA

VENESVELA

Milliaria Germanica
Milliaria Hispanica

Engraved for Middleton's Complete System of Geography

The first Interview of Christopher Columbus with the Natives of America.

The Lesser Antilles are comprised of a long archipelago of islands that stretches from the British and U.S. Virgin Islands in the north to the ABC islands in the south: Aruba, Bonaire and Curaçao—an arc so overwhelmingly beautiful in its gifts of nature, that, from Columbus on, its discoverers have been tempted to yield up the rest of their lives to its allure.

With the exception of islands like Barbados, which is a coral reef formation, the Lesser Antilles are part of a 1,000-mile (1,600-km) stretch of mountainous volcanic islands with tropical climates and vegetation. They are therefore subject to the vagaries of both volcanic eruption and hurricane assault. The 1902 fireball eruption of Mt. Pelee in Martinique destroyed the then capitol city of St. Pierre in a few brief moments, killing 30,000 people, while in 1977 the eruption of Soufriere in St. Vincent forced the island government to evacuate a large section of its village population for months on end.

Hurricanes, spawned in their breeding grounds somewhere to the East of Barbados, can have an equally deadly impact on the islands. A typical Caribbean hurricane can destroy a whole city in a matter of hours. In 1979 hurricanes David and Frederick destroyed the entire agricultural economy of the small island of Dominica within a few days.

So just as California is earthquake country, the Antilles are volcano and hurricane country. Like Californians, the people of the region seem to accept their geographical environmental hazards with feelings of fatalistic equanimity. They do have their compensations, of course. The trade winds, within a subtropical setting of sun-drenched luminosity, make life comfortable. There is, here, none of the oppressive heat of the Persian Gulf region, or the uncomfortable summer humidity of the Atlantic seaboard area of the United States.

Determined by geography: Geography also had an impact on the economic culture of the islands. A rich, fertile soil, perpetual warmth and adequate rainfall have allowed the cultivation of a wide variety of raw tropical products: sugar, coffee, cocoa, nutmegs, rice, sea island cotton and bananas. For a long time, the best-known of these products was sugar. Just as the economic culture of the American Midwest has centered on corn and that of the Middle East on oil, the economic culture of the Lesser Antilles, until the late 20th century, has centered on sugar. The climatic conditions have sponsored a massive tourist industry, which for many island governments has become the chief source of taxable revenue.

The geographical environment has had two further consequences. The distances between islands are never very great and neighboring islands are often divided from each other by narrow sea passages, like the ones between the Virgins and Puerto Rico, or between Grenada and Trinidad. Once Columbus made his first landfall somewhere in the Bahamas (the particular site is in dispute), it was easy for him to discover the other islands. In the Pacific, Captain Cook, on the other hand, only discovered the Tahiti islands by accident.

This geographical proximity has led, from the very beginning, to massive movements of peoples among the islands, by way of inter-island schooner, steamboat, small inter-island aircraft and, of course, jet airliners. Intraregional migration has been the order of the day. In the Eastern Caribbean, laborers go south to work in the oil refineries of Aruba, Curaçao and Trinidad, and others go north to seek jobs in the tourist economy of the U.S. Virgin Islands. Whole settlements of contract workers, both bonded and illegal, become part of their adopted homes: Antiguans and Kittitians in the Virgin Islands, Grenadians in Trinidad, Haitians in the Bahamas, East Indians in Guadeloupe.

Small-island psyche: Another consequence of the environment might be termed small-island psychology. The populations of the islands are not much larger than a moderately sized small American township. This leads to a sort of psychological insularity of temper. These are small communities tied by close kinship patterns. In economic life, small peasant squabbles over land rights can become vicious and divisive. Yet there also exists a real sense of small island community. The balance between people and their environment is much more human and manageable than in the modern-day metropolis elsewhere. However citified they may become by experiences abroad, most Antilleans are immensely proud of their village or small-town birthplaces. And though the small farmer is disappearing, the individual peasant's dream of returning home to own a small piece of land and a house still remains.

Preceding pages: the Caribbean, circa 1660. **Left,** an 18th Century engraving of Columbus presenting tokens of friendship to a West Indies tribe.

THE COLONIAL PERIOD

Accounts by Spanish *conquistador* historians and other European travelers tell of a vibrant Indian civilization existing before the arrival of Columbus. In fact, much of what is known about the Indians comes from these accounts. Such observations have to be read with care because, with the single exception of Padre Las Casas, the defender of the Indians, they were filled with the *hubris* of a European man who saw the native inhabitants as savage children hardly fit for missionary enterprise. Alternatively, some of the accounts presented the inhabitants of this new world in Utopian terms, in contrast to the decadence of European life. Beatriz Pastor, in *Discurso narratvio de la Conquista de America,* has shown how these psychologically conditioned responses oscillated between two opposite pictures; either savage cannibalism or romantic primitivism. European visitors saw what they wanted to see.

These Indians, Arawaks, Caribs and Tainos lived in fishing and agricultural communities of a quite sophisticated character. Ruled by a chieftain, *cacique,* they possessed their own system of laws and government, based on patriarchical lineage. Their ceremonial grounds indicate complicated games. Their boat technology was advanced. Apparently, they traveled all the way from the Guianas to Cuba, passing through the Lesser Antilles. Perhaps, as many of the European travelers noted, they possessed a folklore and religious cosmic outlook of startling complexity. Unlike the European religions, the Indian religions showed a noticeable lack of concern with the moral problem of good and evil. Man was much more the center of their universe. Human life was governed by the supreme being Yocahu, a God morally indifferent to the wishes of his devotees, who could be reached only through stone idols, *cemis,* inhabited by the spirits of deceased *caciques*. These Indians also believed the natural universe was created by magical effects. For instance, they thought the oceans were created when the mythical father Yaya, killed his rebellious son and placed his bones in the branches of a calabaza tree, only to discover that they spawned a multitude of fish and oceanic waters.

Indian pride: The travelers often wrote of Carib pride. Even Pere Labat, who stigmatized

the Caribs for what he saw as their sloth and idleness, acknowledged their violent feelings of liberty. Such pride made the Indians unreliable servants and fed their open contempt for the social hierarchy of whites and the servile status of the blacks. One anonymous Carib chief remarked to French soldiers, "We have not gone over to your country to take it, so why have you come over to take ours." De la Border reported the Indians as saying, when told that they lived like animals, that the Europeans were more so because they did not live the Carib way. He also noted that the Indians had a horror of clothes equal to the Europeans' horror of nudity.

All of the European observers also remarked on the Carib life of ease, in which all were seen as equal, none richer or poorer than another, restricting their wants to what was necessary. Each man does what pleases him, wrote Labat, and permits no one to give him orders. Finally, there were the travelers who wrote of Indian liberty and love for their island homes. Columbus reported in one of his letters to the Spanish Crown how Taino captives, rescued from their Carib captors, swam ashore at night in order to embrace the soil of their beloved Borinquen (Puerto Rico).

Much of this Indian civilization disappeared under the pressures of European conquest and colonization. English and French soldiers and settlers undertook what were in effect genocidal wars against the native populations of the Leewards and Windwards islands during the 16th and 17th centuries. Today, only a handful of the descendant Indians, the Black Caribs, exist on reservations in St. Vincent and Dominica.

There were two general consequences of the Indian presence in the islands. The first was the growth of a European utopian literature. European writers, using the travelers' accounts, invented the fiction of a natural, idyllic life situated in an imaginary island in the Antilles or the South Seas. Defoe's *Robinson Crusoe* is the best-known example. The second consequence was the refusal of the Indians to become enslaved; very few Arawaks or Caribs were prepared to play Man Friday to the white man's Crusoe. Thus European colonizers turned to the African slave trade for an alternative source of labor power.

Three-century legacy: The 16th, 17th and 18th centuries were the major formative period of the Lesser Antilles. It was a time marked, successively, by war and rivalry, the establishment of settlements and colonies, the introduction of the sugar economy, the organization of the slave trade, the implantation of chattel slavery, the rise of white superiority and the slave rebellions.

Left, early tribal life in the Antilles.

By 1700 the four great powers of Caribbean economic and military aggression—the French, Dutch, Spanish, and English—had established flourishing island and mainland colonies when the Atlantic seaboard colonies of Massachussetts and Virginia were hardly beyond their first stages of settlement. The Europeanization of the islands and of the Spanish Main produced cities rivalling those of Europe in size and magnificence.

Practically every European nation joined in the scramble for control of the region. The Danish kingdom ruled the Virgin Islands group for more than two centuries. The Dukes of Courland once occupied Tobago, and Sweden ruled the island of St. Bart's from 1784 to 1887.

The period of war: To begin, there was the period of war. The early Spanish claim to the Indies was rapidly challenged by its European

victims of the international anarchy brought in by the Europeans. That condition was described in Dutchman Esquemiling's book of 1674, *The Buccaneers and Marooners of America.*

"...*certain it is that no coasts or kingdoms in the world have been more frequently infested nor alarmed with the invasions of several nations than theirs. Thus from the very beginning of their conquests in America, both English, French, Dutch, Portuguese, Swedes, Danes, Courlanders, and all other nations that navigate the ocean, have frequented the West Indies, and filled them with their robberies and assaults.*"

This warlike condition lasted right into the period of the Napoleonic Wars, when the political map of the region was finally settled by the 1815 Treaty of Vienna. As long as it lasted it meant almost uninterrupted insecurity for the islands.

rivals—England, France, Denmark and Holland. The Spanish hegemony was anchored mainly in the Greater Antilles—Cuba, Hispaniola and Puerto Rico—although there was a brief Spanish episode in Trinidad. Because they were the first ports of arrival for the invading European fleets the Lesser Antilles bore the brunt of the inter-state rivalry. They constituted a sort of Atlantic frontier. The massive military fortifications of Havana and San Juan meant that neither Cuba nor Puerto Rico were ever seriously challenged, except for the unsuccessful English attack on San Juan in 1797. Jamaica remained English, uninterruptedly, after its takeover by Cromwell's Western Design war in the 1650s. The ravages of war, then, were felt more by the Lesser Antilles and they, from the very beginnings, were the first

The political ownership of any island could rapidly change. The native populations could wake up any morning to discover that they had a set of new masters. One West Indian historian, Dr. Eric Williams, called it a condition of 'in betweenity'. The island of St. Croix, for example, changed sovereignty at least eight times in a period of less than 100 years, including a brief rule by the Knights Templars of Malta.

A precarious existence: The European powers used the islands as naval stations, like Nelson's Dockyard in Antigua. In fact, the islands' position—stretched like a line of watchdogs across the route between Spain and her seaborne New World empire—made it the scene of perennial warfare between each European colonizing power as it arose within the region and its emerging rivals eager to despoil it of its riches. Indeed, if, as the saying goes, the battle of Waterloo was won on the playing fields of Eton, then it is equally true to say that the battle of Trafalgar was won in the naval stations of the Lesser Antilles. Some of the most decisive battles took place in the region, most notably when Admiral Rodney destroyed the French fleet in the Battle of the Saints off the Windwards in 1782. He then destroyed the commercial port of St. Eustatius, which had become a supply center of gun-running arms for the anti-English forces in the American Revolutionary War. Even today, Statians remember Rodney's sack of their island, the Golden Rock, just as Southerners remember Sherman's burning of Atlanta in the American Civil War.

The governments of both the mother country

Welsh Royalist, the Dutch Jew, Cromwell's transported prisoner, the obscure Spanish soldier, the Puritan merchant-adventurer, the Catholic friar, all crowded into a society of brutal vigor and tropical brilliance, in which personal greed and cupidity could assert themselves free from the caste and class restrictions of Europe.

Profit of paradise: However, the history of the New World, called the Enterprise of the Indies, was not just war. War was simply the prelude to Trade, for the main purpose of the conquest was colonization and profit. The European powers saw their new tropical possessions as an opportunity for enriching the emergent state systems of post-Reformation Europe, Catholic and Protestant. And such capitalism could only develop with peace, not war. For that reason, European chancelleries and war ministries were willing, in

and local colony were forced, often at ruinous expense, to build defenses like the Brimstone Hill fortifications on St. Kitts against such calamities. For the small town populations of the time life must have been marginal and precarious. St. Croix alone, the island center of the Danish West Indies, was occupied in one brief year,1650, by three different European war parties.

Also, every sort of European adventurer ventured to the Antilles eager to obtain his share of the legendary spoils of the New World. The

Far left, an English island lord. **Left**, Governor Woodes Rogers of Bahamas. **Above**, battleships, a constant sight in the 1700s.

the early period, to use their pirates to harass their enemies (Henry Morgan started his infamous career as a British licensed privateer), and then later decided to dispense with them because they had become an anachronism. Governor Woodes Rogers' suppression of the pirate stronghold in New Providence in the Bahamas in 1722 marked the end of Piracy. Once the European powers had more or less settled their respective 'spheres of influence'—Trinidad, for example, was finally ceded to Britain in the treaty of 1763 that ended the Seven Years War—the Lesser Antilles settled down to its socio-economic-cultural development as peripheral economies of the European states. That meant the introduction of sugar as a staple crop and the sugar plantation economy. It also meant the beginning of the slave trade.

The slave trade, which lasted from 1500 to 1860, was the necessary prologue to the establishment of the plantation economy—for the growth of sugar cane on the islands required a large and cheap labor force capable of doing heavy unremitting work under brutalizing tropical conditions.

Of the more than 12 million slaves the majority ended up in Caribbean and Brazilian plantations. Some islands, of course, were unsuited to the enterprise; St. Thomas was too hilly and Curaçao too arid. Yet as trading centers that derived their prosperity from the sugar economy, even those islands were part of the general slavery system. Even the lilliputian islands, like Anguilla, Barbuda and the Grenadines, as dependent wards of large sugar islands, were also affected. In any case, fuelled by the new European insatiable taste for sugar, the islands, with few exceptions, became arrival ports and slave markets.

The horrors of the Middle Passage have been frequently described. Pere Labat wrote of the whiplash marks on the bodies of disembarked slaves as if it were the most natural thing in the world. Another traveler wrote that they were bought and sold in the same manner as cattle. Suffice to say that the plantocrats of the Leewards and Windwards were the most obstinate and vociferous in their opposition to the abolition of slavery, which the British Parliament finally decreed in 1807.

So, the triangular trade, between the African trading posts, the European mid-passage ports and the Antilles, laid the foundations of slavery as a domestic institution in the islands. The leading sugar colonies were in the Greater Antilles: English Jamaica, Spanish Cuba and French Saint-Domingue; but the Lesser Antilles islands also spawned a plantation slave-based economy. Ligon's early *History of Barbados* (1659) described how the small holdings of the early lower-class white immigrants were replaced with large-scale sugar plantations. Later, Richard Sheridan's study of the rise of the colonial gentry in Antigua in the the 18th century showed how no entrepreneur in that society could hope to survive unless he was also a planter-merchant.

Strange melting pot: The entire house of Antillean society was built over this slave basement. It became a strange melting pot of white

colonists, black slaves, indentured servants, freed Indians, Catholics, Protestants, heretics, Jews, transported political prisoners, felons, 'poor whites', all mingled in a fascinating exoticism under tropical skies. It was a *picaroon* world of all colors and creeds, slowly learning to co-exist with each other. Naturally enough, it was a society of ranking status. One 18th century English traveler, John Luffman wrote:

"In the slave society of the Leeward islands at the end of the 18th century, the white minority had successfully imposed its claims to superior status upon the overwhelming black majority of the population, who were generally immobilized without hope of escape in the lowest ranks of the social structure, and upon the growing proportion of people of mixed blood making up the groups of colored freedmen and privileged slaves, who were already occupying the marginal position of a middle class, between the depressed lower class of blacks and the dominant upper class of whites. The social order of the whole community hung upon the distinctions established between its constituent races."

Antillean creole society was then a three-tiered structure, composed of upper-class whites, mulattos or freed persons of color—the consequence of the Antillean miscegenative habits—and slaves.

White plantocracy: Each group had its own pride and prejudices. As numerous visitors noted, the whites were racist. They regarded their slaves as lazy, irresponsible, grossly sexualist, potentially rebellious, and rationally inferior. In turn, they saw the group of 'free coloreds' as social upstarts, presumptuously claiming to be 'white when in fact they were black.' As a class, the white plantocracy was arrogant, racist, and socially gross. In fact, much of its own ancestry in the islands was suspect: Pere Labat noted in Martinique that his slave owner neighbors like Monsieur Roy and Monsieur Verrier were originally engaged servants. These observations hardly made Labat popular in those old creole communities and explains why, after some 14 years, he was recalled by the European Catholic superiors and never allowed to return.

The islands at this time were overcrowded not only with African slaves, but also with the white riffraff of Europe who hoped to become plantation owners and escape their lowly origins. Their skin color gave them a new status in the islands; and their sexual irresponsibility shows how they used it to unscrupulously advance their careers. In this sense, the social history of the islands during this period is in part the sexual exploitation

Preceding pages: a 19th-century romantic interpretation of Columbus. Left, slaves found some relief in music and dance.

of the black woman by the white plantation males, whether overseers, accountants, indentured servants, or even masters. Better, after all, to be a *gran seigneur* in Martinique than a lowly serf in Provence.

This, then, was a three-tiered society, not only racially mixed but also psychologically mixed-up. All of the three groups were trapped in a New World environment from which they could not escape. In order to survive, they had to learn the lesson of mutual tolerance, however fragile it might be. They lived in what became culturally and ethnically pluralist societies, rooted not in will but in force, in order to apprehend the ever present danger of slave rebellion. The fear of rebellion was a brooding omnipresence in the daily lives of the planter class, requiring the almost continuous presence of a friendly naval

Martinique early on developed a small creole middle class of professional elite, while Guadeloupe remained mainly peasant. This distinction survives even to the present day. In the Dutch Antilles, Curaçao became another commercial trade center, while Bonaire developed a small salt-pond industry and became a prison for intractable slaves. All in all, it was this intriguing variety of topography, economy and society which established the *magie antillaise* that caught the attention of the European *conquistadores*, *voyageurs*, and others.

Slavery and the arts have rarely gone together—except, perhaps, in the ancient Graeco-Roman world—and it is not surprising that the Antillean slavocracy became, in its own day, a byword for crass materialism and cultural illiteracy. The notable exceptions were the Codring-

unhy	Domestic	Labourer	Males	Females	Names	Age	Colour	Country	Domestic	Labourer	Males	Females	Names	Age	Colour	Count
bastian	£			1	Ruthy	12½	Black	Barbadian	£			1	Mingo	40	Black	Barbad
"	£			1	Peggy Ann	12½	"	"	£			1	Scipio	57	"	"
"	£			1	Nancy Molly	12	"	"	£			1	Cato	55	"	"
"	£			1	Pamela	11½	"	"	£			1	Typhaw	54	"	"
"	£			1	Eve	11½	"	"	£			1	Apphia	54	"	"
"	£			1	Sally Ann	11	"	"	£			1	Will Solm	30	"	"
"	£			1	Molly Quash	10	"	"	£			1	Jeffrey	26	"	"
"	£			1	Eliza	11½	Coloured	"	£			1	Billy	25	"	

squadron or a reliable home regiment.

From north to south these islands shared a common pattern of colonialism and slavery. Of course, there were differences between the individual islands. For instance, Barbados was English and Guadeloupe French. But there were more subtle differences too. In the north, St. Thomas, under Danish rule, developed from the beginning as an important commercial trade center, while St. Croix, also under Danish rule, developed as a sugar plantation economy. In the south, Trinidad emerged as a Franco-Hispanic Catholic society while Tobago became an English-speaking Protestant society of small farmers and fishing folk. Antigua became a sugar colony while mountainous Dominica had little to do but develop an infant lumber industry. In the French Antilles,

tons, a bajan plantation family which left a trust fund for the education of poor children. Most of the slave-owning class were vulgar to a degree. They lived in continuous fear of slave rebellion. Danish Virgin Islands Governor Gardelin's slave mandate of 1733 was typical in its severity of punishments for slaves guilty of bad behavior, not to mention slaves guilty of rebellious behavior. In the French Antilles the official *Code Noir* of 1785 reflected the negrophobia of the time, listing some 128 grades of color, by which every person in the colony was awarded a status.

Few visitors failed to note the ostentatious display of wealth and the extravagant style of entertainment practised by the planters, one of the causes of their perennial indebtedness. Absenteeism was endemic and plantation profits were sent to the absentee owners in England, who wasted them on a lifestyle of prodigality that disgusted even 18th century observers.

Gens de couleur: Centuries of miscegenation produced the second group in Antilles society, the 'free colored' or *gens de couleur*. They were a highly significant group, in part because they occupied a marginal position between the whites and the slaves. Also, their numbers were growing while the numbers of whites tended to decline. After all, it was a rare white person who did not father colored children, except for the descendents of the Scottish-Irish 'poor whites' of the 17th century, known today as 'Redlegs' in Barbados. The history, then, of the Antilles during much of this period was the story of this mulatto group's struggle for social status and for political and civil rights. The first breakthrough in politi-

ing. They resented their own subordination, but did not resist the social structure of which it was a part. They needed the white group as a role-model in their search for social respectability ,and the whites needed them as allies against slave unrest and, even worse, slave rebellion. The coloreds also had to stay on good terms with the white governments, both local and abroad, in order to gain concessions. A typical example was the remarkable royal edict of 1831 in the Danish Virgins, permitting the legal registration of colored persons as white citizens on the basis of good conduct and social standing. The coloreds responded to those concessions by developing their own extravagant life style, which the government tried to curb. The Danish colonial statute book of the time is laden with measures seeking to punish behavior patterns regarded as presumptuous—

cal rights occurred in the late 18th century in Antigua, when free persons of mixed race possessing the necessary property qualifications were allowed to vote at elections. The same thing took place in Montserrat. This movement was aided by the humanitarian anti-slave trade agitation in England.

This long drawn-out rise of the people of color was important for two reasons. In the first place, though hardly a revolutionary movement, it did revolutionize the society. Like the whites, the mulattoes had important interests in slave hold-

the wearing of precious stones and silk stockings, the holding of masked balls, and the use of ceremonial gunfire at funerals. Social snobbery thus supplanted common racial brotherhood, and the Antillean free coloreds, at least in this formative 18th century period, became known as a group given more to lavish social display than to racial mental activity.

Long, silent revolution: Secondly, what was taking place was a long, silent social revolution. Lafcadio Hearn wrote about the racial drama in his book on Martinique, although it took place in all of the islands.

"The slave race had begun to exercise an influence never anticipated by legislators. Scarcely a century had elapsed since the colonization of the island; but in that time climate and

Left, a register listing slaves, with age and race. **Above**, a typical slave market of the 1800s.

civilization had transfigured the black woman...Travellers of the 18th century were confounded by the luxury of dress and jewelry displayed by swarthy beauties in St. Pierre. It was a public scandal to European eyes."

This drama played itself out in all of the islands. Noticeably and significantly, it was an achievement, before anything else, of the Antillean brown woman, the belle *affranchie*, the *fille de couleur*, the colored lady of the household. She appears in all the prints and engravings of the period, from Martinique to Barbados. Her social ambition, as much as the political ambition of her menfolk, brought about the change. In one way, it could be said that it was a movement of feminist protest, although naturally nobody at the time saw it in such terms.

The third group of Antillean society was, of

We know too little about the daily life of the Antillean slave. As the eminent Caribbeanist Gabriel Debien has said, the report of the Caribbean slave experience comes to us only indirectly, it having been written in the main by others, and those most frequently hostile to the slaves. The African tradition was tribal and oral; only the occasional ex-slave like Equiano wrote accounts of his experience.

The daily experience of the slave, of course, was work in the cane fields and the sugar factories. John Luffman described the typical work discipline as it existed in the Antigua of the 1780s.

"The negroes are turned out at sunrise, and employed in gangs from 20 to 60, or upwards under the inspection of white overseers...subordinate to these overseers are drivers, commonly called dog-drivers, who are

course, the slave population. They were, generally, of West African provenance. Philip Curtin, in his definitive book, *The African Slave Trade*, estimated that from its beginnings in the early 16th century to its termination in the late 19th century, some 12 million Africans were brought to the New World by means of the triangular trade. They arrived as unnamed chattel slaves, later to be renamed by their slave owners and masters, which accounts for the Europeanized names of their descendants. The reversion to African names is a phenomenon of the 20th century Black Power movement. The loss of name was, in a psychological sense, important because it was a part of the total loss of liberty that deprived the African of his right to be regarded as a human being.

mostly black or mulatto fellows of the worst dispositions; and these men are furnished with whips which, while on duty, they are obliged, on pain of severe punishment, to have with them, and are authorized to flog wherever they see the least relaxation from labour; nor is it a consideration with them, whether it proceeds from idleness or inability, paying, at the same time, little or no regard to age or sex."

Slaves at play: Yet there was play as well as work. "Every people," wrote Edmund Burke, "must have some compensation for its slavery." And so, from the very beginning, the slave brought with them their traditions of song and dance. Music played a very large part in the life of the slaves; a music that emerged out of a blending and meeting of both the imported European musical forms and the various African song and dance formulations. Slave musicians incorporated the European forms—the waltz, the mazurka, the polka, the reel and the quadrille, into their own musical events—the fêtes, plays, religious wakes, and early carnival forms. These encounters gave rise to completely new forms of dance and music which became uniquely Antillean.

In the Danish Virgin Islands, the *bamboula*, the dance-drumming style, was used by musicians on socially important occasions. In St. Lucia, there was the *kutumba* and *kèlé* ceremonies, the former primarily associated with wakes and the latter with memorial rites for the ancestors. In the small island of Carriacou, off Grenada, the 'big drum dance' encompassed a large repertoire of distinctive singing, drumming, and dance styles.' In

loupe there emerged the *gwoka*, associated with celebrations of various sorts, including sporting events and parties. In the Dutch Caribbean emerged the musical tradition known as *tambu*, with, once again, call-and-response songs sung in the local creole language, *papiamentu*.

Two examples from literature illustrate the process. At the very end of the 17th century Pere Labat tells of how, on Christmas Eve in Martinique, he saw French Catholic nuns dancing the forbidden *calenda* by themselves in the local church chancel. Just before slave emancipation in the 1830s, Captain Marryat described the pleasing hymn-singing of the Barbadian black and colored Methodist congregations, taken from the English Nonconformist hymnals of the time.

This sort of musicological intercourse was not always amicable. The planters, for example, of-

Left, slaves toiling on a sugar plantation. **Above**, a British emancipation society's interpretation of the horrors of slavery.

Trinidad the *kalinda* or *calenda* dances centered around intricately choreographed stick-fighting. These dances were often accompanied by a stamping tube that was beaten rhythmically against the ground, the *tamboo-bamboo,* an instrument outlawed by the colonial authorities because of its supposed relationship with slave plots and rebellions. In Trinidad there was also the *congo*, or *kongo*, sometimes used at weddings and christenings, and later, the *rada* and *shango,* two forms that employed the well-known African style of call-and-response singing. In Guade-

ten feared the slave's drumming dances were secret calls to rebellion (sometimes with cause). But what took place was an interpenetration of European and African music-religious art-forms that helped to create the modern Caribbean of the present century.

Linguistic amalgamation: A similar process of creolisation took place, during this early formative period, with Caribbean language. If the Lesser Antilles seems to be a hodgepodge of different languages and dialects, it's because the region was a meeting ground for Europe, Africa and later, Asia. The Arawak, Taino and Carib languages were replaced by the new European languages and, a little later, by the arriving African languages. In the New World setting— planter, overseer, slave, with all of their respective duties and obligations—had to learn to understand each other. Society means communication, and communication means language. The problem was solved, *ad hoc*, by the invention of creole *patois* language. Columbus and the *conquistadores* had managed with a few interpreters. But that was too awkward for a permanent relationship and understanding as the New World became a series of settler colonies.

From the beginning, there was a cultural process of linguistic amalgamation. Since different conditions of language contact gave rise to different languages, the process differed from island to island. In Trinidad and Grenada, a form of English strongly influenced by the French-based creole gradually became the majority tongue. In St. Lucia and Dominica, the same French-based creole maintained its position as a mass vernacu-

day. To speak 'bad English' is a mannerism of class prejudice. This prejudice is so entrenched throughout the Lesser Antilles that to speak 'proper English', which means speaking like an Oxford-trained announcer of the British Broadcasting Corporation, is regarded as a mark of social esteem. The irony is, of course, that in England itself that speech snobbishness is now met with much ridicule. Colonial habits remain entrenched long after they have been abandoned in the 'home country.' In short, creole has a long way to go before it becomes respectable.

Religion of slaves: But the most lasting and representative expression of the emergent slave culture was found in religion. From the beginning there was a cultural conflict between the European religions and the African ones. The European man was shaped by the Renaissance and the

lar, although it was later threatened by an English-based dialect. Conditions in Barbados proved to be more favorable to a closer approximation of conventional English—today 'Bajan' English is regarded as one of the 'pure' expressions of colonial English.

Where less favorable conditions were present, as in Antigua, Montserrat and St. Kitts, a language situation described by linguists as a 'postcreole continuum' evolved. In those islands different graded levels of speech showed different degrees of approximation to the standard norm of English. There emerged a tendency for upper-class people, of whatever color, to speak a more standard English and for lower-class people to speak a more creolized form. This low status of the creolized form remains even to the present

Reformation, and later, by the 17th century scientific revolution. The African man was shaped by quite different forces. The one was a literary tradition, the other an oral tradition. For the European man, knowledge sprang from experimentally observed experience; for the African man, it sprang from faith in cosmologic principles not susceptible to experimental proof.

In the early period, Antillean religion was a struggle between these two conflicting universes of discourse. Much of the slave religion was underground and secretive. Later, in the 18th century, a typical process of cross-pollination took place. The European religious missions developed their conversion practices, giving rise to the well-known Antillean systems of black bible Christianity. Those missions included the

Lutherans, the Baptists, the Quakers, the Anglicans, the Methodists and the Moravians. In that process, the mission teachers and preachers weeded out what they regarded as the more objectionable 'pagan' elements of slave belief, such as spiritism; while the slave church and chapel congregations took enthusiastically to the new religious modes of hymn-singing and personal confessional testimony. It was a long uphill struggle. The mission reports to their European superiors make it clear that the missions throughout had to combat two hostile forces: the African *obeah,* with the system of *obeah* practices, and the planter-dominated local Assemblies that saw any kind of education of the slave as a dangerous and subversive enterprise.

These missionaries did little to further the cause of slavery abolition. The missionary societies, and their local agents, had to make their peace with the plantocracy just to get permission to do their evangelizing work. Their message, basically, was one of social quietism. The more general tone of the missions was to teach, conservatively, the duties and obligations of slaves and masters to each other. There were individual exceptions. At the very end of the period, before emancipation, a stubborn and fiery Irish-Catholic priest, Anthony O'Hannan in Trinidad, used his ecclesiastical position to promote the cause of freed coloreds and slaves. In St. Kitts, a Protestant minister, James Ramsay, spent nearly 20 years in the island battling the planters' interest.

Rebellion in many forms: Admittedly, there were no slave uprisings in the Lesser Antilles that matched the tremendous struggle of the slaves of St. Domingue-Haiti who, between 1793 and 1804, defeated the crack regiments of Napolean's army, almost in the manner of Spartacus. But there were sporadic plots, uprisings and revolts, nevertheless, though all failed.

The habit of what was called in the French islands *petit marronage*—of running away from the estate for short periods of time to visit a woman friend, or attend a prohibited church meeting, or just simply to feel a taste of freedom—often escalated into rebellion. Such rebellious attempts, all crushed with severe cruelty,

occurred in St. John in the Danish West Indies in 1733, Antigua in 1736, St. Croix in 1759, Grenada in 1795, and Barbados in 1816. Certainly these rebellions showed that slaves had a capacity for insurrectionary leadership. There were leaders like Tackey and Tomboy in Antigua, who planned to rebel, to kill all the whites, and set up an Ashanti-type black kingdom in the island. There was the woman leader, Nanny Grigg, in Barbados, who told her followers, according to the official record, that the only way to get freedom was to fight for it. Then there was Daaga, who led, although after Emancipation, a brief mutiny of the 1st West India Regiment in Trinidad in 1837. He told his interrogators, on the eve of his execution, that the seeds of the mutiny were sown on the passage from Africa.

Left, aspects of plantation life: main house, mill, slaves, owner, slave huts. Above, the good life of colonials as depicted in 18th Century cartoon.

The slave resistance took on more forms than open rebellion. For instance, there was cultural resistance. The slave populations managed to retain a way of life, in dance, music, and religion, that endured alongside the life of the white minority population.

Secondly, in the daily slave life there were innumerable forms of quiet, covert protest. They included malingering, feigned illness and ignorance, slowed-down work habits, sabotage of property, and even the poisoning of masters. There was also, at times, slave suicide. Barbadian planters were warned that their slaves threatened with punishment might hang themselves before the punishment could be carried out. Certain defense-mechanisms evolved to make life tolerable. Slaves disguised their feelings and adopted exaggerated attitudes of deference to the point of pretending to be the stupid black person in which the white mentality believed.

Many accounts also tell of how slaves fashioned a 'divide and rule' strategy, pitting master against overseer, or house slaves against field slaves, thus matching the whites' own 'divide and rule' strategy. Craton, in his study, summarizes what all this meant.

"Slaves always resisted slavery and the plantation system, rebelling where they could or had to. Their aim was that of all unfree people—freedom to make, or to re-create, a life of their own in the circumstances in which they found themselves. This desire, simple and informal though it was, amounted to a popular ideology even more important than that which justified and explained the slaves' subjugation."

Slave resistance demonstrated that slavery could only be maintained by force, a proposition which the public found objectionable by the time of the early liberal-democratic revolution of the 19th century.

There were two other forces that helped destroy the slavery system. First, there was the economic factor: the system died, the argument goes, because it became increasingly unprofitable. Slave labor was more costly and less efficient than free wage labor; an over supply of sugar led to catastrophic drops in world prices; and finally the West Indian planters lost their privileged position in the British market as the British government moved to open world free-trade policies. Then there was the influence of the British religious-humanitarian movement, led by Wilberforce and Clarkson, that finally convinced British public opinion of the un-Christian character of the system.

Slaves unloading cotton, circa 1865.

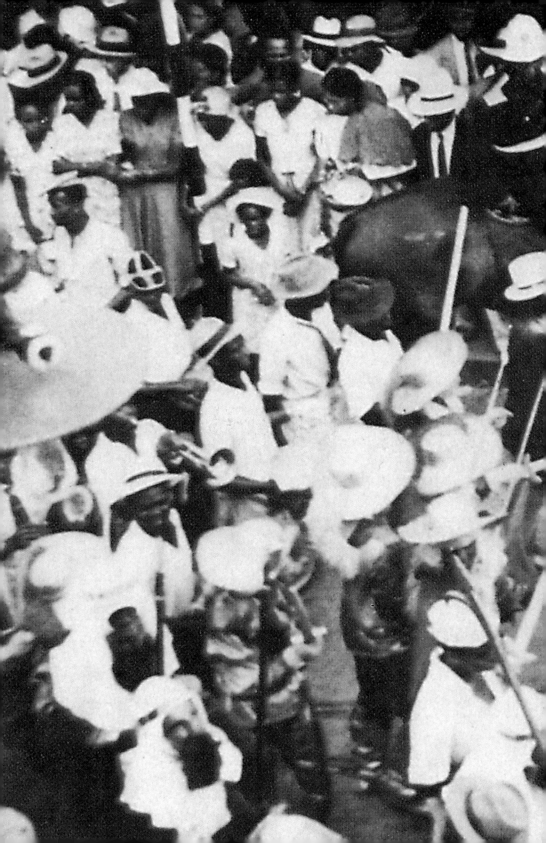

With abolition achieved—in 1834 the British islands, in 1848 the French islands, and in 1863 the Dutch islands—the post-Emancipation period lasted until the vast social and political changes unleashed by the Second World War (1939-45) led to national independence for the majority of the islands. These changes were similar to those unleashed by the Napoleonic Wars (1793-1815) which helped to accelerate the decline of the old slavery plantation order. Wars, everywhere, upset social habit and custom and set in motion long, silent social revolutions. So the Lesser Antilles would never be the same after 1815, as they have never been the same since 1945.

After emancipation there began a process of land reclamation on the part of the ex-slaves. The earlier plantation system had systematically denied land to the slave. Now they bought up parts of abandoned estates, fought for the use of Crown lands, and organized networks of staple crop production and sales outlets in the towns. They were joined by thousands of Indian indentured contract workers brought to the region between 1838 and 1917 to work on the labor-starved plantations.

Land ownership allowed the slaves to develop for the first time an independent economic life. Over the decades they became the nutmeg farmers of Grenada, the fishermen-farmers of Antigua and Barbuda, the small banana growers in St. Lucia, the small sugar producers of St. Croix, the small cocoa farmers of Trinidad and the market women, or 'higglers,' who became the mainstay of the developing town market economy .

New Caribbean farmer: These newly-emerging Caribbean farmers were not like their medieval European counterparts, helpless before the exploitation of medieval landlordry. Nor were they like the sharecroppers of the American South, for they almost always owned small plots for their own use. They were, in fact, a new economic type, neither completely rural nor completely urban. Much of what they produced were cash crops, destined for sale in the local market or even for sale abroad. They were peasants in the sense that their life-style, with all of its old kinship patterns of family, was rural; but their economic values were capitalist. They operated, often with characteristic shrewdness, as sellers and buyers in a free-market island economy. As a class, indeed, they were stratified, like all classes, for there were at once rich farmers and poor farmers, as is still the case today. Sidney Mintz, the leading authority on the typology of these people, has noted their peculiarities.

"The Caribbean peasantries that evolved during the nineteenth century did not consist of people aiming to cut themselves off economically from the outside world, but rather of people who intended to be a free and active part of it. Through possession of land they hoped to escape from the stigma of slavery and from the drudgery of plantation wage labor on the land of others. But because of a combination of factors—official favoritism towards the plantations, limited technical and financial assistance through extension (such as credit, tools, and seed), regressive taxation, and inability to influence agricultural developments elsewhere—Caribbean peasantries have usually been unable to become independent of the local plantation economy or of the commercial and financial sectors outside the plantation system. More serious, those segments of the peasantry that can subsist without selling their own or their families' labor off the farm have always been tiny minorities in Caribbean history."

In short, the small Antillean farmer has always been an endangered species. Only their love of the land, their industry in using it, and their talent for building up, in more recent times, such things as benefit clubs, producers' associations and savings clubs, has guaranteed their survival to the present time.

But more than farmers entered this Antillean working class during this long period. During the latter part of the 19th century and the early part of the 20th century, an urban work force evolved that was concentrated in the large townships like St. Thomas, Fort-de-France, Bridgetown, Port of Spain and Willamsted. These towns were thriving centers of trade and commercial import-export businesses, controlled in Barbados by the white commercial oligarchy of families and in Trinidad by the East Indian business family concern. Another urban work force developed around the oil refineries in Trinidad, Curacao and Aruba, and around the transatlantic sugar companies like the Geest group in St. Lucia and the *Companie Generale Transatlantique* in the French islands.

The arrival of oil refinery companies was of special importance. With the oil companies came

Preceding pages: mounted police watches over a public gathering. Left, a young indentured laborer from India on her arrival in Trinidad.

a full-scale process of industrial and financial capitalism into the region. Just as, earlier on, commercial capitalism had brought the dependent West Indian economies into the network of the Atlantic commercial system, so the new industrial capitalism brought them into the network of the Atlantic industrial system.

The results were technological dependency, the growing separation between the European economies and their colonial economies, a growing imbalance of trade between the two, external ownership and control, the influx of a foreign managerial personnel, and a general system in which the West Indian colonies sold cheap and bought dear. They became, in effect, economies that produced what they did not consume, and consumed what they did not produce.

Slums of the empire: For the inter-war period porting an estate labor force by means of an exploitative task work system. In St. Kitts and St. Vincent, the wage level had barely advanced beyond the daily shilling rate introduced after Emancipation a century earlier. There was gross malnutrition and chronic sickness in the population; a housing picture characterized by decrepit, verminous and unsanitary conditions, as found in the barracks or 'ranges' system of the Trinidadian and British Guianese East Indian estates; and a working class, when it had work, in a state of economic servitude to a well-organized employer class. The defense-mechanisms of a strong trade union movement were stultified by the existence of punitive legislation. Only British Guiana had passed legislation to protect unions against actions for damages consequent upon strikes. Children, noted the report, were perhaps

of 1919 to 1939, the native workers served as a dependent, low-paid docile labor force for industry, commerce, and agriculture. Conditions that were bad enough in the 1920s were made worse by the onset of the world Depression in the 1930s. During this period the colonies became known as the 'slums of the empire.' Such conditions led to the labor riots that swept through the English-speaking islands between 1935 and 1938 and to bloody encounters between workers and police, especially in Barbados and Trinidad. The conditions were described in the findings of the British Moyne Royal Commission.

Perhaps the most critical and comprehensive Royal Commission report ever published on the West Indies, the Commission noted a generally dismal picture of a declining sugar industry sup-

the most exploited of all West Indians. They were denied opportunity for the healthy development of either mind or body, since they lived in small, unlighted hovels with wooden shutters closed tight at night in order to shut out evil spirits or thieving neighbors. In addition, their educational system was marked by serious absenteeism, obsolete curricula, a cheaply-paid teaching staff composed mainly of pupil teachers, and dreadfully inadequate school buildings.

The report concluded that the future of even the lucky West Indian child was bleak. If he was fortunate enough to continue his education until school-leaving age, which was usually 14 in the towns and 12 in the rural districts, he entered a world where unemployment and underemployment were regarded as the common lot. Should he find work as a manual laborer, his wages provided only for bare maintenance and were far from sufficient to enable him to attain the standard of living set before him by new contacts with the outside world. If he were fitted by education and intelligence for clerical posts, competition for which was intense, he had the prospect, at best, of a salary on which, even in Government employment, he would find it a serious struggle to keep up the social position and appearances which he and his friends expected. He would have leisure hours but few facilities for recreation with which to fill them.

The 1935-38 riots, plus the Commission's report, helped to further the formation of new worker movements. These movements brought about a new and militant class consciousness in the islands, and helped, later on, in the formation

known as 'pluralist' societies; societies marked by racial mixture and cultural ethnicity. In these societies the different resident groups, whether defined by color or by ethnic background, had to develop a new system of more or less peaceful co-existence. In most of the smaller islands it was a simple matter of black, brown, and white. In societies like Trinidad it was a more complex matter. There, in addition to the matter of skin color, existed the question of ethnic differentiation between West Indian and East Indian, the latter being descendants constituted of the East Indian indentured servants. With slavery abolished, all of these groups had to formulate a new social contract. New status badges, modes of behavior and inter-personal attitudes had to be shaped. Thus, a new system of race relations and color relations thus slowly developed, setting the

of new political parties seeking, first, internal self-government and, second, independence. Some of the credit goes to Sir Walter Citrine, head of the British Trades Union Congress of the time who, as a member of the Commission, held public lectures throughout the islands, instructing workers and their leaders of the need to form trade unions. The colonial influence, thus, could be progressive as well as regressive.

New social contract: The long post-Emancipation period saw the rise of what later became

Left, Manumission certificate freeing slaves upon a plantation owner's death. **Above**, young farm hands pause in a cornfield.

formative base of the new order that has lasted, in many ways, up to the present day. That new order also perpetuated the element of social class; for the abolition of slavery did not mean, nor was it designed to mean, the abolition of social class structure.

This Post-Emancipation new society is perhaps best illustrated in Jean Rhys' well-known novel, *Wide Sargasso Sea*. The novel sees the world through the eyes of the young white creole girl, Antoinette and her young English lover, Rochester, both of whom are members of the white declining gentry trapped on an island they cannot escape because of limited financial means. Antoinette is surrounded by free colored and black servants who treat her with disdain and whose chatter seems ominous. Rochester never understands the island or its people, and he feels surrounded by a dark and hostile tropical beauty from which he must escape.

There occurred in Rhys' novel, as well as in other literature—Phyliss Afry's *The Orchid House* and V.S. Naipul's *A House for Mr. Biswas*—certain themes that still tell us much about Antillean life. There is the theme of 'old' families being displaced by social upstarts, and of the new affluent colored families with 'big names,' who enjoy upward social mobility while still craving approval from the whites. And there is the theme that Antillean society is somehow a sad and sinister place with little hope. Stories, mostly sexual, tell of how the scions of the old white families survived living on declining incomes and depending on the colored women who loved them. There is the more optimistic theme of

relations in this stage of Antillean life were different from the evolution of race relations in the American South, and even in American society after 1865. In America the classification system became one of a simplistic black-white dichotomy. In the Antilles, quite differently, the classificatory system became one of a more subtle and more benign 'shade' prejudice. Social status depended upon fine degrees of skin color. Wealth and income also made a difference, giving rise to the concept of 'social color'. The more prosperous a person became, the more 'white' he or she could claim to be. In American society, money talked; in Antillean society, money whitened. Color became the crucial determinant of status. This led, of course, to evasive habits of identity, summed up in the Martiniquan phrase, *peau noir, masque blanc* (black skin, white mask), an eva-

the rise of class consciousness among the estate tenantry, and finally the growth of urbanization and social mobility. Both urbanization and professionalism helped slowly to eradicate the old social rule that regarded occupation in the world of work as a function of race or color.

Eventually there was a gradual evolution of mutual tolerance and acceptance among the various groupings of these pluralist societies. But it did not mean, of course, that color pride and prejudice disappeared. They remained as virulent as ever, but now in new forms of expression. The whites, after all, did not disappear, as in the new black republic of Haiti, where as the saying went, 'black rules white.' The whites' early economic power was certainly weakened, but whiteness was still regarded by all as the ideal image. Race

siveness practiced by the middle class colored groups. The whites of the Lesser Antilles kept their pure identity by marrying within their own group. Particularly in the French Antilles, marriage across the 'color line' was regarded as a sin, a betrayal of the creole bêke tradition, and was punished accordingly.

Paltry raffle of colony faction: The post-Emancipation society was also characterized by a continuing colonial rule marked by gradual changes of constitutional forms and political struggles. Island governors and administrators, as well as their administrative staffs, were still appointed from London, Paris, Copenhagen and the Hague. The mother country colonial offices introduced a limited suffrage based on property qualifications, periodic elections for such a limited electorate, and governing machineries composed of a governor or administrator, a nominated executive council whose members owed loyalty to the chief executive and legislative chambers of elected members.

For a century or more it was a closed political system, with little if any popular participation. Only riots could force a colonial government to take some kind of action in favor of the popular cause, such as the so-called Federation riots in Barbados in the 1880s and the so-called Water riots in Trinidad in 1903.

Generally speaking, the politics of the day consisted of factional fighting between the more privileged groups. The colonial governor or administrator, often an outsider, would invariably find his friends and political allies in the local plantocracy, seduced by their legendary

when the Trinidad Workingmen's Association was formed, led by Captain Cipriani, a white creole descended from Corsican immigrants, and a member of the old racing set of estate proprietors of Edwardian Trindidad. There were other exceptions, such as Barbados, where the old representative system of the 17th century remained untouched by the new Crown Colony system. Consequently, the Barbados political struggles continued to center around the old English Whig argument that Barbadians were fighting for their ancient rights as overseas Englishmen. But, all in all, it was a rather narrow and unedifying political situation; what Adam Smith contemptuously called 'the paltry raffle of colony faction.'

Change of power: It was only towards the end of this long period in the 1920s and the 1940s that this system, so seemingly impermeable, began to

hospitality. The opposition factions would normally come from the groups of the well-to-do free coloreds and free blacks, fighting for their civil, political and religious rights.

Sometimes, of course, the politics were complicated by ethnic factors. For a long time, politics in Trinidad revolved around the 'British' party, as the new English colonials were called after 1783, and the party of the Spanish-French 'old colonists'. That particular situation even carried on into the later Trinidad of the 1920s and 1930s,

Left, farm workers breaking cocoa around the turn of this century. Above, urban blacks stroll through Port of Spain's largest park around 1903.

break down. The changes, as already noted, were brought about by the impact of the two world wars. Wars, as Marx said of revolutions, are the locomotives of history. They suddenly accelerate profound changes almost overnight. The whole region was caught up in the debacle. Politics were transformed as new working class movements and workers emerged. One of the earliest examples came in the Virgin Islands after 1917, precipitated by the so-called 'transfer,' the Danish Crown's sale of the islands to the U.S. government. Overnight, Virgin Islanders found themselves under a new colonial master, with new problems to face. The transfer brought at least two major constitutional disabilities. First, the islands, like Puerto Rico, became unincorporated territorial possessions, ruled not by the full mandate of the U.S. Constitution, but by Congress and the President, as well as the Federal regulatory agencies. For the initial period of 1917-1934 they were under the jurisdiction of the U.S. Navy. The appointed governors were Navy officials, hardly trained to rule a colonial civilian population. The result was a running political war between successive naval governors and a new brand of local politicians and newspaper editors, fighting against the indignity of being governed as if the islands were a Navy base. When the Virgin Islands were transferred from the Navy's jurisdiction to the Department of the Interior in 1934, the struggle continued anew. The new civilian governors were little better than the old Navy governors. The fight for more internal self-government ended in 1969 with the Elective Governor Act, which finally replaced Washington-appointed governors with locally elected governors.

A similar struggle took place in the British islands. The 1935-38 riots generated a new political leadership. Some of the new leaders, like Grantley Adams in Barbados, were black middle-class lawyers. Most of the rest were grassroots leaders—Vere Bird in Antigua, Uriah Butler in Trinidad, Robert Bradshaw in St. Kitts, Ebenezer Joshua in St. Vincent, Eric Gairy in Grenada, among others. Since they were all influenced by the British Labour Party, the parties they founded were also, in the main, called Labour parties. Their socialism, therefore, was the gradualist, constitutional form of British Fabian socialism. Not until the later part of the 1960s and 1970s did other parties of a more radical ideology emerge. The struggle of these leaders at that time was a heroic one. They had to fight against the cultural, racial and social prejudices of colonialism. Their dilemma was summed up in the report published by a conference of these parties issued in 1932.

Powerless to mold policy, still more powerless to act independently, paralyzed by the subconscious fear of impending repression and therefore bereft of constructive thought, the West Indian politician has been inclined to dissipate his energies in acute and penetrating but embittered and essentially destructive criticism of the government on which, nevertheless, he has waited for the initiation of all policies intended to benefit his people, and which he has expected to assume the full responsibility for all necessary decisions. His political life, overshadowed by a government too omnipotent and too omnipresent, has had little opportunity for independent growth.

Crooked path to independence:

The general situation began to improve a little later, however, as a combination of factors—the 1930s riots, the war, the advent in Britain in 1945 of a more friendly Labour Party government and the end of the British Raj in India in 1947. Even then it was not a straightforward march towards independence. Before that happened, the movement was derailed by two diversions. The first was the movement in favor of federation, which ended in the short-lived West Indies Federation of 1958-62. That experiment broke up in 1962, mainly because the member-states, and especially Jamaica and Trinidad, were not prepared to sacrifice any of their sovereignty to a central federal government. They were reluctant to accept federal taxation, as well. The end of the Federation left the smaller Leeward and Windward islands out in the cold and gave London the opportunity to change their constitutional status in 1967 to 'associated states'; a status that gave them the right of internal self government but left the jurisdiction of foreign affairs and defense in the hands of London. It was inevitable that, in the next decade, they would follow Barbados and Trinidad and become independent states. Regrettably, however, none of them managed to produce the kind of leadership that Dr. Eric Williams, the scholar-politician, brought to Trinidad-Tobago. His magnetic and powerful personality managed to keep his Peoples' National Movement (PNM) in uninterrupted power for 30 years (1956-86).

The smaller English-speaking islands, the 'Little Eight' as they have been called, did not seek independence with any marked enthusiasm. Colonial loyalty died hard. Britain evacuated its colonies after 1945, but many of the Antillean islanders were as dismayed about it as Winston Churchill. Only in Trinidad, where Dr. Williams educated his electorate in the theory and practice of an informed and sophisticated black nationalist consciousness, did a different attitude prevail. That no independence movement developed in the British Virgin Islands, just as, similarly, no anti-American movement developed in the U.S. Virgin Islands, is evidence of the old-fashioned loyalty to the 'mother country.' The 'status issue,' as it is called in the politics of neighboring Puerto Rico, just does not exist in either of the Virgins group. To paraphrase Shakespeare: some states are born independent, some achieve independence, and some have independence thrust upon them.

Independence of the Dutch and French:

Political and constitutional developments, of course, were different in both the French and the Netherlands Antilles. After abolition, conducted in both cases by liberal-minded home governments, colonial political activities never questioned loyalty to the Dutch Crown or to the French Third Republic. Following the arrival of the oil companies in the early 20th century, political and union leaders in the Netherlands Antilles were more involved in their relationships with the companies than their relationships with the Hague. There was, of course, the same old inequity of power between

52

the mother country and the colony, an imbalance somewhat alleviated by the innovative Dutch Kingdom Statute of 1954. The terms of the Statute gave the colonies direct representation in the Dutch cabinet and parliament by plenipotentiary ministers nominated by their own governments. These same ministers participated in matters directly affecting their interests. The terms also stipulated that the colonial partners were not to be bound by international agreements except by express consent; and that any amendments to the Statute would require a special procedure approved by the Antillean leaderships. There was a certain departure from this continuing relationship when the Hague granted independence to Dutch Guiana (Suriname) in 1975. Perhaps the other territories did not eagerly follow suit because of the negative results of Suriname's inde-

1940), generally siding with the Republican Left in the bitter internal struggles of the Republic. The sympathy even survived 1939-45, when the islands were under the control of the forces of the reactionary Vichy regime of Marshal Pétain. It was not surprising that the islands enthusiastically accepted full assimilation into the French union. The *loi cadre* passed by the Paris National Assembly in 1946 established the islands as overseas departments, *départments d' outre mer* (DOM), enjoying all the rights of French citizens, and with equal representation in the national politics.

What, then, is the final summing-up on this post-Emancipation period? The system of bonded slavery might be forgotten but could never be forgiven. But once it was abolished, a new period of accommodation between mother

pendence. In 1982 the military regime that came to power in Paramaribo killed 15 rival politicians and unionists. That chilling episode must have given many supporters of the separatist movement in Aruba grounds for second thoughts.

The French Antilles have been equally marked by a close relationship with France. Slavery abolition in 1848 was engineered in large part by the noble figure of the Martiniquan creole, Victor Schoelcher, a disciple of de Tocqueville. Martinique and Guadeloupe continued that radical republican sympathy in the Third Republic (1871-

Farm workers on strike in the 1940s.

country and islands grew up. To the credit of the European colonizing powers, they came to see, over a long period, that empire and democracy could not in the long run co-exist, because they represent mutually irreconcilable principles. Whatever the motivating reasons, they finally accommodated themselves to the needs of the time. That explains why there never appeared an Algerian-type colonial war in the French Antilles, or an Ulster problem in the English Antilles. The colonial powers thus came to recognize the inevitability, indeed the desirability, of change. They were responding to the central idea of liberty which has been at the heart of the modern democratic revolution of the 18th and 19th centuries.

In this period, the Antilles finally entered the modern world of political and constitutional democracy, if not social and economic democracy. Universal suffrage was finally established and the masses were incorporated into the decision-making process of the society. This occurred in 1936 in the American Caribbean through the new Organic Act, and in the English-speaking Caribbean in 1944 with the new constitution of Jamaica. As the old colonial empires disappeared, the new states were taken over by a native leadership arising from the ranks of the new creole middle classes, the regional 'black bourgeoisie.' While politics became more democratized, there remained a social class politics. Most of the leaders were lawyers, doctors and businessmen, with later recruitment from university academic people. The new nation states also saw the rise of a new and more modern government. Native trained civil servants replaced the colonial 'expatriate' administrative staff. Also, there was the increasing involvement of the state with the economic sectors. Certain industries were nationalized, and governments became majority shareholders in others. For example, in Trinidad after the oil boom of the 1970, the central government by the 1980s had become involved in oil, gas, fertilizer, chemicals, airlines, shipping, telecommunications, banking and finance, food manufacturing and hotels. This change in the nature of the Caribbean state reflected and expressed wider socio-economic-cultural changes in the area.

Forces of change: Industrialization started early in the century with the oil refineries in Trinidad and the Netherlands Antilles. But after World War Two, it received new impetus with the so-called program of 'industrialization by invitation.' Island political leaders and planners invented a whole series of incentives, including cheap labor and handsome tax exemption systems, to attract outside capital investment, especially from the Americans. It is worth noting that the theoretical framework for the program was written by the Antilles-born economist, Arthur Lewis, in a series of important analytical essays in the 1950s, arguing that industrialization was the only cure for the general West Indian condition of economic stagnation. Industrialization came first to Puerto Rico, in part because the British preferred to keep the rest of the islands as overseas

English tropical gardens. Among other things, the growth of an electronics industry in Barbados, a new oil refinery in St. Croix and twin-plants in Dominica (co-operating with other branches in Puerto Rico), were fashioned after Puerto Rican models, as was the expanding tourist industry, with the Hilton chain of hotels in Barbados, Trinidad and the U.S. Virgin Islands, and the Club Med hotel type in the French Antilles.

Modernization, of course, is in part industrialization, since the displacement of the farm by the factory results in the upsetting of a social order. But it is more than just that. In this period many

of the new states acquired their own national airlines—an insignia of national pride—like British West Indian Airways (BWIA) in Trinidad and the Leeward Islands Air Transport (LIAT). New education systems were founded, like the famous Barbadian private school Lodge, Harrison and Combermere, and the regional University of the West Indies (UWI), with its main campuses in Jamaica, Trinidad and Barbados. Privately-owned condominiums, tracts of middle-class housing, and public housing projects were also built. These, indeed, reflect the process of urbanization in the region. Trinidad is a gross example: 70 percent of its population lives in the overcrowded centers of San Fernando and the Greater Port-of-Spain East-West corridor. Modernity has its price. In the Antilles it has

Left, Eric Williams, Oxford graduate and First Prime Minister of Trinidad. **Right**, a downtown church overshadowed by a towering financial complex.

meant a vast movement of rural depopulation as people flock to the urban centers.

Westernization, in its turn, is best seen in the areas of Antillean religion and politics. The whole region, after all, was originally Christianized by the Protestant and Catholic European colonizing powers , and even the immigrating African and Indian religions became Christianized over a period of time. Today the main religious impulse comes from the evangelical, fundamentalist sects with origin, in the main, in the religious melting pot of the United States: Jehovah Witnesses, the Seventh Day Adventists and the numerous Pentacostal groups. The region is, in fact, a sprawling 'Bible belt'. The Westernizing influence, in its most general sense, is also evident in the area's political life-style. Everybody accepts the electoral voting system, even

other regions, not only in obvious economic fashion but also in the more subtle and pervasive social and cultural fashion. The American-type shopping malls and supermarkets that have appeared in the region have helped Americanize practically every item of life—dress habits, food tastes, speech mannerisms, entertainment modes, social relationships, even moral values. American radio and television add to this saturation of transmitted American-style attitudes and behavior patterns. These forces combine to encourage, as in American society, a lively consumerism. Antillean people, of all classes, want what they see: the BMW , the Gucci shoes, the Calvin Klein jeans, the fancy boutique finery, the video-cassette, the expensive household gadgets—or at least the nearest equivalents they can afford. And here, as elsewhere, television has indeed replaced

the more radical minority parties such as the National Joint Action Council (NJAC) in Trinidad, and Tim Hector's Afro-Caribbean Movement (ACM) in Antigua. Tiny factions that opt for armed struggle, as in Martinique and Guadeloupe, get little if any mass support. In his study of the electoral process, Patrick Emmanuel has shown that between 1961 and 1982, a total of 56 general elections were successfully held in the English-speaking Leewards-Windwards islands, accompanied by high voting levels. This Westernized orientation also appears in the generally pro-Western foreign policies of the new states.

Americanization was in part a composite of all of those other processes, but also a distinctively recognizable and different phenomenon. The American influence has permeated the region, as

religion as the opiate of the masses.

These, then, are the forces that contributed to the shaping and reshaping of the Lesser Antillean societies. Yet it would be wrong to think of them as absolute processes. Industrialization, for example, did not mean a complete industrial revolution. Sugar is dead in Antigua, but still survives as a thriving commodity in the economies of Martinique-Guadeloupe, St. Vincent, Barbados and Trinidad, due mainly to its protected status in the European Economic Community (EEC) market. Modernization is far advanced in the U.S. Virgins and Trinidad, and much less advanced in Montserrat, St. Vincent and Bonaire. Westernization is advanced throughout the entire region, although there is a counter-current in the recent movement of Latin-Americanization. Both the

Netherlands Antilles and Trinidad, only a few nautical miles from Venezuela, feel that current. Americanization, on the other hand, is as inconsistent as it is pervasive. There are differences, island by island. The U.S. Virgin Islands have become almost totally Americanized. On the other hand, the French and Netherlands Antilles are too French and Dutch, respectively, to embrace unreservedly the American way of life. The English-speaking countries, although generally pro-U.S., are not completely influenced by the American lifestyle, and most of them established diplomatic relations with fidelista Cuba after 1972, despite the displeasure of Washington.

Ensuing challenge: As the Lesser Antilles enter the modern period, they, just like their sister islands to the north and west, face a series of grave problems. Their social integrity and political

of Dominica was convicted of a scheme, in alliance with army soldiers and a South American connection, to overthrow the elected government of his successor; a top cabinet minister in Trinidad fled to Panama after being accused of making money on a race-course complex project; and a St. Lucian private airline shipped arms to Angola, perhaps with governmental connivance. The money involved in these scandals often originates from international drug rings, arms merchants and organized crime syndicates. Thus, the small island politician is entrapped in a world of high-stakes intrigue for which he is ill-equipped to deal.

Private lives, public secrets: It has been said that when there is no corruption, there is immaturity. This statement has particular application in the political world of the Antilles. Admittedly,

stability depend on how they meet the challenge. First, there is the problem of island domestic politics. The recent general elections of 1986 in Barbados and the U.S. Virgin Islands have shown how the constitutionalist habit is well entrenched. Also, the election of 1987 in Trinidad showed how a disaffected electorate can turn out a discredited government by massive landslide votes. Yet everything in the garden is not rosy. Money and politics mix to encourage government corruption: a prime minister and cabinet colleagues of the Turks and Caicos Islands were convicted of drug trafficking in Miami; an ex-prime minister

Left, pre-fab houses being assembled on an American base. **Above**, protesters.

there are political leaders of high caliber, like Julio Brady in the U.S. Virgin Islands, "Son" Mitchell in St. Vincent, Errol Barrow in Barbados and A.N.R. Robinson in Trinidad-Tobago. But in the small islands, the politician is typically illeducated, suspicious of intellectuals, hungry for power, intolerant of dissidents and vindictive towards opponents. He manipulates a system in which personal charisma is more important than ideology. Power is obtained by a system in which votes are exchanged for favors and thus an elaborate network of family, friends and job-holders is held together by patronage. Since government is the main employer, the plums are appointments in the local civil service. In small island political systems the politician must show handiness, likability, quickwittedness and, especially, a ready tongue with which to woo voters and intimidate opponents. Usually, he is a merchant or man of property turned politician, rather than a professional politician. It is a kind of market square politics that emphasizes crowd oratory. In this kind of political arena, private lives, especially of opponents, become public secrets. In Trinidad it is called *picong, mauvais langue,* robber talk. To listen to its most skilled practitioners at a West Indian political meeting is to understand the West Indian gift for talk, its spirit of ribald irreverence, its street defiance of the high and mighty, all pulled together in the famous Trinidadian calypso form.

At the same time, this small-island-machine politics is immature. It does not educate the electorate, it simply entertains it. It offers the voter short-term satisfactions but fails to address

all calypsonians, the Mighty Sparrow, is Grenadian by birth. The old opprobrious epithets·like 'coolie' and 'nigger' once used in Trinidad and Guyana are no longer permissible. There is very little anti-Semitic feeling against local Jewish groups, perhaps because the Jewish presence goes back to the very beginning. In Barbados, again, 'Bajans,' both black and white, live more or less harmoniously with each other, and the differences that emerge, frequently intense, relate more to class than to color. In Trinidad-Tobago, where voting by race has long been the custom, a remarkable breakthrough took place in the 1987 election when the three major segments of the society—the French Creole and business groups, the oil-workers trade union, and the black middle and working class formed a national alliance that finally defeated the 30-year-old government of

itself to the fundamental long-term problems of the island economies. Practically everything revolves around the distribution of the 'pork barrel.' This can result in all the system's built-in personal animosities getting out of hand, causing the kind of savage internal contest that ravaged the St. Lucia Labour Party in the 1970s.

Conflicts of race and culture: Then there is the problem of enthnicity. To begin with, and to look on the bright side, there is much mutual respect and tolerance between different groups in these multi-ethnic societies. There are reservations of Caribs in both Dominica and St. Vincent, which are protected by Carib Reserve Acts, although there is occasional tension with the local governments. A large Grenadian immigrant population lives in Trinidad, proud that the most famous of

the Peoples' National Movement (PNM). In sum, there is little in the Lesser Antilles comparable to what separates Sinhalese and Tamils in Sri Lanka, or Hindus and Sikhs in India.

Yet the region is still not yet a full ethnic democracy. There are still problems. Prejudices galore survive in the Antillean collective psyche. In the U.S. Virgin Islands the 'native Virgin Islanders' look down on the thousands of immigrants, both bonded and illegal, who have come from the Leewards looking for work in the territory. Trinidadians still disdainfully regard Grenadian immigrants, and others, as 'small islanders.' In Trinidad, East Indians and Creole blacks manage to maintain stereotyped images of each other. Barbadians remain universally disliked in the rest of the region, perhaps because, as the visiting English novelist Anthony Trollope wrote, they are a set of men arrogantly assured that they and their occupations are the main pegs on which the whole world hangs.

These covert ethnic prejudices take on more overt racial prejudices in the Netherlands Antilles and the French Antilles. In both cases the old black-white struggle has taken on new forms and expressions with the arrival of new white dominant immigrant groups — the expatriate Dutch in the ABC islands and the newly-arrived French metropolitans in Martinique-Guadeloupe. In both cases, the unequal distribution of social and political power and resources gets reflected in racial animosities. In the Netherlands Antilles, the town riots of 1969 in Willamsted were led by the new political group, *Frente Obrere*, agitating for workers' rights. Since their employers were

with the local people. In this context, politics frequently becomes a struggle between white French *prefets* and local Assemblies controlled by the colored political class.

In sum, there are new tensions to aggravate the old racial feelings. Much of it is the normal stress of aches and pains that take place when peoples of different cultural backgrounds intermix. The Antilles—despite the books published by excitable visitors who do not comprehend the long, rich history of race relationships in the region—are by no means on the verge of a racial war.

Bicycle economies, cadillac tastes: There is also the problem of economic development. The processes of industrialization and modernization have really been a process of Americanization, if only because the Antilles lie within the American orbit of influence. This has resulted, over the last

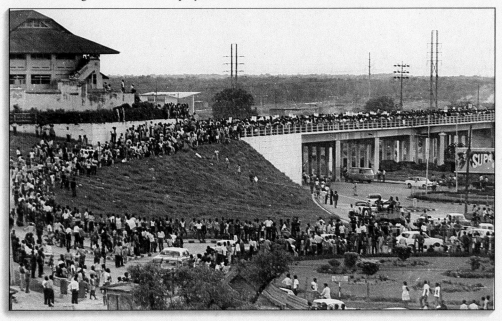

mainly Sephardic-Jews and Protestants, the movement inevitably took on ethnic tones. Again, in the case of the French Antilles, as Michel Leiris shows in his study, political assimilation has meant the growth of a corps of Paris-appointed administrative functionaries who, while liberal-minded in the matter of inter-racial marriage, generally identify with the upper-class creole white in social habits and attitudes, and are hostile to the preservation of the local creole culture. Even when the *blanc metropolitain* is well-intentioned, his ignorance of local culture leads him into crass mistakes in his relationships

30 years, in obvious material benefits. A new, affluent middle class has emerged; and the basic standards of life, in housing, education and health, have improved immeasurably.

There are also qualitative measurements that have to be considered. Movies and television series portray a style of life that the Antillean viewer wants to emulate. Consumerist tastes are encouraged which can hardly be satisfied in these underdeveloped societies. It generates expectations that cannot be realized. As a former Montserrat Prime Minister, W. H. Bramble, has put it, the small Antillean countries have become bicycle economies with Cadillac tastes; and as Prime Minister Errol Barrow of Barbados said, it is not a problem of the high cost of living but of the cost of high living. Absolute standards of life

Left, political graffiti urging independence. **Above**, Black Power demonstrators.

have improved, but relative standards of income inequity between different classes of the societies have likewise increased.

One culprit in this whole process of cultural pollution is the Antillean tourist industry. From the Virgins to the ABC islands, the landscape is dotted by luxury hotels owned by overseas hotel chains. They drain the local agricultural sectors, because the average lower-class worker prefers to be a maid or a bartender in the hotels rather than remain on the land. They foster a new black-white image, as can be seen in the tourist advertising that shows black hotel workers serving white hotel guests.

Many of the region's economies suffer from unemployment rates of 25 percent and more. Agriculture has become a neglected sector, thus hindering the emergence of a regional food plan.

Among other consequences, starting in the 1950s, governments and planners have been driven to encourage mass emigration, thus in effect exporting their poverty and losing much of their skilled work force. Soon, as Dr. Williams once wryly put it, there will be no West Indians left in the Caribbean. Worst of all, development by import capital has increased immeasurably the structural dependency of the region's economy upon international capital from multinational corporations. Some of them seek cheap labor, others—like the pharmaceutical companies—freedom from restrictive environmental legislation in their home base. Others—especially in the more recent stage of finance capitalism—set up off-shore operations that enable them to do a worldwide business. These situations become particularly vulnerable and hazardous when a small-island becomes host to one single industry, thus creating a single-industry economy. In 1984-85, for example, the oil companies, including Exxon, evacuated Aruba and Curaçao almost overnight, leaving the host economies in a devastated condition.

Place in the sun: In retrospect, the history of the Lesser Antilles has been rich, exciting, colorful. It shows how strains from Europe, Africa and Asia met and mixed, over the centuries, to form a New World society unique and special in its character. It is a pity, in a way, that accomplishment has often been overlooked when compared with the history of the Caribbean as a whole. Indeed, the Lesser Antilles have frequently been reduced to a Cinderella role within that larger history.

The very term itself, Lesser Antilles, may be regarded as derogatory, comparing it with the Greater Antilles. In the very beginning, the Eastern Caribbean islands were used by the European colonizers as simply a stepping stone to the richer prizes westwards of Hispaniola, Jamaica, and Cuba. In the present period, again, they are identified within the Caribbean Community as the lesser developed countries (LDCs). Even within the regional university—where more sensitive language might have been expected—the less affluent countries are known as 'non-campus territories,' in comparison to the campus centers of Jamaica, Trinidad and Barbados. All in all, the 'small islanders' have to spend too much time and energy defending their right to an equal place in the sun.

This is unfair, if only because the islands have contributed much to Antillean arts and letters, indeed proportionately far beyond their size. The record in this cultural field is indeed impressive. In the 19th century there were remarkable painters like Michel Jean Cazabon in Trinidad and the impressionist Camille Pissarro in the Danish West Indies.

In the present day period there are the historians C.L.R. James and the late Eric Williams from Trinidad, the poet-playwright Aimé Césaire from Martinique, the poet-playwright Derek Walcott from St. Lucia, the novelist George Lamming from Barbados, the novelist Vidia Naipaul from Trinidad. If to that is added the Catholic festivals of St. Lucia, the crop-over ceremonies of Barbados and, most noticeably, the tremendous fête-bacchanal of Carnival in Trinidad, then the picture is complete of a small region rich in cultural creativity. There are few other regions of comparable size that can match that record.

Left, a young Antillean wanting to have her cake and eat it too. **Right**, a friendly Carib.

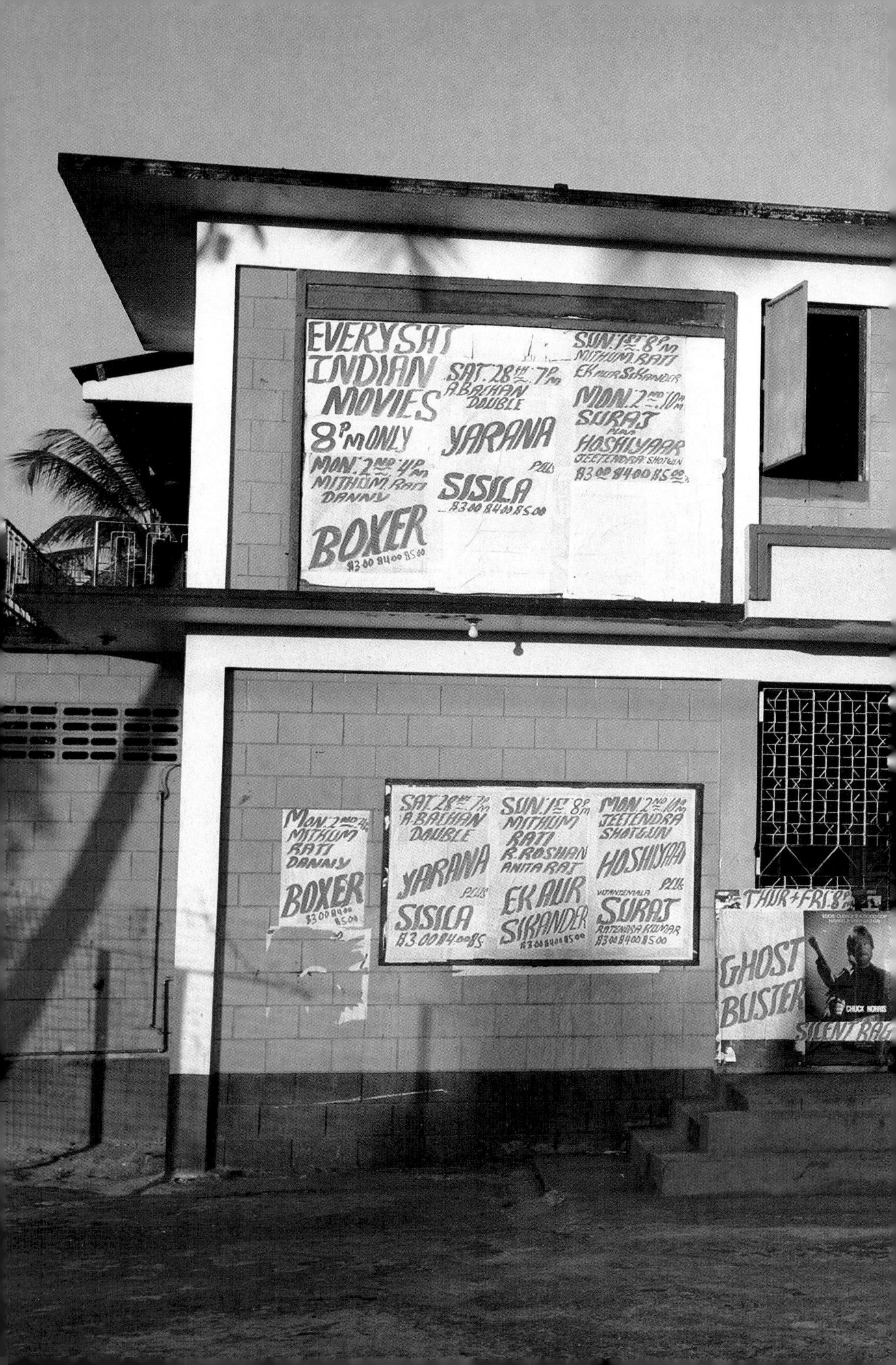

PLACES

It seems that nature and history have conspired to produce an endless array of surprises in the Lesser Antilles. For instance, in Dominica there exists a reservation of Carib Indians, the fierce original inhabitants of these islands whom the Spaniards claimed were cannibals. Thirty miles (48 km) to the north are the unknown satellite islands of Guadeloupe: Marie-Galante, La Desirade and Les Saintes, where a century-old community of white, Breton fishermen have survived undiluted by intermarriage. Further south, on Bequia, a small community of men still hunt 70-foot whales with hand propelled harpoons from sail-powered boats. And it's not unlikely that during your travels you'll happen upon people who claim African, Portuguese, English, Scottish and Danish ancestry. Such complicated bloodlines are not uncommon in these regions.

The terrain is equally surprising. One island has a volcano, another is full of long, rolling fields that look like Scotland, another has a salt lake. On Dominica there is a vast rain forest where cockroaches can grow to be a foot long. Tiny and steeply vertical Saba is practically beachless, while flat and arid Anguilla has a staggering number of beaches.

Also, each island conveys a different mood. St. John is idyllic, St. Thomas only a few miles away is bustling and vigorous. Tiny St. Barthelemy is as chic as the Left Bank; Barbados is as English as they come. On 32-square-mile St. Martin, Spanish, Papiamento, English, Dutch and French are spoken. Nor is there any consistency in political situations. You'll find territories, colonies, independent nations. The U.S. Virgins are part of the U.S.; Guadeloupe, Martinique, St. Barts and St. Martin are all Departments D'Outremer of France, and Dominica recently gained its independence from Britain.

Quite simply, you never know what to expect, not only from island to island, but past the next bend on their narrow roads. And that is one of the true pleasures of the Lesser Antilles.

Preceding pages: Guadeloupe farmers; church in Portsmouth; movie house, Trinidad; visible proof of the trade winds, Diamond Rock in the background. **Left,** a lifeguard demonstrates his acrobatic skills.

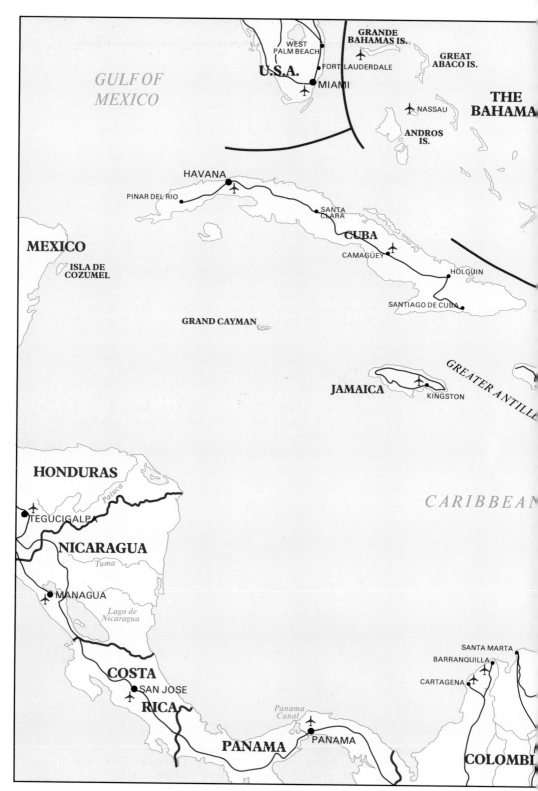

GULF OF MEXICO

WEST PALM BEACH

GRANDE BAHAMAS IS.

GREAT ABACO IS.

U.S.A.

FORT LAUDERDALE

MIAMI

THE BAHAMA

NASSAU

ANDROS IS.

HAVANA

PINAR DEL RIO

SANTA CLARA

CUBA

MEXICO

ISLA DE COZUMEL

CAMAGÜEY

HOLGUIN

SANTIAGO DE CUBA

GRAND CAYMAN

JAMAICA

KINGSTON

GREATER ANTILLE

HONDURAS

Patuca

TEGUCIGALPA

NICARAGUA

Tuma

CARIBBEAN

MANAGUA

Lago de Nicaragua

COSTA

SAN JOSE

SANTA MARTA

BARRANQUILLA

CARTAGENA

RICA

Panama Canal

PANAMA

PANAMA

COLOMBI

WEST INDIES & THE CARIBBEAN

0   300 Kilometres

0   300 Miles

ATLANTIC OCEAN

CAICOS
ISLANDS

TURKS ISLANDS

GREAT
INAGUA

SANTIAGO

DOMINICAN
REPUBLIC

AU
CE

SANTO
DOMINGO

HISPANIOLA

HAITI

U.S.VIRGIN ISLANDS

SAN JUAN

MAYAGÜEZ

PONCE

PUERTO RICO

BRITISH
VIRGIN ISLANDS

ANGUILLA   ST. MARTIN
ST. MAARTEN   ST. BARTHELEMY
St. CROIX   SABA   BARBUDA
ST. EUSTATIUS   ST. KITTS
NEVIS   ANTIGUA
MONTSERRAT
GUADELOUPE
POINTE-À-PITRA

LEEWARD ISLANDS

LESSER ANTILLES

WINWARD ISLANDS

DOMINICA

FORT DE
FRANCE   MARTINIQUE

ST. LUCIA

BARBADOS

ST.
VINCENT   BRIDGETOWN

SEA

THE
GRENADINES

ST. GEORGE'S   GRENADA

LA BLANQUILLA

TOBAGO

TRINIDAD &
TOBAGO

PORT OF SPAIN

TRINIDAD

LESSER   ANTILLES

ARUBA
CURAÇAO
BONAIRE

CORO

ISLA LA
TORTUGA

ISLA DE
MARGARITA

MARACAIBO

MACARAY   CARACAS
VALENCIA   BARCELONA
BARQUISIMETO   MATURIN

VENEZUELA

Apure

CIUDAD BOLIVAR

Orinoco

73

EXPLORING THE U.S. VIRGIN ISLANDS

St. Thomas is called "Rock City" because it is essentially one big mountain—its highest point at 1,500 feet—with one main town, **Charlotte Amalie**, the capital of the U.S. Virgin Islands, on its central south shore. The remainder of the island's coastline is a garland of beach resorts around a wooded interior of private homes—bright red, corrugated tin roofed eyries set into the steep hillsides. There's a crowded feel to St. Thomas: the **Cyril E. King** airport runway juts out into the sea—there was no other place for it—a paved stretch of landfill which jumbo jets have to negotiate like aircraft carriers. If you stay at any one resort beach too long, you begin to feel like you're on your back in one of those fancy hotel lobby ashtrays, with the insignia impressed in the perfect white sand. In the end, it's that sense of confinement that compels you to move about and discover what a diversified place St. Thomas, the most populous of the three U.S. Virgin Islands, really is.

To break into the open country outside Charlotte Amalie might take you some time. At first you'll have to make the transition to driving on the left. It's like *Alice Through The Looking Glass*: you just pass over to the other side and then try to behave as you would normally. And before you get the knack of island driving, you'll have to endure the good hearted jibes of the island's veteran drivers. "Wat kinna drivin' is dat, mun?" Then you have to deal with the traffic jams, a constant factor in the vicinity of town. But they're peculiarly "island" traffic jams—not so much the result of too many cars as they are of a certain lack of urgency in the average islander's driving; a kind of inbred disdain for rushing around. When two friends pull alongside each other, you've no choice but to wait out their conversation.

Once outside of town, the roads twist and tumble drastically, and seem to want to pull you seaward to the little lanes that lead off to yet another posh resort. (One features live alligators in a moat around the beachside swimming pool.) As you drive, you'll get two views of the island. At first, it's an extension of America; a nice little island dream that the large continent is having. After a while, you have the pleasant realization that it's a place unto itself, completely dependent upon tourism—the only vital industry, besides rum-making, left to these islands—and yet somehow very removed from it all.

The local life: A small sign reads **"Dollar Stop."** It dangles from a roadside shed with an extended porch front where some people sit in the shade with their beers. The place looks like a derailed caboose in the dust. Umba, the Rastafarian bartender, sits under the shed's front wood flap, which is propped open like the hood of a broken down truck, two customers on stools opposite him, looking in. The conversation, low key and sparse, is in nearly indecipherable patois. An old radio, perched on the sill of an open side window behind the bar, is barely receiving from the warm evening air what Umba describes as a "safball game from St. Croix." Then he flips the dial and we hear reggae Christmas carols again. Just across the road, some guys are playing basketball under the lights of an adjacent ball field, overgrown now with weeds. One of the players, his body gleaming with sweat, steps up to the side window, buys a coke and asks Umba if his girlfriend has been by.

"She pass, ya know," Umba says.

"She pass when?"

"She pass down."

Umba says that he grew up on St. Thomas and was a trombone player in a local reggae band that toured a few years ago in the northeastern U.S., between Boston and New York. He thought it was nice up there but "too fast", so he came back and got a house across the bay in St. John. He now rides the ferry back and forth to his job in St. Thomas because he says life got too fast here, too.

Umba also talks about St. Thomas and the recent elections in the islands for a new governor (elections are held every four years). He talks about the losing candidate, Aldeburt Bryant, who stirred things up with his outspokeness in defense of the rights of the islanders, and his demands for tighter controls on the build-up of tourism by U.S. developers so that the islanders might benefit more from the burgeoning tourist trade. "Bryant says there's nathin' wrong wid de hotels," remarks Umba, "bit dey should give something back to the islanders."

St. Thomas, like all the U.S. Virgin Islands, is an unincorporated territory and has a non-voting delegate in the House of Representatives; anyone born in any of the U.S. Virgin Islands is a citizen of the U.S. The government is structured like the U.S. Federal Government, with three branches: executive, legislative and judicial.

Next to Umba's bar is **Eunice's Terrace**.

Preceding pages: the ultimate travel dream. Below, a fruitstand in St. John.

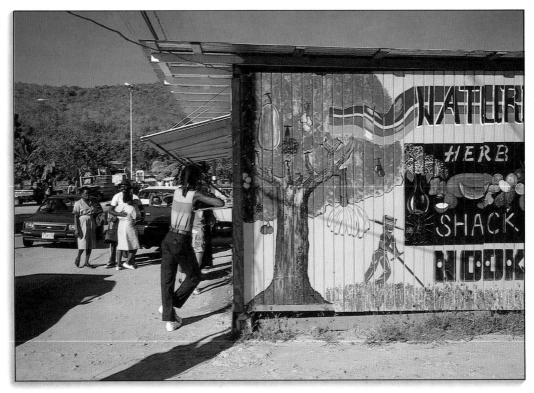

It's more like an open wood deck on stilts above nothing but jungle brush. It also has rolled canvas flaps to guard against the frail brief rains that pass over these islands like a much-needed seasoning for the otherwise bland stew of an unchanging and even over-perfect weather.

One of the specialties of Eunice's is a sweet, steamed white fish called *Gutu*, surrounded by vegetables and various West Indian staples like fungi—a grit-like mixture of yellow cornmeal, okra and butter—local sweet potatoes and plantains. There's also cane rum from Tortola, with sea grapes, cashews, peanuts, and a local root, called *caconga,* all thrown in and sitting on the bottom like dense soil. It tastes like boiled peanut shells, passes through your body in a crescendo of warmth, and makes you pretty dreamy.

Virgin sites: For a small island, there are a number of tourist attractions. There's **Coral World**, a "unique" underwater observatory in which you become the contained curiosity, and the fish become the passing curios. There's also **Mountain Top**, "the highest point on the island," where one can get the "world's best banana daiquiris." **Drake's Seat** offers an expansive view of the island, and **Magen's Bay**

Beach directly below was voted "one of the 10 most beautiful beaches in the world" by *National Geographic*. The story is that Sir Francis Drake used the spot as his personal lookout. Two islanders wait up there all day with two flower headdressed donkeys, so you can take what they insist is a once-in-a-lifetime photo. Instead, most tourists train their cameras on the view; the almost perverse beauty of Magen's Bay—a bright green teardrop in a shell of white sand—toward St. John; Tortola and Virgin Gorda in the British Virgin Islands; and the countless smaller islands and outcroppings all spread out like broken dishes from the same sunken shelf of land that makes up the Lesser Antilles chain. There's a sense of newness to the geography here, as though land and water are still maneuvering for position. Perhaps that explains why everyone snaps pictures so urgently, as though the scene might not hold its pose much longer. Also worth visiting in Charlotte Amalie is the **Virgin Islands Museum** in the former dungeon of **Fort Christian**.

The road from Mountain Top winds down with a view towards Charlotte Amalie and St. Thomas harbor, which during the evening, with all the boat lights, look like felled constellations bobbing on the water

A birthday party at Moyers Bay.

below. In the evening, St. Thomas' nightlife kicks into full gear as tourists and sailors gather to dance in the bayside bars. St. Thomas offers the greatest variety of night-life in the U.S. Virgin Islands. But if you'd like something more subdued, you can wander along the town's narrow streets, lined with old Danish shipping warehouses now converted into fancy duty-free shops and restaurants. Above them, the filigree balconies of private living quarters give the downtown area the feel of the New Orleans French Quarter. All the streets retain their Danish names on plates, displayed against corner buildings—*Vimmekshaft Gade, Dronningen's Gade,* and so on. These nameplates, and the driving-on-the-left business, are the two Dutch traditions that the U.S. has preserved since buying the islands back in 1917, for $25 million. The Danes held possession of the island from 1666, when they took over from the French West India Company.

Along the wharf in the harbor, chances are you'll find lines of docked boats, sleek yachts and sailboats with names like *Windjammer* or *Kon Tiki.* You'll also find the inter-island cargo ships: oafish, roundbellied boats with smoke stacks and circular windows; rusted hulls and lamp-lit, lived-in cabins furnished with little cooking stoves, clothes-strewn bunk beds and radios. Here are the *Lady Jenny,* the *M.V. Effort,* the *Bomba Challenger* and the *M.V. Dianne,* each with a backboard hanging off the side rail, listing their destinations: "Accepting cargo for St. Martin, Dominica, St. Lucia and St. Kitts." There are cars on some decks, on others, stacked window frames, piles of lumber, plumbing and so on, all the disparate parts of people's lives waiting to be shipped off and assembled on other islands.

An entirely different paradise: A sea plane—"It's fun to land on water," said the sign at the St. Thomas Terminal—takes you to **St. Croix,** 40 miles (65 km) to the south of St. Thomas. As you drive through the main town of Christiansted to your hotel, you'll get a notion of just how different St. Croix is from St. Thomas. For one thing, it takes longer to get from place to place, and from East to West there is a dramatic change in the landscape — from low, grassy seaside hills that remind you of Cornwall, England, to lush rain forests. Nearly 20 miles (33 km) long, St Croix has room enough for changing climates; it's more arid to the east and subject to drifting, lingering mists over the west end.

One of the main attractions on St. Croix is

Sugar mill in St. Croix.

Buck Island, a small platypus-shaped hump of land just off St. Croix's northeast shore. It's mostly covered with prickly pear and organ pipe cactus, though there's a nice stretch of beach off the west that boaters like to dinghy up to. The main attraction is the **Underwater National Park** off the east end of the island, with a marked underwater trail. The trail provides a series of little white arrows on submerged headstones and an occasional sign warning you not to touch anything, the surrounding coral being very brittle. It is kind of a sunken china shop out there—the delicately-designed fish floats free from the coral shelves, and you can just about reach out and take one. Here, the sea's most exotic and psychedelic renderings float past you like a pre-arranged fashion show: the dusky damselfish, the redbanded parrotfish, the yellowhead wrasses and the lookdown moonfish—you can just check them off in your program.

But then, you may never leave your hotel. One hotel, the **Cane Bay Plantation**, is the highest on St. Croix. Built onto the side of **Mt. Eagle**, it has one of the world's most ideally located bars—perched above a swimming pool at the level of the rain forest tree tops. Sometimes, from the telescope set up at the bar, you can see whales bounding across the sea on their way south.

In the bars you'll hear many conversations comparing one island to another, declaring what one has over the other. You hear a lot of that from the resident aliens who make up one third of the population here—those from other Caribbean islands who've migrated to the U.S. Virgins to find work. They're known as *garotes*, after a local bird that flies from island to island. For instance, one "continental" talks about how he wants to keep St. Croix quiet and modest, developing the island's tourist trade gradually so things don't get out of hand as they have in St. Thomas.

Caribbean suburb: If St. Thomas is "Rock City", then **St. Croix** might be considered its pastoral suburb. The island's expansiveness, its largely undeveloped inner landscape of old sugar plantations—with names like *Jealously*, *Upper* and *Lower Love* (names the Danish plantations owners gave as tributes, of sorts, to their different island mistresses—which makes you wonder about the plots called *Bold Slob* and *Barren Spot*)—all give the place a provincial feel. Many of the sugar mills have been restored as private homes.

One of these, the **Whim Great House**, is open to the public and houses a museum

with exhibits from the period of Danish rule.

You hear often about the seven different flags that have flown over St. Croix since Columbus first sailed up this island's **Salt River** in search of fresh water (he found hostile Carib Indians instead). The Spanish, English, Dutch, French, Danish, and even the Knights of Malta, have each held the island at one time or another, before the U.S. took over in the interest of protecting passages to the Panama Canal during World War I. Still, you feel the Danish influence everywhere, especially in the main town of Christiansted, where all the cream-colored buildings are made of bricks that the Danish ships brought over as ballast. Somehow, the Danish perfected a weighty architecture that barely interrupts the air. Christiansted is a town built to house its off-shore breezes, and walking through its streets you feel like one of those figures in a Chagal painting, too light, always floating up out of the frame.

At **Jelthrup's Bookstore**, in the middle of town, you can find cookbooks of island cuisine. One of the most famous is *Herbs and Proverbs*, by Arona Peterson, a woman famous in the islands for her West Indian cooking. She closed down her St. Thomas restaurant recently to research the use of local herbs for healing as well as cooking. Among her discoveries: *Pissy Bed Bush* is used to help cure bed wetting and to wash sores; the *Moon Plant* is used for foot pains; and the crushed leaves and bark of the *Casha* are used to treat proud flesh.

Not far from the book store is Christiansted's red light district, about a half block long. One of the bars, the **Echo Hotel**, is situated over a furniture store with a sign in its window that reads: "For Sale—One Night Stand." And it's in one of these bars that a famous Crucian drink, the *fantail*, was once sold. People would travel from all over the Caribbean to fall under the spell of this potent drink, apparently concocted by a woman named Beulah. There is a story that Beulah had a pet lizard who'd run down a pole from the thatched roof over the bar, lap up one of these mystical *fantails*, and go belly-up with a kind of fixed laugh on its face. Someone finally analyzed one of the drinks and found that, among other things, there was *belladona* in it (also referred to as "deadly nightshade," a poisonous plant and potent hallucinogen).

More traditional tourist sites in Christiansted include **Fort Christiansvaern**, which the Danes built in 1774; **The Steeple Building**, which in the 1800's served as a bakery and hospital, and is now a museum of the island's early history; **The Government House** on **King Street**; and the **Strand**, a fascinating maze of arcades and alleys lined with shops and restaurants.

Traveling from Christiansted, you can take the **North Road**, which runs along many of the island's better beaches. Then you take **Mahogany Road**, which leads you through the heart of St. Croix's rain forest—a rich, bowered darkness with vines hanging from a variety of trees; giant mahoganys and kapoks, and the tibit, also called the *mother-in-law tongue* for the way its long seed castings rattle in the wind. On the other end of Mahagony Road, 17 miles (28 km) from Christiansted, is Frederiksted, St. Croix's other coastal town. Nothing much happens in Frederiksted, with its quaint gingerbread architecture, which is why people like living or visiting there.

St. John's, a mere charm: The ferry from St. Thomas to **St. John** pulls you right across **Pillsbury Bay** into **Cruz Bay** and the town of the same name, the only town on the island. Essentially, St. John's fate was sealed by the Caribbean itself, which lapped up enough of the island's coastline to render it a mere charm, larger than an atoll but not so large that one man couldn't buy up most of it, as Laurence Rockefeller did. Only nine miles (15 km) long and five miles (eight

A view of the harbor in St. John.

km) wide, the bulk of St. John is a national park, criss-crossed by trails, with the island residents living on its periphery. The population hovers around 3,000.

Cruz Bay is like a little Cape Cod town: people come in to meet a friend at the ferry, pick up their mail, get some groceries, and then retreat back into the woods. The town square, just opposite the ferry dock with its little wooden guard house for the ticket vendor, is a raised curb bordering a patch of grass. It has an x-shaped cross walk, some tall trees and a little fenced-in mound of dirt (either it's a sacred Arawak Indian mound, or the town statue only works part time). Taxi drivers mill about and there are T-shirt shops, moped rental shops, open food stands and down-and-out bars next to nicer tourist restaurants.

Things seem pretty clear-cut on St. John. People come here to hide away and feel good; businessmen falling off sailboards, college girls sneaking through the woods to isolated arches of white sand so they can get all-over tans. To be honest, everyone seems to pass disinterestedly through St. John's only two public attractions: the ruins of sugar plantations and the nature reserve. You can go up a hill and take a 30-minute walking tour of the old **Annaberg Sugar Mill**, where there are the barest remains of old slave quarters and villages. Further on, one can find various remains of the mill they slaved away in. The mortar between the stones of the buildings is made of flour, molasses and sea shells, so you've essentially got very old, hard chocolate cakes in front of you. There's a great view up there of **Leinster Bay** and the nearby British Virgin Islands. The trail back down to the visitor's parking lot is lined with small, low growing, fern-like plants known locally as *greeche greeche*. As if bearing some long held grudge, the plant's tiny leaves retract and fold up at the touch of a human hand.

The walking tours with park rangers through the national park reserve are actually quite interesting, especially if you're curious about the indigenous flora and its various medicinal applications or dangers. The poisonous *manchineel tree*, for example, has been marked-off all over the island with red blotches of paint. Even rain drops which roll off the leaves can burn your skin. In a sense, the *greeche greeche* and the *manchineel* are metaphors for this island and the rest of the U.S. Virgins; a place set up so that nature and man may co-exist without encroaching too much on each other's terrain; a kind of civilized paradise.

Below, youthful attitudes.

EXPLORING THE BRITISH VIRGIN ISLANDS

The British Home Office once designated the **British Virgin Islands** as "the least important place in the Empire." A slight the islands, in some ways, deserved. Since Columbus first sighted the BVI's more than 400 years ago, very little has happened on this cluster of approximately 40 or so islands that line the Sir Francis Drake Channel. Their history has been undistinguished, their exports have been and are few, their population has remained sparse and development has been minimal.

But this is the era of the anti-hero, the tragicomedy, and the British Virgin Islands have come into their own. Somehow they managed to evade the whirlwind of change that enveloped the rest of the Antilles and can now boast that they offer nothing. Indeed, the main treasures of these islands are simple ones: a pleasant, gentle citizenry and long, unspoiled beaches bordering clear seas that give new meaning to the word blue.

Tortola and Virgin Gorda are the two largest of the cluster and they, like the smaller islands, exude a feeling of neighborhood—a feeling that may result from similarity of terrain. With the notable exception of Anegada—a flat reef island considerably to the north of Tortola and Virgin Gorda—the islands are hilly, rising rather precipitously from the sea. For the most part, they are also narrow; for example, at no point is Tortola more than three miles wide.

But the narrowness should not be misleading. Because the islands are all extrusions of the great volcanic chain that comprises much of the West Indies, they can be crossed only by climbing from sea level to 1,000 feet (303 meters), or perhaps even more. Sage Mountain on Tortola rises to 1,780 feet (539 meters), while Gorda Peak rises to 1,370 feet (415 meters). Consequently, until the recent introduction of a paved road that circles part, but not all, of Tortola, the only way that someone from Sea Cows Bay on the south coast of Tortola could visit someone at Cane Garden Bay on the north would be by donkey over a dirt track.

Guava jelly: The human component of British Virgin Island life is both multi-national and multi-racial. The era of an all-black Tortolan or Gordian society, an era that lasted quite a long time after emancipation, is now over. Tourism has been elected as an island product and it has brought to the island a whole new society of hoteliers, divers, sail charterers and shopkeepers. Yet the development of tourism has, in general, been done with a certain amount of conservatism. There aren't and probably won't be any multi-storied hotels or casinos in the future. However, it is local entrepreneurialism that has brought cruise ships into the harbor and developed a fleet of taxicabs—both unknown 10 years ago.

The fruits of tourism are certainly shared by the established black families, families bearing names that reach directly back to the plantation era; Penn, Callwood, Pickering, Hodge, Lettsome, to name a few. Some of the traditional island occupations are receiving a new infusion of vigor: stonemasons and gardeners are in demand. There may no longer be many of the old island sloops in service, but there are many new boat-related jobs for which "belongers" are preferred candidates.

Some of the island women are finding a new outlet for their culinary skills. Mrs. V. Thomas has been decorated by the Queen for her guava jelly and mango chutney that are for sale in the modern air-conditioned superettes. **Sugar Mill Hotel** near **Apple Bay** on Tortola has long boasted the cooking of its local women chefs, and one of their long-time retainers has branched out into her own business. Now Mrs. Scatliffe fills her veranda every evening with dinner guests who've made reservations to sample her papaya soup, homemade coconut bread, chicken in coconut, and soursop sherbet. Mrs. Scatliffe's restaurant at **Carrot Bay** has probably inspired the recent opening of **The Apple**, at **Little Apple Bay**, where West Indian conch, whelks in garlic butter, and local fish of the day are served.

Just how much new affluence has penetrated into the interior of the island is a matter of conjecture. But it is useful to keep in mind that Tortola and Virgin Gorda are not large islands and the interior is not far away. However, the concept of the "interior" in the physical sense might serve as a metaphor for the private life of the older folk. While a traveler can drive with comparative ease up Ridge Road to such mountain communities as **Green Bank**, **Meyers** and **Challwell**, he is not likely to share the private lifestyle of those who may still make their own charcoal, ride donkeys, fear duppies and praise the Lord in the old ways.

Here the old ways are still expressed by a gentle kindness and almost elaborate politness that will probably perish. "Good Morning" and "Good Afternoon" are still offered to anyone—stranger or friend—with whom one makes eye contact along the road. Much hurt is unknowingly inflicted by tourists who do not respond or who fail to initiate the greeting. Relative remoteness in the interior helps to insulate against such hurt, but the remoteness also helps to accentuate the differences between mountain folk and the town folk.

Gentle, generous and shy: Busy as the ferry dock at **West End** on Tortola may be during the tourist high season, the interior of the island remains undisturbed. Here small wooden houses cluster along the **Ridge Road**, catching the prevailing trade winds that blow from the East, across the entire Atlantic Ocean before they sweep across Tortola.

Along the interior Ridge Road and down the narrow dusty tracks that lead off from it, travel the slow-moving donkeys. Each donkey has an elderly man carrying his work machete. Often the donkeys also carry a load of their own fodder, a huge pile of deep green, coarse razorgrass. Neither man nor donkey hurry, in contrast to the younger men down the mountain who drive their cars along the few paved roads. The inhabitants of the little hamlets along these mountain ridges tend to be a bit more shy, a bit more gentle, a bit more generous than the rest of the island.

Roadtown in Tortola is the capital of the British Virgin Islands. Its name refers to the old maritime concept of a large harbor area to shelter ships. The tertiary definition of "road" in Webster's is the one that relates to the name of Tortola's major town: "a place, less enclosed than a harbor, where ships may ride at anchor." Not a large town, Roadtown has grown in recent years with the addition of architect-designed modern shops clearly tailored to suit the tastes of the new expatriates and sailboat charterers. These shops are located mainly on new landfill creations named **Wickham's Cay** and **Wickham's Cay II**.

The heart of Roadtown is still one main road, **Main Street**, where cars and pedestrians compete for passage on the road. The true, old West Indian architecture can be seen along Main Street—rectangular wooden buildings with corrugated tin roofs. Main Street has yet to be invaded by plate glass storefronts and not one neon sign glows at night anywhere on the island. For that matter, there isn't a single sign anywhere in the British Virgins.

In Roadtown, there is a good, although very small, museum of local artifacts that has been established by a Tortolan. Also in Roadtown is a rather handsome Episcopal church, **St. George's**. Here one can attend Sunday morning service to the scent of incense and the feel of the constant trade wind that comes through large windows whose wooden shutters have been opened wide for the parishioners' comfort.

Early on Saturday mornings there's a market. Like West Indian markets throughout the islands, this is one held mainly under a large canopy of corrugated iron. Men and women from the mountains leave early in the morning to travel into town with their produce and hand products. Island-made candy, cassava bread, little bunches of genips, soursops, and all the root vegetables indigenous to the islands are for sale. During festival—the celebration of emancipation rather than an observance of the beginning of Lent—a greater variety of treats is available. At the fairgrounds in Roadtown one can purchase goat water, hot *roti* (an East Indian filled pancake that has come from down-island), cold soft drinks and beer. At that very special time, one should plan to get into town to wait along Main Street for local steel band groups.

From Roadtown there is also a well-paved road that crosses over the mountain to Cane Garden Bay. Another paved road stretches along the ridge of the mountain range that constitutes the island. This is **"Ridge Road,"** and it provides for commutation from Roadtown to such mountain communities as **Green Bank**, **Meyers** and **Challwell**.

Backwater empire: But the major road in Tortola is the **Queen's Highway**, named for the 1966 visit of Her Majesty Queen Elizabeth II when she and the Duke of Edinburgh came to see these unimportant islands. Indeed, the British Virgin Islands are still part of the Empire-that-was, for they are designated as a "territory" and they have not exhibited any strong desire to separate themselves from their mother country.

The islands have their own Legislative Council made up entirely of islanders. In addition, there is a Governor who represents England. This office has always been filled by a man, usually one distinguished by a long record of experience in numerous other outposts of the empire. Recent Governors have come from service in Kenya, Bermuda, and the Turks and Caicos. More often than not, the civil servant sent to govern Tortola is at the end of his career. After a stint in Tortola, he can look forward to retirement. And so, in a postcolonial man-

ner, it might be said that Tortola still represents to the British a backwater of the empire.

At one time, Tortolans seriously considered petitioning for adoption by the United States as part of the U.S. Virgin Islands. But that movement has died down in a somewhat judicious recognition that there is much to gain from identification with the British Commonwealth of Nations as with the CARICOM community. With consummate political sagacity, its local politicians appreciate the economic help received from England. They and their countrymen also feel considerable loyalty for the mother country.

Generally, however, politically or geographically designated clusters such as the British Commonwealth or CARICOM seem remote. St. Kitts, for example, is very much "down island," and Kittitians coming to work or live in Tortola may be viewed with a fair amount of suspicion. Tortola and its sister-island, Virgin Gorda, sit rather happily surrounded by their own cluster of smaller islands.

Fat Island: Christopher Columbus named the entire Virigin Cluster "*Las Once Mil Virgines*", but Saint Ursula and her 11,000 martyred virgins are more readily evoked by the many small islands of the British Virgin Islands. "Many" is an admitted equivocation: "about 40" is more concrete, but the exact number varies from authority to authority. However many British Virgin Islands there are, Virgin Gorda is generally considered to have been Columbus' Saint Ursula.

During the early history of the islands, Spanish Town in Virgin Gorda was the capital of the island group. The capital was shifted to Roadtown in Tortola in 1741, and Virgin Gorda became a "secondary" island. Because Virgin Gorda lacks the hustle-bustle of a capital, it has retained a more pastoral atmosphere, and, indeed, now comes closer to the ideal remote West Indian provincialism projected in travel literature.

Just when and how "Santa Ursula" became "Virgin Gorda," nobody knows. It is even unclear why Virgin Gorda is so-named. Granted there is one significant hill—Gorda Peak—but otherwise there is little reason for the island to be designated "fat." The first census of the island was taken in 1717, at which time reference was made to "Spanish Town" rather than "Virgin Gorda". (Certainly, an island with only 625 inhabitants could hardly be considered

A place to avoid: prison in Tortola.

"fat," although at the time Tortola's inhabitants numbered only 335.)

Virgin Gorda has been developing a significant tourist industry over the past decade or two. Its attraction for travelers, most of whom are from the United States, was initiated in 1964 when Laurence Rockefeller built Gorda's first resort hotel: **Little Dix Bay**. Not far from Spanish Town, which has become part of "The Valley," Little Dix is also close to Virgin Gorda's airfield—the primary access to the island from the United States. A dirt landing strip until recently, the runway is still short enough—with one end greeted by a substantial hill—to startle travelers inexperienced with small plane maneuverability.

In a *Cruising Guide to the Lesser Antilles*, Donald M. Street describes the opening of the airstrip in Gorda. "An airport has also been built. It has a crosswind runway that is a good test of a pilot. Some don't pass the test. On the day of the airport's inauguration ceremony, the first plane to land on the new strip crashed, killing the pilot and four passengers."

No silent nights: Because Gordians, and Tortolans too, are somewhat retiring for the most part, it is unrealistic to believe that a one or two week vacationer is going to tap the roots of island folklore, or enter into the homelife of a local householder. Consequently, it is advisable to concentrate instead upon the natural beauty and diversity of the island.

Equipped with comfortable shoes and a hat, the visitor can walk from Spanish Town to the Southern tip of Virgin Gorda. Along the road, one learns the meaning of "cactus tropics." Little rain falls in the Virgin Islands; Virgin Gorda is no exception. Further, the southern end of Gorda—a narrow strip—is flat and sheer, making the heat more palpable than elsewhere. And the cacti are everywhere.

There are large aloes that are useful to know about if fair skin is blistered by the sun; there are the ubiquitous magueys that are used in Mexico for making tequila but which, typically, are used for nothing here. There are barrel cacti—sometimes called "Turk's Cap"—that offer themselves as a delightful curiosity, and there prickly pears whose fruit is sometimes used to make a cooling drink. The tall Pipe Organs are not seen so readily along the flat road although they do grow along the steeper slopes elsewhere on the island. One can see the famed Century Plant, or agave, that takes 10 years (not a century) to produce its flowery yellow

The hula hoop craze hits Tortola.

spike.

If cacti are ubiquitous along the roadside, so are their companions, the little goats who nibble throughout the day, sometimes tethered and trapped by cruel-looking chains, sometimes roaming free.Their dry-sounding bleat seems appropriate to their environment, mixed as it is with frequent rooster calls that characterize the British Virgin Islands' soundscape. Roosters in the British Virgin Islands do not honor the time schedule observed by their North American cousins. They do not wait until dawn to crow, but start randomly around 4 a.m. and continue to crow randomly throughout the day and into the early evening. They stop only when it is time for the tiny tree frogs to begin their nightlong cheeping. There is no silent time here; nature asserts itself in background sounds: rooster caws in the heat of day, coqui chirps in the cool of evening.

Scurrying through the dry vegetation are many varieties of small lizards. Reputedly, the smallest lizard in the world is indigenous to Virgin Gorda: the rare Virgin Gorda Dwarf Gecko that is at most only three-quarters of an inch long. And surprisingly enough, there are also a few giant lizards in the British Virgin Islands. High on **Biras Hill** on Virgin Gorda can be seen the six-foot (180-cm) iguanas that look like dinosaurs. On **Angegada**, the only coral-based island in the British Virgin Islands, there are a few remaining Angegada Iguanas, listed in international registers as highly endangered. But such do not appear along the road to the tip of Virgin Gorda.

White beaches: Whatever else the British Virgins may lack, they do not lack beautiful beaches. Other more lush, more tropical West Indian islands like Dominica, St. Kitts, or even Martinique have all the jungle and parrot appeal of the Hawaiian Islands, but they do not have as many long, beautiful beaches as the Virgin Islands, both American and British. Tortola's **Cane Garden Bay** beach has become almost too famous, now attracting power boats from as far away as Puerto Rico on a long weekend or holiday. Neither sail nor power boaters have yet been attracted to Tortola's beautiful **Long Bay** beach, perhaps because of the reef formations that guard it. **Brewer's Bay**, **Josiah Bay**, **Beef Island**, and **Smuggler's Cove** are other accessible Tortolan beaches. The Caribbean sea laps gently against the Western side of Gorda's southern peninsula. Coming across reefs that are themselves temptations for exploration, the sea brings finely ground sand to form exquisite white beaches. Here there are a series of little-frequented beaches: **Valley Trunk Bay**, **The Crawl**, **The Baths**, **Devils Bay**. One must know where to find the trails that lead off the road to these beaches, or else one is forced to come in by boat.

The great natural curiosity of Virgin Gorda's Caribbean shoreline is a group of boulders known as the **Baths**. The boulders are eight to 10 feet (two to three meters) high and smoothly rounded. They are huge white rocks that look as if they were tumbled into place by a giant who left them after he wearied of his play at the beach. They are doubtless the remains of some remote cataclysm, a mute reminder that these islands, like the entire archipelago, are volcanic in origin.

For the swimmer, "the Baths" offer unusual pleasure because the boulders sit just at the edge of the beach and the sea washes in among them, forming a labyrinth of cool, dark pools. As the tumbled boulders rest against one another, they form an overarching ceiling. One should plan to swim through the dark water tunnels formed by the great tumbled boulders. The beach here is very beautiful with fine white sand. One can start by walking from the beach into the Baths, and then swim in the bathing pools formed by house-high rounded boulders. Shafts of light enter between the boulders and the pools are lovely, safe and quiet. They are more visited nowadays as the word has gone out about their beauty.

Another option might be to plan a week at **Guavaberry Spring Bay**, the colony of hexagonal cottages built by Wing Commander Charles Roy and his wife Betty. Guavaberry Spring's beach is right next to "the Baths," but no beach in the British Virgin Islands is restricted by ownership. All beaches are public, so no one—traveler or resident—can be prohibited access to any beach in the islands.

Also on Gorda, at Copper Mine Point are the ruins of an old stone smelter, perched high above the Ocean. It is believed that the Spanish in Puerto Rico started to mine this southeastern tip of Gorda in the 1500s.

Population of 10: Many of the British Virgin Islands are uninhabited. Some islands have only a literal handful of residents. **Salt Island**, for example, has an approximate population of 10 although its salt-gathering population numbered as high as 100 at one time. Ginger Island remains uninhabited while Cooper Island has a few homes owned by expatriates.

Dead Chest, which is believed to be where Blue Beard marooned some of his men with only a sword and a bottle of rum is uninhabited. **Peter Island** has a small, growing population because of the luxury resort there now. Anegada has only 132 residents, whereas **Norman Island, Little Jost Van Dyke, Little and Great Thatch Islands, The Songs**, and **Fallen Jerusalem** are among those that are generally uninhabited. For the wealthy hermit, **Norman Island**, widely believed to be Robert Louis Stevenson's *Treasure Island*, is currently for sale. The entire island, 610 acres (244 hectares), is offered for the price of $6,000,000.

Few travelers, and fewer tourists, are hermits, however. Goats, lizards and tree frogs go only so far in providing companionship. There are, it is true, a remarkable number of guard dogs (at night they help to keep away the duppies) and some pet dogs on the islands. Further, there is a large population of very small, hungry-looking cats who do not receive kind attention.

Over on **Jost Van Dyke**, there appears to be a more militant desire to perpetuate the old ways. 'Jost,' as it is affectionately called by Tortolans, has a small population of its own families: Turners, Ringes, Grants, Callwoods. The expatriate influence has been felt to a lesser degree: mysterious fires that burn out expatriate houses and beach

resorts tend to discourage development. The bareboat charter crowd has discovered Jost as a good party island for an evening. After sundown, small boats filled with bathed and shaved sail charterers and private yachtsmen from the States descend upon **Foxy's**, **Rudy's**, **Abe's**, and **Happy Laury's** for pig roasts, drinks and dancing. After the bacchanal, the revelers return to their ships to sleep it off. Then they sail away, leaving Jost Van Dyke looking much as it must have looked 100 or 200 years ago—and how Tortola must have looked 50 years ago.

A day's hike along the dirt tracks of Jost Van Dyke and some exploratory swimming brings a traveler close to the realities of life there. Bulls engage in power fights along the track, manchineel trees offer their deadly shade along picture postcard beaches, and scuttled wooden sloops guard an attractive anchorage. And in dramatic juxtaposition to the dangerous subtleties of life on a small British Virgin Island is the vision of life-after-death expressed on a tomb in Great Harbour:

"When the saved of the earth shall gather
Over on the other shore
And the roll is called up yonder
I'll be there."

Below, a beachfront police station.

EXPLORING ANGUILLA

Anguilla, the most northerly of the Leeward Islands and a British colony, is a serene, remote place. Its empty beaches are smooth with coral sand white as snow. Although the steep blue hills of St. Martin are visible from its south shore, Anguilla feels more like a raft floating alone in a vast sea than a fixed place in an archipelago.

So today it's strange to learn that once, not very long ago, the island's name was splashed across the world's headlines. The reason for this celebrity further defies comprehension—in 1969 Britain invaded little Anguilla while the island rebelled.

The story of the rebellion begins with another island state, St. Kitts-Nevis. For administrative expediency, Britain lumped its colonies Anguilla and St. Kitts-Nevis together. Proximity, tenuous at that, was the most that Anguilla shared with the state to the south. St. Kitts-Nevis is mountainous and lush, with a large and landless peasant society grown tense on sugar and slavery. Anguilla is flat, dry and calm, with a tiny population and a history colored more by self-determination than slavery. At the time of the rebellion St. Kitts-Nevis and Anguilla detested each other. Kittians liked to think of Anguillians as hicks, calling them "Bobo Johnnys" and using them as the butt of moron jokes. The Prime Minister of St. Kitts-Nevis expressed his attitude towards Anguilla in saying, "I will put salt in their coffee, bones in their rice and salt in their sugar." The Prime Minister denied Anguilla any real representation in their shared government and flogged the smaller island's fragile economy relentlessly. Anguillians were both offended and oppressed by the Kittians' superiority complex.

In 1967, doing its best to lose its Caribbean colonial baggage, Britain tried to force Anguilla into a lasting union with the dreaded St. Kitts-Nevis, through the independent and *de jure* status of "Associated Statehood." Anguilla, desperate to sever rather than strengthen ties with Kittians, rebelled. Protestors brandished Union Jacks and placards flaunting slogans like "We Don't Want Statehood, We Want England." This peculiar rebel call was not the least of reasons why the world, and even most Anguillians, came to view the rebellion as something of a comic opera.

Britain, still blind to Anguilla's plight, could not be deterred from its tidy solution

to its Caribbean clutter. In February, 1967, the Associated State of St. Kitts-Nevis-Anguilla was signed into law. Anguillians marked the occasion by solemnly parading a black-draped coffin labeled "Statehood" around the island. Tension mounted and Anguillian rebels burned down Government House and Her Majesty's Warden fled. The rebels sent home the 12 policemen installed by St. Kitts.

St. Kitts responded by cutting off rebel Anguilla's mail, the island's only source of cash. (Until very recently, most men worked and lived at least part of the year off-island and sent earnings home to support their families.) Still, Anguillians rallied together to survive. The isolation imposed by the rebellion gave the island a chance to learn how to govern itself. Rebel Anguilla enlisted a Harvard Law professor to write a constitution and sent a representative to the United Nations to plead its cause. Meanwhile Britain, finally paying some attention, albeit misguided, to Anguilla, adopted the domino theory and decided that Anguilla was "mounting a disturbance" which would cause a Caribbean-wide "effect". Actually, all the island was saying was that it wanted to remain a British colony.

Red-faced Brits: Heedless, Britain invaded Anguilla on March 19, 1969, with a battalion of 338, including Royal Marines and Red Devil paratroopers. This elite fighting force was met at Sandy Ground by children bearing flowers and candy bars, by broad-smiling parents singing "God Save the Queen," and by the usual contingent of goats. Not a shot was fired in the invasion, which *Time Magazine* tagged: "Britain's Bay of Piglets."

World reaction shamed the British government into rethinking its position on the Anguillian rebellion. Some troops were ordered to stay on the island to help Anguillians build roads, a telephone system and a long-needed pier. Britain reassumed full responsibility for the island, and Anguilla is once again, in its own right, a Colony of the British Commonwealth. Despite the quirks, the Anguillian rebellion became, finally, a people's serious and successful attempt at self-determination.

Today Anguilla has a new constitution and is governed by a ministerial system and a seven-member House of Assembly, including a Chief Minister. The local government handles almost all domestic affairs, while a British Governor takes care of the civil service, police, judiciary and foreign affairs. Anguillians are content with their status and don't anticipate independence in the near future. It is a fortunate arrangement, for the island governs itself but relies on capital funding from the Commonwealth.

Buried treasures: Despite European invaders and pirates, two remarkable houses survived Anguilla's strife-torn centuries. **Wallblake House** was built in 1787, of cut stone hauled arduously across the island from the East End or Scrub Island. Burnt coral, shells and molasses are mixed into the mortar. Clever carpenters, most likely native shipwrights, carved its intricate woodwork. The interior of the cozy, staunch-looking structure is hung with "inverted-tray" ceilings, their edges decorated with carved "roping" in true West Indian style. The Catholic Church now owns the house and garden, and next door sits a tiny modern chapel with walls of open stonework, through which trade winds whistle into Mass.

A succession of Magistrate-Doctors, representing the British Crown, lived in **Old Island House**, circa 1800, in the Valley. The two-story wooden structure has been restored by the Gumbs of Rendezvous Bay and is now painted apple-green. Old Island House is now an art gallery with a restaurant serving local dishes and bread baked in the original brick oven.

Slaveless society: Survival—animal, vegetable or mineral—on Anguilla has always been a question of beating the odds. Drought plagues the island's climate, and the hurricane season is often fierce. Anguilla means eel in Spanish and Italian and the island is flat and thin, 16 miles (25 km) long and no more than three miles (five km) wide. Topsoil is scarce, and only a few acres are fertile enough to support hardy crops—pigeon peas, cassava, yams, corn and tropical fruits. Elsewhere, the 35 square miles (90 square km) are tangled with low tough scrub, foraged by hundreds of goats.

This impoverished land endowed Anguilla with a social history that, like its political history, is quirky. The British colonizers tried to plant tobacco and, later, sugar. Because of the dry climate and poor soil, these cash crops never took root and neither did plantations or slavery. Still, slaves were duly imported, although they were freed long before Emancipation in 1833. Eventually, the land was left to poor whites and Anguillians of African descent. (Even slaves worked their own land, because beleaguered planters, who could hardly afford to feed their own families, let their slaves free four days a week to grow their own food.)

Anguilla's poor soil left its people free of

the scars of slavery, and they appear strong and savvy, not oppressed. Anguilla, left on its own, evolved into an extraordinarily egalitarian and color-blind society, where everybody owned their land and helped each other through the frequent droughts and hurricanes and to overcome the lack of fresh water and arable soil. Nevertheless, one resource, besides characters, was left to the Anguillians—the sea. Unlike other West Indians, landlocked by the success of plantations, Anguillians became expert boatbuilders, sailors and fishermen, their fame as wide as the Caribbean.

Boat people: Boats, then, have always been Anguilla's lifeline, but to build and shelter boats, Anguillians had to overcome enormous obstacles. The island is without timber or a single hurricane-proof harbor. Still, brashly, her fleet of home-built schooners thrived, from the 18th to the mid-20th century. Although plantation islands were all better endowed to support a fleet, indigenous shipping was scarce elsewhere. Anguillians' sea trading was further remarkable in that the crew shared in each voyage's profits, rather than taking a monthly wage. One captain remarked, "If the owner is buying a car, we (the crew) are buying a chair."

The Anguillian schooner **Warspite** sailed for most of the 20th century and holds a significant place in the island's history. Her roster of owners and skippers makes up an Anguillian Who's Who, including a Chief Minister Emile Gumbs. The schooner traded goods and carried Anguillian men to and from half-year stints in the sugar fields of Santo Domingo. She carried salt harvested from the ponds at Road Bay and West End to the oil refineries in Trinidad; and relief crews and provisions to the lighthouse 40 miles (65 km) offshore at Sombrero Island. The Warspite is particularly famous for bringing 300 Anguillian cane cutters home from Santo Domingo in three and a half days' journey which broke all records for speed. Acting as a patron saint, a print of the Warspite hangs today at David Carty's **Rebel Marine**. Here racing boats, cruise boats and the sporty ferries which slice the waters to St. Martin are designed and custom-built.

Fishing on Anguilla has always been a booming business. Brightly painted, prosperous-looking fishing boats neatly span the beach at **Island Harbor**. After the day's catch, fishermen spill sacks of spiny lobster on the sand to display for buyers. Anguilla's lobsters are sweet and luscious and so plen-

Preceding pages: fishermen swim in Neads Bay; fishermen bring in their catch of the day. **Below,** a colorful example of island architecture.

tiful that they are exported to St. Martin, Puerto Rico and St. Thomas. However, the lobster's taste remains a mystery to the fishermen, most of whom are Seventh Day Adventists and follow dietary laws which prohibit shellfish.

Other Anguillian fish specialties are red snapper, conch and whelk. Fresh lobster and fish are grilled and served creole-style at the hotels and also at locally owned restaurants like **Lucy's Harbor View**, the **Aquarium**, **Johnno's Fish Pot** or the **Old House**. The local restaurants serve delicious West Indian dishes, as well, like goat stew, pumpkin soup and even Anguilla's own, Perry's Soda Pop.

Anguillian fishing boats are now powered by outboard motor, but the fleet flourished once under sail. In their small boats, the fishermen would race home together for safety, for their work would take them as far out at sea as 30 miles (50 km). Racing became a passion for the sea-daring Anguillians, and today, the traditional wooden boats are built and sailed solely for that purpose. The sport is so popular that Anguilla is the only British West Indian island where cricket has been eclipsed in popularity. Starting from the beaches at **Sandy Ground**, **Meads Bay**, **Blowing Point** and **Rendezvous Bay**, the boats race to a marker out at sea and back. On holidays and during Carnival, the whole island comes out to watch the races and place bets.

Homecoming: Carnival is a new festival, which takes place in August, to celebrate Anguillian pride and promote tourism. Dancing parades begin early in the morning, and barbecue rigs on the beach grill chicken, ribs and fresh-caught fish throughout the day. Lots of pageants are staged for Carnival, including contests for Calypso Queen, Prince and Princess, and Miss Teenage. Every guest house room is taken, and every private home brims with Anguillians returned from elsewhere in the Caribbean and abroad. More Anguillians live in Slough, Great Britain, and Perth Amboy, New Jersey, than on the island itself.

Anguilla has long been a place of homecomings and pilgrimages. Centuries before Columbus, Arawak Indians canoed to Anguilla's Fountain cavern to perform religious rites. The **Fountain**, near **Shoal Bay**, provides the island's only natural spring. Some islanders are old enough to remember times of drought when, as children, they would seek the cool, fresh waters of the Fountain. Clambering down through the entrance hole marked by an ancient yucca,

Below, **Sunday** **afternoon** **rough-** **housing.** **Following** **pages:** **Sandy** **Island.**

called the "Signature Tree," the children would carry buckets to fill in the mysterious depths. Little did these children know that their chores were being observed and perhaps blessed by Jocahu, the supreme God of the Arawaks.

In 1979 a team of archaeologists explored the Fountain and discovered a magnificently preserved, 2,000-year-old petroglyph of Jocahu. (The only other Jocahu petroglyph had been found in Cuba, sawed in half, and sent to the United States.) Twelve more petroglyphs were also discovered in the Fountain, along with various shards, pots, bones and stone tools. The team identified 18 other Anguillian sites rich in pre-Columbian artifacts, making Anguilla one of the most archaeologically interesting places in the Caribbean. Now a National Park, the Fountain's archaeological treasures are easily accessible amongst the cavern's gruesome stalactites and stalagmites.

Tasteful tourism: Today, perhaps what is most unusual and most compelling about Anguilla is its to-date, tasteful approach to tourism. Anguillians swear they have learned a lesson from watching the gross overdevelopment of other islands, particularly St. Martin. Development on Anguilla is being restricted to small, expensive resort-hotels. However, the granddaddy of the island's hotels, the **Rendezvous Bay**, is moderately priced. Built before the Rebellion by one of the founding fathers of Anguilla, Jeremiah Gumbs, the hotel is infused with his sprawling personality. Roosting on Rendezvous Bay's beautiful half-moon-shaped beach, the hotel's commodious veranda hosts family-style meals and an open bar.

The other hotels, all opened since 1982, are lavish, with tennis courts, watersports and gourmet restaurants. (The list below is partial.) One of the Caribbean's most costly hotels, the **Malliouhana** (from the Arawak name for the island) is an exclusive, jet-set haunt. Security is tight and its huge rooms are hung with a glorious collection of Haitian art. Bathrooms are gargantuan with big mirrors, deep tubs and bidets. The wine cellar stocks 30,000 bottles. The restaurant, overseen by a famous French chef, charges US$14 for a hamburger.

The **Mariners** on Road Bay beach is managed and part-owned by Anguillians, deluxe and happily relaxed. Traditional, West Indian style gingerbread cottages nestle between a seagrape grove and a beautifully landscaped garden, lush with oleander, hibiscus, Barbados Pride, flamboya,

bougainvillea, guava, pawpaw, lime and orange trees.

Cinnamon Reef's 14 villas are built to withstand hurricanes and look a bit like tanks, especially with their cute, color-coded flags. Inside, however, the villas are lovely, spacious and very private, each with its own terrace, where a rope hammock swings in the breeze. Tennis and watersports are free at this wonderfully hospitable, American-owned place. Even locals feel at ease in the bar and dining room, perched aside **Little Harbour**, drinking and listening to local calypso and reggae performers. **Cul de Sac**, a tiny hotel associated with Malliouhana, hosts Anguilla's **Mayoumba Folklorica Theatre**, a local singing group which draws much of its material from the island's history.

Luxury condominiums are also available to rent, most notably **Shoal Bay Villas** on the island's most gorgeous beach. The more moderately priced **Easy Corner Villas** are perched on South Hill with a sweeping view of Road Bay.

To the unschooled eye, Anguilla seems to be experiencing a permanent building boom. Partly constructed concrete houses are everywhere. They are not, however, another testament to the new economy, bullish on tourism. Instead this slow construction is a holdover from the remittance economy and also marks a kind of coming of age. The first thing every island boy does on graduation from school is to lay down the foundation for a house. Then over as many as 15 years, as his earnings trickle in, the house is built.

Much of Anguilla's charm today lies still in what it lacks. No jetport means no mass market package tours. **Wallblake Airstrip** can only take small, island hopping planes. (Most arrivals are, instead, by sea at Blowing Point, on swift ferries from Marigot, St. Martin, just 20 minutes away). No town means settlement is scattered over the island, each house on its own roomy lot. No streams or fresh water ponds mean no mosquitos.

Not many people, only 7,000 full-time residents, means courtesy reigns. Everybody knows one another and cars don't pass each other without a nod, a wave or a honk. The solitary disco on-island caters mainly to West Indians and is open only on weekends and holidays. There are no casinos, and it is not likely that there ever will be. The church is still the center of Anguillian life. The Methodist, Anglican and what islanders call "sideways" churches, mostly Baptist and Seventh Day Adventist, all claim large and active congregations.

The Rebellion did, however, launch Anguilla into the 20th century, and today the island shows some signs of the times. Although there is no shopping to speak of, young women dress fashionably off the racks of the Parisian boutiques on St. Martin. The island has no movie theater, but it does have cable T.V., VCRs and several video stores. Little Anguillians breakdance and rap in the schoolyards, as radio brings American music to the island. It's more popular than any native sound, more so even than Bankie Banx's, Anguilla's own recorded reggae star.

Anguilla's small Rastafarian population includes three civil servants. In fact, the Rastafarian Movement was founded by an Anguillian named Althyi Rogers. In the early 1920s in Newark, New Jersey, Rogers wrote and published the Holy Pibi which became the central text of Rastafarianism and "living righteously." He founded a church in South Africa before he killed himself. His Holy Pibi lived on to inspire Marcus Garvey and the Back to Africa Movement.

The island has no drug problem but is cooperating with the U.S.A.'s drug war, as the illegal trade moves to the Eastern Caribbean. Anguilla suffers from a rash of teenage pregnancies, but the problem is not epidemic as elsewhere in the West Indies. The Rebellion made Anguilla something of a pariah in the Caribbean Community, because its rejection of independence was seen as backward. The Community is now beginning to forgive Anguilla, which is joining many Caribbean-wide economic and political institutions.

Once again Anguilla looks to the sea for its future. Now the sea brings tourists and the first affluence that the island has ever experienced. Since 1982 when the first new resort-hotels opened, the twin problems of unemployment on-island and seasonal emigration off-island have virtually been eliminated.

The biggest question facing the island is whether this new wave of prosperity and opportunity will sink it. Anguillians are aware that they could lose their serene way of life unless they place strict limits on growth. They continue the struggle to hold back the tide of overdevelopment and bring in tourism sensibly, on a small, high-end scale, but greed is a strong force too. Most Anguillians pray that they will find the strength to keep their place quiet and simple while allowing tourism to keep their economy buoyantly afloat.

EXPLORING
ST. MARTIN

According to legend, **St. Martin**'s border was defined when a Dutchman and a Frenchman stood back to back, then walked around the island until they met face to face. The Dutch side is smaller supposedly because the Dutchman was fat, or slow, or drinking gin as he walked, or all three. A more likely version holds that small groups of French and Dutch prisoners escaped their Spanish captors and drew up an agreement to divide the island between them.

Whatever its origins, St. Martin's border bisects the smallest landmass—38 square miles (96 square km), in the world shared by two countries. The smaller, more developed southern half is Dutch while the northern side of the island belongs to France. As of 1946, French St. Martin is technically an *arondissement* of Guadeloupe, which is a *departement* of France (in the same way that Hawaii is a state of the Union).

Fittingly, this two-nationality island is composed of two contrasting landscapes: the west end of the island is an atoll of low land surrounding a lagoon, while the east end consists of a range of conical hills, like a plate of candy kisses. Actually, St. Martin is folded into two parallel ranges. One stretches north-northeast from **Cole Bay Hill** and includes the highest peak, **Mount Paradise** (1,360 feet); the other runs from Pointe Blanche to Oyster Point, creating the steep rocky cliffs along the weathered south-east coast. In the slight depression between these two ranges lie Great Bay with its Salt Pond, the valley of Belle Plaine and the smaller salt ponds at Le Galion.

This is an island that offers charm, not drama. The hills are low and easy to climb, the beaches are sheltered, the feral boars of Terres Basses are long gone. It's a fertile landscape of soft hills and pasture, cattle and horses. Green and hawksbill turtles nest here, and offshore the fishing is good .

Secret languages: There's a sly elusiveness about identities on this island. For instance, it's unclear whether residents are to be called St. Martinois or St. Maartener or St. Martinian. Even the population figures are mysterious: for 1986 various sources give figures ranging from 15,000 to 25,000 on the Dutch side, from 8,000 to 18,000 on the French, and thousands of illegal aliens are said to enter the island's booming labor market every year.

One reason for this elusiveness is an

extraordinary linguistic situation. The principal languages are Dutch, French, English, Spanish and Papiamento. Coincidentally, the Caribs, too, had multiple languages: ordinary Carib, a secret "men's language" forbidden to women and children, and the Arawak spoken among the captive women—a language that Carib men of course did not learn, but Carib women apparently did, taking advantage of it as an exclusive *women's* language.

Throughout the Caribbean, language is a political force. As a rule English (like French) is viewed as the conqueror's language, and some form of creole as the mother tongue, the "national language". On St. Martin the reverse is true. English is the mother tongue, the intimate language of family life on both sides of the island. Also, it was the early commercial language of the region, gaining importance when the youthful United States became a major trading partner, and it has always functioned as a neutral *lingua franca* amid the raging hostilities of Holland, Spain, and France.

On the Dutch side English is the language of primary school and is expected soon to be the language of all instruction. On the French side, predictably, schooling is always in French; and though most students speak English already, they do not study it until secondary school. There seems to be no distinctive local form of English, but the inflections of the whole eastern Caribbean can be identified: St. Croix, St. Kitts, Antigua, even Barbados and Trinidad. The unmistakable sound of Rastafarian speech is also evident.

Papiamento, on the other hand, which more than one guidebook has mistaken for the mother tongue, is widely regarded by islanders as the argot of interlopers. It is a pidgin, developed primarily in Curaçao from Dutch, English, Spanish, Portuguese, and some African languages. The men of St. Martin may have learned it in the oil refineries, but it was not heard on the island until after 1960, when it arrived as the language of an imported labor force. Spoken Papiamento can be baffling, but it's not difficult to read if you know a language or two. Mostly it looks like Spanish written down by a Dutchman: *aki* - here (aqui), *kaya* - street (calle), *awa* - water, *pan* - bread. *Majan* means tomorrow (manana), though one says *luna* for month, like an Indian in a western. Dutch and English are also recognizable: *buki* - book, *motosaikel* - motorcycle, *konsekuensianan* - consequences, *masha danki* - many thanks. There is a Papiamento newspaper, *La Prensa*, available in Philipsburg.

Placid history: By Caribbean standards the history of St. Martin has been rather placid. In the half-millennium before Columbus, the Caribs made their way up from South America through the Antilles, displacing the less aggressive Awaraks. Remains of a half dozen or so Indian camps have been unearthed to date, especially around the beaches of Lowlands. These Amerindians seem to have thought of St. Martin as a resort or hunting ground: the Caribs referred to the island as Sualougia, "a place to get salt" and Oualichi, "a place to get women."

There were probably a few Caribs on the beach just after hurricane season in what would come to be called 1493, when Columbus passed by somewhere to the south. Characteristically, the most significant event in the history of St. Martin happened somewhere else; Columbus was too far away even to see this island. What he sighted and named St. Martin's Day during his second voyage was Nevis, or possibly St. Kitts.

For more than a century the passage of Columbus had few consequences here. In the 1620s Europe began to take an interest in the eastern Caribbean, and for about a generation there was a burst of activity. The Spanish, French and Dutch all made appearances. It was salt, finally, that led the Dutch to lay claim to the island. Holland was at war with Spain, and Spain had a monopoly on European salt, an essential commodity for the preservation of food in the days before refrigeration. When the Dutch built a fort in 1631, Spain responded quickly by capturing the island in 1633 and building a second fort across the bay at Point Blanche. The Dutch soon tried again. In 1644, young Peter Stuyvesant was appointed governor of Curaçao. In the same year he attempted to recapture St. Martin, but left without a battle after losing his leg to a Spanish cannonball at Cay Bay (three years later he became governor of the Dutch colony on Manhattan). Only four years after Stuyvesant's failure, the Spanish abandoned the island. At that point, French and Dutch inhabitants divided the territory between them.

Though there is some question whether the European government ever officially recognized the local Treaty, the border has survived unchanged to the present, despite several armed incursions in both directions, persistent attempts by the Dutch in the 18th century to buy the French side outright and the fact that the island has changed hands 16 times since 1648.

Unlike many of the other islands, St. Martin is not averse to its present or past colonial connections. Here the rhetoric of independence and self-sufficiency is rare. As in several of the smaller Caribbean nations, economic independence is recognized as an impossible ideal. If anything, opinion in the bars and cafes on both sides of the island leans toward a surprising preference for more direct governance from Europe. Some islanders are particularly eloquent in their irritation at being ruled from another small island rather than from a "real" country. After all, 600 miles separate Saint Maarten from Curaçao, while five English islands and two Dutch intervene in the 150 between Marigot and Guadeloupe. Marigot seems actually to have lost some autonomy, and there is a general, if rather nostalgic, sentiment that under direct rule St. Martin would be less encumbered by bureaucracy and at the same time would have better access to real executive authority and resources.

Sand and salt: In 1733 a town was founded on the sand bar that separates the **Salt Ponds** from **Great Bay**. It was named **Philipsburg**, in honor of John Philips, the Scotsman who did so much for the early development of Dutch St. Martin. The sand is still very much in evidence; all over town there are unobtrusive welcome mats to keep as much of it outdoors as possible. What's left of the Salt Ponds, however, is easy to ignore, a stretch of stagnant water much reduced by the landfill expansion of the town. Anguilla still invites visitors to observe the harvest from two working salt ponds, but here the traces of the profitable industry that once supported the whole island are few and easy to miss. There's some rusted equipment, but who would realize that when **Back Street** takes a strange course just behind the **Sea Palace Hotel**, it's avoiding the ghost of a huge storage pile, 30 feet high and perhaps 100 feet long?

Philipsburg is a lively town—a smaller version of Charlotte Amalie: its two main roads, **Front Street** and **Back Street**, are linked by a series of narrow alleys supporting a cruise ship port, several hotels, and "the shopping center of the Leewards." In the middle of everything is the **Courthouse**, built in 1793. A whole book has been written about its history, but now this is the place to buy stamps and pay parking tickets. Directly in front of it, the town's characteristic excitement begins as ships' tenders unload crowds of passengers, all bent on the same task of spending money for pleasure.

Preceding page: hot dog and religion; tiny gambling establishment, Philipsburg. Below, a beach on the French side.

Moving along Front Street the eye at first meets nothing but shop windows—Gucci, Kohinoor, Little Switzerland—but soon the ornamental fretwork known as West Indian "gingerbread" comes into focus, and next, the buildings themselves. The characteristic architecture that developed in the 18th and 19th centuries is still evident in two-storey structures with a warehouse or shop below, living quarters above, and steps from the street up to a front gallery or veranda. There are many examples around **Oranje School** and **Wathey Square**, former merchant residences that became shops as the population moved back out of the developing town. This neighborhood is still the place to find such local haunts as **Oranje Bar**, **Risdon Snack Bar**, and **Gordon's**. A bit uptown is the **Pasanggrahan**, originally a government guest house, and now the oldest inn on the island, maintaining its atmosphere of dishevelled charm only a few steps from Front Street. Out of the limelight on Back Street is the active **Cultural Center**, opened in 1960. Not far away, the **Jubilee Library** is not only bright, comfortable, and popular; it also has a very impressive circulating collection of books from and about the Caribbean in several languages. Few public libraries in the region could match it.

Nearby, Front Street ends at **Vineyard**, a notable country house right at the edge of town.

Shoppers delight: After the hubbub of Philipsburg, **Marigot** seems deserted. This is a more typical West Indian town, though there's more than a touch of Southern France here, especially in the dappled shade of the little **Post Office Square** and in the Mediterranean light of the sea-side cemetery along **Rue De La Liberte**. There is shopping to be done here, especially along **Rue de la Republique** and in the boutiques around **Marina Port La Royale**, but the open-air market on the quay is a sign that what Marigot chiefly offers for consumption is food. Significantly, the town still takes a siesta from noon until two, much more conducive to digestion than to commerce, and unthinkable among the driven merchants of Philipsburg, where midday belongs to the cruise ships.

On a map, the two towns look very similar. Both are laid out in comparable grids three streets deep, facing the sea. But Philipsburg is essentially one street, full of incoming traffic, and the center of town is defined by the intersection of that street with the daily infusion of cruise passengers, often four shiploads at a time. Because Phil-

Cafe in Philipsburg.

ipsburg is linear and traffic-oriented, it is not really possible to "wander" here, though one guidebook desperately suggests that "you will enjoy meandering from one side of the street to the other." There is no place to pause without stepping out of the flow altogether, into a hotel or restaurant. In fact, there is no such thing as a park in Philipsburg. Even the beach seems somehow out of bounds. Philipsburg keeps its back turned to the sea.

By contrast, the main road runs behind, not through, Marigot. The heart of the town is a multi-purpose open space full of activity, but set off from the flow of vehicular traffic and the intrusion of harbor traffic. The Marigot quay is wide open to the sea, a welcoming recess. The town meets the sea with an embrace.

One of the pleasures of travel is an illusory participation in the life of a new place, and this Marigot provides better than its counterpart. Philipsburg invites you to plunge in and buy; it does not invite you to stop and watch. Marigot does. With its market square and cluster of cafes, the street grid acknowledges and uses the sea front. Even the recent **Marina Port La Royale** development repeats this pattern, surrounding its boat basin with shops and cafes. The

town boasts several little parks, and it seems natural to think of going down to the quay with no particular purpose; or of sitting in the horseshoe of the Marina to watch the yachts. There is no equivalent in the dynamics of Philipsburg, where the center of things ought to be **Wathey Square** and the pier: but no one for sport watches the cruise ship tenders come and go, or the taxis, or the vendors of wood carvings. Two restaurants, one frankly cheap, the other not, are perfect observation points, but it seems to be against the spirit of the town for anyone to spend his time this way.

In Marigot on the other hand, it seems entirely right to sit and watch the ferries loading for Anguilla while you eat chicken barbecued over a halved oil drum, or salt cod (the old slave food) served with rice and peas, or fresh fish with lime and garlic and spices—Caribbean fare served in English. Or, if you prefer, to survey the market square over espresso and pastry in a cafe like **La Vie en Rose**, where, in true French fashion, English *will not* be spoken. And yes, drive over to Marigot simply for the coffee, an almost unattainable pleasure in the English-speaking Caribbean, where you find either stale instant or, as in Jamaica, locally grown coffee cooked (that's the

School-children in Philipsburg.

right word, alas) in what can only be called the British style.

In Philipsburg, you can watch Saba, often invisible in the light of day, materialize out of nowhere at dawn and dusk, its peaks as ominous and alluring as a phantom island in a fairy tale. Marigot, too, had its phantom across the bay: the ruins of **La Belle Creole**, an extravagant resort begun with much fanfare, never completed, and abandoned in ruins for about 20 years. But in 1986 it was refurbished into a Hilton, and now lights up the night like a cruise ship. With neat irony, commercial Philipsburg is haunted by a mystery, and sleepy Marigot, by a specter of world-class tourism.

Dutch forts: In Barbados the roads are not only narrow but frequently walled. Jamaicans drive like soccer players; Trinidadians like anarchists on holiday. In St. Thomas the driving is forthrightly American, but the island is choked with cars. In St. Martin, driving is sweet. True, some roads in **Lowlands** are more like streambeds, but you can drive all day and never hear a horn; the hill roads are wide enough, and traffic still stops for conversations on Front Street.

In the countryside there has so far been little effort at preserving historical sites. The largest relics on St. Martin are the ruins of three forts around Philipsburg: **Fort Willem on Fort Hill**, **Fort Amsterdam** commanding Great Bay from the west, and **Old Spanish Fort on Pointe Blanche** (a fourth, **Fort St. Louis**, overlooks Marigot). As the locations of the forts suggest, the earliest Dutch settlements were on the sand bar and around **Little Bay**, but many historical sites are clustered in the hills behind Philipsburg. For a sense of plantation life, visit **Mary's Fancy** up in **Cul de Sac**, a group of plantation buildings transformed into a hotel. Nearby is **Little Bay Cemetery**, bordering John Philip's former estate. His tomb is here, on the foundation of the **Dutch Reformed Church**, which had already been demolished at the time of his death in 1746, so that the materials could be used to rebuild in the prospering town that bore his name.

Further along is a justly famous vista of the Lagoon and the neighboring islands from the brow of **Cole Bay Hill**. Beyond, the road drops to **Simpson Bay** and to the hotels and beaches that circle the west end: **Maho, Mullet Bay, Cupecoy, Long Bay, Plum Bay, Rouge Bay**. These beaches are the island's whitest; limestone and marl sediment laid in nearly horizontal beds has

Haggling over prices at a roadside market.

created low, richly colored cliffs along the shoreline that are the special charm of Cupecoy.

Driving the long curve of Marigot Bay you return to the hills of the French side. Here, around **Grand Case**, were many of the 18th century sugar plantations. The crop must have been introduced to St. Martin around the time of the Treaty of 1648. It ushered in a long period of prosperity, increased settlement and slavery, which lasted into the latter half of the 19th century. The settlers came from neighboring islands rather than from Europe, and the first blacks came with their migrant owners. Things were relatively calm here (rumors of poisoning that periodically spread among the planters probably originated in other French islands). There is little evidence of revolt or escapes—probably not because resistance was unnecessary, but because it was hopeless. St. Martin was deforested quite early; it is apparent that cane was planted virtually on the hilltops. The small size and hospitable terrain that now make the island friendly to visitors meant there were no hiding places for runaways.

During the height of prosperity some 50 sugar mills were in operation on the island. But the end of slavery was tantamount to the end of agriculture, and the end came to the French side (after several false starts) in 1848. For 15 painful years there was slavery in the south and not in the north, on an island where plantations often straddled the border. But freedom came to the south in 1863 (Caribbean emancipation nearly always came in July or August; that is, after the sugar harvest). Within a decade sugar production had come to a halt, and with only salt, cotton and few cattle for export, the island went into a long decline that continued until about 1960.

Borrowed cuisine: It has been said of the little town of **Grand Case** that its only industry is eating, but there is an art gallery here (the paintings of Gloria Lynn and sculptures of Martin Lynn are worth a visit), and of course, a beach. The sand at **Grand Case** and **Friar's Bay** is darker, not white, and the light seems different on this side of the island, with tones of ochre and gold. The road leads on through the rolling countryside of the **French Cul de Sac** to the mangrove swamps that face **Islet Pinel** and the isolated beaches north of **Orleans**. This town served as the capital of French St. Martin until 1768, but only graves and the old dueling ground recall those days.

Beyond are the beaches of **Oyster Pond**,

A farm in Lower Princes Quarter.

and reefs that lure scuba-divers to their caves and cliffs, or to the wreck of the frigate H.M.S. Proselyte, sunk nearly 200 years ago and still sporting cannons and anchor amid the coral. The coast itself is wild, with windswept scrub and cactus, including the striking Pope's Head and other endangered species, around **Guana Bay** (named for the iguanas that use to be found here in abundance). Once this trip ended dramatically with a sort of salt water geyser at **Devil's Cupper**; but changes in the rock formation due to construction have eliminated that. Now it ends less spectacularly, with a sundowner in Philipsburg.

The most touted creole creativity in St. Martin is culinary. One brochure claims there are 180 restaurants! Paradoxically almost nothing is now grown on this "restaurant island." Higglers (called "tray women" here) used to carry trays of fruit from the fertile **Columbier Valley** to market in Marigot and even Philipsburg; now virtually everything is imported. The tomatos and oranges for sale on Marigot quay, for example, come from California. One seafood restaurant in Philipsburg proudly announces that all its fish are flown in fresh from New England.

There is no local cuisine as such, though you are more likely to realize you're in France in a restaurant than anywhere else on the island. The Indonesian restaurants offer an opportunity to sample *bami goreng* and *rijsttafel* (a Javanese smorgasbord). Some restaurants offer the dishes of the ABC islands (hard to find elsewhere): *keshi yena*, (Edam cheese stuffed with a very rich stew), *stoba* (a stew of lamb or goat), and *funchi* (or *fungi*), a corn meal dish like Italian polenta or the *coocoo* of the Eastern Caribbean. Creole cooking is at its best with seafood, and Philipsburg has one incognito Trinidadian restaurant in which local lobster, conch, and fish are treated with particular respect. The **West Indian Tavern** is notable for the audacious creole imagination displayed in such confections as conch marinated in lime, lavender and coriander, or grouper sauteed with hazelnuts, bacon and cream.

Ghosts and spirits: On the whole, St. Martin shares the usual regional folklore of jumbies (ghosts, evil spirits) and soucouyants (though the local term for these vampire women seems to be *soucanaire*). The proverbs and popular dances are those throughout the Eastern Caribbean. Some of the larger hotels offer weekly calypso and carnival shows throughout the year; these

Hotel beach at Oyster Pond.

are entertaining, but of course not indigenous to St. Martin, and the quintessential sting of calypso, the social and political satire that Trinidad calls *picong*, is necessarily impossible here on the "friendly island."

Though St. Martin has no rich cultural heritage, there are stirrings of artistic life. Strangely, the force of French metropolitan culture seems to have acted against local cultural development. No newspaper is published here in French, and there is no library in Marigot. The Dutch side is considerably more advanced, thanks to its cultural contacts with the Anglophone Caribbean. In addition to the contributions of individuals, there are ventures like the Cole Bay Folk Group, the Cole Bay Theatre Company, and Motiance Dance Company. The Council on the Arts, from its center on Back Street, has been an important force in artistic education and performance. The Center has a respectable theater space, which supports drama classes and amateur productions. The Center has successfully staged West Indian plays to good audiences—a risk not always taken even in Kingston, the theater capital of the Anglophone Caribbean. A number of artists spend time in St. Martin, among them Jasper Johns and Romare Bearden.

The poet Derek Walcott also has connections here (his mother comes from St. Martin), but only one local poet is currently in print. Lasana Sekou has produced several volumes of poetry, and has been publishing *Island Newsday: The People's Paper* since 1976. His poetry dreams of independence, but more significantly it bears witness to a local history of political activism dating back to the day of Marcus Garvey and Pan-Africanism—a history of which few other traces survive. Like other young poets in the region, he uses his island's various languages and registers of dialect as a powerful literary resource. While some of his poems lapse into thin revolutionary rhetoric, his vigorous political invective comes as close as St. Martin gets to the spirit of calypso.

Diversified accommodations: St. Martin experienced a long economic decline after the end of sugar production. The opening of oil refineries in Aruba and Curaçao during the 1920s provided jobs, but the social cost of migrant work was high. Family life was disrupted as the island became a remittance society, depending on infrequent mail for news and money from absent husbands, sons and daughters. By 1950, the 300-year-old salt industry on the Dutch side had been abandoned, and the resident population had shrunk to a mere 1,500. When in the early

Long Beach.

50s the refineries were automated and much of the work force returned home, St. Martin reached an economic nadir.

Among the few visitors to what was then a fairly inaccessible island were entrepreneurs, mostly from the United States, who recognized possibilities here. The first tourist hotel, **Little Bay**, opened in 1955. At about the same time the island saw its first cruise ship and, incredibly, its first bank. By 1960 shops had begun to appear, there was a Tourist Bureau, and for the first time electricity was available 24 hours a day. The reversal of the island's fortunes was apparent when it became a labor market, attracting workers from the ABC islands. But the best symbol of this reversal came in 1968, when desalination began. After centuries of separating salt from water, St. Martin now separated water from salt.

Despite the rapidity of development, few horrors were perpetrated. A truly gargantuan project on Little Bay never materialized (it would have included a hotel, several eleven-story buildings, 100 villas, a system of canals, and a cable car). There are only a few instances of the special depravity by which self-contained resorts are ornamented with mock-ups of the traditional local architecture visitors would see if they only got off the grounds. But in St. Martin there are real French villages. On the whole, St. Martin is notable for the rich diversity of its hotels, ranging from idiosyncratic guest houses and opulent hideaways for the wealthy to all-inclusive ghetto resorts. Beyond what it shares with the rest of the Caribbean, the island's appeal can be traced to several factors: the small size that makes its genuine diversity easy to explore, the human scale of its beaches not yet distorted by too many humans, the frankness with which it invites familiarity. More than 300,000 visitors annually find something that suits them here.

St. Martin manages its new industry with real finesse. Yet dependence on tourism entails social risks. The surplus jobs attract imported labor which could be turned into an army of unemployed residents by something as likely as an increase in oil prices. Current prosperity makes higher education abroad accessible to the island's youth, but a decline in the industry could create another generation of expatriates. Economic conditions may be on St. Martin's side this time, but in such matters a degree of social planning is called for that seems inimical to the island's style, and even to its political philosophy.

Cultural identity is also at issue. In a sense, the island has had a split personality since 1648, but if the friendly face of tourism begins to feel like a mask, there is risk of more serious schizophrenia. A few symptoms have already appeared. *St. Martin Events*, a locally written guidebook, honorably draws attention to the poor condition of some native homes, but then feels obliged to pull on the mask: "actually, though, these paint-worn homes serve to add atmosphere to an island which is rated as one of the most 'unspoiled' in all the Antilles." In the long run, St. Martin must find ways to define itself in terms of some identity other than tourism.

Its true identity may still be unfathomable; in the absence of dramatic history or geography, its character must emerge from its people, and this is a very young country. More accurately, it is two non-countries, and in their adjustment to that fact the people of St. Martin may best reveal themselves. The absence of customs officers may seem a public-relations gimmick, but its roots are deeper. Jean Glasscock, whose book, *The Making of an Island*, is a vivid and insightful look at St. Martin, sees the place as "a triumph of people over governments." The symbol of that triumph is the border, originally defined by local people without official approval, and freely exploited for centuries by their descendants in order to escape slavery, smuggle contraband, or find a job. Its significance is at once commemorated and contradicted by a monument that straddles the line beside a road named Union, on a hill called Concord. The fact that this little island owes allegiance to two governments seems, superficially at least, to annul the whole idea of governments.

Under various names—resort, tax haven, pirates' den, Freeport, even Qualichi—St. Martin has always offered a way to *escape* civilization and its discontents. There's always that open border to slip across. Yet the "lawlessness" is extremely civil. What the traveler finds here is an ideal commonwealth, where there are no rules, because, by a kind of enchantment, nothing untoward will ever happen. The spell is fragile, but in good hands: the ancient Martin, famous for dividing his cloak to share it with a beggar, is an apt patron for this amicably divided island. His feast-day, Nov. 11, is appropriately several holidays in one: besides celebrating the saint, the supposed discovery by Columbus, the Treaty of 1648, and (for that French) the Armistice that ended World War I, it also marks for everyone the start of the tourist season.

Right, a tourist and her sunburn in Philipsburg.

116

EXPLORING
ST. BARTS

Surface statistics provide an unarousing and incomplete impression of the tiny island municipality of **St. Barthélemy** in the French Antilles. The total area of saxophone-shaped St. Barts, as it is popularly known, is only 10 square miles (25 square km). By such measurements, New York's Manhattan is more than twice as grand, and Chicago 20 times greater. Yet for this diminutive geographical entity the precepts of finite space, its availability and usefulness, have everything to do with what the island was and is. . .and perhaps most importantly, what it can never be.

An island in sync: As with any place worth a look, the numbers applied to St. Barts can only present unnaturally compressed descriptions, opening windows but closing doors to understanding. Here they express a claustrophobia and an insignificance that poorly reflect the character of the island or the sensibilities of the people who are not unhappy believing that less is more. Steep-sided mountains brindled with torch cactus and stunted wild frangipani; a convo-luted coastline sewn full of blue pockets trimmed with exceptional beaches; kaleidoscopic panoramas, that when encountered, create a feeling of endless topography. In the same way an undersized athlete may overcome his limitations with superior speed or intelligence or strength, so has nature compensated St. Barts with a rugged and irregular beauty. And history has nagged it often enough for the island to have a role in the epic of the New World. Add to these its fundamental feature of whiteness, and you have the components of St. Barts' personality. These traits, shared nowhere else in the Antilles but on the nearby island of Saba, keep St. Barts remarkably unassimilated into the more typical West Indian ethos of cultural and racial syncretism.

The island's rocky arid hills and almost total lack of savannah made a sugar and syrup industry unthinkable, so it is not an island of plantations. While it once exported small quantities of tobacco and cotton, it did not have—nor could its land justify—a slave-supported agricultural economy dominated by a plantocracy. This is not to imply a slaveless history; yet even in its colonial heyday, the ratio of black to white was never more than one-to-one. Compare this to 18th century Haiti where whites were

Preceding pages: a windswept tree. **Below**, one of many boutiques.

outnumbered by their slaves 15-to-one. There are fewer than a hundred blacks in St. Barts today; their ancestral memory of bondage is dim and they do not identify themselves with it. The old black families came here from the neighboring English-speaking islands during the last century to work as stevedores, sailors, and small merchants. Harmony evolved on its own schedule. "Long ago, but in my lifetime," remembers an elderly man, "people used to say, black *this*, black *that*; but everything has changed completely. We live in unity and good Christianship." Racial conflicts, if there are any, are not apparent. "We are as one," says a black youth, smiling and shaking his dreadlocked head. "It's a mystery."

Although there are the barracudas, the land developers, there is no overt corruption on St. Barts, for political and technical infrastructure are, like the island itself, lean. The mayor and his municipal council, all 23 elected every six years, may not be the most efficient record keepers, but the government is too small to shoulder a fat bureaucracy. Nor is there room for more than one ideology here. Candidates for the local administration are perennially right wing. They are much more comfortable with the conservative Chirac than with Mitterand

and his state socialism. Unlike their sister-citizens in Guadeloupe and Martinique, the people of St. Barts are not banking the fires of autonomy. "It's good to have a nation like France looking out for you," says a shop clerk in the capital city, Gustavia. "Independence? Don't speak about that. Crazy people want it."

Here there is no underclass to be placated, suppressed or promised, for unemployment is virtually non-existent, as is not the case in most of the other islands of the Antilles. For the moment, at least, its fishermen, businessmen, builders, and laborers all have plenty to do, spurred on by an industrious ethic that seems incongruously northern and urban. (The apparent incongruity is perhaps explained by history, the Swedes having governed between the first and the present French governments.) As once happened when Sweden took control of this "little pebble" in the 19th-century, people are trying to get *on* the island, not off. Since the port of emigration is wide open, undocumented immigration has become more of a concern and a possible future threat to the notion of "We are as one." The mood of the youth of St. Barts is unlike that of much of the rest of the islands in this part of the world. It is more accurately represented by

A deserted street in Gustavia.

the imagery of cocktails and surfboards, or even cocaine, than by Kalishnikovs or leftist fantasies. Here poverty is associated with individuals, not with the system or with an unjust social order. And although the young reject the conservatism of their parents, their radicalization has been preempted by a perfect capitalist microcosm functioning at full capacity…and in the sun. Thus, travelers who might want to taste from the volatile cauldrons of the Third World are out of luck on St. Barts. The island has full right to its reputation for peace and security, the most influential selling points to its elite expatriate community and its wealthy tourist trade.

The five municipal policemen have trouble recalling crimes of the last several years, but slowly, yes, a suicide, a motorcycle accident. Their eyes brighten as they laugh at themselves for momentarily forgetting the big case: the unsolved disappearance of a woman on Lorient Beach, which they suspect was self imposed, a lovers' intrigue. They worry about drugs and a widespread intemperance that infrequently results in some sloppy street-fighting. Rape? Robbery? No. Almost never.

"No bums, please": St. Barts, declares the island's own tourist guidebook, "is ready to welcome upmarket visitors but doesn't want bums." The source of this sort of hubris, of course, is a presumption about the island's manageable size. But there are no beggars, hucksters or indigents. There are no ramshackle rumshops, no local rums, no native recipe for a patriotically singular rum punch. No colorful, aromatic street market clogs the waterfront of Gustavia, but only four makeshift vegetable stalls on a side *rue*, operated by a half dozen black women who sail the 125 miles from Guadeloupe on weekdays. No hot pepper sauce—the local whites don't like it. Instead of steel bands the visitor is greeted by the rhythm of cement mixers and the siren music of table saws. The island dogs are uncommonly healthy and pampered, though it is true that an unclaimed mutt was exterminated a few years ago.

Perhaps the most poignant evidence of St. Barthélemy's uniqueness in the Caribbean is olfactory—the bankruptcy of its smells. It lacks the woodsmoke of the charcoalmakers and slash and burn farming, the incense of freshly harvested spices, the malodorous whiffs of urine in the streets which typify the West Indies. Is this the Caribbean? Yes, for still the sun is relentless, the sea magnificent, the trade winds comforting, the mosquitoes annoying.

The age of things is everywhere apparent,

especially in Gustavia, which clearly exists on the ruins of its past. And despite the glaze of imported sophistication, there is a tangible rawness in the temperament of the place—a friction in the dynamics of the island's soul—that is categorically West Indian. And there is caution, too, in the face of phenomenal growth in tourism. "We are young in all things modern," says the woman from the tranquil fishing village of **Corossal**, young herself, who started the island's tourist board singlehandedly in 1983, to see what could be deduced about the hoards of visitors overruning St. Barts' 3,500 inhabitants. Over 100,000 visitors arrived in 1984 and the current rate of increase is 21 percent. The protective arm of land that forms the **Port de Plaisance** saves Gustavia from tourist ships, its innards too rough and shallow for their large drafts. Still, caution is essential. "We have to be three times stronger than we have ever been in the face of changes, because we are changing too fast."

Despite the concerns for loss or what might be gained it its place, those people of St. Barts who are not independently wealthy or just newly arrived are dependent on a chain of events directly related to the natural and social attractions of the place. The bringing of wealth from elsewhere for two weeks or the life of a retirement or a fancy is at the core of St. Barts' economic life. As elsewhere, irony plays a role, as the seeker of privacy follows hordes of others; yet somehow each seeker is absorbed as a marsh absorbs hermit crabs of whose presence we are normally unaware. There are few complaints, for the beaches sought are plentiful, from grand to small: going west, the **Anse of Public** on the way to tradition bound Corossal, and on that village's other side a wonderful and quiet beach at the end of a double-back road; the **Anse des Flamands** on the route back toward Gustavia by way of a detour near the Quartier du Columbier, but a hotel and club share this beach, so intimacy cannot be a consideration. The northern shore holds its pleasure places: the **Anses de Lorient, de Marigot, du Grand** and **du Petit Cul de Sac**. Surfers come for **Anse de la Grande Saline**, while others seek the privacy of **Anse du Gouverneur** at the island's southern end. And their money comes with them, creating work…and change that sometimes has a way of occurring well before absorption is possible.

No one lives with a more expanded notion of the scale of St. Barts than its oldest generation of women, the *grandmeres*.

They are an introverted tribe of survivors, thoroughly Caucasian, West Indian by birth and experience, but provincial French by heritage, fiercely loyal to home, village, and tradition. Their habits are as circumscribed and vertical as the land itself; they are no more inclined to venture beyond the familiar than a crab from the vicinity of its hole.

The reasons for their self-imposed insularity are historical. Before the tourist boom in the '70s, the island's woefully static economy presented few alternatives to subsistence farming and fishing, or maritime trade and smuggling. At best, the population could manage to export a few straw hats and modest quantities of corned fish and salt, sell the occasional chicken or goat to a passing schooner, buy rum in Guadeloupe or cattle in St. Kitts to retail to other islands. Bleak opportunities at home had a predictable effect: males turned anxious and packed their seabags.

From the beginning of the 20th century the young men went off to nearby St. Martin and St. Kitts, or over the horizon to Guadeloupe and St. Thomas, to seek work. When they had earned sufficient money they returned to St. Barts to focus their energies on courtship, engagement, and house building. With that attained they again emigrated to fill their pockets for marriage and fatherhood. With replenished savings they returned, married, and stayed long enough to impregnate their new wives, only to go off once more. Back and forth, back and forth, in perpetual quest of what was required.

Faced with the absenteeism of their husbands, the women had little choice but to withdraw into their daily routines, raising their average progeny of eight or nine, and tending the household's garden and livestock. The arrangement demanded an iron-willed independence and the women, resigned to a sedentary existence, cultivated shyness as a defense against their isolation. Their seclusion, and the vulnerability it inferred, is no more vividly symbolized than by the *caleche*, the traditional European peasant bonnet, as shielding as the cowl of a nun's habit, that so severely protected the wearer's face that the monastic headgear was nicknamed *quichenotte*—kiss-me-not—a blunt discouragement to the advances of visiting sailors. (Twenty-five years ago, women indistinguishable in appearance from these West Indian grandmothers could still be seen on Tangier Island in the Chesapeake Bay. The descendants of 17th century Cockney seamen, they wore a *caleche* and long-sleeved workdress

Flight of the pelicans.

identical to their Norman counterparts in the tropics.)

Gustavia, the harbor and careenage on the south leeward shore, graced with an anchorage as geometrical and calm as a swimming pool, has long served as the primary crossroads for the island, but it was from the *carrefour* of the bay of St. Jean, on the windward side, that St. Barts was originally divided into two administrative sections—Quartier du Roi (King's Quarter) to the west, Quartier d'Orleans (Orleans Quarter) to the east—which formalized an already established chauvinism. The islanders stand-offish behavior, at times xenophobic, applied as well between one half of the island and the other. They were all the descendents of French settlers, sharing only a few dozen surnames throughout centuries of cohabitation, but no matter. The people of the western quarter, in the villages of Colombier, Corossol, Flamands and Anse de Cayes, traced their ancestry to Normandy; the families in the eastern quarter from Brittany, Marseilles, Isle Jersy, and other corners of France. Each quarter accused the other of having an impure accent. Each insisted their *caleches* were superior in design and construction. Men and women preferred to marry within their district rather than experiment with the unknown prospects to the east or west.

Only the most pressing business or impetuous curiosity would stir the inhabitant of one side of the island over into the peculiar, mirror-like realm of the other. Until the 1960s the citizens of Gustavia, many of them English-speaking blacks, called the people out in the villages "country buckees," reclusive folks who shunned the metropolitan temptations of the sleepy port except to buy a franc's worth of nails or to complain to the mayor of a neighbor's praedial larceny. Even today, a rivalry of indifference persists between the east and west, windward and leeward; hence a villager from Colombier may take a certain pride in his lack of interest in life in Marigot, four miles distant.

One islander's tale: Mademoiselle Bernier, well into her sixth decade, is one of the islanders who continues to measure the scope of St. Barts by the humble world of her youth. In the 1980s, her cloistered way of life is a fading vestige of the pre-tourism past. She remains where she was born, in a two-room frame house built at the close of the last century by her father, a shopkeeper, atop Morne Vitet, the island's highest pitched roof. (St. Barts is the only island in

A dalmatian on a Gustavian street.

the Lesser Antilles where all the roofs of the traditional houses are pitched.) Partitioned by a plank wall and curtained doorway, parents slept in one room, its space adequate for a double bed, a dresser and wardrobe, and a chair. Their offspring, like Dickensian urchins, lined the floorboards of the other on mats and rugs, brothers with their heads against one wall, sisters' noggins against the other, and everybody's feet in the middle.

There was also a *carbrette* on the property, a lime-pack cottage in the style of the earlier colonists short of lumber on an island with few trees. The walls, low and squat, resembled adobe, two feet thick with a center of stone, the exterior whitewashed, architecturally muscular, eminently hurricane-proof. Some of these archaic dwellings remain standing; comfortably occupied, peasant dollhouses on a windward knoll, painted bright yellow, blue or green. The modern world trend, however, favors the tropo-generic construction of concrete and tile.

Meals served in the Bernier house were dictated by the facts of life on a dry, impoverished island. The spartan diet consisted mostly of fish—salted or fresh, though many of the tastiest varieties caught in local waters are carriers of the ciguatura toxin— garden vegetables restricted to sun-baked conditions, ground roots such as sweet potatoes and yams, and *fungui*, the national dish made from corn meal cooked into a pudding much like Italian *polenta*. Only at weddings or on holidays was meat roasted, grilled or stewed, but since Miss Bernier's father supplemented his meager income by fattening cattle in his pasture to sell at the abattoirs in Gustavia or St. Kitts, the thought of beef at the table tantalized appetites. Water, collected off the wood shingled roof from erratic rainfall, was channelled into a mortared cistern behind the house, the volume never sufficient for the needs of the family and the garden; nor were there streams or springs or wells on St. Barts to make up the difference.

Miss Bernier, whose *paterfamilias* arrived on the island about 250 years ago from Chateau Chenon in France, has the stay-at-home heart not of a mother or a matron but of a true rustic, a daughter of the soil, underprivileged and forgotten, yet with no argument to raise against those conditions. As a girl she would go on errands to the neighbors on Vitet, and on Sundays she descended the narrow footpath, now an overgrown impassable ditch, to the coastal track on a two-hour walk to the Catholic church in Lorient, worshipping under the marvel of its 25-sided vault. Her intermittent visits to Gustavia were undazzling, and lacking a reason to journey over rough paths to the western quarter of the island, she never set foot there.

One by one, her siblings drifted away from the family compound. Her eldest brother, gone by the time she was two, departed on a trading schooner that plied the islands, showed up in Europe in time for World War Two, was an enforced laborer during the German occupation of France, the Chief of Police for the allied Displaced Persons camp at Wiesbaden after the liberation, and finally, the head baker for Famous-Barr in St. Louis, Missouri. He repatriated himself to St. Barts several years ago, and now lives on the mountainside above his sister in a modern house. Toe to toe again, brother and sister—the present and the past, today and yesterday incarnate; he contemporary experience and the recalcitrant legacy, he cautious of her fragility; she confident of the legitimacy of her orthodox values. As her health fails, he visits her daily, and though he is 14 years her senior, sometimes he will tease her gently about her old-fashionedness. "He can think and behave the way he wants," she responds. "He is American. I am Creole."

Because she is often ill these days, a taciturn cousin, not unlike her in age or attitude, has moved in to assist with the daily chores and to provide the reassurance of empathy. Leaf-thin and cat-faced, her long silky white hair startlingly offset by thick black eyebrows, her housedress prim and clean, Miss Bernier perches on the edge of the main room's single bed, her plump cousin settles in a wood chair, their bare feet scuffing the worn floor, and in the natural light of the day they plait inch-wide strips of dried Latania palm to supply to the more dexterous craftswomen when the tourist season fires up in December. They pray together as they braid the palm straw, weaving grace for the Lord and souvenirs for the jet set. Their eyes are too cataracted, their fingers too arthritic, to stitch and bind the plaits into the Panama hats St. Barts was once famous for. With pride free of wistfulness, Miss Bernier will bring out a hat she made 15 years ago to show a visitor, its weave as tight and fine as the most delicately meshed snakeskin.

The blue-painted walls of her house are posted with religious cards, hand-colored portraits of the saints, sepia-toned pictures of parents and relatives. The Christian pantheon inspires discipline and devotion, the family gallery unsentimental remembrance. There is no nostalgia for the past or rejection of the present in these women as much as a self-absorbed fidelity to coherence and continuity. The house is without plumbing and electricity, although the first power plant was built on the island in 1968. But Miss Bernier does not concern herself with the changes modern times have brought to St. Barts because, like many of her peers, she is accustomed to being unaffected by the outside world or the actions of others. As long as her serenity remains undisturbed, the transformation of the island has no special relevance, it cannot matter. She and her cousin constitute an anachronism; they know it and respond with shrugs. They are two old spinsters, husbanded by Jesus during an era when men were scarce, wrapped in a web of lost time, spiritually free, the direct descendents of pirates and New World pioneers.

"The old women wearing the *caleche*," a retired fisherman observes, "there are maybe six or seven in Corossal, three or four in Colombier, maybe a few over in the eastern quarter. When they die, no one will wear the *caleche* anymore. You'll be able to see it in books, that's all. The younger women won't do it. It's too hot, for one thing. And too backward. "Truly, with the passing of the elders more will be lost than their lives alone. Following them into the grave, like a rosary clutched in the hands of the deceased, will be the three centuries of St. Barts' past, the idiosyncratic habits, the undiluted race, the 17th century rural French dialect, of the original settlers. As recently as 10 years ago, an American expatriate living on the island could accurately remark that St. Barts "is probably more like the Normandy of 1650 than the real Normandy is today." The isolation that generated and recycled a living heritage has exploded in the decade since. Now the destiny of St. Barts is programmed by computers, and promoted by the first neon sign. "Old ways are falling fast," says a grey-haired gentleman painting trim at a school under construction in Gustavia. He is one of the minority of natives who seems to honestly mourn the transition.

Origins: The people of St. Barts believe that Columbus discovered the island on his second voyage between 1493 and 1496, naming it for his younger brother, Bartholomew. But the diaries do not substantiate that belief, according to the late journalist-turned-historian, George Bourdin, to whom any student of the island's past is indebted. At any rate, the island first

A Caribbean squall.

appeared as a mere flyspeck on a Spanish map in 1523, identified as San Bartoleme.

In a sea of fecund, resource-laden islands, St. Barts was inimitably undiscoverable, bypassed even by the Carib Indians except as an overnight rest stop on their raids to places more deserving of inhabitants. After the Pope gave the whole New World to Spain in 1494, the *conquistadores* arrived to take a few perfunctory pokes at the Lesser Antilles and decided them not worth conquering. Inevitably, Spain's neighbors, on the advice of royally commissioned privateers who had managed a fair bit of plunder after the cut for their appropriate kings, decided to exploit her disinterest in the smaller prizes of the region. Thus, both French and English settlements were established on St. Kitts around 1629. Five years later, Pierre d'Esnambuc, who would become known as the father of the French colonization, landed on the island, pronounced it to his liking, and set off for home to hustle patrons.

After pleadings through Richelieu to Pope Urban VIII, d'Esnambuc set sail for the Indies with three ships and 532 colonists, mostly impoverished peasants and wharf rats from Normandy and Brittany, and the Pope's blessing to colonize. The half who survived the trip saw the mother country's flag planted first on St. Kitts, then Martinique and Guadeloupe eight years later.

When d'Esnambuc died in 1637 he was replaced by dePoincy, a 57-year-old Commander of the Order of Malta. He enlisted 52 brave or otherwise naive men to occupy the uninhabited St. Barthélemy, and some cultivation of the land took place there, but the main idea was to claim the land before others did. Alas, the relative success of the venture caught the attention of the Spanish who began to make sounds that did not speak of good health for the Commander, so he cleverly pawned St. Barts and the French section of St. Martin to the Order of Malta, which neutralized the Spanish threat, only to see it threatened by the aggression of Carib warriors. They paddled ashore one night and treated the French rather badly, planting their heads on stakes along the beach where they might gaze, sightless, at the waves forming on the reef now most popular with surfers. Thirty additional hardy souls were convinced, after a long siege of talking from the Governor of St. Kitts, to give it another go, and so by 1664 the number of those who took on the venture had grown to 100.

The airport.

The island became a clandestine rendezvous for pirates, whose ships the residents supplied, and who were more reliable buyers than more thoroughly organized entities. Over time the island population grew, avoiding the seesaw of ownership that its neighbors suffered, and became a tenaciously French isle considered by the home government in a report to be "good people, very poor, honest, rather ignorant, and quite quarrelsome," this latter contentiousness surviving to this day in what appears to be an intramural sport. Outsiders were dismayed to note that the 355 whites worked alongside the 141 slaves and five persons of mixed blood.

In a most unexpected and bizarre trade, the neglectful government of Louis XVI gave the island to King Gustaf III of Sweden in exchange for some warehouse in Goteborg. The Swedes, practitioners of the benevolent school of despotism, took on this new property with the enthusiasm of Pygmalion. What was described in the saddest terms by a French diplomat was turned seemingly overnight into a model possession. The capital was given its decidedly non-French name of Gustavia while, with the encouragement of Thomas Jefferson, the port was declared free of all duties. Spared the terror and dissolution about to overtake her French sisters in a battle with the aristocracy, the island flourished. The local administration worked to organize the indigenous population, not as Swedes, but as people of St. Barts with their own traditions and heritage. A rational pattern of streets was laid out around the harbor, warehouses were built, the roadways cobbled. By 1806 the island wallowed in relative prosperity, with Gustavia's population bloated to about 5,000, while 1,500 people lived in the countryside.

As booms go, the Swedish one was sweet, but it was a star-crossed romance that rushed its intoxicated partners to the altar of optimism. By 1807, Gustavia's population had already declined by 1,000. English piracy was disrupting the maritime routes; cotton prices had slumped, and the folks in the countryside were exhibiting some of their former gauntness. The newly-declared free port of St. Eustatia and the Danish Virgin Islands began siphoning off trade, and the ports of the young United States were reopened, after 40 years, to British shipping. By 1819, the population had decreased by another 1,000 souls, and a violent hurricane stamped an absolute end on the halcyon days of Scandinavian stewardship, leaving in its wake physical ruin and an epidemic of yellow fever.

Fair weather merchants, itinerant tradesmen, opportunists from around the Antilles, cleared out, as did some of the remaining blacks, freed from slavery in 1847. Once more life on St. Barts became brackish and forlorn, the core group of families who had been there since the beginning embracing the detachment they preferred and the poverty they understood as a condition of their permanence. Gustavia, now a somnolent village, was ravaged by fire in 1852, not to be rehabilitated until the advent of the tourist still more than a century ahead. Even in 1967 the town's population numbered only 398.

The Swedes, after brooding over St. Barts dissipation for 60 years, dumped the island back into the lap of the French in 1878. The reconveyance stipulated that St. Barts be permitted to retain its free port status, and its population, accustomed to the liberal-minded Swedes, was guaranteed that their immunity from taxation would be upheld, as it still is, though not without controversy. The Swedish flag, having flown over St. Barthélemy for 92 years, was lowered as the Governor from Guadeloupe stepped ashore to show his face, welcome these born-again Frenchmen into the colonial flock, and then vanish back to Basse Terre, where their petitions and cries for assistance would not be so loudly heard. The islanders, however, could now elect their own mayor, and seat a municipal council. Also, they were allowed to send a consul to the administration in Guadeloupe.

In the meantime, the islanders' welfare depended heavily on the charity of Catholic and Protestant clergy. Worker emigration speeded up after World War I. Not until 1946, when the Republic of France passed legislation abolishing the colonial status of the French West Indies was St. Barts officially declared a commune in the Department of Guadeloupe. Remy de Haenen, a Caribbean version of Africa's Denys Finch-Hatton, landed his Kearwin-Porter biplane on the short, grassy savannah of St. Jean in 1947. It took 18 more years for a STOL (short take-off and landing) runway to be poured down the length of the tiny field, but then only nine more years for television via satellite—an electronic force that rivaled the old imperial powers as an agent of change.

Superimposed on the centuries-old epoch of the grandmothers is the golden aggregate of the grandchildren, and stuck in between, like the musculature separating organs and skin, is the transitional generation, the adults outcast from a future that's already begun to shut them out from the tradition-rich lives of their parents and the up-to-the-minute thinking of their children. An outsider can identify them easily enough from their expatriate neighbors: the middle-aged natives of St. Barts look like transplanted factory workers from Quebec. They dress in subdued, sensible work clothes and their feet are bare by choice. The men use tonic to comb their hair back, the women, for the most part, roll and pin theirs into tiny buns. They conduct their business with a Gallic dourness, and deal with everyone in a humble and polite manner. They appear less arrogant and snobbish than the 1,000 resident expatriates (60 percent French, 15 percent U.S.).

Changing times: Shedding the peasantry of their youth, they are the group most jostled by change as they are willingly recreated in the image of the bourgeoisie. Like suburban families in the United States 30 years ago, they are grateful for their newly achieved affluence, even as their children already take it for granted. They are owners—land, house, automobile (120 new vehicles arrive each year), color television, telephone. Their garbage is collected and their mail is delivered. Although they are

Grande Cul de Sac.

loyal Catholics, they are not as religious as they once were, and attendance at the island's three Roman churches has fallen sharply. The masses are no longer said in Latin, which irritates them, and the priests aren't severe anymore. "Now the priests are intellectuals," a local policeman says, voicing a common complaint. "They talk and talk and nobody understands. We need someone simple."

Amid all its vicissitudes, St. Barts is faring well, much better than any other island in the Caribbean in the past decade. Nevertheless, in the floodtide of prosperity, there is a growing desire to reevaluate the pace as family bonds weaken, lifestyles alter drastically, and sensibilities are infiltrated, especially among the youth, by external values.

On roads that were unpaved and trafficked by donkeys 25 years ago, the new generation races through the gears on motor scooters, owning the length and breadth of the island with an insouciance unheard of in their ancestors. A young woman lives in Gran Cul de Sac on the eastern end of the island, works at a trendy boutique in Gustavia, eats her lunch at a cafe in St. Jean surrounded by tourists, suns herself on the beach at Colombier on a weekend picnic. "It's wonderful to live on St. Barts," a 24-

year-old carpenter says, munching on a fresh-baked baguette at Eat and Go, a fastfood kiosk in St. Jean. "You know where everything is here." Mainlands boggle him with a feeling of being inescapably lost.

St. Barts can provide an education for its children up to the age of 14, when they are shipped to private schools in Guadeloupe, then to a university in Paris or the States. Sophisticated but not seduced by the continents, they come back, because the island is now a terrific place to be. In the nuclear age of tourism, St. Barts is one of the chic destinations on the planet. Jimmy Buffet has a restaurant and bar in **Lorient**, the only establishment on the island that regularly stays open past 11 p.m. Bob Dylan anchors his sailboat in the Gustavia harbor and ties up his dinghy to schmooze with the local salts. One of the Rockerfellers has a hideaway on the beach in Colombier. Jean-Marie Riviere, a notable in French showbiz, has a vacation house tucked away behind lush landscaping. Sunday afternoon NFL football games cram the **Santa Fe Snack Bar** with 300 raucous Americans. The World Series is broadcast live on the channel from St. Martin, along with Tom Brokaw and the evening news. From the station in Guadeloupe comes the World Cup

and updates from Paris. Supermarkets carry Le Monde and the International Herald Tribune, and they stock butter from Germany, pimento paste from Tunisia, and pates imported from the motherland. There is a video club, a Fast-Photo service, Canon copiers, the most current rock and roll, enough glamor to choke on, and, for the local youth, astronomical wages. A construction worker can earn as much as a civil engineer in France, while a waitress takes home earnings equivalent to those of an executive secretary in Miami.

Alarms have begun to go off in the collective consciousness. "St. Barts in high season makes New York look mellow," says a travel industry wholesaler who purchases block space from the island's 20 hotels, supplemented by 2,000 rooms available for rent in private villas. Altogether, 400 units for tourists per square mile.

Fifty years ago, when Marius Stakelborough, the retired proprietor of Gustavia's favorite gathering spot, **Le Select**, was a boy, he would peddle the town baker's bread throughout the countryside. Seeing the mulatto hue of his skin, women would step quickly behind doors, children would hide behind bushes. Now blacks have moved out of Gustavia into rural areas, racial intermarriages are accepted, and in the villages where people still live today, once hidden from outsiders, tens of thousands of foreigners pass through monthly from November to May, and it is, by all local accounts, a strange phenomenon.

"You can't call St. Barts a great place," grouses a fisherman on the strand at Corossol. He left at 5 a.m. to check his lobster traps. It's almost noon now, and he's home for the day. Twenty years ago, he could catch 600 pounds of fish in 10 pots. Today, the same pots, set for the same amount of time, will yield only a third of the catch. Ten lobster traps were once plenty for what it takes 30 to do today. "There's big problems ahead for our children and grandchildren," he says. "They are in danger of losing their home and their heritage. It's being stolen from them in the most exciting way—by success."

Another fisherman, whose father was killed in a 1928 hurricane sailing home from St. Thomas, adds his opinion, speaking in the high-pitched patois heard on this quarter of the island. "Life was misery back in the old times," he says. "When I tell my children about it, they don't want to listen. They say *impossible, impossible*, nobody could live that way. Now it's difficult to even to talk to my kids."

Fishing is the main occupation of St. Bartians.

The widening generation gap, and the prospects of the young, are the island's most passionate themes in the 1980s, and they draw a third fisherman into the conversation. "For the young," he tells his cohorts, "the changes are good because they can stay on the island and make a living. For the oldest, they find that they don't like it too much, but they have to accustom themselves, because that's how life goes. But I prefer the way the young are living now to the way they used to live back in the old days."

The three watermen reminisce about the time before everyone had outboard motors, how they used to row out to the reefs in their pirogues when the wind was contrary, and race each other back in under sail. They grumble about the habits of the youth and agree that you couldn't pay a young person today to row a boat.

"Listen," interrupts the first fisherman, steering the discussion back to a larger concern, "if you have a family, you have a problem today in St. Barts. Unless you have land to give them."

First Americans in search of an undiscovered tropical backwater began buying land and building on it, then the French came seeking the same luxurious intimacy of the place, then entrepeneurs from Guadeloupe, and the mega-rich, until land speculation spun out of control as a result of the island's popularity with the world's elite. The price of land has escalated beyond the average islander's means, and today a square meter of space in **St. Jean** (Tourist City, the people call it) is more expensive than its equivalent on the Champs Elysees. Local income is high, but there's no local-oriented economy. Prices are the same for tourist and native alike. In 10 years, says a statistician from Paris, the people of St. Barts will be economic slaves to outsiders. Perhaps this is the greatest irony, that the original settlers abandoned France to flee the oppression of the aristocracy only to discover three centuries later, that the aristocracy has followed them here.

Unofficially, everything on St. Barts is for sale. Unofficially, even the future—and the people of the island are starting to think hard about how to get it off the market. "You better get it now," Marius Stakelborough warns, "because sure as hell things going to slow down." That's history speaking, a cloud in the depths of the communal memory. But perhaps now history can no longer repeat itself on St. Barts, and there's a bittersweetness to that achievement.

The Western shore.

EXPLORING SABA

Four Dutch Alpine villages perched on a mountain rising out of the tropical Caribbean—this unlikely conglomeration is **Saba**. The island is small, just five square miles, and seems to angle straight up everywhere. The first European settlement, established by Dutchmen from St. Eustatius, was destroyed by a landslide in 1651. The settlers moved to higher ground and took to defending themselves by piling boulders at the tops of sloping ravines; when invaders landed, wooden props were removed and the rocks descended.

Through the centuries, even friendly visitors have had to struggle against gravity on Saba. The first road on the island was not built until 1943. Before that, all who arrived at Fort Bay, the harbor, had to climb a steep path, with 200 steps, to the nearest town, which sits 800 feet above the level of the sea and is called, inappropriately, **The Bottom**. Everything that landed on Saba walked or was carried up that path, from pianos (which required 12 men to haul them) to a visiting bishop (four men and a sedan chair). "Baggage and freight are borne up—on the heads of Negroes whose lung power amazes panting visitors," the *National Geographic* reported in 1934. And The Bottom was just an initial resting place if cargo was going anywhere else on the island. Saba's second town, **Windwardside** (which the road did not reach until 1951), was 900 steep steps farther up.

It is little wonder, therefore, that many Sabans confined their regular travels to their own home towns. Island residents today tell of grandparents who spent most of their lives in **Hell's Gate**, the village beyond Windwardside, without ever visiting The Bottom. "As a boy I often heard old people saying that they had never had the time, inclination, or desire to visit any other village," Will Johnson, an island politician and editor, recalled in his book, *Tales From my Grandmother's Pipe*. This on an island of five square miles, where the population peaked (in 1915) at 2,488. Even now, natives of the four villages speak with four distinct accents.

There are 1,000 Sabans today. Half are black and half are white, an unusual racial mix in the Caribbean. The blacks are descended from slaves imported to work the island's small farms (and to carry goods up and down its paths). Saba's vertical geography made large plantations impossible, so slaves never outnumbered their masters, as they did on other islands in the region.

The white residents of Saba aren't sure exactly who *their* ancestors were. It is known that the original Dutch colonists were soon joined by settlers from the British Isles. In 1665, the English privateer Thomas Morgan captured the island and deported the Dutch. (Dutch authorities soon reclaimed it, but the Dutch settlers did not return.) When Morgan departed, a number of his men stayed behind, giving rise to claims by some Sabans today that they are descended from pirates. Other authorities suggest that Saba's British settlers were Scottish refugees or exiles from the British civil wars of the 17th century. And it is not unusual to ask Sabans about their ancestry and hear the reply "I'm Irish…I think."

Lots of Hassells: They do *look* Irish, but no one can say for certain where they came from. It has been established, however, that by the last half of the 17th century the island was dominated by English speakers. A census list from 1699 includes several Johnsons and Simmons, both still common Saban names, and seven Hassells. The Hassells thrived; roughly half the islanders today, white and black, bear that name. A recent issue of the Saban newspaper notes that island commissioner Vernon Hassell had attended a conference on St. Martin, that "Mr. Carl Hassell of Booby Hill will be butchering pigs every other weekend from now until Christmas," that Mrs. Elizabeth (Lizzie) Hassell had been elected president of the Lionesses Club, that Danny Hassell was disbursing industrial loans on behalf of the Development Bank of the Netherlands Antilles, and that Vincent and Louise (*nee* Hassell) Hassell wished to thank all their friends and relatives for helping them celebrate their wedding.

Hassells and other Sabans have made their marks off the island as well as on it. Fishing and sailing were the dominant occupations of Saban men for centuries. Until the advent of the airplane, Saban vessels commonly plied the Caribbean trade routes, carrying all manner of cargo and passengers. One Saban captain ferried French prisoners from Cayenne, the capital of French Guiana, to Devil's Island and other penal colonies. Another, working somewhat at cross purposes, is reputed to have specialized in escaped French prisoners, smuggling them to Trinidad in exchange for gold nuggets.

Many sailing Sabans gravitated toward the United States. An entire wall of the

Saban Museum in Windwardside is hung with licenses granted by the U.S. Coast Guard and Department of Commerce to various Sabans to work as masters and mates on steamships.

In his book, Johnson reports that more than 100 Sabans served as officers in the U.S. Navy in World War I. (He also reports that Saban seamen passing through New York adopted as a sort of clubhouse a clothing shop run by Herman Kaliski, a Russian Jewish merchant in lower Manhattan.) Other Sabans emigrated to the United States and pursued non-nautical vocations. Johnson cites a number of Sabans who distinguished themselves there, including Theodore Hassell, who worked in the American space program; Moses Crossley, a prominent chemist; Howard Hassell, who worked on the Manhattan Project; Cyril Hassell, who won a Bronze Star in Vietnam; and Arthur Hassell, who taught business at the University of Hartford.

If some of these accomplishments do not seem worthy of great fame, keep in mind that Saba is a very small island. The Saba Museum displays a 1940 certificate from the Packard Motor Car Company identifying A. C. Hassell of Syracuse, New York, as a Packard Master Service Manager.

In the years following World War I, many Sabans, looking for work, emigrated to Aruba and Curaçao, the sites of large oil refineries. So many men left the island seeking jobs that the population skewed heavily toward the female. In 1924, there were 1,011 women on Saba and only 604 men. Today, the men have come home. Money flows into the island from the central government of the Netherlands Antilles, and there is no longer a desperate necessity to seek work abroad. Today the world comes to Saba.

It wasn't always easy for it to get there. Columbus sighted the island in 1493, but the first Europeans known to land there were some Englishmen shipwrecked in 1632. Perhaps no one could figure out how to get ashore on the rocky coast. Until the construction of a pier in 1972, one could not, in fact, land on the island without getting wet. Ships anchored in Fort Bay, which is less a harbor than a slight indentation in the coast, and passengers and cargo were ferried to shore in wooden longboats. (The island's first car, a Jeep, rode in on two longboats, lashed together, in 1947.)

On the other side of the island, Saba's airport opened in 1963, although some would say just barely. Constructing an airport on an island that is all peaks and ridges

and steep valleys was an unlikely task. There was, however, a peninsula called Flat Point. The airport builders seized it and got every inch of flatness out of it that they could. The runway is 1,312 feet (398 meters) long, a bit longer than the deck of an aircraft carrier. At each end it drops off in a sheer cliff to the sea below. Service is limited to short-takeoff-and-landing aircraft, which fly in from nearby St. Martin and St. Eustatius.

With emigration slowed and Saba accessible to the outside world, foreign influences flow in. These are apparent during one not atypical evening at Saba's only Chinese restaurant, an establishment operated in Windwardside by Saba's only Chinese family. At 6 p.m., the music on the stereo is a polka. A sign over the bar reads, "No Dirty Words Please." Beyond the window, palm fronds are waving in the cool evening breeze. The Chinese proprietress sits behind the bar, crocheting. A few feet from her is her small son, who plays with a stuffed whale. Outside, the tropical night descends on the mountain village.

Around the island: Windwardside looks like a Caribbean Brigadoon, the mythical village out of time. It sits like a perfect picture on a rich green saddle between mist-covered **Mt. Scenery**, Saba's dominant peak, and adjacent **Booby Hill**. Immaculate small houses, with uniform white walls and red roofs and gingerbread trim, reinforce the fairy-tale atmosphere. There are a few jarring notes—a Datsun with a bumper sticker reading, "You toucha my car, I breaka you face"—but their incongruity only enhances the contrasting marvel of the place.

From the narrow streets, one climbs or descends steps to reach the houses, whose gardens are likely to contain banana trees, a concrete catchment for gathering rainwater (the island relies on cisterns for its drinking water), a couple of old family graves, and perhaps a cow. One American living on Saba recalls the day she went outside her rented house to plant some flowers: "My neighbor up the hill started shouting and ran down to warn me not to dig where her grandparents were buried."

A 150-year-old cottage in Windwardside now serves as the **Saba Museum**, which houses a full old-style island kitchen (still used to prepare meals for island celebrations), examples of the fine lacework traditionally done by Saban women, and some darker mementoes of the region's past, including an 1829 receipt, signed on St. Eustatius, for "the Sum of two Hundred and fifty Dollars Current Money of the Island Being for a boy Sold Named Sambo." Near the museum is the island's deluxe tourist spot, a graceful old sea captain's house that has been converted to the **Captain's Quarters** hotel, where guests dine on a terrace under breadfruit and mango trees and look down on the Caribbean 1,800 feet below.

There are no tourist facilities in **Hell's Gate**, the tiny village even higher up the mountain. An excellent way to spend an hour is to walk there from Windwardside on the Saban highway, which twists and climbs and backtracks all the way. The road, which runs from the seaport to the airport and links all four villages en route, was built under the supervision of a Saban named Josephus Lambert Hassell. Dutch engineers, it is said, concluded that building a road on Saba would be impossible. (That may just have meant that it was impossible to build one at a price Holland was willing to pay.) Hassell, undeterred, took a correspondence course in civil engineering and proved them wrong. With the labor of part-time workers, many of them farmers, the road was begun at the port in 1938. It took five years to reach The Bottom, less than a mile away (but 800 feet up), and another 13 years to reach Windwardside, but the job was finally done. A plaque to Hassell stands on the road today, commemorating the "engineer of this road 'that could not be built.'"

Hell's Gate is a charming terminus for a hike. Its houses are built on the slope, with one family's chimney beneath another's garden. Once the most isolated of Saban villages, Hell's Gate's residents still speak with a distinctive brogue that is apparent even to an untrained ear. There are no cafes in the village, but a thirsty tourist need only inquire of anyone he meets to be directed to the diminutive wooden house of a lady who serves Coca-Cola in her sitting room; there may also be some conversation about her cousin who is a lawyer in Pennsylvania.

The Bottom, Saba's capital and largest village (with 350 residents), is a long hike or short cab ride from Hell's Gate. It and the adjacent village of **St. John's** are mostly black (Windwardside and Hell's Gate are mostly white), and The Bottom has what passes for congestion on Saba, with its government buildings, a hospital, and a few bars and restaurants, but it is no less picturesque for it. The Bottom also boasts the island's sole athletic facility—a single tennis court that doubles and triples as a volleyball and basketball court. Girls' volleyball games on Wednesday nights are popular events for players and spectators alike.

Pedestrians on the main road in Windwardside.

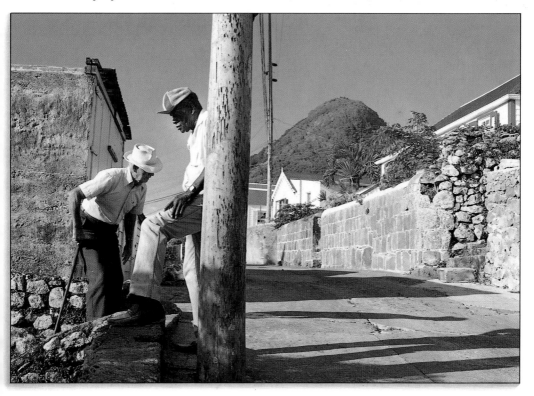

Despite the limited athletic facilities on Saba (there is no place large enough and flat enough for a soccer field), it is still possible to get plenty of exercise. The most rewarding workout for a visitor is to climb Mt. Scenery, the 2,900-foot peak of a dormant volcano that dominates the island.

Mountain high: The top of Mt. Scenery is often covered by a cloud (clouds seem, in fact, to appear from nowhere just to hover around the peak), local guidebooks advise tourists to wait for a perfectly clear day before hiking up the mountain. That advice is best ignored. A spectacular view of the sea and neighboring islands can be obtained from many points on Saba, including wayside-stations up Mt. Scenery even on a misty day. In fact, it is only on a misty day that one can both enjoy a hike into a tropical rain forest and experience an eerie yet satisfying feeling that the rest of the world has been obliterated.

The path up Mt. Scenery, which begins just outside Windwardside, requires no mountaineering skills. It is clearly marked and steps have been built into it. Local residents report that Queen Beatrix of the Netherlands climbed it in high heels (and declared when she reached the top, "This is the smallest and highest place in my kingdom"). That doesn't mean that the climb isn't tiring. Yes, steps are provided, but there are 1,064 of them.

Small lizards scurry about as one begins the ascent, climbing past delicate red and yellow wildflowers. If there is mist on the mountain, one starts out below it in sunshine and enters the mist only gradually. At first, it just adds coolness to the air. One can see right through it to the village below and the sea beyond. One does not seem to be *in* it.

Farther up, the vegetation grows more extravagant. Vines hang from treetops by the hundreds; they dangle beside luxuriant shrubs with leaves as large as tablecloths. The mist closes in, billowing through the dense forest and cutting off all the views of the world outside. The path grows slippery. Birds call from the wood. There is a rich damp smell.

Approaching the top, one hears a ferocious rushing of wind. On the peak, there is a surprise—a massive 210-foot microwave relay tower built of heavy steel girders, with concrete buildings at its base (all lifted by helicopter, on a sunny day). Beyond is the peak, and a sheer drop-off. The wind gusts up from below, pushing branches and climbers alike away from the edge of the ridge and roaring as it blows through the

A bar in Windwardside.

limbs of the radio tower. Looking down, one can see nothing but gray, and feel the mist, and hear the wind. Then the hike back down, into the sunshine and a first view of Windwardside, its houses charming from above in haphazard clusters on the green slope. Near the bottom of the path, a sign one passed on the way up: "Welcome At Rendezvous. You can get Soft Drinks and Cold Beers. At the White house. You are welcome. Again."

Island economics: The Saban people are nothing if not industrious. For centuries their island was a neglected corner of the Dutch empire, largely left to its own devices. Sabans grew their own food on small mountain plots, and the men went out in the world in search of jobs. The women, left behind, made a cottage industry of "Saba lace," a type of lacework brought back to the island in the 1870s by a local girl who learned it in a convent school in Venezuela.

Today the island still grows most of its own food, and Saban lace is still crafted, mostly by older women, who sell it to tourists. Local fishermen supply the island and export to St. Martin. "Everybody does two or three things to keep going," a local resident explained. "They go to a job at seven, finish at 3:30, and then go to another job, or farm, or fish." Or they run a little shop on the side. There seem to be nearly as many shops on Saba as people. Many of the stores have carefully-painted and prominent signs, although why they need signs at all is not obvious. On an island of 1,000 people, doesn't everybody know which buildings are hardware stores?

Despite this earnest private enterprise, the government is Saba's largest employer, providing jobs for about 65 percent of the island workforce. Most of the local government budget comes from the central government of the Netherlands Antilles. "A false sense of security has been created," says Saba's Commissioner Vernon Hassell. "We have become too dependent on outside money."

The Sabans have this on their minds as they contemplate the future. "The Dutch are talking about an independent Netherlands Antilles," says Will Johnson, who represents Saba in the territory's parliament. The Netherlands Antilles comprise Bonaire and Curaçao, both just off the coast of Venezuela, and St. Martin, St. Eustatius and Saba, hundreds of miles to the northeast. Curaçao officials, who have economic problems of their own, may object to providing indefinite support for their distant sister islands, Johnson says. "Curaçao is saying, 'Who appointed us godmother of these other islands. *We* didn't colonize them." On some occasions, Johnson adds, Dutch officials have talked about an independent Saba. "They come here, see the situation, and say everybody should be independent. You want to choke them." Johnson advocates maintaining at least St. Martin, St. Eustatius and Saba as a single political unit linked to Holland.

The future of Saba and the rest of the Netherlands Antilles will likely be debated for years. In the meantime, Saba is looking to increase its small tourist industry in a controlled fashion. As of 1987, Saba had only 31 hotel rooms. There was talk of building several new small hotels, and officials had a plan for a large yacht harbor. (Yachts used to call at Fort Bay, but the opening of an ill-conceived stone-crushing operation there, which constantly showers the harbor with dust, has driven the yachtsmen away.)

Saba will be selling itself to tourists largely on its charm, as it has no beaches, the traditional Caribbean drawing card. (It does have excellent scuba diving, however.) Saba's abundant charm lies in its storybook villages, manificent physicaly setting, and its unusual blending of peoples and cultures.

The distinctive flavor of Saba was on display one afternoon behind the Anglican church in Windwardside. A dozen Saban boys, black and white, and one local scoutmaster suddenly appeared carrying an odd selection of athletic equipment. "I bat first," one boy called as they arrived. "I second," called another. They put their things down next to a bust of Simon Bolivar and proceeded to play baseball—after a fashion.

The field was clearly inadequate (or at least so it would appear to outsiders). A tall tree stood directly behind the spot designated as the pitcher's mound. A large hedge stood between the shortstop and left field. On Saba, this was the best ball field that could be found. The only larger, flatter place in Windwardside was the graveyard.

While the first batter stepped up to the plate with a baseball bat, the boy on deck took practice swings with a cricket bat (which was ultimately ruled illegal). The pitcher threw a tennis ball. The batter swung and hit the ball into the stone wall jutting across the first base line. The ball bounced back to the catcher, who fielded it and threw it toward first. It hit the runner in the back and rolled away. The runner was called out. This was baseball as played nowhere else in the known world. Only in Saba, where it seemed just right.

EXPLORING
ST. EUSTATIUS

The air of ruin in **Oranjestad**, the only town on **St. Eustatius**, is a curious one. Local residents go about their business in the fine sunny weather, seemingly oblivious to the widespread crumbling evidence that their small island home, now so obscure, was once a very important place. The most imposing church in town, the **Dutch Reformed**, has not been used since 1680 and stands in ruins, its tower intact but its roof gone. The second-oldest synagogue in the Western Hemisphere is here—also a ruin. Its walls of handsome yellow brick still stand, as does an exterior staircase, leading nowhere. Looking down to the seafront from the upper town (which sits atop a 130-foot cliff), one can see straight through the dazzling turquoise water to the sands beneath it and the submerged remains of the foundations of vanished warehouses, homes and shops, which once sprawled two-deep for a mile (two km) along the shore and bulged with samples of all the riches of the earth.

Foreign impressions: In 1775, at the height of St. Eustatius's reign as a Caribbean trading center, when as many as 10 ships a day were calling at Oranjestad, a touring Scottish gentlewoman strolled along this seafront and recorded her impressions: "From one end of the town of Eustatia to the other is a continued mart, where goods of the most different uses and qualities are displayed before the shop-doors. Here hang rich embroideries, painted silks, flowered Muslins, with all the Manufactures of the Indies…Next stall contains most exquisite silver plate, the most beautiful indeed I ever saw, and close by these iron-pots, kettles and shovels. Perhaps the next presents you with French and English Millinary-wares. But it were endless to enumerate the variety of merchandise in such a place, for in every store you find everything."

Today, that same shore boasts two small hotels (one of them quite elegant), an abandoned power plant, a dozen gaily-colored fishing boats on a small beach, rows of ruins, and a scuba shop. Where has everyone else gone? An old man walking a puppy by a broken warehouse wall has the answer: *"Dey gone all over in de Outer World."*

Left behind are the 1,800 Statians of today. (St. Eustatius is universally referred to by its residents, quite sensibly, as Statia. (The island has no connection with the saint;

historians conjecture that the old Indian name for the place sounded something like "*Estatia*" and was transformed by the early Spanish explorers, who liked to name things after saints.)

The islanders are, by and large, the descendants of slaves who worked the island's now-vanished plantations and passed through Statia by the thousands when it was, among other things, a major slave-trading center. European merchants presided over the island's "golden age," when a favorable location, free trade and smuggling combined to make it a major port. They departed in the early 19th century, when the end of the slave trade and the independence of the Unites States altered Caribbean trading patterns, and the island declined into insignificance. In 1790, Statia had a population of 8,124 (5,140 slaves, 2,341 whites, 43 freemen), more than four times the number it has today.

One moment in history: Though off the world stage today, Statia holds on to a few memories. The **Doncker-De Graff House** in Oranjestad, once the home of a wealthy Dutch merchant, has been meticulously restored as an historical museum. The house itself once entered history, serving in 1781 as headquarters for British admiral George Rodney, who conquered (and looted) the island and held it for 10 months. Rodney's invasion was motivated in part by what is today the most widely recalled moment in island history—the occasion in 1775 when the guns of **Fort Oranje** boomed a salute to a warship from the rebellious British colonies in North America.

The Statian salute was the first fired by foreign authorities to a warship bearing the flag of the United States. The salute was acclaimed by the Americans and denounced by the British; it is remembered and honored by the Statians.

Every November 16 is Statia/America Day, a public holiday when the anniversary of the salute is marked by ceremonies at Fort Oranje (now restored and housing government offices). Islanders gather and sing the Statian anthem, including the lyric: "Statia's past you are admired/Though Rodney filled his bag./The first salute fired/To the American flag." Over the fort are hoisted the flags of the 13 American colonies (donated by the Kiwanis Club of Yonkers, New York, and the Yonkers Bicentennial Committee). Plaques presented by Franklin D. Roosevelt and the St. Eustatius Commission of the American Revolution mark the spot.

Preceding pages: an illusion of autumn in Gingerland; a summer rainshower (the guill is in the background). **Below,** fort in Oranjestad.

History casts some doubt on the popular local view that the Statian salute was motivated by the islanders' love of liberty. The actual salute fired was not of the type accorded foreign warships but rather that accorded merchant vessels. (Dutch authorities later assured the irate British that no recognition of sovereignty had been intended.) And even if the island sentries realized the significance of the American flag, which they had never seen before, it is certain that any welcome granted to North American ships must have been largely motivated by the fact that Statian merchants were having a field day supplying American rebels with weapons, gunpowder, and other provisions at substantial profits.

A matter of economics: More than 200 years later, the salute is still entangled in economic motives. An island tourist board press release appeals to Americans by describing Statia as remarkable "in a world in which the United States is all too frequently castigated and reviled." There is also some local sentiment that a debt was incurred and should now be repaid.

"The feeling here is, 'Look what our ancestors have done to benefit the United States. Now that the United States is a powerful country, it ought to do something to help us,'" says Lt. Gov. George Sleeswijk, the island's chief administrator.

Statia can use some help. There is a surface appearance of prosperity, with televisions, VCRs, and automobiles visible in abundance, but the island's economy is built on no firm foundation. (Why there are so many cars on a not-rich island 5.5 miles long and 2.5 miles wide, with one solitary town , is an interesting question. Asked where all the motorists drive to, one Statian explained, "In circles. Having a car is a matter of delight, not a necessity.")

The island's sole industry of any size is an oil terminal that employs 80 people. Agriculture was important long ago. The first Dutch colonists arrived in 1636, and by 1638 Statia-grown tobacco was being sold in Europe; later cotton, coffee and sugar cane were established. But the plantations took second place to trade during the island's boom years, and, after emancipation in 1863, the slaves were happy to leave the land. Discouraged by erratic rainfall and other uncertainties, their descendants have had little interest in returning. The government has sporadically tried to encourage agriculture, and one new private venture began outside Oranjestad in the early 1980s. Its first products include rabbits for local

Playing dominoes outside a bar in Oranjestad.

consumption and seedless limes for cocktail slices in the hotel bars of nearby St. Martin. As of 1986, however, only 65 Statians were employed in agriculture.

The island's biggest employer by far is the government. Some 266 people, 38 percent of those with jobs, are employed by it. Most of them work for the Public Works Department, which doles out jobs on a political patronage basis. (There are three local parties, distinguished more by personalities than ideologies, and local elections are vigorously contested.) Island observers blame the patronage system and the government jobs, many of which are less than all-consuming, for a lack of initiative among Statians. There is also concern that the system cannot work this way forever. The local government budget, which is substantially supported by the central government of the Netherlands Antilles, is in danger of suffering cutbacks as Netherlands Antilles is in the throes of an austerity program.

Statian authorities are looking to tourism to boost the economy. So far, the tourist industry barely exists. There are a mere 124 rooms on the island, including hotels and guest houses. In 1985, fewer than 5,000 foreign visitors arrived. Some were on business; of the tourists, most were on day-trips from St. Martin.

Local charms: For those who come to stay, however, the place has distinctive charm. The scarcity of tourists means that the profession of tourist hustler has not developed here (unless one stretches the definition to include a taxi driver who pleasantly hands out cards saying, "For Peace and Love when visiting Statia ask for H. Richardson Rental & Taxi 5 Convertible Tours Shalom"). Scuba divers have the thrill of exploring ancient warehouse ruins and numerous shipwrecks beneath the clear waters off Oranjestad, and anyone from a busier place can profit from a long stroll across the small island.

At 11 a.m. on a Saturday morning, the Seventh Day Adventist Church in Oranjestad, which has a large and enthusiastic membership, is in the midst of its service. The minister's voice booms out through open doors and windows: "It is necessary for us to depend on the grace of the Lord."

The narrow streets of the Dutch colonial village are empty. **Kool Korner** is closed (it will open in the afternoon to vend drinks and freshly-baked bread). Radio music is heard from houses with pastel-painted shutters and red corrugated steel roofs. The older houses have arcaded porches and balconies adorned with peeling gingerbread trim.

Flowering trees and shrubs decorate their gardens.

The few pedestrians wave to one another with the island greeting: "Okay." Although Statia has been Dutch for most of the last 350 years, English is the local language. The Statian version can—almost— be understood by outsiders; Statians easily switch back and forth between the local idiom and more standard English, depending upon whom they are talking to.

On the outskirts of the town, there are newer concrete houses of pink, yellow and blue, as well as a Chinese restaurant. The road runs on, across the island's central plain and past the **President Roosevelt Airport**, which is bounded by fields, a few of which are cultivated. Cattle and goats wander freely, to the constant outrage of the authorities, and irritation of some of the residents. ("Due to the uncontrolled manner in which livestock and cattle are making use of the public roads, despite the fact of my various warnings and notices…all cows, donkeys, sheep and goats which are found unattended on the public road, one week from today, will be dealt with drastically," Lt. Gov. Sleeswijk decreed in 1985. Some animals have indeed been shot.)

Behind the road, towering over the southern end of the island, rises the **Quill**, a dormant volcano of classic formation. Its slopes rise 1,980 feet (600 meters), lush and green, to the lip of a crater, 990 feet (300 meters) across, which shelters and conceals a tropical rain forest. Both slopes and crater are accessible to hikers, who will find there insect-sized lizards and hummingbirds, wild orchids, wild bananas and feathery creepers hanging from tall trees. Most startling are the hermit crabs, far from the sea, who come tumbling down the mountain paths, bouncing along the rocks in the borrowed shells they inhabit.

Across the central plain from Oranjestad, at the end of the road, lies a small hotel on a beach. This is the loveliest beach on the island, flat sand in a curved bay, the panorama extending to the slope of the Quill, and beyond that, the island of St. Kitts rising in the distance. The hotel's proprietor, a Frenchwoman, recalls the last time there was any excitement in the neighborhood. "Dutch Marines invaded last year," she says. "It was an exercise. They set off charges in the water and killed a lot of fish. Then they landed on the beach."

"You have to show your presence," explains a crewcut Dutch marine who happens to be sitting at the hotel bar. Then he sips his rum punch. This trip, he is here on vacation.

EXPLORING ST. KITTS-NEVIS

All seems at peace in these two Lilliputian "fragments of Eden." Long before dawn come the first chirrups, a cock crow, the asthmatic braying of some irritable donkey, and the yap of dogs lying in dust hollows under clapboard cottages. A chorus of cooings and warblings begins, a sound of enticement, an invitation to rise or to sleep on. Then the breeze begins, bringing the slightest murmur of leaves rubbing together, the sudden staccato showers of dew drops on tin roofs, the dry rattle of tamarind pods hanging like rusty machetes among the mango and breadfruit trees, and the sensual scents of bougainvillea.

The sun yolks up over curls of pink-golden sand washed by the surf; shadowy blossoms of frangipani, hibiscus and African tulips erupt in sparks of reds, purple and white. Over by the well, a plump pawpaw drops and rolls down a path to rest near the nose of a fat black pig tethered like a pampered pet on the steps of a lopsided one-room cottage. The heat comes quickly. Spirally wisps of morning mist over the banana trees vanish and floorboards creak in the clustered homes of the village. A blue cotton-cloth "door" is tied back and a young girl emerges in a loose frock to start the fire outside for a breakfast of stewed cornmeal and fruit. Inside, a wooden bed takes up most of the room. Pinned to the painted wood walls are two magazine cutouts, one of Cicely Tyson (a Nevisian made good), the other of Dallas' Bobby Ewing, next to a white plastic crucifix and a child's pastel drawing of a smiling Christ with arms outstretched, standing by a field of tasseled sugar-cane. The girl picks two wild mangoes and a bunch of plantains from trees near the path. "You gotta be awful lazy to starve on our island," say the older Kittitians smugly.

"Nothin' much going on man": Caribbean nationals occasionally make fun of the islander's lackadaisical "lyming" lifestyle that requires no more than modest self-efficiency—a little fishing, a little gardening, some cutting days in the sugar-cane fields (which form the prime economic base of St. Kitts), long pauses during the midday heat for chats with friends under shady fig trees, and maybe a few Carib beers to while away the time before the next meal. *"Nothin' much going on man, nothin' much t'all."*

Couched in the gentle southward arc of the Lesser Antilles, these two green volcanic blips offer a cocooned Caribbean of yesteryear with quiet beaches, remnants of the old British plantocracy, and dreamy days under the silk-cotton trees, wrapped in the scents of flamboyants and frangipani. While the native Arawak and Carib Indians called St. Kitts, the larger of the two islands, "Liamuiga" (the fertile isle), today's static combined population of around 43,000 on a land area little more than the size of Providence, Rhode Island, and an economy still far too dependent on sugar, might suggest a chronic case of backwater blues. But, in fact, this nation-in-miniature is dealing enthusiastically with the challenges of a go-it-alone economy, while at the same time, celebrating a varied and vibrant history.

Christopher Columbus, Horatio Nelson, Captain Bligh, Alexander Hamilton and, more recently, Queen Elizabeth II, have all contributed to the nation's rich heritage. Columbus, who occasionally waxed poetic in his namings, bestowed the elegant title of "Nuesta Senora de las Nieves" ("Our Lady of the Snows"—in reality, clouds) upon Nevis in 1493, but then resorted to a little self-glorification by calling St. Kitts - St. Christopher.

As was often the case in those hectic colony-collecting days, claims of sovereignty were largely forgotten and the Carib population continued to smoke the "cohiba" tobacco, and delight in their diet of turtles, iguanas, "pepper-pot" stews and "mawby" liquor, oblivious to the future. But then, in 1623, Sir Thomas Warner and a bunch of hardy British settlers arrived on St. Kitts followed closely by a group of French colonists, and the peaceful island became a microcosm of traditional Britain vs. France antagonisms. Over a century and a half of conquests and counter-conquests ensued until the 1783 Treaty of Versailles formally acknowledged British sovereignty.

Agro-economy: By that time the Caribs had been wiped out (most of them in the terrible massacre at Bloody Point in 1626) and over 10,000 African slaves had been brought in to run the tobacco and sugar plantations. Tiny Nevis had become a more significant commercial center than New York, a veritable Caribbean social nexus ("The Queen of the Caribees"), complete with palatial planter's mansions and a fashionable hotel-spa. Horatio Nelson was an attractive and eligible addition to the social whirl although, in his initial role of enforcement officer for the Treaty of Versailles, he

Preceding pages: Great Salt pond; a retired fisherman. **Below**, the daily catch ready for sale at a Charlestown market.

152

created considerable turmoil among the planters when he summarily dismissed all American traders from the isles. Under the treaty, American independence had been recognized and her ships were now labelled "foreign" and forbidden to trade in British Colonies. But personal charm, sound legal advice and the power of the British monarchy eventually made him a welcome guest in the Great Houses and led to his marriage with Nevis-born Fanny Nisbet at Montpelier House in March 1787.

Alexander Hamilton's relationship with the island was less fortuitous and for many years he attempted to keep secret his "foreign birth" on Nevis in 1757 and his subsequent ignominious departure for St. Croix at the age of five, following the bankruptcy of his father. However, Hamilton's subsequent fame led to the establishment of a museum at his birthplace in the capital, **Charlestown**, now one of its principal attractions.

At the time of Hamilton's departure there followed a prosperous period of sugar and cotton production which continued—with infrequent recessions—way beyond the emancipation of slaves in 1834. While occasional calamities such as the abrupt disappearance of the Nevis capital of Jamestown in a 1680 earthquake, intermittent outbreaks of malaria and yellow fever, and even, more recently, the loss of 200 islanders following the capsizing of the Christena ferry in 1970, provide dramatic historical markers, the overall ambience is still relatively untouched by the frantic pace and economic realities of 20th century life.

Political aspirations: Yet there are those who would prefer a little less peace and a bit more ambition and productivity from their political representatives. Lee Llewellyn Moore, ex-premier and leader of the Labor opposition party regularly attacked the PAM (People's Action Movement) government of prime minister, Dr. Kennedy Simmonds. "After seven years in power," Moore declared, "there's nothing to see—after seven years they can't even agree on the outline for a National Development Plan!" His party's newspaper, *The Labor Spokesman,* also criticize the Government and every day, outside the paper's offices in Basseterre, screeching denunciations of official ineptitude and corruption were scrawled on the public blackboard. One proclaimed: "You see to please their $12,000 a month supporters they abolish income tax and now twist and turn themselves into the letter "S" to introduce taxes

A participant in the island's semi-annual horserace.

to hurt the little man for they can get nothing to borrow. Schemes, tricks, propaganda and lies. Wait till you see the wage increases of some of the dunderheads who don't know their necks from their elbows. The laugh of the Caribbean!"

Just around the corner from the opposition, in the newspaper offices that occupy the modest government headquarters building on Church Street, such regular tirades are regarded as "a healthy expression of island freedom." According to Claudia Nisbett, the official public relations spokesperson. "We were once islands of slaves—now we're an independent democracy. And this is how democracy works on St. Kitts-Nevis!"

Occasionally though, government tolerance is stretched to breaking point. Following a particularly vicious accusation of official sanctioning of bogus money-laundering banks and drug trafficking, Lee Moore was arrested and briefly imprisoned before being bailed out and carried away on the shoulders of his supporters. A fiery evening meeting in the "Masses Yard" behind the newspaper offices, drew a crowd of over 1,000 Kittitians who clapped, stamped and high-fisted the lively rhetoric and then strolled home smiling as they might have after a particularly enthralling game of cricket, a favorite island pastime. Somehow all the fun in no way detracted from the popularity of the Eastern Caribbean Debating Competition being held nearby in the local high school. By the weekend when a mass rally was called to support Moore and his opposition colleagues, interest in the whole affair seemed to have dwindled.

Bertram Gilfillan, teacher, watch-repairer, philanthropist and journalist, explains—"We're only a little country of two tiny islands—we've hardly got going on our own really. Independence from Britain finally came in 1983 and we've hit difficult times. We sell sugar for less than it costs to produce. Tourism is growing but not very quickly. Something needs to be done to get up and go. We're not really lazy people—not at all—but on St. Kitts there are problems we've got to sort out." He paused to make a note for his next column in the local paper (his desk was littered with notes on tiny scraps of blue paper). "For a start most people don't own their land—that's why the houses are built on piles of stones so they can be moved off quickly if there's trouble. There's a phrase we use: 'Who ain't got nothin' don't care for nothin'—and it's true. Then there are the remittances—many

A spectacular poolside view.

154

families receive money from abroad, from other family members, particularly the young ones, working the U.S.A., Britain, or other islands. They can't do without that money but it has a way of sapping initiative." Bertram talks slowly—like the schoolteacher he once was, and tinkers with his watches laid out in various stages of disassembly on the small table in front of him. "We're at the proverbial crossroads I suppose. But," he adds, "at least we've got our own freedom now to make up our minds."

Freedom: The actual attainment of that freedom was a rather messy process. In 1967 the three islands of St. Kitts, Nevis and Anguilla, long jointly administered, became an Associated State of the United Kingdom. Almost immediately Anguilla ceded, much to the chagrin of the British government which dispatched, in true-blue colonial fashion, two frigates bristling with paratroopers, and a dozen or so London bobbies. But all to no avail. Anguilla proudly regained its Crown Colony status and the islands of St. Kitts and Nevis—never very compatible bedfellows—were left to sort out a joint constitution prior to their formal independence on September 19, 1983. Tiny Nevis feared the economic dominance of St. Kitts and made sure it had guarantees of partial self-government and even an "escape clause" if the union proved unworkable.

But, in spite of these often mean-spirited machinations, the sudden emergence of "freedom" brought a surge of exuberance—a new pride. Scrawled on a wall near Basseterre in red paint is the message:
Together we will stay, Forward ever, backward never, St. Christopher and Nevis forever.

The red was bright. It had obviously been repainted many times since independence. And there were others in similar spirit: *"Dignified and Black, no one can take my freedom back!"* and *"Hey man, make no fuss, independence is a must."*

Plantocracy exists: Nonetheless, independence hasn't cured the island of its social and economic inequities. Critics have suggested the presence of a new persuasive but more hidden "plantocracy." Descendants of the old plantation owners still live and prosper on-island; some, like Pam Barry at the **Golden Rock Estate** on Nevis and Phillip Walwyn at **Rawlins Plantation**, run refurbished Great Houses as exclusive inns. Others are relative newcomers, attracted by tax and other investment incentives, who establish businesses and small factories

employing primarily female labor. While such concerns are sometimes fickle in terms of loyalty and longevity, they at least provide the framework for urgently needed alternative island economies in the face of a rapidly imploding industry. Englishman Morris Widowson's **Caribelle Batik** workshop in the **Romney Manor Great House** at Old Road Town is one of the island's best examples of diversification; others, notably the large shoe-production plant in Basseterre which attracted considerable government investment, closed recently for lack of orders.

But then along come plans for the distillation of island gasohol from surplus sugar products, experiments near Sandy Point by the Republic of China in dry-land rice production, the cultivation of "luxury vegetables" for island hotels, and Baron de Rothchild with his factory for the production of sugar-cane wine, and the future begins to take on a more rosy hue.

"The real motor of the future economy must be tourism," claims Larkland Richards, Director of Tourism. "In terms of industrial development it's hard to compete with the low wage scales of Haiti and South America. We need new hotels, more condos, more cruise ships, more outside trade to generate local employment and spur demand for new-farming technologies to replace our dependence on sugar."

But caution still reigns here. While the future seems full of possibilities, many islanders regard rapid change with suspicion, even fear. They like things pretty much the way they are. They enjoy the lyming lifestyles, the laidback stop-for-a-beer-anytime spirit, the "pocket a mumps" attitude that suggests a pocketful of wages is cause for abandoning work for a while and enjoying the fruits of labor.

Quiet charm: And to such citizens, **Basseterre** (population 15,000), capital of St. Kitts, seems "jus'bout right" the way it is. To Caribbean connoisseurs, the town may appear a rather dowdy place, lacking the monied sparkle of other more highly-developed resorts. Critics will point out the lack of a marina and boats in the harbor, the rusting remains of a launch beached in a long-gone hurricane, and a bedraggled waterfront devoid of the usual touristy fripperies. But compared to the other sleepy communities scattered like loose beans on a string around the circular island road, Basseterre booms with an irrepressible West Indian vigor. Crisply-dressed traffic police sort out the snarls at the intersections around **The Circus** where an ornate cast iron clock tower, **The Berkeley Memorial** (painted a ghastly Victorian rust-brown), regards the swirling scene with the pompous aloofness of a colonial plantocrat. Reggae and a dozen skip-beat variants blast from stores and cafes; bemused visitors and locals peer down from the balcony of the **Ballahoo Cafe** at the frenetic salesmanship of city cab-drivers ("Man—you gotta want a taxi—s'way too hot to walk man"), and everyone seeks shards of midday shade along the narrow sidewalks, pausing at corners, hoping for Trade Wind breezes.

Down along **Bay Road**, just by the nondescript strand of gray sand, an impromptu fish market draws a crowd of choosy buyers who nudge, poke and sniff the bonito, snapper, grouper, king fish and fantasy-colored parrot fish. The official government-run market across the road is almost empty. One stall displays a line of old bottles with sun bleached labels containing such oddities as Dr. King's Sulphur Bitters, Eno's Fruit Salts, Zube's Cough Mixture, and Andrew's Liver Salts.

Founded by the French, Basseterre became the official British capital in 1727, was decimated by fire in 1867 and rebuilt in a kind of Franco-British colonial style with such delightful Caribbean nuances as high pitched, no-awning roofs (to lessen their vulnerability in storms), shutters to reduce sun-glare but retain the essential movement of air through the hot interior spaces, and occasional self-conscious outbursts of carpenter Gothic trim. A dash of fresh paint, a few more boutiques, bars and fancy restaurants, and Basseterre could blossom into your typical Caribbean nexus. But the residents seem to prefer the place the way it is. They like the chickens and goats nibbling at scraps in the narrow alleys, and the ragtaggle jumble of colorful fishing boats on the narrow beach. They relish the smell of island cooking from local bars and restaurants—curried goat dishes, fried plaintain, Creole red bean soup, conch chowder and boiled saltfish stew, the broad views across the bay from the pool of the Ocean Terrace Inn, the brown pelicans dive-bombing the waves off Fisherman's Wharf, and snoozy socializing in sidestreet pubs.

Inside St. Kitts: If Basseterre basks in a sleepy haze, then the rest of this little island, as enjoyed on the 32 mile loop drive, may appear virtually comatose. The only real road wriggles through villages of pastel-shaded wood and breeze-block cottages with tin roofs overlooking black sand beaches, and backed by miles of sugar-cane,

The ferry from St. Kitts to Nevis.

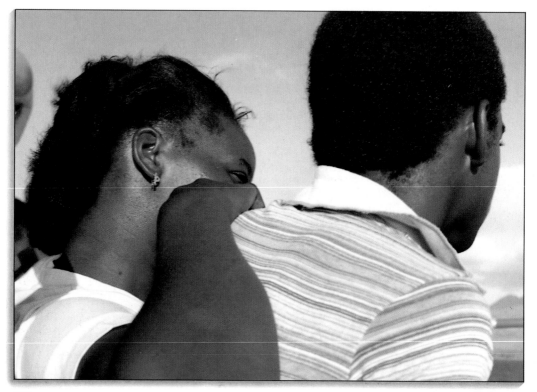

climbing up to the fringes of the rain forest surrounding Mt. Misery (now renamed **Mt. Liamuiga**). Remnants of old sugar mills abound, tall stone chimneys and broken walls among vines and scrub patches inhabited by mongooses and stray goats. As on Nevis, a handful have found a more productive use as elite island inns and private homes, but in spite of the busy little sugar-cane railroad, the slow demise of the sugar industry is evident everywhere.

Dotted along the roadside are tiny clapboard stores selling traditional staples—Argentinian corned beef, tomato paste, soap, sardines, bread rolls, cake, beer, ketchup, candles and the inevitable bottles of Irish Guinness, one of the islander's favorite drinks. Large black ladies in loose pinafore dresses sway by with prize-pumpkin sized bundles of washing on their heads; schoolchildren in neatly pressed uniforms dawdle home from school in the scorching afternoon sun, dallying in pools of shade cast by calabash trees; big butterflies—orange sulphurs, malachites, mimics and Caribbean buckeyes—skim on fresh breezes following the familiar afternoon shower, when canefields steam and the earth smells young again.

History interjects itself, sometimes subtly in the form of Carib rock drawings in **Old Town Roa Village** and the sad little ravine at **Bloody Point** where over 2,000 Carib Indians were massacred on a hot afternoon in 1626 as they were about to launch an attack on island settlers. Sir Thomas Warner, who supervised the slaughter is buried up on the road in **St. Thomas' Churchyard** at **Middle Island**, in an ornate tomb topped with his rather self-serving epitaph: "First read, then weep, when thou art hereby taught That Warner lyes interr'd here, one that bought, With loss of Noble bloud the Illustrious Name Of a Commander- Greate in Acts of Fame…"

Brimstone Hill is history writ large atop an enormous volcanic plug of andesite edged by limestone protrusions. A great graystone fortress peers out over a panorama of ocean and the two Fuji-shaped cones of St. Eustatius and Saba islands are clearly visible to the northwest. Begun in 1690, the fortress was confidently known as Britain's "Gibraltar of the West Indies," until its humiliating capture by the French in 1782, just prior to their final ejection from the island a year later. Today a series of small museum rooms give a useful overview of island culture and history for the many tourists who climb the long flight of

A local poolhall.

steps to sit among the cannons, admire the broad blue vistas, and wait expectantly for the appearance of the local (and very elusive) Vervet monkeys.

High above the fort, the rainforest begins abruptly—a deep green line fringing the sugar-cane fields. Those enjoying the security and companionship of a group usually join one of various organized walking tours to the 750-foot (227-meter) deep, picture-postcard volcanic crater of **Mt. Liamuiga**, or take a jeep trip to the remains of Chuck Norris' *Missing in Action* movie set, hidden in the hills above Sandy Point. Others, willing to endure the tensions and tribulations alone, follow sinuous paths up through the cane and enter the gloom where the balmy Trade Wind breezes suddenly cease. Big blue butterflies flash in shafts of sunlight that become less frequent as the darkness deepens. The path quickly narrows to a series of tight toe-holds between sinuous roots and thick patches of ferns; vines hang like snakes from towering banyan trees; buzzings, slitherings and rustlings in the undergrowth suggest a lively retinue of jungle residents. Although few creatures have the audacity to reveal themselves, solo voyagers sense watchful presences in the shadows. To add to this discomfort is the intense heat. Pools of fetid air fill the tight spaces between the trees; sweat douses the body, turning neatly pressed leisure outfits into heavy sags of soaked cloth. Breath becomes shorter; lungs resist the soupy intake; paths keep disappearing, bringing panic—the fear of being lost forever in this dank tangle of vegetation among the rotting carcasses of fallen trees.

Slow boat: While regular short-hop flights are available between St. Kitts and Nevis every day, the old green ferry boat linking Basseterre to Charlestown provides an unforgettable 45 minute, 12 mile, nautical experience—a slice of island life in its most chaotic and charismatic form.

The boat wallows alongside Basseterre pier near the domed customs house as the loading takes place—a mini-mountain of boxes, baskets, sacks of vegetables, a crate of startle-eyed chickens, two trussed pigs (alive and squealing), three old bicycles and five enormous axes with brightly honed blades. A bunch of bleary-eyed musicians from Antigua watched their young admirers spinning home in the dawnlight, and now, four hours later, they stand mute and morose wondering if their equipment will ever make it safely to Charlestown for the evening show. A case of canned soup is

A house in Charlestown.

dropped and disappears with a flurry of bubbles in the churning water between the boat and the pier. A brief moment of concern is followed by recognition that recovery is impossible and everyone bursts out laughing, except, of course, the musicians, who are now totally convinced that they should have stayed at home.

The ride is choppy as the ferry rolls past the velvety hills of the south-east peninsula, skirting **Balast Bay**, **Bugg's Hole**, **Nag's Head**, and catches the bigger waves in **The Narrows** between the two islands. An old man with no teeth sits hunched at the back of the boat among boxes of breadfruit, sipping a bowl of "goat-water" (a thin soup made from goat meat and vegetables); a couple of deck hands share a bottle of spiked "maubi," an island concoction made from tree bark, and most of the other 40 or so passengers doze in the stuffy heat of the cabin. Outside the spray-splattered windows, the classic volcanic profile of **Nevis Peak** rises 3,232 feet (979 meters) into its perpetual cloud-cap. Dense rainforest shrouds the higher slopes; lower down are tree-bounded fields and the remnants of old sugar mills and below that the long line of **Pinneys Beach**—four miles of golden sand shaded by palms—underdeveloped, unspoiled, the

perfect Caribbean strand. A black horse gallops through the skittering surf, its rider hunched so low he becomes part of the creature's rhythmed movements. Two people swim in the blue shallows. The rest of the beach is deserted.

Charlestown (population 1,200) emerges from its palmy setting, a colorful sprawl of pastel walls, tin roofs, and shady gardens. A hand-painted sign reads "Welcome to Nevis. Birthplace of Alexander Hamilton," and once again comes that sense of tangible history—flickers of familiarity.

The town has seen bad times. An American traveler, Hyatt Verrill, described Charlestown in his 1907 journals as: "forgotten, neglected and of so little importance that few ships ever drop anchor here—a pathetic place, passed away forever perhaps, but beautiful, even if dead."

Of course Mr. Verrill picked a rather inauspicious time to visit the tiny town, during a decline in the island's sugar industry and following a combined earthquake and hurricane that had damaged the Great Houses and blown the sails off the sugarmills. Since then, although the population of the island continues to decline (9,500 in 1980, and thought to be less than 7,500 today), the capital retains a quaint dignity

The final yards of the semi-annual horserace.

and architectural unity in its high-roofed, verandah-shaded buildings on main street and around **Walwyn Plaza**. Huckster ladies sell vegetables and trinkets near **Don Williams' Longstone Bar**, where expats congregate for darts, devilish island cocktails and Don's irreverent daily monologues on island life and scandals. Nearby at the **Nevis Handicraft Coop**, local fruit wines are for sale in old soda bottles—pawpaw, sorrel, genip, gooseberry and bottles of fiery homemade pepper sauce. Around the corner at the **Nevis Philatelic Bureau**, visitors flock to buy frequently-issued first day editions of colorful Nevis stamps (a useful source of revenue in this subsistence-economy island). And on Saturdays the place is bursting with life by 7:30 a.m. as Nevisians pour in for the weekly fish, meat and vegetable market down by the docks.

By comparison, the remainder of this 36 square mile volcanic blip seems a sleepy, pastoral place. The 18-mile-long road around the island meanders up past the shell of the once-fashionable **Bath Hotel** (the subterranean sulphur baths are still open to visitors), and wriggles past bursting bushes of bauhinias, shrouded by wild almonds and untidy bark-dripping gum trees. The spine-laden trunk of a sandbox rises out of a tangle of Mexican creepers and lantana. The openness of the roads on St. Kitts, bounded by endless fields of sugar-cane, contrast here with an exuberance of wild fecundity. Sea island cotton was once found in large plantations, over 3,500 acres (1,400 hectares) in the early 1950s, but today less than 150 scrawny acres remain. Much of the land has returned to scrub, punctuated by the scattered gardens of islanders on the long slopes of Nevis Peak.

The past lives: There's little evidence of concern for the future and the old ways persist. *Obeah*, traditional island voodoo practices, continue secretly; *Myal* men still use ancient herbal cures for sickness and islanders retain their respect of the mystical powers of big fat toads—the crappos. Even the names of newly-baptized baby girls at the methodist chapel in **Taylor's Pasture** have a softness, a tranquility of sound, that seems to capture the old spirit of Nevis: Carrisa, Shani, Kahani, Petronella, Joyah, Angelica, Varina and Tulipina.

The spanking new air-conditioned villas of the emerging "American colony," hidden in cool folds high up near the rain forest, seem far removed from island culture. At the tiny Newcastle pottery near **Nisbet Plantation**, local clay is fashioned in the

A siesta on the Brimstone Hill Fortress.

traditional Caribbean manner and fired over coconut husks in the open air. Plans for expansion and the introduction of more efficient processes are met with polite disinterest. On the north and west coasts beautiful white beaches, fringed by palms and mangoes, are quiet and deserted—ideal places to relax, Robinson Crusoe fashion, and watch the humming-birds among the wild orchids.

Visitors, however, are not entirely uncatered for. History-buffs make straight for the **Hamilton Museum** in Charlestown or the nearby **Morning Star Estate** where Philadelphian lawyer, Robert Abrahams, displays his outstanding collection of Nelson memorabilia. Just up the road is the stone-built **St. John Fig Tree Church**, where the Admiral's marriage to Fanny Nisbet in 1787 is formally recorded. Others revel in the five-day riches of the Culturama festival in July, featuring island folk art, music, masquerades, "big drum" dances, and food galore. Most divide their time between the six restored plantation inns where lobster lunches and hours by the blue pools leave many questioning the rigorous work-ethic routines awaiting them back home.

Jaunts off the circular island road along the narrow byways provide insights of Nevisian life-rhythms. Down **Buck's Hill** from **Taylor's Pasture**, for example, a narrow track winds toward the hidden beaches of **White Bay** past typical cameos of island life—more pockets of tranquil self-sufficiency. A tiny lime-washed breeze block house with tin roof, door and window frames painted bright blue to discourage "jumbie" spirits, hides in a dell, shaded by coconut palms and breadfruit trees. A domed brick oven stands in the earth yard where chickens scratch for tidbits; a small garden brims with yams, cabbages, sweet potatoes and a couple of dusty pumpkins. The Creole aroma of a pork stew—*souce*—eases up through the trees; a little girl in a bandana-red dress pounds pumpkin chunks into an orange goo and adds flour, fresh lime juice, onions and a sprinkle of hot pepper sauce (a Nevis specialty) to make spicy fritters for dinner. A radio plays one more fire-and-brimstone American preacher (self-proclaimed High Priest of the Church of the Immaculate Power of South Bend, Indiana) promising just about everything in return for "a little gift to God."

A man sits outside the house on a broken bamboo chair sucking the cottony white flesh of red "Fat Pork" berries, and talking

Sunset view of Basseterre.

cricket to a neighbor, comparing the records of such world-class Nevisian cricket heroes as Elquemedo Willet and Derrick Parry with the latest performance of Keith Arthurton at nearby Grove Park cricket pitch. A couple of split fish he caught in the early morning with a surf net hang against the wall of the house, turning gold in the sun. The trees are heavy with ripe fruit. Life is simple and good.

In the evenings at the old Great House inns, charming hosts help guests recapture the atmosphere of the old plantocracy days. Fan-cooled cottages set in explosions of flowering bushes, are scattered around the swimming pools. Ice tinkles in tall high-balls as the evening chirpings of crickets and tree frogs begin below the rain forest around Nevis Peak, which may (on rare occasions) lose its cloud-cap and turn crimson in yet one more perfect sunset. On the lower slopes shadows ease across a patch-work of tiny fields and gardens surrounding the scattered hamlets.

Then the gong booms and guests stroll across the lawn to their places around a finely polished mahogany table in the dining room, performing the politeness they feel appropriate to plantation-life etiquette. Portraits of planter-family ancestors peer down on an impromptu Agatha Christie-styled mixing of honeymoon couple, famous lawyer, obviously wealthy real estate broker and diamond-encrusted wife, architect with arty girlfriend in tow, mysterious femme-fatale who smiles but never talks, aging writer with full Hemingway beard, and bouncy host and hostess-owners, determined to include everyone in country house-party conversation through all the candlelight courses, to coffee in the garden under the stars.

"Breakfast from eight o'clock," the hostess smilingly reminds her guests, 'in your room or on the patio, as you wish." And even after the filling dinner, visions of morning fruit baskets brimming with custard apples, shaddock, soursop, mangoes, guavas, passion fruit and star apples, all served with hot Johnny cakes and home-made kumquat marmalade, send guests to bed grinning like greedy schoolkids.

Hubcap chicken: Across the valley, lights still glow in Dame Eva Wilkin's home on **Clay Ghaut Estate**. The island's beloved "artist-in-residence" began her residency in 1918 when she came to live on her father's sugar plantation and eventually took over the windmill as her studio when operations declined in 1940. Now well into her 80s, the

House in Middle Island.

diminutive Eva still creates her evocative pastels and watercolors of Nevis life and tells her tales of earlier island escapades to a stream of daily visitors who drive up the rough track from the main road in their opensided mimi-moke hire cars.

Further around the island in **Butler's Village**, **Dick's Bar Disco** shifts into high gear around midnight with a live "steel-reggae" band in the open courtyard and a couple of hundred young Nevisians (many of whom have walked more than five miles for the high times) dancing on into the dawn. Across the road there's an aromatic trade in "hub-cap chicken" which is precisely that—chunks of chicken dipped in spiced batter and deep-fried in dented truck hub-caps by two enormous women whose sweat drips rhythmically into the boiling oil, making it spit and crackle.

And way at the northern end of the island, lovers stroll the long curved beach at the **Nisbet Plantation Inn**, a sensitive restoration of the 18th century Great House. The sand shimmers in silver moonshadows, night breezes keep the palm fronds clicking (and the coconuts falling), and the skittering surf sparkles with luminous phosphorescence. It's hard to imagine a more idyllic setting for romantic trysts, straight out of a Harlequin novel; a short distance away up the tree-lined walk from the beach is a cozy bungalow with fans slowly turning, night doves cooing, stars in the windows, and crisp linen sheets turned down invitingly…

"And this is exactly what we mustn't lose," says Richard Lupinacci, the popular American-born director of the Bank of Nevis and owner of his own inn, the **1740 Hermitage Plantation** in **St. John Fig Tree Parish**. "Sure we must keep up with the times. We don't want to create a typical Caribbean "busboy" scenario either. Nevis is special—it's not like other islands. Things have been pretty quiet here since the Treaty of Versailles and we want to attract visitors who appreciate the way things are. That doesn't mean no development or change. It might be a good idea eventually to form stronger links with other Antilles islands—there are proposals for federations flying around and they may make sense. We also need more hotel space, we need a longer airport runway on Nevis—but what we don't need is change just for the sake of change. The people are proud of their islands and I live here too—I'm as proud as they are. It's all a matter of balance really."

In the case of St. Kitts-Nevis, it's a case of "so far, so good!"

School girls tarry on the way home.

EXPLORING ANTIGUA

From a few miles off shore, **Antigua** looks much as it did when Columbus sighted it 500 years ago during his second voyage to the New World. The forest which then covered the island has long since disappeared, replaced initially by sugar plantations, but now taken over by the bush, grassland and thickets which still give it, from a distance, a wooded appearance. For anyone sailing among the Lesser Antilles, Antigua from seaward looks pleasant enough but rather uninteresting when compared with the mountainous islands to the south and west. This is a most misleading impression, based on the false assumption that the inhabitants are no different from the people of the other islands around.

When the mariner draws closer he will realize that the low, rounded outline is merely a plain back-drop to a spectacular coastline. It is only from close-up that Antigua reveals its deep bays, secluded harbors and the numerous coves and inlets—all set in waters ranging in color from the deepest blue to the brightest green, and fringed by stretches of eye-achingly white sand. This deceptive outward appearance of the island is reflected in the character of its people. The rather formal, distant attitude encountered at first will soon be found, given the right approach, to be no more than a facade.

Because of its excellent natural harbors and its pivotal position on the arc of the Lesser Antilles, Antigua has always had regular seaborne contact with the outside world. Once advantage of its terrain to construct an airstrip was taken in the 1940s, the island assumed an importance to the communications of the region which it has never lost. These factors helped to produce an outward-looking population, used to travel, and made up of people with antecedents from all over the Caribbean. It is their adaptability and enterprise, as much as the island's natural attractions, which have created the modern Antigua—a stable, democratic country with a leading place among the island nations of the eastern Caribbean.

Imported sugar slaves: Columbus did not land but he did bequeath the name, Santa Maria la Antigua, after a painting of the Virgin in Seville Cathedral. It retained its virginal state, as far as the Europeans were concerned, until 1632 when a group of English settlers arrived from the nearby island of St. Christopher. Although it seemed ideal for planting, Antigua had one great drawback—no permanent running water or lakes. The shortage of fresh water remains a problem today, although greatly alleviated by wells, cisterns, reservoirs and the use of de-salting plants. With rainfall usually restricted to brief heavy showers, the climate is excellent, probably the finest in the Lesser Antilles. The combination of high air temperature and a fairly high relative humidity is tempered by the trade wind, which blows with great consistency throughout the year. Though such conditions were not ideal for intensive agriculture, by the beginning of the 18th century the whole island had been cleared and divided into plantations. And until 1972 sugar remained the island's most important product. To create the plantation, a huge labor force was needed and slaves were imported from Africa soon after the first settlement. By the time slavery was abolished in 1834 there were 30,000 slaves, together with about 4,000 'free coloreds' and less than 2,000 whites. Today the population is approaching 80,000, of whom about 95 percent are of African descent.

Antigua's first settlement started only twelve years after the signing of the Mayflower Compact. Little has happened since then. It changed hands only once during the colonial period. The French captured the island for a few months in 1666. Otherwise it played little part in the struggles which occupied the European nations in the Caribbean during the 17th and 18th centuries. After these wars ended in 1815 Antigua entered a long period of stagnation. Sugar became less and less profitable to produce, estates were abandoned or incorporated into larger holdings, and half-hearted attempts to grow other crops met with little success. For the majority of the population the events of 1834 made little material difference to their way of life, and improvements came slowly during the next hundred years. The sharp divisions between races and classes, and an absence of social, civil and economic amenities, can be said to have ended in Antigua only with the outbreak of the Second World War. For the poor in 1939, and most Antiguans were then very poor, their daily lives differed very little from those of their forefathers a century earlier.

Modern Antigua: Two events were largely responsible for bringing the island into the 20th century. After a Royal Commission investigated social and economic conditions throughout the British West Indies in the late 1930s, the workers in each island were encouraged to form trade unions. The formation of such a union in Antigua in 1939 not only helped the workers to improve their conditions, but also provided the leadership for a labor-oriented political party to oppose the white oligarchy which then ran the island through the colonial Legislative Council. The creation of this party was delayed by the start of the war, but in 1941 the second catalytic event occurred. When the United States entered the war, Antigua was selected as a suitable site for military bases, and the island soon saw the arrival of American servicemen and contractors in large numbers. The impact of this friendly invasion on many aspects of island life, together with the assertion of workers' rights through trade union activity, meant that by the end of the war Antigua was firmly in the 20th century and most ordinary Antiguans were motivated for change. After 1945 changes came—compared with the lassitude of the previous 300 years—with incredible speed: full adult suffrage in 1951, a ministerial form of government in 1956, internal self-government in 1967, and finally in 1981 complete independence from Great Britain. Throughout this period one man dominated the political stage and played the leading role in bringing the island squarely into the modern world.

Vere Bird became president of Antigua's first trade union in 1943 and three years later was elected to the Legislative Council, beginning an association with the government which has continued to the present day. Since 1946, except for the years between 1971 and 1976 when he was out of office, he has been the undisputed leader of both his party and his country; holding the offices of Chief Minister, Premier and now Prime Minister. Despite his many achievements, and his place as one of the Caribbean's most experienced politicians, he has remained a modest man. British orders and decorations have been rejected, a personality cult firmly discouraged, and his portrait is seen in very few public places. His only departure from this abstemious attitude was to allow the airport to be renamed in his honor in 1985.

When Bird entered politics the economy was based almost entirely on sugar. The activities of his union and his party did much to help the workers in the sugar industry, but at the same time they hastened its demise. Agriculture generally now plays little part in the economy. Instead, light manufacturing and tourism have become the mainstays. A change was stimulated by an outside demand for Caribbean vacations and by foreign investors wishing to cater to it, but it was accomplished mainly by the readiness of Antiguans to adapt and to profit from their innate friendliness. Bird's main achievement has been arousing the spirit of enterprise and directing the initiative of the Antiguan people.

Sharing the island: About one third of all Antiguans live in or around the capital, **St. John's**, on the north-west coast. The remainder are spread evenly throughout the island, in over 40 small towns and villages. A few of these, like **Falmouth** or **Parham**, are as old as St. John's, but most of them came into existence during the past 150 years. **Liberta** and **Freetown** were the first free villages founded after the abolition of slavery. The growth of the villages in the 19th century—many of them near the coast with excellent views to seaward—foreshadowed the island's tourist potential. In 1950 there was one beach hotel for visitors who arrived at an airstrip abandoned by the U.S. military, or who, because there were no port facilities, landed by launch from ships. Now, decades later, some aspect of tourism is found everywhere. The primitive airstrip has become a full-blown airport, a deep water port has been constructed in St. John's Harbour, and visitor accommodations are spread thinly all around, utilizing some of the many beaches for which Antigua is renowned. The absence of any specific "tourist quarter" means that residents and visitors share the island equally.

There are a surprising number of different regions in the 108 square miles (280 square km) that make up the island. These range from a small area in the north-east with an almost semi-desert appearance, complete with eroded rocks and cacti, to a range of hills in the south-west which contain the nearest thing to a tropical rain forest. With the virtual cessation of agriculture, much of the land elsewhere has reverted to bush and woodland. As a result most of the island's color comes either flowering trees and shrubs or from the brightly painted houses.

English Harbour contains the finest and most famous of Antigua's historical sites—the former British naval dockyard now named (for reasons which have more to do with attracting visitors than anything he did there) after Admiral Horatio Nelson. **Nelson's Dockyard** is the focal point of Sailing Week and the center of all yachting activity throughout the year. The buildings all have been restored and put to some use not too far removed from their original purpose. Because of this, the modern visitor gets a very good impression of what the dockyard must have been like in its heyday as one of the most important British bases in the Caribbean. This feeling of historical continuity is also apparent, if to a lesser degree, among the remains of the fortifications built on the hills overlooking English Harbour.

The various barracks, batteries, magazines and other military buildings which make up **Shirley Heights** is not so well preserved as the dockyard, but it is well sign-posted, easily accessible, and plenty of information about them is available. None of this is true of another stronghold about two miles away, guarding Falmouth Harbour. **Great George Fort**, on top of Monks Hill, was intended as a citadel in which the inhabitants of this part of the island could take refuge if attacked. It can be reached only by walking, or bouncing in a cross-country vehicle, up a mile-long track. The discomfort of the approach is far outweighed by the pleasure obtained from the stupendous view from its walls. Anyone who walks up will gain some idea of the effort which went into its construction in the late 17th century, and of the difficulty in keeping it manned and supplied.

From the fort there is an all-round view of the coast except to the west where it is overshadowed by higher hills. These hills occupy about 20 square miles (50 square km) of the most remote and rugged countryside on the island. They are crossed by good walking trails which provide access to some of the least frequented of all the beaches, as well as to the 1,300- foot (400-meter) summit of **Boggy Peak**—the highest point of Antigua.

No road signs: Normally, it is necessary to climb to appreciate the scenery in Antigua, yet one of the most attractive parts of the island is a valley which runs into the hills from the north-west. A dirt road meanders through this countryside which in places resembles an English park, with tall trees, grazing animals and small lakes formed by damming a stream which flows whenever it rains; only the occasional coconut tree destroys the illusion.

This valley, and another to the west, which has a road joining **Bendals** to the most remote Antiguan community at a place called **Sawcolts**, has changed little in the past century. To stroll through either of them is to experience something of the rural Antigua which existed between the end of slavery and the advent of the modern era in

Leaving church, St. John's.

1939. Near the village of Bendals is a low hill called **Green Castle**. It is less than 600 feet (180 meters) high, and from the foot not very prepossessing, particularly because there is a stone quarry along the lower slopes....This, like other aspects of Antigua, is a misleading first impression. The rounded, open summit is delightful, with a splendid view of the northern part of the island.

Local opinion holds that the large standing stones on the hill are megaliths. Though undoubtedly a myth, when standing on the summit near the gravestone which covers the ashes of a former British governor, it is not too difficult to visualize the early Amerindian inhabitants wanting to erect a permanent memorial of their visit. Nor is it hard to understand why the ex-governor, Lord Baldwin, asked for his remains to be interred in such an idyllic spot.

Monks Hill, **Bendals**, **Sawcolts** and **Green Castle** are all identified on maps of the island, but are seldom visited; and this is so with may other parts of Antigua. Most of it is waiting to be explored and investigated. Except those for Nelson's Dockyard, Shirley Heights and the Anglican Cathedral in St. John's, there are no guidebooks for any historical sites or places of interest.

There are no marked nature trails or recommended hiking tours. Very little is signposted, and one of the most eccentric aspects of traveling in Antigua is the absence of road signs, village names and distance indicators. It is possible to see this as another manifestation of the Antiguan's independent outlook: the man "cooling out" in front of his house knows which village he lives in, so why bother with a sign displaying his name? If a stranger wants to know where he is, all he has to do is ask—and here everyone has time for a chat. But, a word of caution: one of the worst solecisms a stranger can commit is to omit a "Good morning" when entering a house, an office, or even a store. With this in mind no-one can ever get lost in Antigua, regardless of how few road signs are encountered.

The general shortage of street and traffic signs extends to St. John's , although "city" is really too grandiose a term for what is in fact a small town. Business and commercial life is still concentrated in the few streets which formed the original 18th century town laid out between the harbor and what later became the **Cathedral of St. John the Divine**. Other than the cathedral there are no large buildings, and there remain many private houses still amongst the offices and

Fishing boats in the harbor.

stores. A great deal of the life of St. John's takes place on the main streets, which are all narrow and often without sidewalks.

"At the corners of the different streets are seated hucksters (black or colored women), some with their shallow trays containing cakes of all descriptions, parched ground nuts, sugar cakes and other confections, and varieties of fruits and vegetables; others have piles of cottons, colored calicoes, bright-tinted handkerchiefs, etc., placed by them, or carefully spread along the sides of the most frequented streets, to attract the eye of the passer-by."

This description, taken from the book *Antigua and the Antiguans,* published in 1844, still holds good today. The same type of tray with exactly the same contents will be found at each corner, tended by a genial, usually well-proportioned, lady. Available sidewalks are usually taken up by other vendors selling fashionable clothing and souvenirs. Their trays and stalls can be something of a hazard, given modern traffic conditions, but they do much to enliven the city scene.

Carnival time: The leisurely movement of traffic comes to a complete stop for two days each year. From about the middle of July the city starts to take on a festive air—far more music is heard, garish signs appear on buildings, and stores and restaurants begin to do brisk business. At the **Recreation Ground,** not far from the city center, a huge outdoor stage is erected, surrounded by equally large banks of loudspeakers, and every night for a week a colorful, noisy and vastly entertaining show is staged. This is **Carnival City**, the venue for most of the annual Carnival program. It is opened by the Governor-General, who then (and understandably, as his official residence is next door) departs for his annual vacation abroad.

Although it attracts many visitors, especially Antiguans living abroad, Carnival is very much a local event. Steel bands, calypsonians, beauty queens and decorated floats all have their place, but the accent is on providing an occasion for Antiguans to dress up and "let go." Their participation reaches its climax on the first Monday and Tuesday in August with the frenzy of J'ouvert, and the chance to "play Mas" and to "jump up" to the music of steel bands in the streets for the better part of two days.

Carnival takes place in St. John's only, helping to reinforce the dominance of the city over the entire life of the island. This predominance stems in part from its proximity to the airport, the main seaport and the island's single industrial site. Nonetheless, most Antiguans still live in the villages, and village life continues to exert a great deal of influence—as it has for the past century and a half.

When slavery was abolished the plantation system began to break down, greatly assisted by the decline in the value of sugar. From around the middle of the 19th century land started to become available for ordinary black Antiguans to lease or buy, and a class of peasant farmers slowly came into being. As the number of villages increased, so more and more people could aspire to own something, even if just a tiny wooden house and a few square feet of land. Those who went abroad to work could often afford a larger house and a bigger area of land when they returned.

Today it is likely that the majority of Antiguans own property of some kind, and many otherwise very unassuming villagers possess substantial tracts of land—a situation which is not common to other islands in the region. The evolvement of a broadly-based, property-owning society—not confined to the capital—has had a lot to do with the rapid development of the island in recent years.

Sugar legacy: The sugar estates left behind two permanent legacies: their names and the windmills which used to grind the cane. The estate names, many of them dating back to the 17th century, are still in everyday use as district names outside the villages. The monumental stone towers of the mills, impervious to wind and weather, are seen everywhere. One or two have been converted into bizarre dwellings but most of them stand empty and overgrown, permanent reminders of the past and memorials to the bonded Antiguans who built them. The architectural form used, and the care with which they were built, make them almost indestructible—something which could not be said for a structure put up to commemorate the island's separation from Great Britain in 1981. This was a functionless, three-legged "independence arch" erected in St. John. It collapsed while being assembled, and once it was raised it had to be propped up with stays and guys. It lasted less than four years before being condemned as unsafe and dismantled. It is doubtful whether its disappearance was mourned by many Antiguans. They hardly need a concrete symbol to remind them of something they have known since long before Antigua ceased to be a colony, and which many of their ancestors realized well before 1834—that independence is a state of mind.

EXPLORING MONTSERRAT

The 27-mile (44-km) flight from Antigua to Montserrat is a brief jog in a nine-seater over the warm Caribbean waters. Redonda, an uninhabited island ruled by a self-titled "King Juan," is visible out the tiny window; other than that, it's all blue specked by the white fringes of the waves.

A green shamrock passport stamp prepares a visitor for "The Emerald Isle of the Caribbean," as Montserrat is called, but the area surrounding the airport hardly lives up to that reputation. Here it is flat and scrubby and skinny-flanked cows nibble at sere grass. But past the airport the terrain grows miraculously green, the startling red flamboyant trees live up to their name and the goats seem to be plumper than their brothers further down the slopes. For indeed, the glory of this island studded with lemon-and apricot colored hibiscus, scarlet canna and trumpeting gold allamanda is its physical self. Montserrat's historical preservation society, the National Trust, describes the terrain that burst out of the sea in a volcanic eruption more than four million years ago as one of the few perfect eco-systems left in the world. That means there's enough kelp for the fish, enough fish for the birds, enough plants for the cows and so on.

"Goat-Water" and "Mountain-Chicken": The centerpiece of this magnificent eco-system is **Galway's Soufriere**, an inactive volcano and sulfur spring. After a narrow, rocky half-hour hike to the top, the air thickens with the smell and dampness of sulfur steam. The craggy rock walls are stained with mineral deposits of extraordinary colors: cadmium yellow, deep rust, flat blue. Beneath the rock the sandy dirt is pitch black, and seeping trails of warm water eke down the stones. It feels like a fantasy moon-walk.

Olaudah Equiano, a slave in Montserrat in the 1760s, left a written account of a visit to the Soufriere. "I had taken some potatoes with me," he wrote, "and I put them into different ponds, and in a few minutes they were well-boiled…the silver shoe buckles, and all the other things of that metal we had among us, were, in a little time, turned as black as lead." Two hundred years later, little has changed, except that Montserratians say you can cook an egg, rather than a potato.

The volcano's earlier eruptions left the mountains of Monserrat so fertile that most of the islanders feed themselves off home gardens. A wide variety of vegetables grow in the generous volcanic soil, so the cucumbers, breadfruit, tomatos, pumpkin and cabbages served at local homes and restaurants are native, as are other vegetables less familiar to non-West Indian diners, such as the pale green, squash-like christophene. Many people ride donkeys up and down the steep road to gather and bring these crops to sell at the Saturday morning market

"Goat-water" and "mountain-chicken" are two of the national dishes of Montserrat. The former is a goat-meat stew flavored with "herbs and chible," the local term for scallions and thyme. The latter is not chicken parts at all; it is gigantic frog's legs, cooked any number of ways. Eating a vibrant orange Montserrat pawpaw (papaya) is as vivid an experience for the eyes as for the palate. Pawpaw should be the name for its own color.

There are purposes for island plants other than eating. Use of local plants for physical and spiritual health is common knowledge, particularly among older people. "Bush tea" refers to any kind of plant potion, and a "bush-baby" is a child who is soothed with herbal brews because his stomach can't tolerate milk. *Obeah*, an Ashanti-rooted religion characterized by sorcery and magic ritual, is outlawed on Montserrat. Some speculate that this is because modern practitioners have lost touch with the sources of power and methods they would need to be effective. Nonetheless, this is an island where most people have enough of a sense for their country's particular natural resources to nourish and care for themselves and their families.

Luck o' the Irish: Montserrat's history is typically Caribbean in that its story is one of initial settlement and subsequent colonial aggression and rule. But there are a few twists: Montserrat's greatest European influence is Irish, rather than British, Dutch, Spanish, or French, and it has not been marked by anything near the level of resistance to colonization that has existed elsewhere in the region.

From 400 to 1,500 A.D., Indians migrated up the Leeward Islands chain from South America, after their original descent from Asia via the Bering Strait and across North America. Ciboneys, or, "stone people," arrived first. Next came Arawaks, followed by Caribs, who called Montserrat "Alliouagana," which seems to mean either "island of the prickly bush" or "island of the aloe plant."

In 1943, Columbus sighted the island and named it "Montserrat" because it reminded him of the land surrounding the Montserrat monastery in his native Spain. According to his son's account, he did not land because he had been told "that Caribbees had unpeopled [the island], devouring the Inhabitants." Montserrat's Irish roots can be traced back to 1632, when Sir Thomas Warner ordered dissident Irish Catholics living in St. Kitts to colonize neighboring Montserrat for England. The country became known as a refuge for persecuted Irish Catholics from other English colonies. Today, the phone book is filled with the names of both black and white Ryans, Sweeneys and O'Garros. St. Patrick's day is a national fete, featuring parades through parishes with names like St. Peter's and Cork Hill.

The 17th, 18th and 19th centuries were characterized by power struggles amongst various European and Indian factions. Sugar cultivation began in 1643, and soon after, in 1650, the African slave trade began. In 1678 the population was composed of 2,682 whites, and 992 black slaves. About 100 years later, the picture had changed drastically: 1,300 whites to 10,000 slaves. Emancipation of the slaves came about in August 1834, and people in some areas of the island still sing the original, celebratory ode to black hero Nincom Riley on the first of that month: "*De fus' o' Augus' is come again, Hurrah fo' Nincom Riley. If buckra [white man] nack, me nack ee 'gain, Hurrah fo' Nincum Riley.*"

Today, Montserrat is a British Crown Colony with a resident governor appointed by and representing Queen Elizabeth. The governor appoints a Chief Minister from the ranks of the popularly-elected legislative and executive councils. The elected officials make the laws and run the country, but the governor always has the final authority, in the name of the Queen, to "withold his assent." According to Montserrat's major historian, Howard Fergus, this power is rarely exercised. He quotes a poem from "*Son of the Soil*" which characterizes Montserrat as "a lost chick that has strayed from its mother" that would, if it became independent, "quickly fly back to find food and cover." Whatever the case, Montserrat shows no signs of moving toward full independence any time soon.

Winding tour: The shortest distance between two points may be a straight line, but that is frequently a navigational impossibility on Montserratian roads. The roads wind and wind. To get from "A" to "B" requires hairpin turns and ups and downs through thorny bush. But the view from some of these summits is remarkable and recalls the tufty, deep-green of fictional Scottish moors. Marked lookout points throughout the island with plaques explain the historical significance of each given site. Montserrat is well-suited to wandering with the assistance of a cab-driver. Although you could, you wouldn't want to rush through all of it in a day. Leisurely chance conversations with Montserratians make the sites more memorable.

Downtown Plymouth, the capital of Montserrat, is small but complete: banks, post and government offices, the old-fashioned open courthouse with its custard-colored walls. Supermarkets offer a wide range of foods as well as bottles of bay rum and tins of tea-crackers. A little boy sells knotted ropes of spices on the street; a woman brings leafy greens in a wide basket from her garden. The public library is a cool cave inside the government building where people will stop for a bit in the middle of the day to read magazines or peruse the extensive collection of West Indian literature on the shelves by the front door.

Just outside of town, a woman sells homemade soursop and coconut ice-creams from her living room window. A Trinidadian gentleman named Neptune sells *roti*, delectable curried meat wrapped in pastry, at his rumshop/restaurant, called **"Nepco's"**. Albert Murphy sells fresh fish and dispenses advice by the side of the road at **Carr's Bay**. **The Village Place** is a popular dinner spot for local people as well as for visitors. Taxi drivers know where all of these places and people are located.

Rock stars and royalty: Montserrat is known for **Air Studios**, a recording facility built by former Beatles' manager George Martin. This state-of-the-art studio has hosted internationally-known musicians such as Paul McCartney, Stevie Wonder, Phil Collins and Sting, as well as some local artistes. Visiting musicians often drop in on the **Friday Night Disco** in town. Every week it's packed wall-to-wall with visitors and Montserratians.

The Montserratian Museum is a converted old sugar mill which displays Amerindian beads, flints, crushing stones and other artifacts, as well as early maps and legal documents. **Sea Island Cotton** is grown and processed on the island and sold, as woven table-wear and clothing, from a government-run boutique in the center of Plymouth. **The Governor's Residence**, with its sumptuous, unruly gardens, is open to the public during designated hours. With

Preceding pages: ringing the bells outside an Anglican church in Plymouth; house in Montserrat. Below, cactus perched on a cliff above the Caribbean.

its stately atmosphere and multiple photos of Charles, Di and the Queen, the house itself exudes Brittania. As for hotels and guest villas, **The Vue Pointe Hotel** offers individual cabins on a summit above Isle's Bay. **The Montserrat Springs** has a hot springs pool which allegedly possesses curative powers. **The Coconut Hill Hotel** is a faded flower straight out of Tennessee Williams: "frayed about the edges, but not without its charm."

Though most of the beaches are dark with volcanic sand, **Rendezvous Bay** is lime-white, with excellent snorkeling opportunities. Captain John Martin sails there daily, through the Vue Pointe Hotel's arrangement, because the beach is difficult to navigate by foot and impossible by car. When the boat is anchored, sea wonders are visible below the surface and all around. Full schools of tiny silver fish skim quick as gasps along the surface, followed by larger fish leaping in hot pursuit. Black "cattle egrets" with eight-foot wing spans cruise and circle in the sky; Captain Martin says they have to get a running start off a cliff to fly.

Hi, chief: Twelve thousand people live on Montserrat, and the same faces pass each other many times a day. But it would be unthinkable not to say hello and call a passer's-by name, as if each time were the first. Cab drivers honk in greeting to virtually everyone they pass on the road, and most people say they leave their doors unlocked.

The country is so small, in fact, that a taxi-driver showing a visitor about town is likely to run into his mother, working at the Sea-Island cotton factory, or his brother, selling half-boots at Arrow's Man-Shop. On Fridays, anticipating the disco that evening, perfect strangers as well as friends call out to a visitor, "Are you going to the party tonight?" There is bustle in the streets and people are busy at work, but there is also the quiet comfort of familiarity which comes from seeing the same faces time and again waiting under the huge shade tree at the center of town for the one bus that goes around the island. This is, after all, a country so tiny and so intimate that when Chief Minister John Osborne rides ceremoniously through Plymouth, people in the street wave and call, "Hi, Chief!"

Montserrat's economy is based on agriculture—mostly subsistence farming—as well as real estate, building, textile and electronic assembly work and tourism. Sugar didn't grow well in the rocky moun- **Isle's Bay.**

tains. For a time, limes fared better, and now Montserratians cultivate some cotton. The island has its own elementary and secondary schools, but for children to receive further training, they must go to Antigua, or Jamaica, or further still, to the United States or England.

"Jumbie names": As in many other communities throughout the African diaspora, names and nicknames are two distinct entities in Montserrat. People have their "official," birth certificate name, used for church and school. Nicknames are known as "jumbie names." Jumbies are spirits. If, for example, a child is sick, he'll be given a jumbie name so that evil spirits can't "find" him.

Jumbie names are also given after a particularly distinctive episode. A cab driver, despondent after his girlfriend left him, tried to kill himself by eating rat poison. The poor fellow lived and a new name stuck: "Rat Poison." The phone book lists both given and jumbie names. James Firth is called "Mango," and "Bebeep." One could go for days asking after John Weekes of Harvey Street and only get a smile of recognition at the name "Third World."

Alphonsus Cassell (Jumbie and stage name: "Arrow") is one of Montserrat's most notable stars. He is the king of soca music, so-called because it blends soul with calypso. He lives in Foxes Bay in a house with an arrow-shaped swimming pool, but when he is not touring the world, he is frequently found in his Plymouth "Office": Arrow's Man-Shop.

Both merengue and rhumba influence the traditional calypso base of Arrow's music, which is heard almost continuously on the radio. Arrow says the Montserrat soca is distinguished from other islands' by "a particular strum" and is influenced by the time patterns of the drum beats in the Christmas Carnival's Masquerader's bands.

This celebration is not unlike Carnival in the rest of the black world, except that on Montserrat this particular celebration occurs at Christmas rather than just before Lent. Costumed bands play instruments with onomatopoeic names like "shack shack," "boom drum" and "woo woo."

An 1854 visitor to Montserrat, J. Day, wrote that the island had "the fatal gift of beauty." It is too easy to write about warm water and exotic fruits and flowers, to claim them as our own, but at least one thing is true for anyone who stands on a Montserrat beach when the sun comes up: at that moment, the universe seems vast.

A t-shirt store.

EXPLORING GUADELOUPE

Butterflies have a short life span, but the two unequal wings of **Guadeloupe**—one dry and rocky, edged with its white ring of beaches, the other mountainous, luxuriant and crisscrossed with crystal-cold rivers—have been spread for centuries. This butterfly settled on the Caribbean sea centuries ago, many leagues from the coast of South America, and belying the general reputation of the species, it has survived tribulations that would have destroyed the more fragile of its kind. It is said that when Christopher Columbus first set eyes on Guadeloupe at the end of the 15th century he immediately encased it in a casket and presented the jewel to the very Catholic King of Spain.

The small island of Guadeloupe (720 square miles/1,800 square km) is not only diverse, but also complex. Beaches wash the sides of volcanoes, flat expanses of sugar cane grow alongside winding mangrove swamps, international hotels contrast with wooden huts perched on four stones and major highways cross paths leading over the mountains amidst giant ferns.

One section of the population defends its ties with France, the other, its African heritage, although a growing minority refuses these divisions harking back to slavery and proclaims a "Caribbean identity." Some want to keep the political status of French overseas possession decreed in 1946. Others brandish a red and black flag, stamped with a crab, and demand independence. Some drive to work in their BMWs. Others trundle along in an ox-cart.

Island stops: The plane has landed at Le Raizet, but let's make a hurried exit from this modern airport where, in the high season, three daily 747's from France unleash a flow of tourists and immigrants returning home to savor a few weeks of sun, creole cooking, reputed to be among the best in the world, and family affection (three to four percent of the population leave each year to work in the factories and offices of metropolitan France). **Pointe-á-Pitre** is the main commercial center whose population is inflated daily by an influx of 100,000 workers. If you close your eyes to the low-cost housing developments, similar to those in the depressing suburbs of Paris, and delve into the old town, you will discover its charm.

In some places its balconied wooden houses rival those of the French Quarter in New Orleans. Its many admirers regret that the **Place de la Victoire** and its century-old sandbox trees, where the children's nannies, dressed in Creole costume and three-pointed madras headtie, used to watch over their upper-class protégés at play, has now been converted into a parking lot instead of a meeting place for young lovers. They regret that the magnificent house of the Desgranges, a Creole family, has been turned into the offices of the French Social Security and the Wachter's which lies back from the road in a small garden, has become an hotel. But never mind. The **Place de la Victoire** opens out onto the **Darse** (harbor) and the boats that take you to the tiny, round island of **Marie-Galante**, the last bastion of a ruined sugar economy, have kept the magic of yesteryear's sailboats. The Darse continues along the wharf where for two or three centuries the import-export houses have been selling red herring, lard and codfish. Gone are the ocean liners which sailed for France. All that is left are a few inconspicuous banana freighters and rusty commercial vessels. Once a month, however, a cruise ship throws anchor and its white silhouette blots out the horizon, raising the old magic.

Mingle with the crowd thronging the **Rue Frébault**, Pointe-á-Pitre's busiest street, but avoid entering the shops to haggle over the price of fabrics since the overworked sales staff are often impolite. Make a stop rather at the main market where the women sell sugar apples, sweetsops, soursops, mangoes, passion fruit and tubers such as yams, sweet potatoes, cassava and madera, as well as home-grown vegetables.

On **Grande Terre** the flat landscape of sugar cane fields is dotted here and there by the massive stone silhouette of a sugar mill, the dark green foliage of a mango tree or the scarlet splash of a flame tree. **Beauport,** one of the few sugar factories still operating, stands guard at the entrance to **Port Louis**. You'll have trouble tearing yourself away from the magnificent beach, **Le Souffleur**, faithful companion to one of those cemeteries, peculiar to the island, that are true cities of the dead with their funeral palaces of stone and Italian marble, clinging to the sides of the most humble village.

Push on further north, to the **Pointe de la Grande Vigie,** where the land ends in the dazzling realm of azur. Here the sea meets the sky. Only a few years back this was a wild and desolate place. Still undiscovered by the Club Med, it has become the haunt of scuba diving enthusiasts and the strong swimmer who is not duped by the apparent calm of the blue, blue water. If you're tired of the sea, take a walk along the cliffs and watch the waves rage below, sending up their feathers of spray. Night falls suddenly at the Pointe de la Grande Vigie and in the shadows only the sound of the sea is a reminder of its presence.

Instead of following the coast and taking a swim in one of the many sheltered, hidden coves, head for **Le Moule** (the second most populated town on the island), cutting across country of thornbushes and acacias, by way of **Hauts de la Montagne, les Mangles** and **Bazin**, under the sleepy gaze of peacefully grazing cows. At the entrance to Le Moule make a stop at the **E. Clerc Museum**, which houses a collection of pre-Columbian items, among other treasures. There are not many museums in Guadeloupe. This one is the work of Jack Berthelot, an architect known throughout the Caribbean and a figure in the independence movement, who died in 1984 in a car bomb explosion. Le Moule is symbolic in many ways. Another example is the **Hotel des Alizés** on the outskirts of the town. Previously bankrupt, it has now been taken over by a cooperative of workers who wish to put the colonial past behind them. Le Moule has a series of beaches, and restaurants for lingering over a rum punch or savoring the seafood.

At the **Pointe des Chateaux** the rugged beauty of the landscape is very similar to the Pointe de la Grande Vigie. One can easily tire of the immensity of the sea and sky. So why not visit the marina at **St. François** with its de luxe hotels and tourists in flowery shirts? And what about **Sainte Anne** and its beaches?

Music magic: But if you feel like getting dressed up and going out to dance, try one of the nightclubs in **Le Gosier**. There you will hear new music from Guadeloupe which has undergone profound changes and hit the international scene. For many years only the Afro-Latin rhythms from Cuba and reggae from Jamaica were identified with the Caribbean. Although Guadeloupian musicians such as Robert Mavounzi set the whole of Paris dancing during the post-war period and surprised the black American musicians during their visits, their success seemed to paralyze any subsequent creation. The island seemed destined to produce only imitators and third-rate composers of beguines. The emergence of a certain hard-line nationalism in the 1960s, influenced by Black American radicalism, saw the resurgence of the *gwoka,* the slaves' music that had been forgotten with time. Guy Konket raised it to a fine level of artistry and loaded it with a political message—to affirm an identity of African origin. For many years after that the music from Guadeloupe wavered between two poles. The militant pole used the *ka*, the drum par excellence, and the reactionary pole composed beguines with European instruments. Bogged down in these ideological quarrels, any real music had trouble finding its expression. Then along came the group Kassav. Innovating as well as reviving the plaintive rhythms of yesteryear, taking inspiration from where they could yet remaining loyal to the past, they combined string and traditional instruments, modified the drums and gave a melancholic, wild, throbbing note to their vocal accompaniment. Kassav are not just content to play to full houses in Paris to audiences of nostalgic immigrants, but are also box office successes in Burkina Faso, Zaire and Burundi. Guadeloupe is now giving back to Africa much, much more than it ever received. So dance to the music of Kassav:

"Zouc-là, sé sèl médikamen nou ni ....!"

Today many groups are hot on the trail of Kassav and there is no lack of talent. Old carnival tunes are being revived, but they've been given a new look and produced groups such as Gazolin. Add a touch of James Brown and the charm of female voices and you've got Zouc Machine. But perhaps

before taking you to sweat it out in a "zouc," you will want something to eat. Pass up the excellent hotel restaurants, like the venerable **Vieille Tour**, and go into one of the countless little restaurants owned by the locals. The service is slow, but a series of "ti-punches" helps to pass the time. The Creole cuisine has a well-established reputation and any tourist guide will tell you it combines African and French traditions with a touch of Indian in the *colombos* (curries), spices and essences.

Avoid the usual tourist plates of stuffed crabs, broiled lobster, conch and squid, however delicious they might be, and taste the humbler dishes not to be found on every menu— like breadfruit *migan*. How to explain a "*migan*"? Cut a ripe breadfruit into slices and cook slowly with just enough lemon juice and salt pork. *Bébélé*, the traditional dish of Marie-Galante, combines plaintains, green bananas, congo peas, tripe and once again the salt pork, the cheap staple diet of the slave that fashioned the national palate. This is the real Guadeloupe.

Excursions: Le Gosier, the Cradle of Tourism (so says the sign), lies on the outskirts of Pointe-á-Pitre and here you are back where you started. Now for the western wing, the mountainous **Basse Terre**. It

would be easy to take the tourist buses and keep to the beaten track. Instead, cut across the 60,000 acres of the natural park, its waterfalls, rivers with freshwater crayfish, Norfolk Pines and giant ferns down to the sea and return via the sleepy town of **Basse Terre**, the capital of Guadeloupe. Or climb the volcano, **la Soufriére**, which has remained dormant since 1976, when virtually the entire population of Basse Terre had to be evacuated on a false alert.

A third possibility is to take the boat from the wharf at **Trois Riviéres** to the **Saintes**, two islands without sugar cane, whose population is said to be of Breton origin. Wearing their wide hats called *salakos*, they go out fishing in all weather. Somewhere between **Gourbeyre** and **Capesterre** the bus will make a stop at a "pit" where cocks, drunk on rum, fight it out with their sharp metal spurs.

Don't forget the **Carbet Falls** and, at the entrance to the town of Basse Terre, the admirably-restored ruins of the **Fort Saint-Charles**, dating from the 17th century, which kept the British at bay in their constant wars against the French.

Two sides: There have always been two **Montebellos**. The one down below is composed of ugly, iron-roofed huts and bars where the many jobless in this agricultural region drink the rum from the local distillery, play dice or cards and criticize the mayor who, like all good politicians, is a lot of hot air, so they say. "*Pawol sé van*," goes the saying.

Between the huts and the bars the women set out pitiful heaps of tubers and wild fruit that nobody bothers to buy.

Then there is the Montebello up above, with its summer homes that have now gone to ruin. In their gardens enormous pear trees interlace their amazing roots on the surface of the ground, like the tentacles of an octopus or gigantic snakes. A dozen steps away a parasite, a wild apricot, wraps an ancient mango in its mortal embrace. Everywhere plant life is sumptuous, luxuriant, encroaching and imperious.

Vegetation reigns supreme. From the heights of Montebello there is a view of La Soufriére and the bay of Le Gosier. Sea, mountains: Montebello encompasses everything. A splendid past, a destitute present. But perhaps nothing can return Montebello to its former splendor. The island's economy is moribund; the only lifeline is subsidies from France. One sees little but dice players, drinking and arguing until the bats fly off into the dusk from the tall trees, and

Pointe a Pitre, projects in the background.

Montebello youths pointlessly riding their motorbikes untiringly round the loop road that joins Montebello with Carrére.

In the ailing agricultural heart of the island, look at the rich black soil where the yam, the queen of tubers, sung by many a poet, wraps its vines around its pole. Over there is the sea of sugar cane which despite the mortal blows dealt by its competitor, the sugar beet, still occupies 45 percent of the arable land and provides around 16,000 seasonal jobs. And rising up like a ghost vessel with its black, rusty hulk is the Bonne Mére sugar factory. Like Beauport, it has not kept pace with modern times. In the past gangs of men worked here, mixing their smell of sweat with that of the cane. Today there are no more than 20 workers fighting for their living. Rum is an anachronism in this age of Coca-Cola and long drinks.

Since 1975 a group of agricultural workers, fired with an anger and tired of underemployment, have occupied the land at Galbas, Sainte-Rose. They refuse to be subjected to the tyrannical hold of sugar cane and painstakingly irrigate fields of rice. They have reinstated the old custom of *"cout min"*, collective work, and have built their homes of local wood. They have found a way of expressing themselves, and during the long evenings tell their tales and proverbs to the sound of September rain.

Like their fellow islanders from Africa, the Indians of Guadeloupe have lost their language and speak only Creole. Their women no longer know how to tie a silk sari. But they worship their gods in the shadow of their hearts. There are also the Blancs-Matignons, those Whites that remind one of the Old South, yellowed and mummified in their racial prejudice and their refusal to accept progress.

To discover the writers and artists you don't really need a guide. Just walk into the bookstore, **Librairie Générale**, in Pointeá-Pitre. The manager, a former pharmacist charmed by the alchemy of words, is a real book lover. He's got everything: novels, autobiographies and essays. You'll find every subject from fishing in Guadeloupe to local magic and architecture. The paintings on the wall are by Michel Rovelas, Michéle Chomereau-Lamotte and Claudy Cancelier.

The golden rule to remember: take your time. The tiny island of Guadeloupe abounds in natural beauty. If you rush through your visit this beauty will blind you to other things; you won't see the people for the trees.

Point des Chateaux.

EXPLORING DOMINICA

From every compass point, **Dominica** rears up from the sea like a sort of Caribbean Never-Never Land. Mountains fervent with vegetation rise higher than mountains have a right to rise in this part of the globe. They appear to be borrowed from one of those Hollywood adventure epics where men in pith helmets discover curious tribes and native porters always stumble into bottomless gorges. Breadfruit, palms and thickets of bamboo and elephant-ear (*Chou sauvage*) live at a continuous tilt with existence; to tend his garden, the Dominican must have something of the mentality of Sir Edmund Hillary. Small wonder that Columbus, when asked by Queen Isabella to describe this steepdown island, reportedly hunched up his napkin and said: "Like this, Your Majesty."

In the rain forests of Dominica, 66 foot (20 meter) tree-ferns grow and there is a body of water—the **Boiling Lake**—which steams and bubbles volcanically. The windward coast is a topiary of phantasmal green shapes, sculpted by the trades. Even the wildlife has a Conan Doyleish, Lost World quality. There are gigantic cockroaches called, locally, "mahogany birds." Eight-inch (20-cm) Hercules beetles make Stuka-like assaults on lightbulbs. The spiky carapaces of land crabs puncture automobile tires. The frogs (*crapaud*) are elephantine; they've been known to clog up public water outlets in the capital town of **Roseau**. And somewhere near the leaf-domed summit of Morne Diablotin, highest mountain on the island, there may even lurk a primitive reptile longer than the longest liana vine.

Antillean anomaly: Because of its terrain, Dominica was the last Caribbean island to be colonized by Europeans. For the most part, it was left alone during the 18th century sugar cane boom that turned many of the Antilles into intensive cane plantations. Its tall mountainy slopes did not encourage any sort of massive, orderly planting. And fertile though it was, the volcanic soil had the unfortunate habit of being washed away by torrents of rain attracted by the mountains.

The French, the first Europeans to arrive, persevered. A steady trickle of French farmers began to plant coffee, tobacco and limes in *petite mal* fashion. They gave French names, most of which are still in use, to settled areas along the leeward coast: **Soufriere, Le Roseau, La Grande Baie**

and **Pointe Michel**. Soon slave boats were coming. But since so much extra land was available on Dominica, many slaves were offered gardens of their own, scarcely less large than their masters'. Often the slave could sell enough ground provisions to buy his freedom. If not, he did enjoy a better relation with his master on Dominica than on other islands, for the small estates bred a certain togetherness. Both slave and master were hemmed in equally.

In 1748, the Treaty of Aix-la-Chapelle left Dominica in undisputed possession of the island's inhabitant, the Carib Indians. But almost immediately the island became a pawn in power plays between the French and the British. After the Battle of the Saintes (1782), Dominica was handed to the British. In the 1790s, the French tried to reclaim it, burning down Roseau in the process. At last the French were offered a £12,000 bribe to give up all claim to the island, which they did, though not before some of their planters had left behind a sizable progeny (even today it's not unusual to see a Rastafarian who looks more like Francois Mitterand than he does Bob Marley).

From 1805, Dominica remained a British colony until it gained independence in 1978. Independence brought with it the usual growing pains, but on Dominica it is not a question of whether something will grow so much as a question of what strange growth the deep topsoil will send up next. In 1982, there was a *coup* attempt against the government of Prime Minister Eugenia Charles. The Dominican invasion force consisted of a motley crew of Ku Klux Klansmen, Gay Liberationists, neo-Nazis, and Canadian mercenaries. Called Operation Red Dog, it was backed by the Mafia, who wanted to use the island for drug-trafficking and international fraud. If the Red Doggers hadn't first been captured, they would have joined a group of Rastas and backers of ousted leftwing Prime Minister Patrick John. Only on an island which lacked the more damning racial side-effects of a plantation society could leftist Blacks have greeted White supremacist Klansmen with open arms.

Today a visitor to Dominica will find a Caribbean nation, not a resort. There are only family-run inns, not franchised high-rises. And bananas, not suntans, are the chief export; they are shipped to Britain under contract with Geest Industries. A few estates also produce copra. Bay oil is distilled in eastern parts of the island. Antigua and St. Martin buy Dominican river water; an empty faucet means the waterboat has arrived in port. There is a hot sauce and guava cheese factory, Bellot's, and a rum distillery. Most of this enterprise operates on a very modest, pre-industrial level, for the difficult terrain condemns modern machinery as a Ruth amid the alien corn. Everything seems to move backwards and forwards simultaneously. In agriculture, for instance, the most radical advancement has been the boxing of bananas in the field rather than in boxing plants.

With independence, the island has become a drain on its own exchequer. Occasionally an energetic person will come up with some baroque plan to make Dominica at least solvent. There will be a flurry of activity, under-brush cleared away, offices constructed. One year later a forlorn bit of masonry will be peering out from among the creepers and convolvus, mute testimony to the vanity of human wishes.

Nature isle: Despite its 20,000 people, **Roseau** feels like an afterthought, a shanty town offered to humankind by the tolerant mountains; and indeed, it was an afterthought, quickly becoming Dominica's first town in the 1760s after the intended seat of government, Portsmouth, turned out to be malaria-infested. Like most Caribbean capitals, Roseau is tucked away in the southwestern corner of the island to escape the northeasterly trades. Yet the trades would have been welcome compared to the violent winds of Hurricane David ("Big Master David," in local vernacular) that struck the town and all of southern Dominica on August 29, 1979. Two-thirds of the people were left homeless; 60 were killed. But with help from the European Economic Community (E.E.C.), the International Monetary Fund (I.M.F.), and the Red Cross the town was rebuilt on the same model as the old Roseau.

Roseau is a place of trellised gables, low-slung shingle houses, hilly terraces, and poor drain off. Its charm lies in its resolute lack of charm. Roseau is a genuine community with no frills, no trinket shops, no bars with cute names, and no plumped up historical preservation. Instead, it has a Saturday market fully in keeping with the prodigal variety of fruits and vegetables on the island. It boasts a very good **Botanical Gardens** which nonetheless must be the only such place in the world less lush than its botanical surroundings. And it possesses an example of Dominican town planning in its purest, most surreal form—a public bathhouse in the midst of a cemetery.

The town ends abruptly with cliffsides north and south after which Mistress Na-

ture, Dominica's real Prime Minister, takes over once again. Island roads are not bad, exactly; most of them are even blacktopped. But all roads on Dominica seem to have been declared the personal property of the mountains. And so it is that they curl around the island like demented snakes. Sometimes they display boulders like pieces of discarded statuary. Other times avalanches pock them with giant footprints and pound them into bumper-scraping ruts. Around **Geneva Estate** (childhood home of author Jean Rhys), the mountains would appear to be bored with their plaything. They've tried to fling the road into **Grand Bay**. Here the motorist needs to be on the lookout for quirky tides.

On these roads, the automobile slows to a speed not significantly faster than what can be achieved on foot. Six miles (10 km) is the distance from Roseau to **Scott's Head**, a fishing village with a bed of stones that passes for a beach; it takes nearly 40 minutes to drive there. It is 27 miles (45 km) to Dominica's only bonafide historical ruin, **Fort Shirley**, set among the *savannet* trees of the **Cabrits Peninsula** just north of **Portsmouth**; these 27 miles (45 km) require almost an hour and a half of whirligig movements.

Perhaps owing to setbacks on other Caribbean islands, the gentrification of St. Barts, the loss of the Caymans to international banking and Antigua to tourism, Mistress Nature seems all the more determined to hold on to Dominica. She demands even of the motorist an intimacy with the Spirit of Place. He cannot help but inhale the warm fibrous scent from the earth after a heavy rain. His eyes must take in the women walking along the road, their heads crowned with huge haystacks of arum lilies. He must pause for a man blowing a conch shell to announce the arrival of a skiff laden with needlefish; the man is standing on a part of the road that also happens to be the edge of the sea. And he must even slow down for a boa constrictor or an army of land crabs—on Dominica, right of way is not the exclusive privilege of the human species.

The interior contains no such compromises with pavement, only rustic paths that are a botanist's horn of plenty. One of these paths winds six miles (10 km) through the **Morne Trois Pitons National Park** and ends up at the **Boiling Lake**. This lake is a flooded fumarole, a crack through which gases escape from a foundation of molten lava deep inside the earth. The pressure of the gases forces the lake to seethe like an enormous boiling bathtub, now turning black, now oily-grey, now even blue. It can boil an egg in three minutes (a few unwary visitors have been boiled there, too). Next to the lake are the thermal springs and burnt yellowish rocks of the **Valley of Desolation**. This area reeks of sulphur and seems about as remote from the tropics as an Icelandic volcano. Only the haunting single-note birdcall of the *Siffleur Montagne*, the Mountain Solitary, disturbs the silence.

The Boiling Lake was first sighted in 1870 by a district magistrate named Edmund Watt. It is said that Mr. Watt was so astounded by his discovery that he wandered around in circles for five days afterwards. Imagine: a bubbling, vaporous cauldron 80 meters wide, located in the Caribbean and *unseen* by human eyes until slightly more than 100 years ago. This will give some indication of the degree to which Nature hoards her riches on this most untamed of islands.

Of feet and gardens: Joseph Baptiste is a typical Dominican. He has Carib, Creole, and even some White planter blood in his veins. He speaks a Creole patois heavy on labials, nasal inflections and proverbs about flying witches called *suquiyas*. He was born and raised on the leeward side, in the village of **Coulibistri**, which until recently was so isolated that he needed to walk over several mountains to reach Roseau; to reach Portsmouth he also needed to walk over several mountains. His own garden lies near the top of yet another mountain, for the soil is better there, less leached out than around his home. Several times a week he treks to his garden, over sharp thorns and the exposed fluting of roots, in his bare feet.

These days one of Joseph Baptiste's feet is distended like a balloon. The local *obeah* man contends that one of his ex-sweethearts has cursed him with a "big foot" because he refused to honor his pledge of marriage. As the sweetheart has died, the foot will only grow bigger, and bigger, and bigger. Joseph Baptiste grins. He hardly cares. Adversity is his twin brother. And, after all, he has another foot…A stranger to Dominica might think Joseph Baptiste a rather sorry specimen of humanity and flip him a few coins. Joseph Baptiste would not turn up his nose at these coins. They are income, and he needs to pay the *obeah* man (a hefty US$10 a visit) as well as buy a few yards of madras for his current sweetheart. He has no money just now, or any prospects. Nor do the austere fiscal policies of Dominica include the welfare funds that might sit him pretty on another island.

Small fishing village.

Dominica has by far the lowest per capita income in the Antilles. Agricultural workers earn just enough during a eight hour day to buy three bottles of Red Stripe beer for the evening. Shop assistants earn a little less than that. The universal army of the self-employed, to which Joseph Baptiste belongs, earns almost nothing. So it comes as no surprise that a good many islanders believe that not only a "big foot" but also "wealth" is the result of *obeah*. If a person suddenly comes into money, rumor will get around that he's in league with supernatural forces. Sometimes even the person himself will believe the rumor.

Yet a man like Joseph Baptiste is not, in the root sense, poor. Over his head is a corrugated iron roof which gives off a lovely rattle in the rain. Unlike the Caribs, he owns his own land. And, most important of all, he has immediate access to a rich bounty of food. In his garden he grows breadfruit, yams, dachine, papayas, oranges, tanya, limes, coconuts, and bananas. Outside the garden, free for the picking, he can find ginger, cacao, wild guavas, and *kowosol zombi* leaves, just the thing to quiet the anguish in his foot. On the way down, he can pilfer the odd mango or grapefruit from an estate orchard and no one will know the difference. Can there be such wealth in the great cities of the world?

Joseph Baptiste probably could hawk some of his produce at Saturday market in Roseau if he put his mind to it. But selling things is not his style. He was spawned by a different past; a past which includes flying witches, herb cures, and self-sufficiency. Besides, he'd rather play dominoes in a Coulibistri rum shop than hit the hustle and bustle of Roseau on a Saturday morning. Or he'd rather hunt agoutis and *crapaud* in the rain forest. Such are the ways of his green world. They reflect the cheerful underside of the Carib Curse: nothing works, but nothing matters, either...except, maybe, dominoes.

Carib isle: It was 1,000 years ago that the first Caribs arrived in Dominica. They had tremendous oceangoing skills, and they sailed up from the banks of the Orinoco River in South America in 60 foot canoes hewn from a single *gommier* tree. On Dominica as on other islands, they fought with the gentler Arawaks, whom they easily subdued. They killed or ate the Arawak men and took their women as wives.

The Caribs welcomed all visitors to Dominica with showers of arrows tipped with poison from the manchineel tree. Any

A Carib weaving baskets.

visitor unlucky enough to be captured was stuffed with herbs and spices at once; then he was trussed to a pole and roasted over a medium fire, while Carib womenfolk turned and basted the body, catching the lard in calabash gourds. Tradition has it that the French tasted the best, the Dutch were flavorless, the Spaniards tough and stringy. The Caribs gave the word "cannibal" to both the English and Spanish languages. But they seldom ate human flesh simply to satisfy their appetites; rather, they ate an enemy to render his hostile spirit harmless.

They were a people with a dramatic flair for freedom. They could never understand the European habit of keeping slaves. If they were taken prisoner themselves, they would eat dirt until they died. Such incorrigibility made them a perfect target for missionaries. But even these good men seemed destined to fight a losing battle. The Caribs could not value anything so abstract as the Christian God. A priest-historian, Father Raymond Breton, who labored on Dominica in the mid-17th century admitted that in 25 years he had succeeded in converting "only a few children on the point of death."

As Dominica turned into an island of English planters, Creoles and Catholics, the Caribs found themselves boxed into an inhospitable stretch of real estate on the northeastern coast. There, buffeted by the trades, their numbers dwindling, they lost their customs one by one. They gave up cannibalism and forehead elongation. They no longer made necklaces from the teeth of their enemies.

And on the same inhospitable stretch of windward coast, now called **Carib Territory**, this last indigenous race in the Caribbean continues to make its home. Their land plummets and rises with 3,700 acres (1,480 hectares) of slopes and hillsides spread along eight miles (12 km) of meandering road. Down below, Atlantic rollers thunder against rocky cliffs in a fashion more befitting the west of Ireland than these docile latitudes.

Along the road are villages with old Carib names like **Bataka**, **Salybia**, and **Sineku**—small aggregates of houses that appear to be sprinkled on the landscape by someone who finds the idea of planning intolerable. Between these villages, a sudden clearing will reveal a breadfruit-plank shack and, perhaps, a man hewing out a *gommier* canoe. There might be a woman framed in a doorway of red hibiscus, seated and weaving a basket with the neat angular pattern of a mosaic. And there will always be a group of frolicking children whose high cheekbones,

almond eyes, and copper skins suggest a journey across the Bering Strait from Asia long, long ago.

The Territory was set up in 1903 to give the Caribs a measure of control over their own affairs. It was then called the Carib Reserve. In 1985, the name was changed because the word "reserve" implied a habitat for endangered animals as well as native people. Yet the earlier name has a certain appropriateness. The race is very diluted today because of intermarriage between Carib men and outside women (Carib women, according to patriarchal custom, can't marry outsiders). Of a total population of 1,800, less than 50 full-blooded Caribs remain, most of them elderly pipe-smoking women and men with faces like ancient Chinese sages.

In any event, the Caribs of Dominica have fared better than their brethren who once upon a time lived on Grenada and Antigua. On Grenada, the Caribs leaped off a cliff *en masse* rather than allow themselves to be taken prisoners; the place is duly memorialized as **Morne des Sauteurs** or **Mountain of the Leapers**. And on Antigua, there was a law passed in 1693 that called itself "An Act to encourage the destroying of the Indians." Alongside the title of this Act in the *Revised Collection of the Laws of the Island of Antigua*, brought out in 1805, is printed one lone word: Obsolete.

Guardian spirit: There is a Carib legend about a gigantic boa constrictor, called the Master Boa, which crawled to Dominica centuries ago from beneath the sea, slithered onto land, and set up its home in a fathomless hole on Morne Diablotin. In this hole it is still supposed to live, crowing like a cock and siring broods of smaller boas. To look upon the snake means immediate and violent death unless the person has fasted for three days first and abstained from his wife for a somewhat longer period. Yet a number of Caribs claim to have seen it. They say the snake has a diamond crest riding the back of its head. They point to the **Escalier Tête-Chien**, the Master Boa's Staircase, an outcropping of basalt that twists up a hillside near Sineku. That's where the snake emerged from the sea, they say. They add that the Master Boa is the real reason why Dominica has never been developed, exploited, or even undergone significant change; why the island has an older, more casual, perhaps even sweeter style of Caribbean life. The snake doesn't want its vast lair disturbed. And what proponent of change would dare do battle with a 330-foot reptile that has a diamond crest on its head?

EXPLORING MARTINIQUE

Sign at the small beach at the base of **Fort St. Louis:** *No Taking Away Sand Under Penalty of Prosecution.* In North America we warn people about littering the ground. In **Martinique** they warn people about stealing it.

Christopher Columbus discovered Martinique in—according to various books and pamphlets obtained in the island—1492, 1493, 1494, 1495 and, accurately, 1502. Old, arthritic, eyesight failing, Columbus commented: "It is the best, the most fertile, the softest, the most even, the most charming spot in the world. It is the most beautiful thing I have ever seen. My eyes never tire of contemplating such greenery." But he did not land, and for more than a century the island went largely ignored. Not until 1635 did the corsair Belain d'Esnambuc arrive in Martinique with a hundred men to found St. Pierre and begin the colonization of the island.

Tropical France: At 417 square miles (1,085 square km)—50 miles (80 km) at its longest, 21 miles (34 km) at its widest—Martinique is almost one-third the size of Long Island, N.Y. To the west lies the Caribbean Sea, placid, even lake-like; to the east, the Atlantic Ocean, choppier, more dramatic, "like the coast of Brittany, *en France*," a Martiniquan tour guide was to remark with no sarcasm and with some pride.

A mountainous island, it feeds the eye with its contours that ascend gradually from the irregular coastline and culminate dramatically, in the north in Mt. Pelée (4,656 feet), the now dormant volcano that erupted with a shattering violence in 1902. Pelée is linked to other mountains—**Les Pitons du Carbet** (3,960 feet) in the center, and **La Montagne du Vauclin** (1,500 feet) in the south—by a series of gentler hills, or *mornes*. The temperature, with a yearly mean of 79° F, fulfills all expectations, while the winds blowing in off the sea make for comfortable evenings. Add to this a thick coating of vigorous vegetation and one begins to understand Columbus' enthusiasm.

Today, Martinique is a largely agricultural island with a racially-mixed population of 350, 000 Africans, East Indians, whites and others. Like other West Indian islands, it has been through the historical horrors of colonialism and slavery; but while the British West Indian islands have sought their own paths in independence, Martinique, with its sister island of Guadeloupe, has been absorbed politically and economically into France as full "Overseas Departments" of the republic. So much so that, in a brochure, Jean-Baptiste Edmond, the president of the Office Départemental du Tourisme, describes Martinique, stunningly, as "this corner of Tropical France" and urges enjoyment of "the French atmosphere, hospitality and cuisine."

On the bus: The bus, shaking and rattling, resounds with the local music, a brash, raw-edged blend of Caribbean and Latin American rhythms. The other riders are reserved, well-dressed. Outside in the sunshine, empty fields and commercial buildings file by, heavily littered with empty cigarette packs, crushed soft-drink cans, plastic cups, paper bags, the occasional green garbage bag dumped at the roadside and now ripped open.

From time to time a voice calls *"Arrêt"* and the bus pulls in at the next stop to let someone off.

Cars roar by, overtaking the bus on the intestinal roads in stunning demonstrations of the art of the barely possible. Motorcycles, helmetless riders crouched low in the seats, weave snappily in and out of the traffic, whining engines cutting through and mingling with other engines and the jangle of the music. There reigns on the roads of Martinique a Divine Right of Vehicles, and the pedestrian is merely an annoyance to honk at.

At the end of the line, a concrete footbridge leads across the Riviére Madame, the slow, brown waterway that cuts lazily through Fort-de-France and empties into the Baie des Flamands (Flamingo Bay). There is a busy traffic of people across the bridge, many carrying bags of groceries or sticks of baguette. One old woman, a parcel balanced delicately on her head, treads a slow, weary way through the crowd, descending the stairs to the road with fragile, uncertain steps, as if exhausted by a life that has grown simply longer, not easier. She looks as worn and weary as the buildings that line the Boulevard Alon the Buslégre on the other side of the river.

Fort-de-France: The capital of Martinique is not a large town, but with a population of over 100,000, it bustles with people, traffic and noise until the closing of stores and restaurants in the mid-afternoon heat imposes a somnolence on its narrow, crowded streets. There is a seedy, tropical feel to the town; buildings quickly lose their

newness and cloak themselves in a black mildew born of heat and the humidity blowing in off the sea. But there is, too, an underlying sense of a decayed European-ness, hinted at in the baguettes, the motorcycles and mopeds, the képied policemen walking in pairs, revolvers dangling from their waists and walkie-talkies held to their ears. The setting closely resembles those found in Graham Greene's novels—the old and the new blending together to create a slightly askew colonial vision of a greying town melting in the bubbling humidity and burgeoning vegetation—one wonders if the novelist borrowed his scenes from here.

The centerpiece of the town is the **Savane,** a 12-acre park of lawn, shade trees, footpaths and benches. Young parents, stylishly dressed, relax as their children play. Other young people, well-dressed or shabby, neatly coiffed or dreadlocked, lounge or stroll dreamily around. Old men sit on the benches and rail in jocular tones at each other. In the shade of its clustered ferns and bamboo, groups of men play fervent games of dominoes, the quiet broken only by the swift, over-lapping click-clack of the tiles and little yelps of triumph. The scent of marijuana hangs in the air like an oily perfume.

In one corner of the park, close to the landing where the ferry *Somatour* disgorges tourists from Pointe du Bout on the other side of the bay, stands the small craft market. A turn among the stalls of uncertain watercolors, straw hats, wooden cutlasses, goatskin collages and the other paraphernalia of the tourist trade—all prices posted in French francs and, the target evident, US dollars—is disheartening. The workmanship is bad, the talent thin. In most of the carved objects—urns, statuettes—one detects less the imperfect hand of a human than the self-replicating precision of a machine. The stall owners sit around reading newspapers or gossiping in creole, self-absorption spinning into a desultory salesmanship at the scent of money. "Whaddaya want?" one young man demands aggressively.

West Indian Empress: Away to Napoléon's Joséphine, one of two monuments in the Savane. She stands pristine white in the sun, a portrait of her famous husband in her left hand, her eyes staring across the **Baie des Flamands**, in the direction of her birthplace at **Les Trois Ilets.** Her pedestal shows, on one side, a relief of Napoléon about to crown her; on another, her date of birth (June 23, 1763); and on the third, the date of her marriage (May 9, 1796). Birth, marriage, coronation: they are her most notable achievements, and the island has done her proud in its statue, regal, dignified, accessible.

The other monument, the island's war memorial, is dedicated to the island's human sacrifices in the two World Wars, Algeria and Indochina. A helmeted woman, 10 imposing feet of tarnished bronze, mournfully faces the Caribbean with lowered eyes, a torch of frozen flame, grasped in both hands, raised above her head. Her pedestal reads MARTINIQUE À SES ENFANTS MORTS POUR LA FRANCE; marble slabs to either side list the names of the dead. Behind her like a stiff, stylized cloak falls a white-washed wall; and behind that, in magnificent backdrop, thick, bushy stands of bamboo mushroom high into the sky. It is an impressive memorial, poignant without being sorrowful, a nicely understated act of remembrance. Yet, like much of the town, it is falling into disrepair. The whitewash is thinned and mildewing; two marble plaques, cracked and brown, carrying unintelligible messages; red bricks and slapped-on cement perfunctorily patch one end of a central concrete slab. An air of neglect, shadowed and regretful, hangs over the monument.

Away from the Savane, Fort-de-France is a maze of tiny streets crowded with people, shops and little restaurants striving for a French feel (menus offer few local dishes), but attaining it for the most part only in costliness. There are points of interest: the fish market; the floral park; Schoelcher library, a colorful building crazy with Roman, Egyptian and majolican patterns, and named, like our suburb, for the man most responsible for the abolition of slavery in 1848—but they consume little time and evoke only passing interest.

At the **Musée Départemental de la Martinique**, three floors of well-lit glasscases highlight remnants of the Arawaks and Caribs, the island's first inhabitants whom Columbus, searching for India, mistook for "Indians." By d'Esnambuc's arrival in 1635, the Caribs, warlike and cannibalistic, had long supplanted the more pacific Arawaks; but then they too were decimated, by European weapons, their civilization disappearing in battles of conquest (the despair of defeat lead, at one point, to a mass Carib suicide off cliffs), slavery and disease. They survive now only in historical writings and glasscases, bits of rock and pieces of crockery under light. But the museum, hung with uninformative signs, fails to create a context, gives no

sense of a people. No display arrests; many puzzle. The frustration leads to only one conclusion: that the Arawaks and Caribs were fairly clumsy people.

More engaging is the town's fondness for place names with big connections: Avenue Maurice Bishop, Place José Marti, Place Stalingrad, Heroic Vietnam Traffic Circle. One wonders at this penchant, and maybe Place Monseigneur Romero, a small square of grimy concrete in front of a church, is instructive. A sign offers the following information: "Assassinations while celebrating mass, on March 24, 1980, by fascist killers in the employ of the Salvadoran oligarchy (two percent possessing 60 percent of the land)..." Despite the bluster—the information is essentially accurate—it would have been a moving, unexpected tribute, save for the meagerness of the square, its air of dilapidation and the garbage dumped in a heap at the base of the sign.

Out of the *centreville*, past the temporary fruit and vegetable market—a massive, open-air shed crowded with stalls and women; young, old, gossiping raucously while, off to the side, a thin, aged woman digs painfully into a pile of vegetables discarded on the dank ground—one reaches the water's edge at **Point Simon.** Dumped to the side, in what appears a failed park of stunted trees struggling in the sunshine, is a rental company van stripped of all strippable parts, windscreen smashed into a definition of "smithereens," its abandoned hulk rusting fast in the salty air. The water's edge is railed off; four or five feet down, the Caribbean—a dull mass of greyish blue reaching to the horizon—laps at the garbage-strewn rocks. Yachts sit passively in the distance and, further on, the wall of the fort keeps its heavy watch. Down the railing from us, a young man alone stares vacantly at the water, lazily tossing in pebbles that splash soundlessly as they disappear beneath the surface.

Higher ground: The stone walls and the statue of Christ up above are as if licked by fire, blackened in the greater humidity of the tropical rain forest. The church, we are told, is an exact if shrunken copy of Sacré Coeur in Montmartre.

The road, originally carved out by Jesuits, is as slight as a small intestine; it winds upwards into the mountains, through vegetation thick and varied, a mist-like rain, almost constant, slicking the greenery that is background to explosions of pink and orange bougainvillea, pink bells, and pink and yellow hibiscus. Cars slice past the bus in

Tourists at Club Med.

202

vehicular displays of rapid microscopic surgery. The bus slows. The guide points out a vine from which hangs a christophene, a yellow local vegetable.

The **Jardin de Balata** is a tropical botanical garden with a difference. Isolated in the hills, with distant views of both mountain and water, the calm and quiet of a monastery follow in your footsteps as you wander the meandering paths among the flowerbeds thick with plants of unfamiliar shape and color. Reds, blues, yellows, purples, greens, shades of them, combinations of them: There is, almost, too much for the eye with an even casual interest in flowers. A kind of greed ensues, lapping, for example, at the incredible richness of the anthuriums before jumping, too quickly, to the scarlet, flame-shaped bloom of the basilier, and hardly pausing before skipping to the calming beauty of a lotus pond. There are plants and trees here that might have walked off the set of a *Star Trek* planet, a vegetation wondrous and mesmerizing.

Climbing higher, the land falls away on the left to misty valleys and, in the distance, faded folds of mountains. The vegetation grows thicker, less delicate, dense stands of bamboo and leafy, liana-draped trees blocking the view. Showers of giant ferns and false banana trees pour from the cliff face on the right. Through the window is every imaginable shade of green, and many unimaginable. Occasionally a poinsettia splashes red, and the guide says it is a plant with the character of men, i.e. inconstant, changing color every six months. She gets a laugh. But outside the show continues, dramatizing why the Caribs called the island Madinina, Islands of Flowers.

In the wet twilight of the rain forest, high above **St. Pierre,** the Caribbean spreads out dramatically and the road descends in sunlight to the little town hugging the coast. St. Pierre: the former cultural and economic center of Martinique, the former "little Paris of the West Indies." One becomes aware that somewhere in the surrounding mountains looms Pelée, the sleeping volcano (now constantly monitored) that awoke on May 8, 1902, at 7:50 a.m., in a fireball of seething lava and superheated gases. Fires erupted in the town. The sea boiled. Within seconds, 30,000 people were dead. It is somehow appropriate that, as we enter town, we drive by the cemetery with its large white mausoleum containing the remains of the victims.

St. Pierre never recovered. Today it is a quiet little town, clean, pretty with resurgent foliage, but distinguished only by its former

self and violent end. Ruins offer their mute testimony: the burnt, broken stone walls of sea-side warehouses; the courtyards and foundations, stairways leading to nowhere, the vanished theater (a replica of Bordeaux's) and, on the hill that rises behind it, the cell of the sole survivor, Antoine Ciparis, a convicted killer awaiting execution whose reprieve came not from the governor but from Pelée and the strength of his cell. Ironically, the governor was among those killed; and Ciparis ended up a feature in the Barnum & Bailey circus, displayed in a replica of his cell. A small museum, established by and named for an American, Franck Perret, presents evidence on a more personal scale: large clumps of nails and screws fused by heat, melted bottles, a large church bell deformed by fire, containers of scorched food, enlarged photographs of the devastation. In the silence and the sunlight outside, in the knowledge that, deep down, Pelée still seethes, it is a chilling display.

A sign on a restored slave building at the Leyritz Plantation reads: *SPA and HEALTH CLUB.* The former slave quarters have been converted to tourist bungalows, the sugar mill to a restaurant. The Big House, open to inspection, was built in 1700. It sits on a rise dominating the plantation, its ground floor of thick stone walls, stone floor and heavy wooden furniture—a European sense of solidity, strangely unsettling in the tropical context. Unsettling too to think that here, in this object of tourist curiosity, lived people on whose conscience slavery sat lightly, secure in the knowledge that the church considered blacks, like animals, soulless.

Pineapple fields give way to sugarcane fields which, in turn, become banana plantations, then sugarcane fields again. It is mostly women, we are told, who work the pineapple fields. The sugarcane, in flower, waves fluffy white spears above its mass of tall, green stalks. The young bananas, sprouting upwards in bunches from the stalks, are draped for protection in blue bags of transparent plastic; from time to time, the trees are lashed together in gigantic cat's cradles of thick string, for additional strength.

From behind, a flat, dry, unimpressed male voice says: "Bananas, bananas, bananas. . ."

The banana fields continue, endless, on either side. The same flat voice from behind says, now with just a touch of desperation, "Bananas on the right, bananas on the left, bananas on the right. . ." There is a ripple of sympathetic laughter.

Back in Fort-de-France the sea and sky,

blended, drip dramatic with the color of mercury, the glow silvering the cars, the buildings, the yachts into a mesmerizing, metallic unreality. At the hotel a pianist, flanked by a large potted palm, plays bar standards while, straight ahead past the barman pouring drinks, the Caribbean grows hazy, loses luminosity, settles into a deep, inert blue. There is a melancholy to it, like that of grace denied, of possibility thwarted. The imagination fails before it, cannot leap into an approximation of reverie. From somewhere in the potted palm a frog croaks rhythmically.

Pointe du bout: A miserable morning, grey. At the ferry landing the rain comes down in thick sheets, fine drops. The *Somatour* goes across the bay to Pointe du Bout. Others, locals and a few tourists, wait patiently. One young man passes the time tossing his diver's knife, blade new and shiny, but it refuses to bite into the wooden flooring; time and again it clatters hollowly in failure. A plump woman fusses desultorily over her new baby strapped into its carriage while, behind her, a woman selling edibles chomps with disinterest on one of her own sandwiches and sips Coke from a plastic tumbler. A *Martiniquaise* and her *métropolitain* boyfriend, both snappily dressed, stroll by oblivious to the rain; her high heel slips on the dark wet wood; she has a moment of panic, and as she recovers and walks on, his arm now protectively around her, her eyes swivel back and glare at the spot responsible for her momentary loss of composure and style. Later, once the rain has stopped, they will sit on the plastic chairs in the bow of the ferry and she will have to cool the passion of his kisses and the public ardor of his hands.

After 20 minutes the ferry lands into another Martinique.

The beaches in the north are grey with volcanic ash; here in the south they are pristine. Fort-de-France offers glimpses of everyday reality, Pointe du Bout of a less troubling one. Here, no old women dig in discarded vegetables; instead visiting yachts moored at the marina abandon cats and purebred dogs—retrievers, shepherds—inconvenient in sea travel. Two realities, then, refracted in the same mirror.

"But we've passed the Musée de la Pagerie," the taxi driver says. "But you can walk back, it's not far, just after the bridge at the golf course." He smiles widely, says a hearty, "Bonne journée," and drives off.

"Not far" turns out to be a 45-minute walk, 30 to the bridge at the golf course

Ferry from Fort de France.

(acres of superb field, rolling up and down hill, edged by the sea), and then turning left at a rusted metal sign that points the way to the Musée de L'impératrice, another 15 past open field and a closed botanical garden.

Marie Joseph Rose Tascher, later rechristened Joséphine by her famous husband, left Martinique for Paris at the age of 16, in 1779, to marry the Viscount of Beauharnais. There, flighty and funloving, she was a social success; but 15 years later, in the midst of revolutionary turmoil, her husband was guillotined. Two years after this, at the age of 33, she married Napoléon. When he became emperor in 1804, she became his empress.

It reads like a fairy tale, the island girl from the colonies makes it big in the home country and secures herself a solid place in French history. It is said that it had all been foretold by a clairvoyant black nursemaid whose portrait now hangs in the little stone cottage museum along with those of Joséphine and Napoléon, with their letters and their knickknacks. Small but beautifully put together, it succeeds where the Musée Departemental fails: there is here the sense of a life lived, the objects adding up to a tangible. As we wander around, viewing the ruins of the plantation's sugar refinery, the foundations of the house, destroyed by fire, in which Joséphine was born, two busloads of locals, older, with the look of a church group, join us. They tread quietly even reverentially, from site to site, examining the ancient tools, hefting the rusting slave chains. In the museum, a middle-aged man lets his gaze dwell on Joséphine's portrait. He says, with a hint of surprise, "She was white." The guide, friendly, knowledgeable, quickly replies: "Yes, she was white, but she was born in the West Indies." The man nods, satisfied, and moves on, with the others, quietly reveling in his island's bit of glory.

There are other places to go (the Gauguin Museum, Diamond Rock) and other things to see (cockfighting, cabarets) in Martinique, but the island remains essentially a place to which one comes not for what one can do, but for what one cannot do, a retreat from the ravages of winter and profession.

In Paris, one must see the Eiffel Tower; in London, St. Paul's; in Barcelona, the Sagrada Familia. In Martinique, there is nothing one *must* do, but there are things one *can* do. It is perhaps its greatest charm: it dispenses with even the pressures of travel and offers, especially in the south, a splendid isolation.

Below, a house by the beach in Marigot.

EXPLORING ST. LUCIA

St. Lucia was a pawn in the 200-year French and English struggle for power in the Caribbean. Seven times English and seven times French, the island was taken by force or bartered at the negotiating table. Today the Civil Service, Government House, Royal Mail, House of Parliament and the Royal St. Lucia Police Band are part of St. Lucia's English veneer, but its heart and soul are Creole, a mixture of France and Africa. Most older women continue to wear the Madras head-tie and a modern version of panniered skirts. The names of towns are French, the island is Catholic, and most important, although the official language of St. Lucia is English, its unofficial, mother tongue is Patois.

No one knows for certain when Europeans first lay eyes on St. Lucia, but well before their arrival the island was inhabited by the Arawak and, later, the Carib Indians. The Caribs did not take kindly to European invasion of their home, and early 17th century British attempts at colonization failed. The year 1650 saw the establishment of a successful French colony, and these settlers concluded a treaty with the Caribs in 1660. Thus began the seesaw history that saw St. Lucia change hands between the British and French fully 14 times before the British gained final possession under the 1814 treaty of Paris. During this period, each colonizing nation sought to play the Caribs off the other, until finally the British simply rounded up those that remained and dumped them on a (still-existing) reservation on Dominica.

A colonial tradition: St. Lucia's government, however, is one clear residue of English rule. Although the island gained full independence on February 22, 1979, the official head of state remains the British monarch. She is represented by a Governor General—currently Sir Allen Lewis—who appoints the 11 members of St. Lucia's "upper" House of Parliament, the Senate. In making his appointments, though, he must consult with the majority and minority parties, as well as several important social groups. The House of Assembly—Parliament's other house—is elected. Currently, its 17 seats are divided between the United Worker's Party, with 9, and the St. Lucia Labour Party, with the remaining 8. The leader of the UWP, John Compton, is St.

Preceding pages: a view of Halifax Harbor. **Below,** a view of Soufriere.

Lucia's Prime Minister. A third party, the Progressive Labour Party, also has a strong following on the island.

Any excuse for a party: Chances are, though, if you mention the word "party" on St. Lucia, politics won't be what comes into your listener's mind. St. Lucians delight in having a good time. As you prowl around the island, you may occasionally hear "dance announcements" filtering through the background buzz of Radio St. Lucia. The St. Lucian motto is: "the land, the people, the light". But it might just as well be: "any excuse for a party". Every little town and three corners on the island holds a dance regularly. Take any building of even modest size, a small fee at the door, some chicken, beer, rum, a Hi-Fi with a pair of ear-splitting speakers—and it's a dance. At one point in the mid-80s, dance announcements took up fully 30 minutes of Sam Flood's 90-minute patois news program. Despite the graciousness of island residents, dance-loving visitors may feel—and be perceived as—intruders at some of the smaller-scale dances in the countryside. But if you're interested, ask around; at the larger events, such as the Friday block parties in the town of Gros Islet, you may feel quite at home.

Rich culture, luxuriant surrounds: The singular local culture is matched by an equally lush environment. Oval-shaped St. Lucia is marked by sheer volcanic peaks, deep green forests and strikingly beautiful beaches. It covers a total area of 238 square miles (616 square km), a significant portion of which is rich in tropical flora—hibiscus, poinciana, frangipani, orchids and jasmine.

St. Lucia is quite densely populated: according to the 1980 census, 124,000 people live here, some 75 percent of African origin, three percent the descendants of indentured servants brought here from India, and 2 percent of European ancestry. This mixture of peoples has produced a unique sensibility, nowhere more evident than in the local patois, a mix of African and French grammar superimposed on a vocabulary drawn from French, English and Spanish. When the man on the street makes a joke, it is in patois. When people argue, they argue in patois. Many court cases are tried in patois. Sixty percent of St. Lucians understand patois better than they understand English.

Sights and sites: You will probably want to spend some time seeing St. Lucia's "sights". Taxis and rental cars are one way to do this, but the local "transports"—vans

Working and socializing on a St. Lucian beach.

and mini-buses—are much cheaper and give the traveler a taste of how St. Lucians live. They can be crowded, but the experience and savings make the occasional discomfort worth it.

The capital city of Castries is as good a place as any to start your sightseeing, though, due to a long history of fires and rebuilding, the city itself isn't as interesting as some Caribbean burgs. A few sites of historical interest do remain, but Castries' most enchanting offering is its bustling Saturday market. Here you'll find everything from fruits to fish to chairs, all produced on St. Lucia and sold by people from all parts of the island. Castries also offers a variety of other shopping opportunities, and **Morne Fortune**, a hill to the east of the city, affords lovely views all along the west coast.

North along the coast lies **Pigeon Point**, formerly a retreat of pirates and other seafarers, such as Britain's Admiral Rodney. Historical markers dot the area. The southern section is covered with rainforest. If you venture here, note the causeway (constructed in the early 70s) that connects the former island with the mainland. It may have increased ease of access, but at the cost of serious damage to a neighboring coral reef.

South of Castries lies a number of pleasant and scenic towns, including **Laborie**, **Choiseul** and **Vieux Fort** near the international airport. **Soufriere**, a little closer to Castries, was the first French settlement on the island, and is a sort of gateway to some of St. Lucia's major scenic attractions. First among them are the **Pitons**, those two pinnacles of green-softened rock leaping out of the sea—one of the classic images of St. Lucia, if not the Caribbean as a whole. Experienced mountaineers can ascend the Pitons' half-mile-high peaks. For the less adventurous, the best view of the Pitons may be from the water—but we'll come to that later.

Near the town of Soufriere lies La **Soufriere**, a volcano you can actually drive into; once there, you can stroll around amidst seething mud pools and steaming sulfer springs. Watching a guide cook an egg in the steam has become a sort of cliché of St. Lucia touring. Nearby are the **Diamond Mineral Baths**, natural hot tubs where, for a negligible fee, visitors can soak their aching muscles. Also on hand: a waterfall that changes colors.

The volcanic activity still in evidence at La Soufriere has recently been exploited by the St. Lucian government for electrical generation. In 1981, 60,000,000 kw-hr of geothermal electricity was produced on the island. Apparently, the government hopes to increase production.

Other attractions near the town of Soufriere include the **Moule-a-Chique** rainforest—an ideal and breathtaking area for walking. If you are lucky, you might catch a glimpse of the St. Lucian Amazon parrot, a highly endangered species, like many of its island cousins. Dusk is the best time to look for these birds.

At the southernmost tip of St. Lucia lies the T-shaped Moule-a-Chique peninsula, where the differently-colored Atlantic and Caribbean waters come together, and from which, on a clear day, you can view St. Vincent 21 miles to the south. Close at hand is the Maria **Islands Interpretation Center**, where visitors can gain insights into St. Lucia's cultural history.

Returning to Castries, you might want to take the east coast road along the crashing Atlantic (but don't stop to swim here unless you're with an experienced local person—surf and undertows can be treacherous). St. Lucia's eastern regions are less saturated with hotels and travelers, and offer visitors more of a taste of how island residents lead their lives. **Micoud** and **Dennery** are two towns worth visiting. From Dennery the

Inspecting an uncooperative engine.

road turns inland, and you come to the **Barre de L'Isle**—St. Lucia's "continental divide". Continuing along your way, you'll hook up again with the west coast road, where turning north you come back into Castries.

Along the east coast road, you'll notice lots of land under cultivation, and if you inquire at Denner you can find your way to the La **Caya** banana plantation, one of the island's largest. Bananas are St. Lucia's most important cash crop, accounting for around 45 percent of total export earnings, but this wasn't always the case. The ancestors of most present-day St. Lucians were Africans enslaved to work the island's sugar plantations, and even after Emancipation in 1834, sugar monopolies contrived to pay wages not much beyond slavery. Gradually, though, sugar operations became less profitable, and ceased altogether in 1964. With the departing sugar companies went the harrowing, back-breaking labor of the cane fields, and a tradition of centralized control. Banana production is spread out among several operations, offering workers at least some hope of higher pay through competition. Even so, St. Lucia's 1982 per capita income only amounted to US$980.

A young St. Lucian.

The economy: As a whole, St. Lucia's economy is primarily agricultural, with coconuts, citrus, spices and subsistence crops supplementing banana production. Fishing, of course, is also practiced. Nevertheless, the island is a net importer of food. St. Lucian industry produces rum, soft drinks, beer and ale, fruit juices, textiles, coconut products such as copra, soap and oil, and cardboard boxes, some of which are exported, as well as electrical equipment, car batteries, plastics, feeds, cigarettes and industrial gases. Near Castries, there is a recently completed oil trans-shipment facility. And, of course, tourism is a major component of island economy, bringing in more foreign exchange than all exports put together—although whether this really benefits the bulk of St. Lucians is debatable. All aspects of economic life received a jolt from 1980s Hurricane Allen, which destroyed almost the entire banana crop and left 6,000 people without homes.

To get a sense of what St. Lucian life is like, walk the countryside. Footpaths connecting numerous towns to roads—and to each other allows both a glimpse of the beauty of the countryside, and the hard lives St. Lucians lead. It is a side of St. Lucia that not many visitors see—and a salutary experience after the clean glitter of resorts.

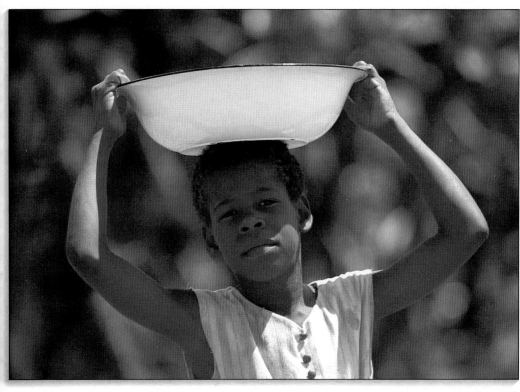

EXPLORING
ST. VINCENT

There is a fort in St. Vincent that the British built sometime in the early 18th century. Now, from lack of care, it has fallen into disrepair. The Vincentians aren't very active about preserving the few pieces of history they have. Grass grows in the cracks of the stone blocks, and in the old guardhouse there is a prison bakery where the island's few criminals spend the day baking bread for the mental hospital.

Hire a guide and it's very likely that his tour will include a short spiel about the few rusty cannons still remaining. But unlike their peers in forts throughout the Lesser Antilles, these cannons are directed inland rather than out to sea. When the fort was built, the Carib Indians, not the Europeans, posed the greatest threat to the British. Still, when you look into the heart of St. Vincent and view its jungles, there's a chance you'll feel like Marlowe, the character in Conrad's *Heart of Darkness*. This landscape can awaken a bit of primordial fear into hearts accustomed to more civilized topography and you'll be glad the guns are pointed inland.

Once you get past their initial reserve, Vincentians are an opinionated people. This particular tour guide—a native Vincentian who claims ancestry from three of the many cultures that have struggled here, Portugese, African and Carib—offers a theory on sexual diseases. He says he once watched a tourist, a rich woman from the States who wore pearls on the beach, kiss her french poodle right on the mouth. This behavior, he says with a knowing look, is how sexual diseases got started.

This is not to say that the people of these islands are ignorant. They are, in fact, more politically aware and involved than the majority of North Americans. On a small island like this, where many people are related in some form or another to a member of government and where there is only one movie theater, politics are like the sexual activities of neighbors; they tend to be discussed with great passion.

Modern civilization has taken a little bit longer to arrive here at the southern tip of the Antilles. Island cultures tend to blur on a ration loosely based on the length of the airport runway. The small one on St. Vincent means only small planes can land here, which means there are fewer tourists and tourist industries. That means you'll find a culture, island and people that have been spared from the forces that have homogenized much of the rest of the Caribbean.

Kingston: In the mornings, the cobblestone streets of Kingston are full of uniformed school children, government workers, dollar taxi cab drivers, Rastafarians peddling sandals, and old women and ragged children selling, from upside-down cardboard boxes, the oddest collection of goods—packs of Juicy Fruit gum, peanuts wrapped in cellophane and pieces of ginger. Hustlers appear out of alleyways to coax tourists on rides to the Soufriere or to the falls of Baleine, or to sell recordings of local calypsonians, like Professor, Vibrating Scakes and De Man Age. And as the afternoon heat grips the town, the government bureaucrats, the bankers and the barristers go to the Bounty, a small cafeteria, to take their lunch.

There's an official zoning law that says no building will rise above the height of a full grown coconut tree. So far it's been obeyed. Nonetheless, this town, little more than a few dusty blocks carved in a rugged shoreline, is the heart of civilization in St. Vincent and the Grenadines.

Here, too, is the apparatus of this tiny nation's government. St. Vincent has a way of making you rethink your idea of just what a nation is. It seems rather inconceivable that this 18-square-mile spot has the same legal status as Canada, for instance. But such has been the case since October 27, 1979, when Great Britain granted St. Vincent its independence.

Because this country is so small, it's not difficult to reach out and intimately view the mechanisms of government. The parliament building on Main Street, which looks like a very sturdy school house, is open to visitors. And you can wander around many of the government buildings spread along King Street. A rule of thumb in this country is that you can tell a person's status by whether or not they have an air conditioner.

But though Kingston may be the most visible source of activity on this tiny commonwealth, the real power comes from the rich volcanic soil. This is an island of farmers, a world where practically every single person knows how to furrow a hillside to plant sweet potatoes. Agriculture is a regular part of the school day and the more fortunate students go away to study it further in one of the West Indian universities.

In fact, the most significant event in this island country occurs every Tuesday, when the large white Geest Industries freighter

Preceding pages: a colorful St. Lucian house; St. Vincent's fishermen. **Below,** a taxi driver.

arrives in port to ship the week's crop of bananas to the rest of the world. In 1976, the banana industry was estimated to account for 60 percent of the total value of St. Vincent's exports and 50 percent of the island's economy.

In fact, bananas are one of the reasons St. Vincent elected to remain within the commonwealth. As members of the British Commonwealth, they receive market protection from Great Britain. Bananas from more efficient, low-cost producers in South and Central America may enter the U.K. only under license.

And on Fridays and Saturdays you can get an idea of just how productive that soil is when the farmers ride dollar taxis into town loaded down with their produce. They congregate inside the airplane-hangar-like market on Bay Street, and from large wooden trestles they sell every kind of fruit and plant known to man, including ginger, breadfruits, cashews, dates and cassavas.

Though per capita income on the island hovers around $600, the idea that anyone might starve here seems absurd. In mango season, for instance, the ground is littered with fruit and the whole island walks around picking the orange meat from between their teeth.

It's not surprising that, like many Caribbean islands, agriculture seems to have dominated the history of St. Vincent. After the 1763 Treaty of Paris, the English began to make serious attempts to take over the island. English settlers came en masse to set up sugar plantations. By 1829 St. Vincent contained 98 sugar estates manned by slaves. Most of these were run by landowners who lived in England. In 1848, a report claimed that only 12 of a total of 100 proprietors were living on the island. And by the end of the 19th century, most of the arable lands in St. Vincent were in the possession of just five owners. It was these largely absentee landlords who controlled the fate of the island.

Inside St. Vincent: It is difficult to explain distance on this island. What would take 10 minutes to drive in a flatter world can take hours here, as you circumvent mountains and jungles. In fact, there are parts of St. Vincent that are accessible only by foot or boat.

The Vigie Highway leaves Kingston from the east and winds through what the Vincentians call the "breadbasket" of their island. On the windward, or Atlantic, side the slopes are gentler and the soil more fertile, and it's here that much of the farming

A graveyard in the hills.

is done. From the unbarricaded highway you have views, somewhat frightening, of deep valleys littered with small farms and banana plantations. Banana farming is hard work. At least three times a day the farmers will inspect each stalk to see if there are leaves pressing against the fruit. Bruised fruit will not be accepted by the buyers.

As the highway continues on toward the coast, you'll pass steep gorges with freshwater streams, shirtless farmers carrying machetes and small towns that consist of little more than an awkward gathering of corrugated houses with red tin roofs, a Hairoun beer sign and streets filled with children.

Now there is a traffic jam on the narrow coastal road that leads from Kingston to Georgetown, once the prosperous sugar capital of the island. A traffic jam on St. Vincent may often be comprised of little more than one car. The cause of this particular one is a fisherman squatting next to a rusty iron scale. Next to him is one large red fish. A crowd of people stand around him watching, only a few actively buying. The traffic jam was caused when a man driving a red pick-up truck full of bananas stopped his car in the middle of the road, yelled "I need something for my dinner", and wandered over to inspect the fish. It seems rather strange that on an island full of fishermen, one red fish could cause such a commotion. Yet such impromptu markets are commonplace.

A little past the traffic jam is Georgetown, the second-largest town on St. Vincent. At one time, when the price of sugar was 60 to 70 cents a pound, this was a prosperous town. But the price of sugar fell and it was rumored that the government was losing millions of dollars. So the sugar plant, which employed most of the laborers in this valley, was closed down. Now the roads of Georgetown are deserted and potholed and there's a sense of driving through a ghost town.

Lurking behind Georgetown is St. Vincent's volcano, Soufriere, which erupted as late as 1979 in a series of explosions which caused no fatalities, but destroyed hundreds of acres of arrowroot and banana farms and forced the evacuation of many of the surrounding towns. An earlier eruption in 1902 did kill more than 2,000 people, but for the moment, the volcano is not in a fatal phase and you can drive to Chatbeler and take the six-hour round trip walk up to the rim of the crater.

Also on the northern end of the island is

Furious activity on the fishing boats.

the Carib reservation, at Sandy Bay. This once fierce tribe has become something of an island scape goat and are the brunt of ethnic jokes. These, however, are the remainders of a tribe of Indians that were fierce enough to keep the vastly better armed Europeans from settling there. Apparently, St. Vincent was regarded as something of a Carib stronghold and many of the Caribs fled here from other islands. It was because of the large Carib presence that the island was declared neutral during the Treaty of Aix-La-Chapelle in 1748.

There is speculation that a Dutch ship carrying slaves from the blight of Benin foundered off the coast of Bequia in 1675, during a hurricane, and that many of those slaves escaped to Bequia, where they were cared for by the Caribs. Other slaves escaped from Barbados and were swept by the trade winds to St. Vincent's eastern shore.

The mixing of the Africans with the Caribs produced a tribe of apparently even more fierce natives called the Black Caribs. These Black Caribs fought with the Yellow Caribs, the French and the British. Their impact on the island ended after a series of guerilla-like battles, the Brigand Wars, against the British. After the battle the defeated Caribs, approximately 5,000, were shipped to Roatan.

Other sites: A half-mile outside of Kingston is St. Vincent's Historical Museum, a few rooms that house artifacts from the primitive tribes who inhabited these islands before the Europeans.

Next to the museum are the Botanical Gardens, the oldest in the hemisphere. Chances are young men will come up to you at the gate entrance and offer you a tour of the gardens that contain, among other things, a 50-foot breadfruit tree, teak and mahogany trees, and nearly every single other flower and tree that can grow in the Caribbean.

In the Buccament Valley, on St. Vincent's leeward coast, you can wander in tropical rain forests, and, if fortunate, hear the St. Vincent parrot and the whistling warbler, two birds unique to the island. Further north are the 100-foot high (30-meter) falls of Baliene, accessible only by boat.

The Grenadines: You have to search a bit for the sea in Kingston. You'll find it by walking down Upper Bay Street, behind the banana crates, rum huts and warehouses. It is here that you'll find the small pier where the schooners and freighters that travel among the rest of the Grenadines dock.

There are only two other countries in the

An ocean-liner visits St. Lucia.

world that use the conjunction "and" with their titles: the Caribbean nation of Trinidad and Tobago, and Sao Tome and Principe, a two-island country off the coast of Africa. The "and" in these seems to imply a certain amount of equality between two land masses.

But somehow Bequia, Battowia, Balliceaux, Pillories, Mustique, Petit Mustique, Union Isle a Quatre, Petit Nevis, Ramay, Savan, Petit Canouan, Canouan, Baleine, Tobago Cays—the separate islands that comprise the Grenadines—seem to have been snubbed in the naming of their country. St. Vincent, the largest land mass, managed to gain top billing.

Politically they claim neglect as well. Most public services receive little attention on these islands. Bequians have long complained about their lack of money to build roads on their island.

Protest can take a more virulent form. A few days after the 1979 election, won by Son Mitchel, a revolt was staged by 50 or so young men on Union Island, whose ultimate goal was to secede from a nation that treated them as a second sister. Led by Lennon "Bumber" Charles, the revolt was quickly quieted by a detachment of St. Vincent policemen. The group escaped to Carico, but were later captured and brought back to St. Vincent to face criminal charges.

Bequia: Bequia is an island defined by its physical circumstances. Remote, it is accessible only by boat and is too rugged to support plantations. The island has forced the Bequians to turn to the sea for their livelihood. Consequently, they evolved into one of the most self-reliant people in the entire Caribbean.

It's not surprising that the focal point of this island is the stunningly beautiful Admiralty Bay, an enormous, clear harbor bordered by steep green cliffs. Here, on the shore, is the main town, Port Elizabeth, little more than a road, a small store and a few tiny restaurants. A small walking path which runs along the water connects the guest houses and cafes that lie among the palms. Along the shore, you'll often find unfinished sloops being built by the locals, and directly off the pier are the almond trees where the resident philosophers of Beguia gather to discuss the world's affairs.

Much of the islanders' skill with the sea comes from New Bedford whalers who used the island as a whaling station during the 19th century, and consequently passed their skills on to the Bequians.

In fact, one of the last true whalers in the

Punaise Island.

220

Western Hemisphere, Aytheneal Oliverre, lives in a small hut on the western side of Bequia. The path to his front door passes underneath the jawbone of a whale, and on his living room wall is a vertebrae of the first whale he killed in 1958.

Every whale killed on Bequia since then, approximately 70, has been harpooned by this man. There were three years when the small, 26-foot sail-powered whale boats left shore without Oliverre on board. But no whales were caught.

Harpooning a 70-foot whale with a hand-thrown harpoon requires a bit of courage. As Oliverre says, many of the island men have plenty of courage in the rum shops, but not so much out on the water. Nor is that surprising. There is always a chance that a boat will be overturned or destroyed completely by a flip of a whale's tail. But because the boats are slow and the weapons inaccurate, the probability of catching a whale, or a whale catching a boat, is slim. There are many years when no whales at all are caught.

Nonetheless, this is still one of the few islands in the world where people are very familiar with the taste of whale meat. Oliverre used to have a teaspoon of whale oil every morning for breakfast. And his brother claims that the best part of the whale meat is the heart. When and if a whale is caught, the island flocks out to little Nevis, where the whale is cut up and sold. This spectacle sometimes attracts as many as 2,000 people.

But like the rest of the nautical traditions on this island, there is a chance that such skills will die out. The young Bequians aren't as keen as their elders in learning such trades.

Mustique: The Mustique airport is little more than a small palm hut, with a runway that appears slightly longer than a driveway. On the bulletin board outside is a poster of a rabid dog's face that says there are no rabies on this island.

Visitors to Mustique are often greeted by the local security force, which consists of one policeman who visits the airport with the arrival of each five-seat plane to see that every visitor has a proper destination.

Not that there are many places to go. There are approximately 80 houses on the three-square-mile island. About 50 of those belong to people like Mick Jagger, Princess Margaret and other royalty, and a contingent of wealthy South American businessmen. There is also a small community descended from the slaves who originally worked the citrus plantations on this island.

Also on the western shore, fishermen set up camp on the beach near Basils Bar, the only public restaurant on the island. They live in tents and shacks and eat quite a bit of conch. There is a small mountain of conch shells along one of the beaches outside Basils.

The other islands: The other islands in the Grenadines should be considered as travel spots for the more adventurous. There is the small, crescent-shaped, undeveloped island of Canouan, the site of the first boatbuilding in the Grenadines. Canouan has two hotels, an abundance of deserted coves, and very little else.

Tiny Mayreau is less than two square miles and is inhabited by about 100 people. There are no cars, no roads, a small salt pond and one very subdued resort. Directly off the coast of Mayreau is a small cluster of five uninhabited islands known as the Tobago Cays. They offer what's regarded as some of the best snorkeling in the Caribbean. Mountainous Union Island is the most developed of the lesser known Grenadines. There is an airport, a number of hotels, and a population of a few thousand. The end point for the Grenadines is Petit St. Vincent, an island devoted entirely to a resort considered to be one of the best in the Caribbean.

Right, a view from the hills.

EXPLORING GRENADA

The island of **Grenada** rises up from the Caribbean sea in steep, green volcanic mountains. Sheer cliffs and scalloped sandy beaches alternate along the rim of the island. In the interior there are crater lakes, natural springs and spectacular waterfalls. A deep, pocket harbor draws banana boats, cruise ships and creaky wooden motor sailers loaded with produce and bulky cargo right into the heart of the capital, St. George's. Inside the wide mouth of the harbor and off to one side, sailing yachts collect in a broad, sheltered cove.

Stone and cement buildings, some ancient, some relative newcomers, wrapped around the waterfront and red-roofed bungalows climb up the hillsides like benches in an amphitheater. The steeples and belfries of half a dozen churches and the high walls of an old fortress reach into the sky.

Some mornings conch fishermen tie up downtown and pile their pearly pink shells on the low seawall after they have scraped out the meat. Foreigners from the yacht basin come across in little rubber dinghies to pick up provisions in the grocery store, maybe buy a paperback or a Trinidad newspaper in the **Sea Change Bookstore** and have a drink upstairs in the **Nutmeg Inn**.

Grenada is a gem of an island. It is twice the size of Washington, D.C., but with a population of about 90,000, it has only one-seventh as many people. Farmers working small plots harvest nutmeg, bananas and cocoa beans and fishermen in wooden skiffs provide fish for the local market. A few people keep horses, cows and goats that sometimes graze along the roads outside the capital.

Even in the rainy season the days are mainly sunny, and the trade winds keep temperatures in the 70s and 80s year-round. There are dozens of species of birds and even some wild monkeys. The waters are clear and there are coral reefs with tropical fish.

The island's most striking beach, **Grand Anse**, is a broad, sandy crescent on the edge of a placid ocean bay on the west coast, a few miles outside the capital. Languorous palm trees collect pools of shade near the water's edge and back towards the road there is a natural hedge of red and yellow hibiscus and tropical shrubs. The beach rises gently from the sea. Waves sweep up the sloping sand, flare and dissolve in frothy fans. A few steps into the water the bottom drops away to swimming depth, then gradually slopes away with perfect, heavenly engineering. Women sell black coral jewelry, batik shirts and dresses, homemade fudge and coconut candy and little straw baskets with assortments of the spices that grow on the island—nutmeg, cinnamon, pimento, ginger and bay leaf. Men with machetes whack off the tops of fresh coconuts to get at the milk and meat. At dusk, lights on a bluff near the mouth of the St. George's harbor begin to twinkle and, often, a cruise ship heads out across the rim of the bay.

Grenada is not the smallest or the most remote place in the Caribbean by far. But it feels small and faraway, alluringly naive and uncomplicated. Foreigners find it a marvelous hideout, good for a week or a month, a year or a lifetime. It is comfortable but not fancy, and with just a little effort the hazy illusion of a beachcomber's paradise can be maintained.

"The rescue": At its core, however, Grenada is a restless island. It has endured ritualistic cannibalism, massacres, slavery, rebellions, strikes and numerous invasions. It has had moments of notoriety, as in the 1770s when its sugar production made it one of the most valuable British colonies. But by the time of the last invasion, carried out by more than 5,000 American troops in the fall of 1983, Grenada was still so obscure that most Americans and Europeans were unable to locate it on the world map, and some confused it with the Spanish city of Granada. Newspapers published maps showing the island located deep in the Caribbean, near the bottom of an arc of islands that dips toward South America, about 90 miles (145 km) north of Venezuela and the island of Trinidad and 150 miles (242 km) southwest of Barbados.

Whether the United States' invasion of Grenada was proper or even necessary was widely debated in many parts of the world. In Grenada there was no debate. To most Grenadians, the American soldiers and marines were saviors. Long afterwards, the Grenadians fondly referred to Mr. Reagan as "the cowboy." For them, the term "invasion" sounded jarring. They liked the Reagan Administration's rubric, "the rescue mission." Often they just called it "the rescue."

For more than four and a half years the islanders had been living under a leftist government that had created economic hardships and restricted civil liberties. A few days before the Americans landed, the government, led by young men who had become enamored of Marxism at universities in the U.S. and England, exploded in stunning violence. The popular leftist prime minister, Maurice Bishop, and seven others were abruptly lined up against a wall and executed, and perhaps as many as 100 others, including many children, were killed in an afternoon of wild shooting. Survivors told of dozens of people leaping off a grassy promontory to escape the gunfire. A 24-hour curfew was imposed, making Grenadians prisoners in their own homes.

The overwhelming force brought to bear by the U.S., with token assistance from neighboring islands, quickly restored order to Grenada. To most Grenadians it was irrelevant whether President Reagan had sent the troops in some geo-political linkage with the truck bomb that had killed 241 American Marines in Beirut two days earlier and whether the hardline leftist faction that had executed Mr. Bishop might have eventually gotten the island functioning again. What was important for them was that the Americans had come.

The American invasion was one of the most significant events in Grenada's history. The invasion and close attention from Washington afterward brought the island a popularly elected moderate government, a burst of prosperity and some of the basics for future development. It also reminded the rest of the world that there was such a place as Grenada and this led to a revival in tourism. As the leftist government had moved closer to Moscow and Havana and relations with Washington worsened, the number of American visitors dropped off and the island's hotels began to fall into disrepair.

Shortly after the invasion, passenger liners started calling in again. People would get off and look around for a day, then head off to another island. Many of the first visitors came out of curiosity.

Bob Loveless, a former Marine who owned a shoe store in Oklahoma City, sailed into Grenada aboard the 526-foot (159-meter) CUNARD COUNTESS. He had wanted to see "what we had been fighting for." His wife, Maxine, had wondered how the people felt toward Americans. "You hear a lot of whether we should stick our noses in a country like this."

The refrain from the Grenadians was consistent. "You start talking with the people and you hear about the Communist influence and as an American you want to put a stop to that growth," said Michael Hendricks, a 25-year-old flight attendant from Skokie, Illinois who had gone to Grenada with his family aboard the cruise ship VIC-TORIA. "The people seem to like what we did," he said.

Cornelia Rudin, a New Yorker who had once dreamed of a career on the stage, moved to Grenada in the 1960s. She and her husband, Bob, who had worked at the Museum of Modern Art in Manhattan, were running an art gallery on the island when the American troops landed.

"If I had been in the States when this happened," Mrs. Rudin said, "I would have been loudly against it. But being here, and having a rifle pointed at me by revolutionary army soldiers when I stuck my arm out the window to feed the dog during curfew, made a difference. There was no way people could wait and see how things worked out. They had us all under house arrest."

Some Grenadians had toyed with the idea of creating a tour of the invasion battle sites. But most of the island's taxi drivers stuck with their old programs.

"We don't show the battle sites," said Victor Lawrence, one of the more enterprising of the drivers. "We take them to the Anedale Waterfall, the crater lake, a high point where they can look down on the city and the botanical garden. The tour has noth-

ing to do with war. If people want to see where the war took place, we take them. But it's not part of the tour."

In the first three years after the invasion, financial aid from the U.S. jumped to more than $80 million from about $10 million annually. Millions more came from U.S. allies in Europe, Latin America and the Caribbean.

Some Grenadians and foreign diplomats worried about all the money suddenly changing the quiet character of the island, one of Grenada's greatest assets. In the beginning, at least, the charm remained. The island just became more functional. A person could still dine on possum and armadillo at a tin-roofed place called **Mama's**; still linger over a drink called a *Bentley*, essentially a limeade with a dash of bitters and a maraschino cherry, at the **Nutmeg Inn** at the edge of the harbor; still watch the sunsets at **Prickly Bay** and hear nothing more intrusive than the rattle of lanyard to mast. The nearly 200-room **Grenada Beach Hotel**, which served as the headquarters for the American troops, had been taken over by Ramada International and elegantly spruced up and there was talk of several projects for new hotels of perhaps 200 or 300 rooms. But the small, well-kept places

Preceding pages: the traveler's dream destination; **Saturday market at St. George's. Below**, midday snooze.

like the nine-room **Twelve Degrees North** with a tennis court, a wooden pier and an honor-system bar by the beach, were still providing succor to well-healed refugees from harsher climes.

Airport import: The foreign aid paid for resurfacing the island's main roads and re-routing some of them to make them less winding and "roller-coastery." It also was used for installing a modern telephone system. (The leftist government had brought in a lot of East German telephone equipment that did not mesh with the original British equipment and American bombs destroyed one of the main exchanges.) It bought new generators and pumps to restore and expand electricity and running water.

But what pleased the Grenadians most was the building of the new airport. They had been wishing for it for nearly 30 years, but there had never been anywhere near enough money to turn their dream into reality. One of the benefits of the relationship the leftists had developed with the Cuban government had been a start on the airport. The airport had also been the thing that worried the Reagan Administration most about the leftist government. President Reagan had insisted that the Grenadian leftists, the Cubans and the Soviets were building the airport primarily for military purposes and that it constituted a menace to security in the region. After the invasion the Americans found huge underground storage tanks that they said proved the airport would have been capable of refueling long-range bombers and surveillance planes and fighter squadrons. They said the terminal was much bigger than the island needed and had really been intended to handle large numbers of foreign soldiers. American military transport planes used the 9,000-foot long runway during the invasion and for months afterward. With the leftists in power, the airport was "a tool for exporting revolution," one senior Washington official said. But with the invasion, he said, it became "a means of revolutionizing the economy of this island."

The new airport, set along the sea less than 25 minutes over coastal flatlands from St. George's, was equipped with radar and other electronic gear that permitted it to operate around the clock in any weather. It replaced the island's first airport, which was built in 1943. The old airport was short and unlighted and a long trip over the mountains from the capital. To land there, one pilot recalled, "you had to fly into a mountain and then down into a valley."

British colonial engineers recommended the site for the new airport, at a place on the southwest coast called Point Saline, in 1955. In 1966, a Grenadian engineer named Ron Smith drew the first plans for the airport and in late 1979 Cuban construction crews started on the project. When the Americans arrived it was about 65 percent finished.

In most countries, said Ron Smith, who remained project manager until the end, the Point Saline site would have been rejected out of hand. The path of the main runway crossed eight spiney 100-foot-high ridges and a small bay. But, he said, nowhere else on the island was there a space big enough to lay down a runway that could handle the biggest international jets without running into a mountainside or plunging into the sea. The Cubans, he said, spent most of their time leveling the ridges, filling in valleys and laying down 10 inches of asphalt. A handful of American companies worked as subcontractors under the Cubans and an American company that had been part of a consortium that did much of the government construction work in Vietnam put on the finishing touches after the United States took charge.

It was gray and rainy when the new airport opened for the first commercial flights on Oct. 25, 1984, a year to the day after the invasion. But thousands of Grenadians put on their Sunday best and went out to watch the marching bands and the children's folk dances and listen to a speech from the governor general, Sir Paul Scoon. Standing in the crowd that day, a 49-year-old farmer named John Francis said he did not know who deserved the most credit for bringing the airport to reality. But he said, "to all those who helped us, we are glad and thankful. This is a good and magnificent thing for bringing business to this country."

Travelers and tyrants: Christopher Columbus and his crew were the first Europeans to lay eyes on Grenada on his third voyage in 1498. He did not bother to go ashore, but named it Concepcion. A few years later, Americo Vespucci, the famed map-maker, came upon the island and, unaware that Columbus had arrived before him, christened it Mayo. Inexplicably, the island began to show up on maps in the early 1500s as Granada. Eventually, the island became a British possession and the name became Grenada.

Men have been fighting over the island for centuries. Before the Europeans started arriving, various groups of South American Indians battled. Some of the first residents, the Arawaks, carved heads and faces into rocks that can still be seen on the island. One big carved rock stands in the bed of the La Fortune River on the Mt. Rich Estate in the northern part of Grenada.

The surviving Indians, who were known as Caribs and who included among their rituals the eating of human flesh, fought attempts at colonization until they were wiped out in 1654 by the French. In the final confrontation with the French, whose presence is still evidenced by many place names and the patois that islanders speak among themselves, 40 Caribs leaped to their deaths off a cliff on the north end of the island rather than submit. The cliff, near the town of Sauteurs, is now known as la Morne des Sauteurs or Leaper's Hill. There is a good beach in Sauteurs and an old plantation house run by a woman named Betty Mascoll who offers visitors a West Indian-style lunch.

The French brought the first slaves to Grenada and ran the island as a huge plantation for more than 100 years, first growing tobacco and indigo and later switching to sugar. The British captured the island in the Seven Years War, which ended in 1763, lost it to the French and then regained control in 1783 in the Treaty of Versailles. For the next 191 years, until independence on Feb. 7, 1974, Grenada was a British colony.

In the mid-1790s a Grenadian named Julien Fedon, a Free Colored who had been born of a slave mother and French father and who owned a large coffee and cocoa estate, collaborated with the French to try to drive the British off the island. Fedon's men captured and eventually executed the British governor and about 50 other leading British citizens. But within a year and a half the rebellion was crushed. Hundreds of slaves had been killed and Fedon disappeared, possibly drowned while trying to flee the island.

Slavery ended on Grenada in the 1830s. Many of the freed blacks began working small, unclaimed plots or sharecropping and the British began importing indentured East Indians to keep their plantations going. By the end of the century, cocoa and nutmeg, which had initially been brought to Grenada from the Dutch East Indies, surpassed sugar as the main crop. Bananas became an important crop in the 1950s, especially after the hurricane in 1955. All the crops were badly damaged in the storm, but bananas recovered quicker than the others. Part of the folklore of Grenada is that breadfruit, which is still a popular food with Grenadians, was brought to the island from Tahiti by Captain Bligh on the Bounty.

Women peeling outershell of nutmeg on Dougaldston estate.

For decades, Grenadians agitated for a greater voice in the political life of their island. Newspapers were started and closed, editors were arrested. There were protracted negotiations and bursts of disorder. Once in the 1920s there was an outbreak of arson and some historians believe the plan was to burn the capital. When independence and freedom finally came in 1974, years of turbulence lay ahead.

In 1949, a slender wisp of a man named Eric Gairy returned home to Grenada from a clerical job at the big oil refinery on the nearby island of Aruba. He had a grand way of talking that made people feel good and made them see how smart he was and for more than three decades he was the most important single figure on the island. He was not always good for Grenada, but he was an enduring presence.

He organized an island-wide strike that made him a hero to Grenadians and a villain to the British and propelled him to victory in the island's first election with universal adult suffrage in 1951. People began to call him "Uncle Gairy," and he won all but one of the next half dozen elections. Once he was barred from politics for leading a calypso band through an opponent's rally and later he was suspended as chief minister on charges of squandering thousands of dollars on government contracts and real estate transactions and refurnishing the government house in which he lived. He showed off in white suits and collected striking women; his business interests included hotels, restaurants, a boutique and a beauty parlor. He spoke of himself as a mystic, said he had been divinely chosen to lead Grenadians and, at international forums, advocated research into the phenomenon of flying saucers. When his influence seemed on the wane, he terrorized Grenadians with a bunch of thugs who came to be known as the "Mongoose Gang."

In late 1973 and early 1974, with independence just months away, many Grenadians, from the Chamber of Commerce to the leftist opposition, argued that the island was not ready to go it alone. Their concern, they said, was determined to shed itself of the colony and in the midst of a general strike and power blackouts. Nevertheless, the Union Jack was run down and Gairy became Grenada's first prime minister.

Five years later he was toppled in the first *coup d'etat* in the history of the English-speaking Caribbean. On the morning of March 13, 1979, when Gairy was in New York preparing to address a session of the

Rounding up goats in Gouyave.

United Nations on the subject of Unidentified Flying Objects, a group of leftists led by a London-educated lawyer named Maurice Bishop seized power. About 40 of Bishop's followers took over an army barracks at a place on the outskirts of the capital called True Blue and captured the one radio station. Three people were killed.

Bishop, like Gairy in his early years, charmed the people. And everyone was glad to be rid of Gairy. But Bishop and the others, in an organization they called the New Jewel Movement, proved merely to be trouble from the opposite end of the political spectrum. Their dreams of making Grenada blossom through socialism never materialized. Because of their mismanagement and the fears of tourists and international business that grew out of their close relations with Cuba and the Soviet Union, the economy shrivelled.

Bernard Coard, a doctrinaire Marxist who had graduated from Brandeis University in Boston, challenged Bishop's leadership and succeeded in having Bishop placed under house arrest. On the morning of Oct. 19, several hundred Grenadians went to Bishop's house, hoisted him on their shoulders and marched him downtown to the old fort that the British colonials had built overlooking the harbor.

Coard and the others who had opposed Bishop conferred hastily. Soldiers and armored cars were dispatched to what was then known as Fort Rupert. The soldiers opened fire on the fort causing panic among the hundreds of people inside. Abruptly the fort fell quiet. Some of the young soldiers led Bishop and a handful of others outside, lined them up against a wall and tore them apart with automatic rifle fire. The bodies of Bishop and the others were later dumped in an open pit and burned to cinders.

Hudson Austin, a former prison guard who had become head of the People's Revolutionary Army, then took charge of a so-called Ruling Military Council that clung to power until the Americans landed six days later. Austin, Coard and a dozen others, including Coard's wife Phyllis, were convicted in late 1986 of murdering Bishop and the other firing squad victims and sentenced to death.

A little more than a year after the shocking upheaval, a 66-year-old self-educated lawyer and former head of government who had silently suffered the leftists, re-entered political life and, with strong American backing, was swept into office as Prime Minister.

Cropduster destroyed in the invasion.

EXPLORING BARBADOS

The breakers of the Atlantic—"white horses", as the Bajans call them—slam against jagged cliffs of **River Bay**, a vast, barren plateau and dry riverbed at the isolated northern tip of **Barbados**.

Ordinarily it is deserted here. But today is Boxing Day. A lengthening line of public buses curves along the road that leads to this rugged area, intruding on the landscape like a monstrous blue and yellow snake. Clusters of people swarm toward a hillside shaded by a grove of long-needled casuarina trees. Women wearing their Sunday best—brilliant turquoise skirts or scarlet polyester dresses that look even brighter next to the muted browns and greens of the landscape—step gingerly across a narrow stream and stake out the best picnic spots on the hillside. The few trees, gnarled and stunted by the ever-present trade winds, provide a canopy under which the women begin to unveil the elaborate holiday fare.

A Bajan picnic is a grand affair, especially on a "bank holiday." A few families have brought the familiar red and white buckets of Kentucky Fried Chicken, but most unveil big casserole dishes filled with homecooked food: peas and rice, chicken stuffed with Bajan herbs (a combination of onions, parsley, thyme, hot pepper, garlic and lime), and the traditional Christmas dish—*jug jug*. And of course, there's the bottle of "devil soup", Cockspur rum, the local favorite.

Gangs of teenagers roam the area, and one boy in each group carries a huge ghetto-blaster; "dub" music played so loud it distorts into little more than a muffled, persistent beat. Watching this holiday scene gives a sense of the Barbados character—serious and playful, with an overlay of British propriety and a subtle, but persistent African beat continuously throbbing in the background. African cultural influences are stronger here than they might seem at first. One feels them in the pulsing of a steel band, tastes them in local foods such as *cou-cou* and *conkies*, sees them in the structure of the family, and hears them in the dialect, the folktales, the expressive proverbs and sayings. They explode through the surface in colorful bursts of calypso, costumes and dance—especially during Crop Over, a month-long harvest festival that brings celebration and song to the streets.

Nicknamed "Little England," Barbados,

with its afternoon teas and starched school uniforms, can appear very British. One 19th century visitor declared it "more English than England itself." Names such as Trevor, Derek, Nigel and Dexter are common. There's a statue of Admiral Nelson in Bridgetown's "Trafalgar Square," and the game of cricket is practically the national religion.

Unspoilt East: Barbados is known as "the singular island," perhaps because it's a bit off the beaten track, 100 miles (161 km) to the east of the Caribbean chain. During the days of sailing conquerors and Caribbean settlement, this isolation provided Barbados with an unwitting defense: it is difficult to sail there from the other islands because of the prevailing easterly winds.

Today, 70 percent of the population is descended from former African slaves, and another 20 percent is of mixed black and white blood. Only seven percent is Caucasian, and the remaining three percent is Chinese, Indian or Arab.

This tiny coral island is densely populated—about 260,000 people live in a space just 14 miles (22 km) wide and 21 miles (33 km) long, yet Barbadians have one of the highest per capita incomes in the Caribbean and claim a literacy rate of over 95 percent, one of the highest in the world.

With a total area of only 166 square miles (431 square km), Barbados has some of the most varied terrain in the Caribbean. The island is divided into 11 parishes, each with its own character and landscape. The north is the least populated section; its shores are punctuated by dramatic cliffs and crashing waves. Equally unspoiled is the scenic east with miles of windswept beaches along the Atlantic coast and the hilly "Scotland District." The south and west coasts have most of the hotels and beaches and are the hub of culture and commerce. The capital, **Bridgetown**, is there, in the parish of **St. Michael**. The center of the island is covered with gently rolling cane fields, rural villages, and lush tropical vegetation.

Although some of the hills are very steep, Barbados is considered a flat island. It is coral rather than volcanic and its highest point, **Mt. Hillaby**, is just 1,100 feet above sea level.

The first Bajans were the Arawak Indians, who came in canoes from the South American mainland around 400 B.C. These gentle fishermen and farmers were eventually wiped out by the more aggressive Caribs, who invaded the island around 1200 A.D. and dominated Barbados for over 300 years.

European adventurers who sailed to the Caribbean in the 1500s tell tales of Carib cannibalism. Anthropologists now say these Indians probably never depended on human flesh for nutrition, but occasionally did eat an enemy's flesh during a ritual to promote courage in battle. According to the reports of one Englishman, the Caribs said that "Spanish flesh caused indigestion, the French were delicate in taste, while the English were too tough."

The Spanish used such claims of "unhumanly" cannibalism, to justify their enslavement of the Indians. Many of the Indians were abducted from the small Caribbean islands like Barbados and taken to work in fields and mines on larger islands.

Whether it was because of this enslavement by the Spanish or famine and disease, all the Indians had disappeared from Barbados by the time the English first arrived in 1627. All the British found was a population of wild hogs, left behind by Portuguese explorers who anchored briefly there in 1536, and who, according to legend, named the island "Los Barbados" ("the bearded ones") after the bearded fig trees they saw on its shores.

"Jewel in the crown": On February 17, 1627, 80 English settlers and 10 black slaves, captured from trading vessels en route, landed on the calm west coast of the island. The first English settlers were an intrepid lot, willing to risk their lives for the promise of colonial wealth and power. Despite the beauty of the island, life was grim at first. An "anything goes" spirit prevailed, and Barbados became a stage for outcasts, gamblers, fighters, fortune hunters, political refugees and kidnappers. Sometime in the 1630s a ship captain remarked to one of the island's judges, that "If all whore-masters were taken off the bench, what would the Governor do for a council?"

Nearly all early settlers were motivated by economics. Many were second or third sons of well-placed Englishmen, who would miss out on the inheritance marked for the first-born. Others were from the laboring classes of England, Scotland or Ireland, and came as indentured servants.

Barbados was, in fact, the first British possession to cultivate sugar on a large scale and by the 1650s, the island had a booming economy based solely on sugar cane. It was so productive that it was called "the Brightest Jewel in the English Crowne." As the sugar cane plantation system evolved, the institution of slavery became firmly entrenched, and between the 1670s and the early 1800s, a number of slave revolts were squelched by the planters. Black rebellion was more subdued in Barbados than in Jamaica, where dense woods and mountainous regions provided asylum for hunted blacks. Barbados, small and highly cultivated, was too wide open for much successful hiding. In 1834, slavery was abolished; it was a quiet reform.

The Anglican Bishop wrote that "such was the order, the perfect silence, that you might have heard a pin drop" as he addressed a congregation of 4,000 people, 3,000 of whom were newly freed blacks.

Post freedom struggle: The problems of reconciling a large black labor force and a small, wealthy leadership class would take more than a century of reforms. The planters' greatest fear was the the loss of their labor force, consequently they tried to bind workers to the plantations through legal means. Nevertheless, between 1850 and 1914, 20,000 adventurous laborers left for Panama to help build the canal, and many came back wearing flashy clothes, their pockets stuffed with U.S. currency, which was used to buy land, educate their children and increase their standard of living.

But after the canal's completion there were few opportunities for black Bajans and most returned to the plantations as laborers.

The poor working conditions there and a lack of political power—about two percent of the population received no national income, and only four percent had voting rights—sparked a half century of intense political and social change.

Perhaps the most noteworthy figure to challenge the ruling white planter class was Sir Grantley Adams, the acknowledged leader of Barbados Progressive League, the island's first mass movement political party. Over the course of the next 30 years Adams and the BPL helped attain fair labor laws and universal voting rights.

Political independence finally came under the leadership of Errol Barrow in 1966, when Barbados declared its independence from England and peacefully became a sovereign state, a decision marked by surprisingly little opposition or fanfare. Ten years later, Tom Adams, son of Grantley Adams, took over. A popular leader, he took Barbados confidently into the 80s. But in March 1985, he died suddenly of a heart attack. His successor, Bernard St. John, continued his policies. In 1986 Barrow was back on the scene, hammering away incessantly at St. John's administration just as Barbados was experiencing an economic slowdown. St. John

decided to hold the election that was due by the fall of 1986 in the spring, in order to avoid the inevitable criticisms from the calypso songs released during the July Crop Over Festival. Despite the early election and a massive advertising blitz by St. John, on May 28, 1986, Bajans went to the polls and voted Barrow in by the largest landslide in Barbados history.

While Barbados managed to forge a political identity, it took much longer to escape a cultural limbo and develop its own indigenous culture. Long known for its "Britishness" and the old fashioned life-style of its people, Barbados' reputation began to change in the 1970s, when the Black Power movement and Rastafarianism had a profound impact on island identity. Yet by far the most powerful influence on Bajan culture in the last two decades has been American television and music. As the island's most famous calypsonian, the Mighty Gabby, sings, "All dem shows on TV, you must agree, are not for we/ Show me some Castle of My Skin by George Lamming [Bajan novelist]/ Instead of that trash like Sanford and M.A.S.H./ Then we could stare in the face/ And show dem we cultural base."

Only in the last five to 10 years have Bajans become interested in trying to preserve aspects of their own culture in the face of foreign influences. After its first 20 years as an independent nation, Barbados is finally coming into its own culturally. There is a growing appreciation of things Bajan, and a movement to preserve aspects of the folk culture that are dying out.

The enthusiasm the annual Crop Over Festival generates is one sign of the new cultural pride. The wildly popular calypsonians have now become a major force in Bajan society. They speak for the people, providing social commentary, gentle political protest, and catchy, entertaining tunes that are played everywhere: on the radio, at beach picnics, discos, at "fetes" or "jumpups" (neighborhood dances) and at the hotels.

Spilling over with rum: It's 2 a.m. on **Baxter's Road**—"the street that never sleeps"—just one narrow road in a rundown section of Bridgetown, lined with small rum shops and restaurants. Every night from dark until dawn these ramshackle establishments open their doors and a human drama unfolds. Tourists mingle with the locals and quite a bit of philosophizing goes on over cigarettes and Banks beer. Out of one rum shop blares the lyrics

Warri, a game slaves brought from West Africa.

238

of the latest calypso hit, *"Bajan Yankees come down and shake their bodies."* A few doors down, it's drowned out by a jukebox playing Madonna. At one end of the street, ample Bajan ladies fry dolphin and kingfish steaks over fires in big iron "buck pots." **Enid's** and **Colin's** are restaurant/rum shops that sell real Bajan fried chicken, fish and rotis—a curried beef and potato stew wrapped in a thin crepe.

The island's rum shops aren't all on Baxter's Road. There are over 1,000 on the island; each little village has one or two, and in the crowded parish of **St. Michael** there's one every few blocks or so. A rum shop is not merely a bar; it is a village store, a community center, an arena for fiercely competitive domino-playing, a place where tongues are loosened, politics discussed and rumors spread. *"Man, leh we fire one on that!"* is the exhortation prompted by a happy event such as a birth, a wedding, promotion or lucky bet on the horses. The *"one"* to be fired is usually dark Cockspur rum—locally refined and not exported.

Rum shops are still largely the province of men. *"Men in de rum shop; women in de church,"* the saying goes. And the number of storefront, revivalist churches rivals the number of rum shops. On this 166-square-mile (431-square-km) island, there are over 143 different religions. The majority of Bajans, however, are Anglicans, in keeping with their English heritage.

Taking in the sights: This tiny island has some of the most varied scenery in the Caribbean—from rugged coastline to lush jungles to heavenly beaches.

In the parish of **St. Thomas** is **Harrison's Cave**, where a train takes visitors on a ride through a spectacular network of well-lit caves, complete with underground waterfalls and giant stalactites and stalagmites. Nearby is **Welchman's Hall Gully**, a deep ravine with an abundance of lush vegetation. The many species of trees and flowers along the footpath are labelled. One can follow another kind of path—an underwater one—near **Folkestone Park** in **St. James**. Along a coral reef just off the shore is a marked trail about one-quarter of a mile long for divers or snorkelers. There is also a sunken barge that attracts fish.

Anywhere one drives, one passes examples of the "chattel house" architecture, which is unique to Barbados. Chattel means "moveable property" and the gaily painted wooden cottages are so named because they can be taken apart and moved. The first chattel houses belonged to plantation workers in the 1800s who did not own the land on which their houses stood. Workers would rent tiny "house spots" from the owner of whatever plantation they worked on, and bring their houses with them.

St. Lucy, the rugged, sparsely populated parish at the northern tip of the island, has quite a few authentic chattel houses. It also has the best picnic spots on the island, most of which are well-kept secrets. **Archer's Bay** is a peaceful, grassy area in St. Lucy shaded by a grove of casuarina trees (graceful, long needled evergreens). Usually it's deserted, unless the local boy scout troop is having a picnic there.

At the very northern tip of the island is the **Animal Flower Cave**, named for the "animal flowers," or tiny sea anenomes that grow in pools on its floor. Here the ocean's relentless pounding has created steep, jagged cliffs and rocky, barren land that resembles a moonscape. The refreshment stand sells delicious homemade lemonade and the proprietor's sheep, Pepita, drinks 7 Up out of the bottle.

A perfect place to wind up a tour of the north is **Cove Bay**, also called Gay's Cove. It lies near the village of **Pie Corner** in St. Lucy, the site of an archaeological dig where artifacts from the Carib and Arawak Indians have been unearthed. At Cove Bay there's a promontory called **Paul's Point**, which some say is the prettiest spot in all of Barbados. It's one of the best and least known picnic spots on the island. The point, on the border of **St. Lucy** and **St. Peter**, overlooks the bay and the entire Atlantic coastline of Barbados. Towering over the bay is an unusual formation jutting out from the white cliffs. Called **Pico Teneriffe**, it rises from the sea in stark grandeur, guarding the eastern coastline like a sentry and appearing much higher than its 264 feet (80 meters).

The **East Coast Road** begins in the parish of **St. Andrew** and is the most dramatic drive on the island. Miles of deserted beaches along the Atlantic shore line one side of the road, and the steep, eroded hills that form **The Scotland District** rise abruptly from the other. Going inland here is like being transported to the grassy rolling hills of Scotland. The village of **Chalky Mount** in St. Andrew is where generations of potters have made hand-thrown pots out of clay from the nearby hills. They sell their work at an establishment aptly named **The Potteries**.

Take a hike: Taking a hike with The Barbados Outdoor Club is an offbeat way to explore the rustic eastern side of the island. The day-long hikes are not well-advertised, but offer a glimpse of Barbados not possible to get by car.

A private minibus pulls up to the hotel at 7 a.m. On it are a few groggy tourists and at the back, an energetic Rastafarian singing and pounding a set of very loud bongo drums. Two Bajan girls dressed in skimpy tie-died costumes dance around the bus and bring people coconut bread and coconut water in bamboo cups. The bus makes stops all over the island, and finally arrives at **Hackleton's Cliff** for breakfast. Eating fresh fruit, peanuts, and more coconut bread, the hikers gaze out over the Atlantic and the entire east coast of Barbados. The "donkey bar" arrives. It is a real donkey, carrying a jug of lemonade on one side and rum punch on the other.

The hikers set off, each carrying a big walking stick. They walk all day, climbing down a cliff, walking through dense tropical forests and abandoned banana plantations, over rolling hills dotted with grazing cows and sheep, and along the rocky coastline, stopping to visit Bajans in their chattel houses along the way. In a simple clapboard shack in the woods is Violet, who's "been 80 for 20 years," has no teeth, cooks on a wood fire and still loves "*workin' up*" (dancing). Next is Mrs. Cumberbatch, who shows the dress she always wears to weddings and funerals. And finally, a family of "poor whites" who live on Martin's Bay.

The donkey bar is lost, never to be seen again. But nobody seems to care. After lunch, which is in a hut built high up on a scenic cliff, everybody is singing Bajan calypsos and "*workin' up*." The happy, frenzied mood leads to a skinny dip in the isolated "natural jacuzzi," a foaming pool created by the waves of the Atlantic as they crash over the rocks. And at sunset, the mood mellows as kingfish is cooked over an open fire on the beach and cold Banks beers are passed around. The bus leaves. During the ride home no one is even sitting—the once shy, groggy hikers of that morning are now jumping around, hooting, dancing in the aisle to blaring calypso and reggae music, and passing pints of Cockspur rum round.

Natural beauty preserved: Run by the energetic Julian Hunt, the Barbados Outdoor Club is sponsoring a movement to have the **Glen Burnie** region of the east coast made into a national park so that its natural beauty can be preserved. It is still a wild and rugged place, unspoiled by civilization. Club lore has it that an early Scottish settler named it after Glenburnie in his native

St. Thomas Church on a Sunday morning.

Scotland because the landscape reminded him of home. The descendents of the Scottish indentured servants still live in the area, at **Martin's Bay** in the parish of **St. John**. Most of them are poor, trying to survive by fishing and farming. They are somewhat pejoratively called "red legs" because the kilts their ancestors wore exposed their legs to the sun.

Bathsheba, a tiny fishing village at the southern end of the East Coast Road, is the setting for a very simple hotel with lots of character, **The Atlantis**. George Lamming, the Bajan novelist who wrote *In the Castle of My Skin*, stays here when he comes from England. Lunch on the breezy terrace that overlooks the fishing boats in **Tent Bay** is inspiring.

Tourism is the biggest industry in Barbados, and fishing is third. Second is the sugar cane industry. Visitors can arrange to have a tour of a sugar factory to see how the grassy stalks become sugar and molasses. The **Bulkely** sugar factory in St. George is the island's most accessible one. Anyone can arrange a night-time tour by calling the supervisor there.

A good way to learn more about the local culture is to see a play at the renovated **Queen's Park Theatre**. It is in Queen's Park on the edge of Bridgetown. This large public park is the traditional gathering place for Bajans dressed in their finest for kite-flying on Easter Sunday and on Christmas morning after church.

On Saturday mornings, women come from all over the island to Bridgetown to sell fresh vegetables and fruit at one of the two lively open-air markets—**Fairchild** or **Cheapside**. "*See de women/ How dey calling, singing/ Come for your breadfruit/ Come for your corn/ Come for de apples/ Fresh as de morn...*" sings The Mighty Gabby in "*Bridgetown Saturday Morning.*"

It is in Bridgetown that the contrasts characterizing Barbados are most evident. While duty-free shops sell luxury items like cameras, crystal and cashmere, a Rastaman peddles coconuts from a wooden cart. A flock of black-belly sheep ambles past a new $8 million office building. The strains of calypso emanate from a juke box in a back-alley restaurant with a sign that says "*It's Time to Eat A Home-Cook Meal at the Swizzle Inn.*" And behind the galvanized fences in the jumbled, crowded neighborhoods on the edge of town, people are watching an episode of the popular American crime series *Miami Vice* on T.V. This is Barbados.

Below, all decked out for Christmas Day in Queen's Park.

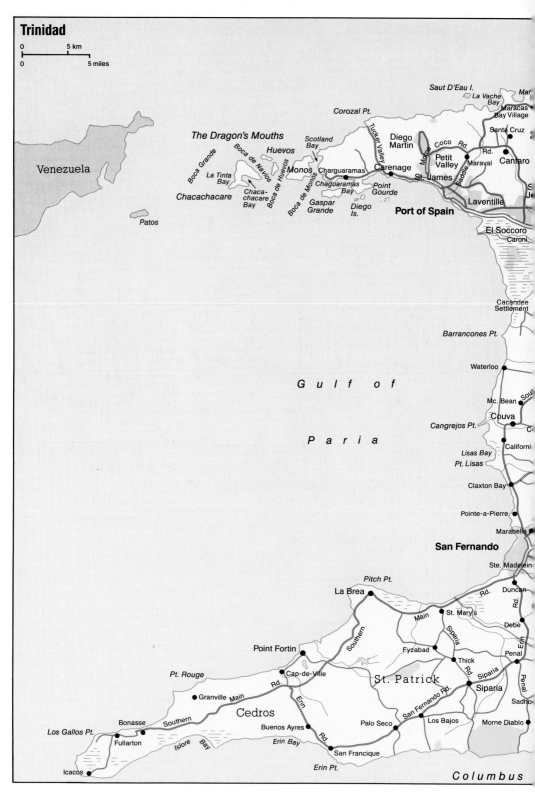

Trinidad

0   5 km

0   5 miles

Venezuela

Patos

The Dragon's Mouths

Boca Grande

La Tinta Bay

Chacachacare

Chaca-chacare Bay

Boca de Navios

Huevos

Boca de Huevos

Monos

Boca de Monos

Scotland Bay

Gaspar Grande

Diego Is.

Charguaramas

Chaguaramas Bay

Point Gourde

Corozal Pt.

Tucker Valley

Diego Martin

Carenage

St. James

Port of Spain

Saut D'Eau I.

La Vache Bay

Mar

Maracas Bay Village

Santa Cruz

Morne

Coco Rd.

Petit Valley

Maraval

Rd.

Saddle Rd.

Cantaro

Laventille

S. J

El Soccoro

Caroni

Cacandee Settlement

Barrancones Pt.

Waterloo

Gulf of

Paria

Mc. Bean

Sout

Couva

Cangrejos Pt.

C.

Californi

Lisas Bay

Pt. Lisas

Claxton Bay

Pointe-a-Pierre

Marabella

San Fernando

Ste. Madelein

Duncan

Rd.

Pitch Pt.

La Brea

Main

St. Mary's

Rd.

Debe

Southern

Fyzabad

Siparia

Thick

Penal

Rd.

Sadho

Penal

Erin

Point Fortin

Pt. Rouge

Cap-de-Ville

Rd.

St. Patrick

Rd.

Siparia

Siparia

Granville Main

Erin

Cedros

San Fernando Rd.

Los Bajos

Morne Diablo

Bonasse

Southern

Buenos Ayres

Palo Seco

Los Gallos Pt.

Fullarton

Islore Bay

Erin Bay

Rd.

San Francique

Icacos

Erin Pt.

Columbus

244

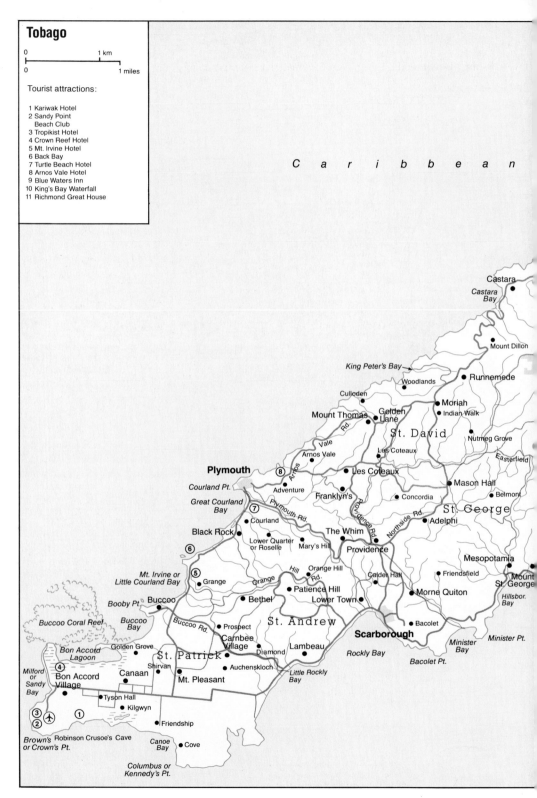

Tobago

0   1 km

0   1 miles

Tourist attractions:

1 Kariwak Hotel
2 Sandy Point
   Beach Club
3 Tropikist Hotel
4 Crown Reef Hotel
5 Mt. Irvine Hotel
6 Back Bay
7 Turtle Beach Hotel
8 Arnos Vale Hotel
9 Blue Waters Inn
10 King's Bay Waterfall
11 Richmond Great House

C a r i b b e a n

Castara
Castara Bay

Mount Dillon

King Peter's Bay
Woodlands
Runnemede
Culloden
Moriah
Indian Walk
Mount Thomas
Golden Lane
St. David
Nutmeg Grove
Vale Rd.
Arnos Vale
Les Coteaux
Easterfield
Plymouth
Les Coteaux
Courland Pt.
Adventure
Franklyn's
Mason Hall
Concordia
Belmont
Great Courland Bay
Courland
Plymouth Rd.
The Whim
St. George
Adelphi
Black Rock
Lower Quarter or Roselle
Mary's Hill
Providence
Northside Rd.
Providence Rd.
Mesopotamia
Mt. Irvine or Little Courland Bay
Grange
Orange
Orange Hill Rd.
Calder Hall
Friendsfield
Mount St. George
Booby Pt.
Buccoo
Bethel
Patience Hill
Lower Town
Morne Quiton
Hillsbor. Bay
Buccoo Coral Reef
Buccoo Bay
Buccoo Rd.
Prospect
St. Andrew
Scarborough
Bacolet
Minister Bay
Minister Pt.
Bon Accord Lagoon
Golden Grove
Carnbee Village
Diamond
Lambeau
Rockly Bay
Bacolet Pt.
Milford or Sandy Bay
Bon Accord Village
Canaan
St. Patrick
Shirvan
Auchenskloch
Little Rockly Bay
Mt. Pleasant
Tyson Hall
Kilgwyn
Brown's or Crown's Pt.
Robinson Crusoe's Cave
Friendship
Canoe Bay
Cove
Columbus or Kennedy's Pt.

S   e   a

North Pt.

Corvo Pt.

Charlotteville   Starwood

Man of War Bay   St. John

Cambleton   Belmont

Hermitage

Anse Fourmi   ⑨

Bloody
Bay

Parlatuvier   Bloody Bay   Tyrell's
Bay

Parlatuvier Bay   St. John   Speyside

lishman's
Bay   Parrot Hall   Trois Rivieres

shman's   Roxborough Parlatuvier Rd.   Windward Rd.

Tobago Forest Reserve   King's Bay   Merchiston

St. Paul   ⑩

Delaford

King's
Bay   Shore Park

Roxborough   Pedro Pt.

Louis D'or

Morne D'or   Pulteney Hill   Kendal Place

Prince's
Bay

⑪

St. Mary   Carapuse Bay

The Lure   Cardiff   Belle Garden

Hillsborough   Pembroke   Glamorgan   Richmond I.   A t l a n t i c   O c e a n

Windsor   Goldsborough

en Hill   Goldsborough Bay

Goodwood

Montrose

Studley Park

Windward Rd.

arbados Bay

Ganby Pt.   A t l a n t i c   O c e a n

St. Giles or
Melville Islands

Charlotteville   Starwood

Belmont

Cambleton

Goat I.   Little Tobago
or Bird of
Paradise Island

Speyside   Tyrell's
Bay

EXPLORING TRINIDAD AND TOBAGO

Trinidad and **Tobago** are like one of those married couples one sometimes meets who are different enough from one another as to be almost incompatible, but who in successfully joining opposing qualities create a dynamic union. Within these two tropical islands that make up the Republic are the cosmopolitan enticements of one of the most sophisticated cities in the Caribbean, the serenity of a pastoral island virtually untouched by internal tourism, the exuberant bacchanalia of Carnival, the quiet of deserted beaches, the wildlife of a South American jungle, the beauties of a Caribbean coral reef, a tumultuous history, and a wealthy and literate present. In short, there is the worldliness, ethnicity and industry of the big island of Trinidad, and the friendliness, languor and natural beauty of much smaller Tobago.

Combined, the southernmost islands in the Lesser Antilles are about the size of the state of Delaware, lying only seven miles (11 km) from the coastal plains of Venezuela. Unlike other Caribbean islands, Trinidad and Tobago are not the remnants of ancient volcanoes or coral reefs, but rather the serendipitous result of a gradual and gentle breech between South America and a small, mountainous region on her northeastern coast. This geological fact creates a sea of difference between these two islands and those further north, and a geography, flora and fauna as multiform as that of the great continent of the south.

Trinidad, with over one and a half million inhabitants, is almost 50 miles (80 km) long by 40 (64 km) wide, encompasses a high level rain forest with over 450 species of birds, two swamps, miles and miles of rich farmland and both Atlantic and Caribbean coastlines. Tobago, only 26 miles (41 km) long by three miles (four km) wide, is a more typically Caribbean paradise, a hump of lush mountain greenery surrounded by miles of deserted white beach.

International occupation: Since their European discovery by Columbus in 1498, Trinidad and Tobago have been fought over by Spain, England, France and Holland. Slaves, laborers and immigrants have come in large numbers from Africa, India and the Middle East, and town names on both islands are a multi-lingual Babylon: Diego Martin, San Souci, Auchenskloch, Barrackpore, Courland, Waterloo and Sadhoowa.

The islands were under Spanish control for almost 300 years, but Tobago was neglected almost entirely by the Spaniards, allowing a series of British, Dutch, and Latvian settlements to grow up and be wiped out by native tribes and disease. Governed separately until the latter half of the 19th century, Tobago was ripe for plantation schemes of other governments, which the Spanish permitted through benign neglect. Trinidad, however, was originally viewed as a source for Amerindian slaves, and as a starting point in the famous search for the gold of El Dorado, and thus was guarded rather more fiercely than her neighboring island.

The Amerindians proved intractable, wily adversaries, and anyway were fatally prone to smallpox; El Dorado remained a distant chimera but, having set up a capital at the inland site of St. Joseph in 1592, the Spanish settled down to wrest whatever riches they could from the cultivation of tobacco and cocoa.

By 1757 plagues had decimated the population of St. Joseph and the new Spanish governor forced a move to a seacoast spot, more accessible and less vulnerable to jungle incursions. **Port of Spain** grew slowly at first, and then more quickly as various settlers arrived, first among them Catholic missionaries sent in the 17th century to civilize the Indians.

Tobacco export met stiff competition from producers up north; cocoa, the next money-maker, fell prey to disease. In 1776, in an effort to realize more of the country's agricultural potential, Spain offered land grants and tax incentives to Roman Catholic settlers who would come to the islands. Consequently, an influx of French planters, largely from French-controlled Caribbean islands, flowed into the country. The French prospered, and by the close of the century they occupied positions of power in government, and spread their patois and customs throughout the land.

In 1797, when Spain declared war on Britain during the Napoleonic Wars, the British sent a fleet to Trinidad. Spain, with bigger things on her mind at home, sent little help, and the Spanish Trinidadians, besieged on both sides by slave uprisings and British war ships, lost to the Brits. Tobago came under official British control in 1815, and was made a ward of Trinidad in 1897.

Remnants of wealth: All the strands of Trinidad and Tobago's multicolored fabric are tangled in a knot in her capital city, Port of Spain. Gingerbread houses and 10-story office buildings stand shoulder-to-shoulder with ramshackle curbside stalls and decaying clapboard storefronts. Twisting lanes lead to neatly designed parks and squares, and tell the story of years of colonial existence recently overlaid with independence and a new source of wealth.

During the oil boom of the 70s, Trinidad, with her offshore petroleum supplies, became the wealthiest nation in the Caribbean (excluding those tax havens such as the Cayman Islands). It was like the Roaring 70s for Trinidad, as suddenly everyone was able to afford a new car every year (giving the old one to the maid, it was said), trips back and forth to Miami and New York, fashionable clothes and other accoutrements of national wealth. Literacy rose to over 90 percent, roads were built, water and electric lines laid, and much of the grinding poverty that characterizes so many West Indian nations was virtually eradicated.

But by the mid-80s the coffers were almost empty, and the challenge of the 90s will surely be to stabilize the economy and ensure conservative management of the country's natural resources. In December 1986, A.N.R. Robinson was elected Prime Minister, the first non-People's National Movement candidate to win since independence in 1956.

On the brighter side, Trinidad and Tobago's wealth has allowed her to eschew tourism as a primary source of national income. The Republic has made a concerted effort to consolidate its culture without the constant intrusion of Europe and the United States, and it was only in the last few years that the government felt ready to actively promote Trinidad as a tourist destination.

Port of Spain's central downtown area, spreading east from the docks toward the foothills of the **Northern Range**, is hot, noisy, dusty and crowded with traffic during the day. Calypso tunes blare from storefronts, while "limers" congregate on street corners and bar stoops and admire the passing trade.

Rags to riches: Woodford Square is in some ways the heart of downtown, surrounded as it is by the seat of Parliament, **(the Red House); the Town Hall; the Public Library**; and **Trinity Church**, the main Anglican cathedral built in 1816 by English Governor Ralph Woodford. Over the years Port of Spain has been a meeting place for various community activists, from a 1903 water rates riot in which the original Red House was burnt to the ground, to the independence movement in the 1950s, led by the former Prime Minister. (1956-1981) Eric Williams, a local boy who made good.

Through scholarships he was able to attend the Queen's Royal College High School, the most prestigious in the country, and from there won an Island Scholarship, a traditional stepping stone toward greater success, which sent him to Oxford University. For awhile he taught at Howard University, where he refined his then-radical politics.

Returning home in 1948, Williams began to give lectures under the auspices of the Teachers Educational and Cultural Association, delivered in Woodford Square in front of the **Public Library**. His eloquence and scholarship attracted scholars, politicians and plain people, and he began to build the widespread support which eventually catapulted him into the Prime Minister's office. Leading the fight for independence from Britain in 1955, he helped form the People's National Movement party. This "black people's party" was to remain in power for 30 years.

South down Frederick Street is **Independence Square**, another focal point for city activity. This long dusty avenue has none of Woodford Square's charm; it is in fact merely two lanes of traffic divided by a wide paved median, and business rather than politics is the order of the day. Here route taxis, which ply definite paths around the city and environs, come to pick up passengers at the beginning of their runs, and create exuberant traffic jams and noise. Governor Woodford's contribution to this nerve center is the **Roman Catholic Cathedral of the Immaculate Conception**, built between 1816 and 1832 from blue metal stone found in local quarries.

Anchoring the northern end of Frederick Street is **Memorial Park**, across from the **National Museum** and **Art Gallery**. Beyond, perhaps the true heart of the city, are the wide, flat grounds of the **Queen's Park Savannah**.

Organized fete: The **Savannah**, about three miles' circumference, has a central horse race course. In January, February, June, July, September and October the Trinidad Turf Club holds a series of races which attract bettors from all over the country. The large open arena on the southern end of the Savannah is called the **Grandstands**, and is the scene for much public entertainment in the Port of Spain, most notably the various events of Carnival in late February/early March.

Not merely a drunken bacchanal (though certainly that), Carnival in Trinidad and Tobago is a forum for all the best in the Trini spirit. Musicians and performers, dancers and designers, all races, ages and religious and ethnic backgrounds join in a nationwide, three day celebration of the carnal pleasures of life.

The French settlers who came in the 18th century brought with them the tradition of celebrating the period between Christmas and Lent with various festivities. While they held fancy masquerade balls in estate houses, their slaves were permitted to celebrate a combination of the customs of their masters and traditions brought from West Africa. They danced in makeshift costumes that lampooned the activities of their masters and revelled in the streets in bands of stick fighters called "*batonniers*."

After the Caribbean slaves were freed in 1832, the Carnival processions became a vehicle for their protests against economic and political situations. The French element of Trinidadian society protected the ex-slaves' right to convene because they saw the British government then in power as inimical to Frenchmen's rights as well. Through this unlikely alliance Carnival was preserved, and eventually spread to include Hindus, Moslems, Christians, Middle Easterners and Orientals as well as whites and blacks.

Carnival is an organized "fete," with clubs around the country planning the themes and costumes for their "band" all year long. Each band has a King and a Queen, who wear costumes that will be displayed in the King and Queen of Carnival competitions at the Savannah. These costumes are frequently as much as 12 feet (four meters) tall, and require small wheels placed strategically around the perimeter to support and balance their weight. The rest of the 500 to 2,000 club members dress in simpler variations on the theme. Recent themes have included "Rat Race," "Sombrero," and "R & R in Rio."

On the Monday and Tuesday before Ash Wednesday, bands parade through the streets of Port of Spain—for spectators and judges to evaluate—drinking and dancing for up to six hours a day. Each section is led by huge flatbed trucks filled with musicians, who play a series of that year's calypsoes at earsplitting volume while revelers sing along at the top of their lungs. When bands cross paths, each truckload tries to outplay the other, and eventually these little battles help decide the winner of the "People's Choice Calypso" for the year.

But the two days of procession are only the culmination of Carnival. Four to six weeks prior to this, steelbands and calyp-

Hindu cremation site.

sonians perform their latest songs in practice yards and calypso "tents" (actually buildings nowadays) across the city, in formal and informal shows. For that matter, bands have been working on their costumes since the end of last year's Carnival. By the week before Carnival, everyone has chosen his favorite to root for during the semi-final events that go on nightly at the Savannah grandstand. All Tuesday afternoon, each band parades across the stage to be judged in the final formal event of Carnival. Parties then celebrate the last hours of bacchanal, ending promptly at midnight.

Innovative music: At the north end of the Savannah are the **Botanic Gardens**, the oldest in the western hemisphere and the **Emperor Valley Zoo**. The Botanic Gardens include specimens indigenous and foreign, as does the Zoo. Also in the Botanic Gardens is the house of the President and Prime Minister, best seen from the nearby balconies of the Hilton Hotel.

Across from the park on **Maraval Road** are the extravagant buildings known as the **Magnificent Seven**. These mansions, built between 1904 and 1906 by various wealthy landowning families, are remarkable for their diversity of architectural style, including a copy of Balmoral Castle in Scotland, a Venetian Palazzo, and a marvel of Victorian fretwork—a German Renaissance behemoth. Unfortunately, they are not well kept.

Immediately southwest of downtown are the mythic lanes of **Laventille**, whose history is inextricable from the growth of carnival, calypso and steel-band. A tough, lower-class black neighborhood, the houses of Laventille perch on the edges of ravines and hillsides, so that in places the roadbed rises above the rooftops. Here the first steelbands are said to have begun, growing out of the gangs of young stickfighting toughs like the Desperadoes, a renowned steelband who still practice in a yard on **Upper Laventille Road**. Some say that it was in Laventille that the first steeldrum itself was fashioned.

Slaves imported from West Africa had always relied on percussion of various sorts to be a part of any celebration or gathering. In the 20th century, this need was satisfied, during marches, rallies, carnival and other gatherings, by beating on bottles, tin cans and the other effluvia of modern society. Eventually, people realized that if steel containers were pounded to various thickness and shaped, definite notes could be produced. Gradually, the bands grew from various individuals beating a "pan" that

Port of Spain racing stables.

hung around their necks to highly organized orchestras capable of playing the Beatles, Beethoven and calypso.

North of Laventille is Port of Spain's first suburb, **Belmont**, a former sugar cane estate (like many areas of the city), given to freed slaves to settle in the 19th century. A maze of twisting streets and close-built houses, Belmont retains the feeling of a village in many ways. It has more churches, schools and lanes than any other area of the city.

After the slaves were freed, cheap labor was in scarce supply. So East Indians, who had little chance of advancement at home, were encouraged to come over as indentured laborers. A number settled in **St. James**, naming their streets Calcutta, Bombay, Madras and so forth.

Here the East Indian festival of Hosein, marking the anniversary of the massacre of the grandsons of Mohammed, is celebrated with tassa drumming and paper mache replicas of the brother's tombs. These confections, covered in bright paper and tiny mirrors, are carried through the streets by devotees for three nights, followed by the drummers and onlookers. On the final night of celebration, huge six foot or larger versions are brought out, and carried in a final procession to the sea, where they are ceremoniously dipped in the water.

Naturalists paradise: While the Port of Spain is the administrative and tourist hub of Trinidad, much of the country's character and wealth emanate from her provincial towns, industries and countryside. It would be difficult to form a true picture of Trinidad without visiting the rest of the island: the sharp cliffs of the north coast, the flat, palm-fringed beaches of the east, the **Caroni Swamp** where Scarlet Ibises nest, the mountain rain forests that are home to hundreds of bird species, **Pitch Lake**, and the oil and sugar-cane fields of the south.

On weekends, Port of Spain residents often go to the beaches of the North Coast, taking the **Saddle Road** through the residential suburb of **Maraval** to the **North Coast Road. Maracas and Las Cuevas** beaches are long, wide and beautiful, and only a half hour or so from downtown. Carloads of friends go up for the day bringing coolers full of beer and rum punch and casseroles of *pelau*. They buy fresh fruit and *roti* (the spicy curried meat or vegetables rolled in an Indian pancake) from the stands that line the highway above the beaches.

The North Coast Road continues along a beautiful shore, with rocky, palm-fringed coves, half-hidden vacation houses and rural villages. Just past the Creole village of **Blanchisseuse** is a turnoff into the mountains that leads to the **Asa Wright Nature Centre**, a Victorian estate house now serving as headquarters and inn for visiting naturalists.

Because Trinidad and Tobago used to be a part of the South American mainland, their flora and fauna have a continental diversity. In the rain forests of the Northern Range are over 400 species of birds and even more butterflies, a concentration unequaled in any area its size in the western hemisphere. Amateur naturalists can enjoy the rustic 19th century charm of the **Great House** rooms, and have tea or rum punch on a screened porch that hangs over a rain forest of declivity.

Guides lead hikes into the surrounding forest to see examples of the rare nocturnal oilbird, or *guacharo,* a cave-dwelling species whose most accessible colony in the world is near Asa Wright. The young oilbirds are about one and one-half times the size of their elders, and South American Indians used to capture the adolescent birds and render them down for their copious fat, used for lamps and torches. Other birds to be seen are white-bearded manakins, swallow-tailed kites, pouis, various hummingbirds, piping guans, channel-billed toucans, honey-creepers and tanagers. Asa Wright can also arrange bird-watching trips to the Arip Savannah to see macaws, cuckoos, flycatchers, and yellow-rumped caciques, or to the Heights of Aripo, where blue-capped tanagers, yellow-legged thrushes, and orange-billed nightingale thrushes live above 1,980 feet (600 meters).

The drive back to Port of Spain through the mountains to Arima passes small roadside waterfalls, groves of bamboo, bromeliads, heliconias, or, in August, the blooming cahconia, Trinidad and Tobago's national flower. As the road twists and turns down the mountain, the sliding-roofed drying houses of cocoa and coffee estates can be seen in small clearings. Here the beans are spread out to sun dry, but during the sudden squalls so typical of the area the roof can be quickly rolled back into place.

Two of the most spectacular and visible trees in the forest are the immortelle and the poui. The towering immortelle was imported to the country in the 18th century to shade low-growing cocoa and coffee bushes, and its dark green leaves and rusty orange flowers can be seen in every hilly or mountainous area of the country, sticking out above the forest canopy. The poui is indigenous, and its flowering in early March/late April is said to herald the coming of the dry season. At this time the leaves drop, leaving only the multitudinous lovely blooms of pink and yellow.

Between Arima and Port of Spain are the **University of the West Indies at St. Augustine** and the **Monastery of Mount St. Benedict**. The monastery is situated on a high hillside overlooking the **Caroni Plain** and the **Piarco Savannah**, and is a nice place to have tea and watch the sun set out at sea. The old capital of **St. Joseph** is just west of St. Augustine. There is little of interest there now save the **Jinnah Memorial Mosque**, a white confection of classical Arabic design.

The far northeastern corner of Trinidad has a wilder geography and more isolated population than the closer north. Here the spectacular beaches of Toco, Balandra and Salybia provide good surf and tremendous swimming. In a few villages, some still speak a French patois and tend to preserve the older, more rural ways of life, farming and fishing.

Mystical South: The Caroni Swamp, south of Port of Spain, is both brackish and tidal, and supports a diverse population of land and sea animals. The 15,000-acre (6,100 hectare) nature preserve is the home of the elusive scarlet ibis. These vivid red, flamingo-like birds are rarely seen during daylight hours, and are presumed to fly to the South American coast to feed and nest. At sunset they return to the swamp in huge squadrons to roost in the tops of the dark green mangrove trees. Guides are available for boat trips through the twisting canals of the mangrove-choked waterways, and can point out some of the other avian species as well.

Further south down the **Uriah Butler Highway** and the **Southern Main Road** is **Chaguanas**, Trinidad's third largest city and the former home of novelists Shiva and Vidiadhar S. Naipaul. Beyond is hilly **San Fernando**, the second largest city, a largely East Indian town serving as a focal point for the farmers and industries of the south. Though central to the economic and political life of the country, the oil refineries and industrial developments of the southwestern coast are none too lovely, raring their stark heads out of the pleasant green fields and calm tropical waters. There has been considerable pollution from these industries, and one of A.N.R. Robinson's main stated programs is an environmental clean-up that will start at the grass roots.

The older business of sugar-cane refining is also important in this area, and at one of

A country road outside Charlotteville.

the factories, **Brechin Castle**, tours are available to interested visitors.

On the southwestern promontory of Trinidad are the **La Brea Tar Pits**, a natural 100-acre (40 hectares) lake of pitch said to be hundreds of feet deep at the center and a million years old. The bitumen from the pits paves roads the world over, and was first used for industrial purpose by Sir Walter Raleigh, who stopped to caulk his ships on one of his 16th century searches for El Dorado. One can actually walk on the "lake" in flat shoes. Amerindian artifacts and bits of fossilized sea shell found trapped in pockets of the tar are on view at the small museum next to the lake.

All the way down to the southernmost coast is the town of **Moruga**, where Columbus was said to have first landed. In August Discovery Day celebrations are held here, with a costumed reenactment of his landing and meeting with aboriginal peoples. Now Moruga is known as a Baptist town, where *obeah* men and women will concoct potions and spells to cure illnesses, jinx enemies or unite lovers. The beach at Moruga is also notable because at low tide the ocean recedes 1.5 miles, stranding fishing boats and other debris in the wet sand.

The Atlantic coast on the southeastern side of Trinidad provides a similarly breathtaking, yet different kind of seascape beauty. Taking the Eastern Main Road through **Sangre Grande**, then to **Rio Claro** and **Plaisance**, one passes through the sugar cane fields of the Caroni Plains. Here beast of burden like buffalypsoes, the local bovine, drag homemade wooden carts filled with harvested cane, while their masters walk alongside encouraging them with switches.

This area is heavily Hindu, and Hindu homes are identifiable by the thicket of bamboo poles stuck in corners of the yards. The various flags attached signal the presence of a marriageable daughter, or mark a death, a holiday, a *puja*, or offering, or any number of events of daily life.

At Rio Claro, one crosses bridges over the **Ortoire River**, where alligators and anaconda snakes live, and then passes through acres and acres of coconut groves. Between **Rushville**, where the beach begins, and **Upper Manzanilla** is over 40 miles (64 km) of beach edged by cocals, or coconut estates. Sometimes the alternating currents of the Caribbean and Atlantic create crisscrossing surf.

Tobago: In Tobago, land life proceeds at a rural pace. Tobagonians go to Port of

Ice cream vendor.

Spain for excitement and jobs, but usually return to the island home they consider paradise. The island is a constant feast for the eyes. Interior roads are usually only 15 or so minutes from glimpses of the sea, and a route through the mountainous interior passes stands of enormous creaking bamboo and dense jungle growth before suddenly giving way to vistas of sparkling white palmy beach, or open pastures grazed by placid cattle and scruffy goats.

The fish-shaped island is circumnavigated by two main coastal roads, but the "head" and "tail" are beyond the reach of this oval, and north of Charlotteville are only paths. Any point on the island is reachable in a few hours' drive at most.

One of the few traditionally touristic spots on the island is the **Buccoo reef**, a small offshore coral fringe much destroyed by pollution, boats and thoughtless tourists and locals. About 15 minutes offshore of **Store Bay** (an Anglicized version of the name of its first settler) the reef lies out beyond the Nylon Pool, an offshore sand bar whose thigh-high pale waters and pristine sand provide a sybaritic bathe. Buccoo Reef is a good example of the cons of *laissez-faire* tourism. While on the one hand it leaves Tobago unmarked by the crowds and Americanization of international tourism, on the other hand no one actively enforces environmental laws that might protect the reef and thus, ironically, create a bigger tourist attraction. The Marine Preservation Act is poorly enforced, and it is only the harder-to-reach areas of this reef and those off the northeast coast that offer attraction enough for the serious diver.

On the way back from Buccoo, the boat may stop at **Pigeon Point** to let off passengers. The beach, pictured in many of Tobago's enticing travel ads, has intense aqua waters, graceful palms and a picturesque thatched-roof dock. But don't get off here unless you want to pay for a taxi back, because it's a half-hour's walk to Store Bay.

Like Buccoo, Pigeon Point is a tourist's necessity, so avoid it during weekends when it is likely to be crowded with denizens of offshore cruise ships. The only private beach on Tobago has a reasonable entrance fee, and the idyllic stretch of beach is bordered by groves of palms where cattle graze the soft green grass like a scene from a Rousseau painting.

Labor shortages: All over the island are many areas reserved for grazing cattle. Until the 1960s these were generally private cocoa estates, then scarce and expensive labor

A typical carnival.

made them economically non-viable. A recurring theme in Tobago's history since European colonization has been the problem of labor. In the mid-18th century, when sugar, rum and cotton were all farmed here on a relatively large scale, the slave to white ratio was so high (20:1) that slave uprisings were practically a matter of course. And a century later, after Emancipation, labor again became scarce, prompting the creation of the "*metairie*," or sharecropping system. This arrangement permitted laborers to farm a small portion of the estates they worked—a land for labor agreement. But within 20 years, when a hurricane destroyed many crops and the estate owners were in financial straits, the metairie system fell apart and labor riots broke out again. These uprisings broke the independent spirits of the planters and led them to agree to becoming a Crown Colony, the first step toward federation with Trinidad.

Natural wildlife: The **Shirvan Road**, leading eastward from Buccoo, is quietly pretty, running near the water through pale green groves of palm and banana. Shirvan turns into the **Grafton Road**, with **the Mount Irvine Bay Hotel** marked by the neatly clipped greens and towering palms of its famed golf course. Mt. Irvine is built on the site of an old sugar plantation, with its restaurant built around the old stone sugar mill. The public beach is next to the site of the estate sugar depot, where ships once deposited their ballast of slate and brick in exchange for sugar, and later, cocoa, cultivated on the estate.

The **Museum of Tobago History** is also on the hotel grounds. A one-room display area contains shells, pre-Columbian and European tools, buttons and tableware from pirate shops and colonials, potshards and a host of other archaeological finds from all eras of Tobago's history.

At the hotel beach one can rent windsurfers, and at the public beach just northeast are changing rooms, showers, and an informal bar and restaurant serving local food. For a really secluded beach, walk northeast down the main highway to a rusted, rickety gate leading into a palm grove. Cross the grove to the sea, and climb down the low cliff to deserted **Back Bay**.

Continuing toward Plymouth, take the shore road along **Grafton Beach**. The long wide beach is usually deserted, and off the road before the hamlet of Black Rock is a dirt driveway leading to the old **Grafton Estate**. When Hurricane Flora struck in 1963, the natural habitats of many island birds

A boatload of goats, Port of Spain.

were destroyed. So Eleanor Alefounder, a former owner of the Grafton Estate, began to provide food and roosts. The pheasant-like cocrico and midnight blue mot-mot, two of the three national birds, were daily visitors, as were tanagers, woodpeckers and other local species. Since Mrs. Alefounder's death the house itself has fallen into disrepair and feedings are no longer regular, but a brief visit may provide sightings.

Northeast of Black Rock is **Great Courland Bay**, once the site of an early settlement of Latvians and now famous for the immense sea turtles which lumber onto the beach at night between March and July to lay their eggs. The turtles, which can grow up to seven feet long, appear unperturbed by human observation. The Trinidad and Tobago Field Naturalists Club organizes nightly trips during the season.

In the residential village of **Plymouth**, **Fort James** stands guard over Great Courland Bay. Built by the British in 1768 as a barracks, it is now used as a storage shed, though the building remnants and grounds are well-kept by the Tourist Board. In the courtyard of a small stone church on the approach road is the mysterious tombstone, so-called because of its cryptic inscription:

"She was a mother without knowing it and a wife without letting her husband know it except by her kind indulgences to him.— Betty Stiven 1783."

Blue waters and pothole roads: The gently curving road out of Plymouth leads inland for a few miles, with the **Arnos Vale Hotel** entrance on the left. Terraced along a small hillside with winding paths through botanical plantings, Arnos Vale offers some of the best snorkeling and birdwatching on Tobago.

Past Arnos Vale, the road continues to curve upwards through rolling countryside planted with the short, leafy banana palms. A half mile or so past the hotel on the right is "Franklyn's Road," and just after the turn onto this bumpy terrace, on the right practically hidden by thick undergrowth, is the original Arnos Vale water wheel, a good example of the colonial structures which used to provide power for estates.

The Arnos Vale Road continues through low, dry hills reminiscent of Africa, past the ubiquitous tethered livestock and tiny crossroads towns where crowing roosters and friendly residents make every day seem like Sunday. The small fishing villages and perfect beaches of **Castara** and **Parlatuvier** provide some of the most spectacular

A small disco.

views and stunning beaches on the island.

Especially on the beach at Castara, one might imagine oneself on the Amalfi Coast, with sharp, dark green cliffs enclosing the town and bay, and deep blue water glittering like diamonds. Like most of the north coast towns, Castara is a fishing village, and most of the 500 or so residents support themselves by a combination of fishing, farming and "government work" (road repair). It is a Tobago conundrum that a great number of island men work on the roads, yet aside from a few main thoroughfares, most are deeply potholed and quite a number in the farther reaches simply don't exist or are not passable. In fact, the north coast road ends unexpectedly about a half mile past Parlatuvier.

There are a number of overland routes to the south side. The **Parlatuvier-Roxborough road** is wide, smooth, and lovely, only a half hour's drive. Another route is via the **Hillsborough Dam** in the heart of the **Tobago Forest Reserve**. This route, through what was for years huge cocoa and coffee estates, takes a few hours, as much of it is on bad dirt roads. Best not to go after a rain storm.

The huge iron pots in some yards along the way were used for boiling sugar, and the neighborhood dogs who were permitted to lick them clean were thus dubbed "pot hounds." Now they are somewhat of a plague in places, serving primarily as objects of misplaced aggression: even small children like to kick and tease them.

The dam is a good place from which to begin a hike or hunt, but don't set out without a guide who knows the area well. Check with the local game warden for guides and hunting permits.

Breathtaking sunset: The interior on the west side of the island, between Plymouth and Scarborough, is more populated and less wild. Near **Patience Hill** is the **National Fine Arts Center**, which houses a permanent collection of old maps and changing exhibitions of local talent.

Scarborough is Tobago's largest and most important town, a market center and port where 17,000 of the island's 40,000 inhabitants live. Compared to some of the more European cities in the Caribbean, Scarborough is ramshackle and provincial with few remnants of a grander age.

The library offers a periodical section with a wide selection of Caribbean magazines and newspapers and the Caribbean book section contains many books on Trinidad and Tobago, some impossible to find elsewhere, as well as copies of all

A farmer's house in Tobago.

monographs and books written by T & Ters on Tobago. **Fort King George**, high above the town, was built by the English in 1779 to protect the town, and later captured by the French. Like Tobago, it changed hands a number of times and now lies in partial ruin above the hospital, surrounded by palms, ferns and green lawns. The views, particularly at sunset, are breathtaking.

The **Windward Road** east of Scarborough passes endless stretches of deserted beach. Just outside the city is **Bacolet Beach**, a long, rough, beautiful crescent used for the setting of the movie-version of "The Swiss Family Robinson." Beyond Bacolet, the **Windward Road** curves to and from the shoreline, offering glimpses of long misty beaches beyond coconut groves and watery estuaries.

Rural life: After Hillsborough Bay the terrain gradually becomes hillier and the road climbs. Here Tobago is more the tiny rural island and less the idyllic vacation retreat. There are only a few lodging places up this end, and all are small and unassuming. Village life reigns supreme here. The roads are traversed by strong Tobago women, renowned for their broad shoulders and ample girth. These women are almost always seen with bundles on their heads or umbrellas unfurled against the sun and passing showers.

The ubiquitous schoolchildren are sassier here, and boys may shout unintelligible but highly amusing remarks to the passer-by. In time-honored Tobago (and African) tradition, these light-hearted verbal assaults are meant as amusement. Though the "picong" may make the visitor feel slightly uncomfortable, generally it is not meant to be taken seriously.

Just outside the hamlet of **Belle Garden**, keep an eye out for the wooden sign to **Richmond Great House**. One of the many old estate homes, Richmond is one of the few to have been restored. The square whitewashed brick house sits atop a knoll overlooking rolling land to the sea, with mountains behind and jungle as far as the eye can see. The unassuming house has lodgings for a limited number of overnight guests.

Continue on to the village of **Delaford**, and right outside, look for a sandy parking lot on the left side of the road. This is the entrance to the **King's Bay Waterfall**. The highest in the Republic (100 feet/33 meters high), the falls are fed by rain and stream water from the mountains, and are full during the rainy season.

Ramshackle house near Les Coteaux.

Back down the main road a bit is the **King's Bay Depot Road**, leading to **King's Bay Beach**. This sheltered bay has deep grey sand and a soft pebbly bottom. Enclosed by the jungle-covered hills, King's Bay seems cooler and wilder than more westerly beaches.

Home for endangered birds: After King's Bay, the Windward Road turns inland until **Speyside**, the jumping off point for trips to Bird of Paradise Island. This small, almost barren little island a mile or so off the coast is the only place in the western hemisphere where the Bird of Paradise can be seen. Indigenous to New Guinea, they were imported here at the beginning of the 20th century, when a former owner of the island learned about the danger posed to the birds by trade in their gorgeous feathers. Forty-eight birds were brought to Little Tobago, as the island is sometimes called, and lived and bred there happily until Hurricane Flora. It is unclear how many birds reside there now. Local boatmen are always waiting on the beach to convey bird watchers to the islands. You might want to check with the Game Warden about the bird count, though the boatmen will all tell you there are plenty to be seen. It's a 20-minute ride to any of the three offshore islands.

Between Speyside and Charlotteville the road winds across the mountains through dense, wet, deep green jungle. Curving and mountainous, it can be treacherous during sudden heavy downpours, and though it is only about four miles between the two towns, the drive takes a good half hour. Midway is a scenic vista from a metal lookout tower placed at Tobago's highest point. **Bird of Paradise Island** is visible across forest and water.

Charlotteville is the most picturesque of many towns on Tobago. Isolated by the mountain to the south and the impassable road to the west, it sleeps undisturbed on sharp, steep cliffs above a deep blue bay. Some of the best fishing and scuba diving can be found offshore.

Though the road to the north side is impassable after a few miles, it is worth a short drive into this almost primeval forest. Everything is covered in a luxuriant carpet of soft green vegetation, with orchids and bromeliads growing from trees, guy wires, telephone poles or anything else that provides a small foothold. The noisy, ceaseless chirping of tree frogs and the small romantic waterfalls edging the roadside here and there combine to create a misty-terrarium-like atmosphere.

View of King Peter's Bay.

EXPLORING THE ABC ISLANDS

Back in the early 17th century Dutch naval officers cruising the far reaches of the Caribbean decided that the island of **Curaçao**, off the coast of Venezuela, would make an excellent headquarters for looking after their interests in the region. As was the custom in those days, they quietly landed a few hundred soldiers and informed the handful of Spanish settlers and Indians that the island was henceforth under new management. The Dutch did not get much resistance and they went on to develop Curaçao into one of the most prosperous islands in the Caribbean.

A little later, more for the sake of protecting Curaçao from some future adventurous task force than anything else, the Dutch took over the neighboring islands of **Aruba**, 50 miles (80 km) to the northwest, and **Bonaire**, 20 miles (32 km) to the east.

The three islands, sometimes referred to as the ABC islands because of their first initials, were blessed with neither rich mineral deposits nor lush foliage. But each has grown into something special in modern day West Indies.

Curaçao, the largest of the islands with 160,000 people and 171 square miles (444 square km) of land shaped like the arched wings of a great sea bird, is as cosmopolitan a place as you'll find in the Caribbean. Its main town, Willemstad, is a miniature Amsterdam, thriving on international banking, shipping and oil refining. It has a number of small, beautiful beaches and good waters for snorkeling and scuba diving.

The sister island of Aruba was luckier when it came to the kind of long, wide stretches of blanched sand that travelers seem to regard as great beaches. The curving west coast of Aruba, known as Palm Beach, is the quintessence of that dream beach. It is lined with a dozen or so resort hotels and the casino is a magnet that causes Aruba to dwarf Curaçao and Bonaire in tourism. That glorious beach, and neighboring **Eagle Beach**, also dotted with resorts, became even more important to Aruba after its big Exxon oil refinery shut down in early 1985.

Bonaire, the least developed of the three islands, has gained a sterling reputation among scuba divers, and bird watchers know it as one of the world's largest breeding grounds for flamingoes. The boomerang-shaped island, which covers 112 square miles (291 square km), is a third larger than Aruba. But it is the least populated of the islands, with about 9,000 residents compared to 60,000 in Aruba. The three islands are connected by daily flights, but only Aruba and Curaçao have international airports capable of handling commercial passenger jets.

The ABCs are bathed by brisk northeasterly trade winds which keep temperatures in the low 80s during the day and sometimes cool enough in the evenings to warrant a sweater or a light jacket. The skies seldom darken with rain clouds, which is not as great as you might think. In order to get drinking water, the islanders have had to build desalination plants that take the salt out of sea water. The landscapes of the islands are more what you'd expect to find in Arizona than in the tropics: vast stretches of parched soil and boulders with legions of candelabra cactus and scrawny, gnarled local trees called divi-divis that rise in a crouch on the barren land, bent by the gusty trade winds like troubled prairie witches, their fine leaves shot forward in scraggly cone-shaped coifs.

Nearly everyone in the three islands can read and write at least one language and many people are fluent in Dutch, English and Spanish. The mother tongue of everyone in the ABC islands is Papiamento, a creole that is believed to have originated among Portuguese and Dutch slave traders and their African slaves. It was derived from Dutch, Portuguese, English, Spanish and several African languages.

The islands have had a long history of good and close relations with the United States and with Venezuela, which is 15 miles (24 km) from Aruba, 36 miles (57 km) from Curaçao and 48 miles (76 km) from Bonaire. The islands supported Simon Bolivar in his independence battles in South America. During World War II, Curaçao and Aruba were swarming with American soldiers, sailors and airmen sent to defend oil refineries that were vital to the war effort.

In 1950 the Antillian government built a rambling house with a roof of striking blue-black tiles on a bluff overlooking Willemstad and presented it to the United States as a residence for the chief of its diplomatic mission in the Dutch islands in gratitude for American military backing during the war. Seven years later, the federation of Dutch islands presented Venezuela with a mansion for its chief diplomat in appreciation for Venezuela's business, its cultural influence on Antillean society and its help in de-

Preceding pages: a swirl of Aruban gulls; a mountain of salt in Bonaire. Below, a moment's rest in midday Aruba.

veloping Curaçao's schools.

The Dutch had to fend off raids from the French and the British and for a few years in the early 1800s the islands fell briefly into the hands of the British. One of the bloodiest stains on the history of the islands was the Curaçao slave uprising of 1795, which the Dutch ended by overpowering the slaves and executing three of their leaders. Except for an outbreak of rioting in Curaçao in 1969 and a rash of protest marches in Aruba in 1985, the three islands have been politically and socially calm for most of this century.

From their base in Curaçao, the Dutch influenced the course of history in the Caribbean and enriched themselves at the same time with a simple, self-perpetuating scheme. They became leaders of the slave trade, then extended capital to finance the start-up and expansion of sugar cane plantations which could only be profitably operated with hordes of slave labor. They created a greater demand for slaves, reaped a healthy interest on their plantation loans and sometimes even brokered some of the sugar.

Instead of cutting loose their Caribbean colonies as the British did, the Dutch, like the French, incorporated them into the mother country, proclaiming in 1954 that they were equal, self-governing partners in the Kingdom of the Netherlands. The ABC islands and three other Dutch islands clustered east of Puerto Rico, which collectively make up the Netherlands Antilles, were permitted to establish a parliament in Curaçao for governing the federation. But they remained dependencies of the Hague, with the mother country responsible for their defense and many foreign policy matters and giving them about $70 million a year in aid and loans. The people of the Netherlands Antilles have full Dutch citizenship and carry Dutch passports.

In January 1986, Aruba was granted "separate status" by the Netherlands, making it separate but equal to what became known informally as the Netherland Antilles of the five. Aruba had been seeking separate status for years, complaining that it had been contributing a disproportionately large share to the central government of the islands and consistently seeing its wishes subordinated to those of Curaçao. Some political leaders in the Netherlands had been trying since the early 1970s to shed the colonial legacy and financial burden of the Netherland Antilles, but they had found the islanders uninterested in going it alone. One of the conditions the Dutch imposed in

Bridge into Willemstad, Curaçao.

permitting Aruba to sever its ties with the five other Antilles islands was that 10 years later, in 1996, Aruba would become fully independent. The Arubans say they hope they won't have to live up to that stipulation. "The whole thing behind separate status never was to get independence," said Milton E. Ponson, who was the president of Aruba's Chamber of Commerce as the island was preparing to break away from the other islands. The motive, he said, "was just to get our own position in the Kingdom separate from the Netherlands Antilles, where in fact we had been put in second place " by Curaçao's size and wealth."

One of the arguments the people in all six Dutch islands made against independence is that affiliation with the Netherlands shelters them from the give and take of international politics. Another, which they are not always so eager to concede, is that they get a great sense of security from the belief that if the islands get into serious financial trouble, the Netherlands will be there to bail them out.

Curaçao: Curaçao, which was briefly governed by Peter Stuyvesant before he went on to become the chief colonial executive in what later became known as New York, has had the most colorful history of all the Dutch islands and the most prosperous.

It does not lack for pleasurable diversions. But it has made its way as a serious place of business, which makes it more interesting than many other places in the Caribbean, but puts it somewhat at a disadvantage in a tourist world that adores sunbathing against a primitive backdrop.

Curaçao's main town, **Willemstad**, is a gem of 17th century European architecture, unique in the Caribbean and so cute and neat that it looks more like a stage set, like a corner of Disney World, than a real town. Tall angular buildings with curlicue gables, ornamented facades and steeply pitched roofs of red-orange tiles line cobblestone streets and one side of a long, bottleneck-shaped inlet leading into a big inland harbor. The colors are pastry shop earth tones of tangerine, lemon and chocolate, trimmed in white. This is no one's fancy or restoration, but an authentic working town that has somehow been kept beautifully intact for more than three centuries.

Forty-one years after the Dutch established their naval base on Curaçao, they declared the island a free port and began promoting trade throughout the region. Within a few years, the harbor master was recording departures of more than 100 ships a day. Curaçao became one of the main

Ramshackle house in Curaçao.

slave trading centers in the Caribbean. Banking flourished. It remained neutral during the American War of Independence and sold supplies to both sides. In 1778 the North American and West Indian Gazetteer noted that the island, with its thin dry soil, was so barren that it could not keep its inhabitants alive for 24 hours, but that, because of its voluminous trade, life was better there than anywhere else in the West Indies.

The end of slavery in the 1860s threw Curaçao into a tailspin which left it depressed for decades. But in the early 1900s oil was discovered in Venezuela and the riches embraced both Curaçao and Aruba. Because of sand banks, ocean-going tankers were unable to make their way from Lake Maracaibo in Venezuela's oil producing region into the Caribbean. So refineries were built on the two nearby islands. People from throughout the Caribbean went to work at the refineries. Aruba's refinery became a favorite work place for Grenadians and three of Grenada's prime ministers, Eric Gairy, Maurice Bishop and Herbert Blaize held jobs there in their youth. A drop in oil prices and consumption and a change in marketing strategies in the mid-1980s led to the closure of the Aruba refinery and a reduction in production at the Dutch Royal Shell refinery in Curaçao. But the Shell refinery remained an important element to Curaçao's economy. These days, while most Caribbean islands scrape by with per capita incomes of $1,500 and less, Curaçao is among the few islands where annual incomes average $5,000 and more.

In the late 1930s, as the threat of war from Germany was increasing, a Dutch lawyer started setting up companies in Curaçao as a place to move assets out of the Netherlands. Now there are thousands of so-called offshore companies in Curaçao, which in many cases consist of only a few pages of legal paper in a file, but serve as the vehicles for multi-million-dollar transactions. The management of these companies and banking, which often dovetails with them, has become a major industry in Curaçao. By incorporating in Curaçao, American corporations are able to borrow billions of dollars in Europe and avoid certain United States taxes. This has led to a long-running battle between Curaçao, which likes the arrangement, and the United States Treasury Department, which would like to put an end to it. Bankers in Curaçao say their profits were significantly reduced by certain measures taken in Washington in 1984.

Tugboat in the shadow of a mighty oceanliner.

Ship repair was one of the first businesses to get started in Curaçao shortly after the Dutch took control. The island's location and its natural deep water harbor, which made it a natural naval base and ideal for trading, were also just what the doctor ordered as a dry dock for vessels criss-crossing the Caribbean and working the coast of South America. Business slowed in the 1980s with the slump in the oil industry and a general decline in maritime shipping. But the Curaçao dry dock remains one of the largest in the Western hemisphere.

Among the most consistent seafaring visitors to Curaçao are the weary-looking wooden coastal traders with their dun colored sails that ply the waters between the island and the Venezuelan coast, laden with fresh fruits and vegetables. They tie up bow to stern along a sidewalk in a canal on the east side of the inlet, sling their sails out to one side as awnings against the sun and arrange piles of oranges, melons, tomatoes and fresh greens on their decks, creating a floating farmers' market.

The shops in Willemstad are filled with goods aimed at foreign customers, the kind of things you find in such cruiseship capitals as Nassau and St. Thomas. There are cameras and binoculars, wristwatches, crystal, linens, perfumes and designer clothing. They are not much of a bargain by United States standards, especially considering the discount stores in Miami and New York. But the Curaçao stores did a booming business in the 1970s when oil was bringing high prices and the economy of Venezuela was humming. There were not only lots of Venezuelan tourists in those days, but a good many small business people who waltz in and buy dresses and suits by the 10s and 20s, pack them off to Venezuela as personal goods, duty-free, and resell them at enormous mark-ups. As the merchants remember it, even the true tourists from Venezuela were shopping, picking up things that just could not be found back home.

Then the oil business hit the skids. In early 1983, the Venezuelan Bolivar was devalued from 4.30 for one US dollar to 10 to the dollar. Things got even worse and the Venezuelans stopped traveling.

Willemstad is not a very big town and it is an inviting place to walk. The streets are clean and many are blocked to vehicles. There are a handful of sidewalk cafes and strategically located wagons and carts with drinks and snacks. There is also a Kentucky Fried Chicken place, a McDonald's and a

Curaçao fishermen at day's end.

Pizza Hut to tide you over until you're ready for one of the island's many fine restaurants. And only a few miles from South America, music shops along the way fairly vibrate with super-amplified favorites from the Latin hit parade.

One of the jewels of Willemstad is its more than 250-year-old **Mikve Israel-Emanuel Synagogue**, which, according to Rabbi Aaron L. Peller, is the oldest synagogue in continuous use in the Western hemisphere. Jews from Spain and Portugal, many of them by way of Brazil, were among the earliest settlers of Curaçao. Some of their heirs are business leaders in Curaçao today.

Jews from Curaçao contributed to the spread of Judaism in America. In 1693 a contingent from Curaçao emigrated to Newport, Rhode Island and founded the community of Jeshuat Israel, later known as Nephutsay Israel. Their leader was Isaac Abraham Touro, the father of Judah Touro, the philanthropist. Over the years, the Jews in Curaçao sent money to the Jewish community in Newport as well as those in New York, Philadelphia and Charleston, S.C. Rabbi Peller, an American from Buffalo, N.Y., who joined the synagogue with a contract for life in 1978, said the Jewish

population in Curaçao reached a peak of about 2,000 in 1750 and now totals about 600. Perhaps as much as 80 percent of the people of Curaçao are Roman Catholics.

The synagogue, which is the congregation's fourth, was opened in 1732. It is a cool, white-washed sanctuary with blue windows, mahogany benches and pulpit, and big brass chandeliers that are replicas of those hanging in the Portuguese synagogue in Amsterdam. The floor of the synagogue is sprinkled with sand daily in a symbolic gesture that is variously said to recall either the wandering of the Israelites in the Egyptian desert during the Exodus or the muffling of the sound of worshippers' feet as they met secretly during the Inquisition. Visitors are welcome to have a look or to attend services.

Across an interior courtyard there are two restored 18th-century houses that serve as the synagogue's museum. There are religious articles and antique furniture, a table set for the passover dinner and photographs and paintings of early members of the congregation. One large painting depicting a military battle is dedicated to the memory of George L. Maduro, a member of one of Curaçao's wealthiest families who was studying law at the University of Leyden

Shopping for produce in a Curaçao market.

when the Germans invaded the Netherlands on May 10, 1940. Young Maduro, who had become a lieutenant in the Dutch light cavalry, was taken prisoner by the Germans and died in the Dachau concentration camp.

Willemstad is divided into two parts by the long, narrow inlet feeding ships into the harbor: the Punda, where the synagogue and most of the shops and government buildings are located, and the Otrobanda or "other side." The two sides are connected by a pontoon bridge for pedestrians that dips and sways in the undulating currents. Twenty or thirty times a day, one end of the nearly 200-yard (182-meter) long Queen Emma bridge is unhinged and swung to the far side of the channel by a putt-putting little marine engine attached to one of the end pontoons. While the bridge is open, a ferry shuttles people across the waterway. Motorists make the crossing on the soaring, 18-story-high lanes of the Queen Juliana bridge further back from the sea.

There are old Dutch forts on both sides of the harbor entrance. On the Punda side, the Curaçao Plaza Hotel, built by the Inter-Continental chain in 1957, rises within the walls of the Waterfort. Ships heading into the port seem to almost brush the windows on one wing of the hotel. The thick stone walls are about all that is left of the Waterfort. Iron links embedded in the outer wall are reminders of the heavy chain that the Dutch used to stretch across the waterway as a barrier to invaders. The anchor point on the Otrobanda side was the Riffort or Reef Fort.

Adjacent to the Plaza Hotel is a third military post, **Fort Amsterdam**. It is a beautifully preserved colonial administrative headquarters with tall buildings and angular burnt orange tiled roofs set like a solid fence around an open quadrangle with old cannons and Dutch marines at the gates. The island government convenes in Fort Amsterdam and the prime minister, cabinet officials and several government agencies have offices there. There is a Dutch **Reformed Church** inside the fort with a modest cupola, steep gables and twin porches with descending stairs that meet in the center. It dates from 1742 and is the oldest Protestant church on the island. Embedded in the southwest wall of the church is a cannon ball fired by British forces under the command of Captain Bligh, which they say bombarded Punda for 26 days in early 1804.

The Hilton and Holiday Inn chains also built hotels on Curaçao, but they, like the

former Inter-Continental and most other hotels on the island, are now owned and operated by the government. Some Curaçaoans say they believe the indifferent service in most of the hotels is at least partly a result of the staff having become civil servants. The former Hilton, which has undergone several name changes, is a high-rise that stands on the edge of Pescadera Bay. It has a big pool, a small but pleasant beach, tennis courts and expansive grounds with palm trees and tropical shrubs. It also has one of the leading gambling casinos on the island, sometimes featuring a kind of island version of the Las Vegas stage review with imported American dancing girls, comedians and sleight-of-hand artists. One of the most charming places to stay is the privately owned Avila Beach Hotel, built in 1811 by a governor of Curaçao and used as a retreat by various governors for the next 100 years or so. It is a small hotel with 45 air-conditioned rooms and a vaguely European feel, particularly its palm-shaded outdoor dining terrace overlooking a small, sheltered beach. At one end of the beach there is an old domed house where Simon Bolivar's sisters lived and where he was once a guest.

Out along the south beach, beyond the Avila, is Curaçao's **Seaquarium**, set among coral rocks and equipped with a system that capitalizes on the trade winds and the tides to keep fresh ocean water constantly flowing through the display tanks. There are dozens of varieties of rarely seen tropical fish. The aquarium, with large sections exposed to the open air, is surrounded by a concrete moat filled with rather substantial looking sharks. The jagged, rusty remains of a Dutch steamer lie on the rocks in front of the aquarium where, loaded with coffee and sugar, she met her demise in 1906. Just offshore, in 10 to 15 feet (three to four meters) of water, is a sunken tug boat that also lost its bottom on the rocks. Beginning a short distance up the coast from the aquarium, encompassing the tug and sweeping to the southeast tip of the island for a total of 12.5 miles (20 km) is an underwater park with a marked trail for snorkeling and 16 bouys for dive boats. Most of the park consists of coral formations created by Mother Nature. But there is also an artificial reef called Bus Stop which was made by piling up the hulks of about 100 old cars.

Though Bonaire is by far the best known of the ABC islands for underwater sports, *Skin Diver* magazine ranked Curaçao and Aruba in the top 20 percent of the diving

The placid beauty of a Curaçao bay.

spots in the Caribbean islands. According to *Skin Diver*, there are 35 to 40 "dive sites" off the south coast of Curaçao, more than half of which are within easy reach of the shore. The magazine found interesting coral formations in the shallows as well as at depths of 80 to 100 feet (24 to 30 meters). Visibility underwater, it reported, is usually 80 to 150 feet (24 to 45 meters), even close to the entrance of the main harbor.

There are a number of sunken ships along the coast that divers like to explore. The most impressive, the experts say, is the **Superior Producer**, a 200-foot (60-meter) steel-hulled freighter that went down in about 100 feet (30 meters) of water just off the beach between the harbor entrance and the former Holiday Inn, now known as the Holiday Beach. The freighter is sitting upright on the flat, sandy bottom. "All the ship's cargo holds, hatches, companionways and quarters are open for exploration," *Skin Diver* reported.

For divers who get into trouble, the 780-bed St. Elizabeth Hospital, one of the most modern hospitals in the Caribbean, has two decompression chambers.

At the Otrobanda end of the pontoon bridge there is an open plaza and a bronze statue of Pedro Luis Brion, a native son who led the Curaçao militia in the defense of Willemstad against the British and went on to work with Simon Bolivar to establish the navies of Venezuela and Colombia. He served as an admiral in the Venezuelan navy and his body lies entombed in the National Pantheon in Caracas.

Off to one side of **Brionplein,** or **Brion Square**, stands the charred skeleton of a three-story building that, until the riots of 1969, was **Touber's Clothing Store**. Mr Touber wanted to leave a reminder of the violence and loss of property and the island government let him have his way. One of the buildings burned in the riots and later cleared away was the Hotel Americano, where many American servicemen were billeted during World War II.

South of Brionplein, part of the old Dutch fort, the **Riffort**, is now used as a police station. Wrapped into the fort's walls are a couple of good restaurants, **Bistro Le Clochard**, which offers French and Swiss specialties, and **Le Recif**, a seafood place. Another of the notable restaurants of Curaçao, the **Fort Nassau**, is located in Fort Nassau on a hilltop that overlooks the inland harbor and the **Royal Dutch Shell Refinery**, which sprawls over 1,000 acres (400 hectares) and manages to function without

Deciding on dinner.

creating great clouds of smoke and ghastly odors. At night the refinery's tanks, towers and steel girders are invisible and it is atwinkle with lights that, in the distance, add a certain charm to dinner at Fort Nassau. For more history and architecture combined with dining, there is **De Taveerne**, a classic country-style Curaçao mansion called a "landhuis," operating as a restaurant with continental as well as some of the best renderings of such local dishes as *keshi yena*, an Edam cheese stuffed with chicken or beef and baked. **The Java Restaurant** in the Stellaris Hotel, a big, rambling wooden affair with broad verandas facing the inlet, offers a modestly priced *rijsttafel*, the Indonesian smorgasbord. For an upscale version of *rijsttafel* there is the **Rijsttafel Restaurant Indonesia,** a short drive from the heart of Willemstad.

Otrobanda is mainly a residential district with some stores frequented by island people. Along one of the main shopping streets there is a little open-front drinking place called the **Netto Bar**, with a battered wooden counter, red Formica-covered tables and bright yellow walls. Ernest Coster, whose friends call him Netto, has been doing business here more than 30 years. He is 71 years old. He serves a lot of the usual

drinks. But he says he gets a lot of call for rum with angostra bitters, fresh coconut milk with Dutch gin and something called a Ponche Kuba, which he makes with cream or milk, rum and raw eggs. Netto also makes his own rum. There are two kinds, one clear as vodka and the other tinted green with limes. Both pack a mule's wallop and go for 75 cents for a double shot.

Across the inlet on the outskirts of Willemstad, **Senior & Co**. operates a distillery in one of the old "landhuisen," producing an orange-flavored liqueur called Curaçao. There are regular tours of the small factory and drinks are free. Senior & Co. makes about 400 gallons (1,538 liters) of the liqueur a week. Its natural color is clear, but it also comes in green, orange and blue versions, all of which taste the same. The liquer is made from laraha, the offshoot of Valencia oranges.

The Spanish brought Valencia oranges to Curaçao in the early 16th century in the belief that the island's soil and climate would provide growing conditions similar to those in Valencia. But the trees shriveled and yielded only an inedible bitter fruit. In the early 18th century, someone discovered that the peel of the orange, dried in the sun, contained a tasty aromatic oil. The nature of

The local bounty.

the orange had changed so much that it was given a new botanical name: citrus aurentium curassuviensis, the golden orange of Curaçao, known locally as the laraha. Several Curaçao families used to make Curaçao liqueur with slightly different recipes. But the Smith family recipe is the only one still in production, although the Smiths are no longer associated with the distillery.

About 10 minutes by car from the heart of Willemstad, in Otrobanda, a 19th-century quarantine hospital for yellow fever patients, was long ago turned into **The Curaçao Museum**. It is a small place with creaky wooden floors, packed with mementos of Curaçao's history; everything from Indian relics, whale bones and stuffed birds, to Dutch and Caribbean paintings, locally made antique mahogany cabinets, old sewing machines, typewriters and musical instruments and the angular metal frame of a seat from a World War II vintage American fighter plane.

Not far from the museum there is a huge plant that looks something like a power station. Actually, it is the desalination station that transforms ocean water into drinking water. Nearby is an amusement park called **Coney Island**, with a ferris wheel and other rides.

Aruba: For nearly 50 years, the main engine of life on Aruba was its big oil refinery. It was the largest single source of employment and it also paid millions of dollars in taxes. It provided medical care, schooling and recreation for its employees and their families. The first, and for years the only, golf course on the island was the refinery golf course. One of the main boulevards sweeping along the waterfront of the capital of Oranjestad is named after an American former general manager of the refinery, Lloyd G. Smith.

The closing of the refinery in the spring of 1985 occurred nine months before Aruba pulled out of the federation of Dutch Caribbean islands. Suddenly, Aruba, which had enjoyed a high standard of living similar to that of Curaçao, was faced with an enormous loss of income, high unemployment and new expenses for the transition to separate status in the Netherlands, including the cost of printing new currency to permit it to stop using Netherlands Antilles gilders and gain a clear measure of distance from the central bank in Curaçao.

As the island headed toward the end of the decade, Arubans were looking to tourism as their salvation. As early as the end of the World War II they had foreseen the perils of

A uniquely appointed house.

their heavy dependence on the refinery and started capitalizing on the gift of their spectacular beaches, crystal waters and mild climate. By the time the refinery closed, tourism was big business in Aruba and Arubans were hoping to make it bigger.

Nearly everyone who visits Aruba comments on the attitude of the people toward visitors. They actually seem to like tourists. They see tourists as good business and they understand that a pleasant atmosphere is as important, maybe even more important, than marvelous beaches. There is probably no such thing as an island of happy natives waiting to minister to weary foreign travelers. But Arubans have gone so far as to imprint on the license plates of their cars the logo, "One Happy Island."

This attitude is a startling contrast to that of Curaçao, where cheerfulness is far from the rule and where waiters and waitresses often seem to be balky, careless, irritable and resentful. Community leaders on the two islands say the different reactions of Arubans and Curaçaons to tourists may have something to do with the history of the islands, particularly in regard to slavery. Aruba is one of the few Caribbean islands where the Indians were not wiped out and where, except for a few domestics, there

Another perfect day in Aruba.

were no slaves. For the first 250 years after its discovery in 1499, first the Spanish and then the Dutch barred foreign settlers from Aruba. Eventually Dutch and other Europeans, as well as Venezuelans, moved to the island. Many inter-married with the Indians and the result was a mestizo population. They were spared the indignities of servitude suffered by most of the ancestors of Curaçao's now overwhelmingly black population.

Before tourism and oil, Arubans tried working the land. One of the most profitable ventures was the cultivation of aloe, a squat, greenish-brown plant with thick, spinney leaves that contain a medicinal liquid once used as a laxative and now used in skin creams and suntan lotions. In the 1920s Aruba was producing 70 percent of the world's supply of aloe. But because of a drop in demand and the advent of the oil refinery, which offered relatively high wages, Arubans lost interest in aloe. There are still acres and acres of aloe growing on the island and in the mid-1980s some Arubans began making a business of it again. For decades, the yellow pods of the wild divi-divi tree, which is perhaps even more plentiful in Aruba than in Curaçao, were marketed as a source of tannin for

dyeing leather. Some people also made a living raising a kind of insect called a cochineal. Found mainly in Mexico, the insects eat cacti, which are plentiful in Aruba. The cochineal insects were once used to make a red dye, but synthetics came along and no one wanted Aruba's tannin or its cochineal insects.

Gold was discovered in Aruba in the 1820s, but no one was able to find much of it. Efforts to mine it were abandoned during World War I when it became impossible to get spare parts for the smelters. The ruins of the **Bushiribana Mine** are one of the stops on the island tours that several companies run out of Oranjestad. The mine, with its walls of cut stone, are sometimes erroneously described as a pirate's castle. According to local lore, pirates were frequent travelers to Aruba. But the mine did not exist in their day. Phosphate mining began in the 1870s, but it was stopped during the World War I, due to insurmountable competition from other countries. The phosphate works had been in **San Nicolas**, a community near the southern tip of Aruba. It was blessed with a natural, deep-water harbor and blossomed as the home of the big refinery which opened in 1929.

Compared to Willemstad, the capital of Aruba is a sleepy village, much less reminiscent of Europe. There are touches of Dutch architecture here and there, but the overall feeling is tropical-modern. The streets are wide tarmac; the buildings stucco and glass, functional rather than charming. A dominant vision in the downtown harbor is the swoop-roofed, floating Bali restaurant which, of course, specializes in Indonesian dishes, such as *rijsttafel*. Nearby there is a little fleet of wooden-hulled coastal traders with brownish sails pulled close to the dock and offering fruit and vegetables from Venezuela, just as they do in Curaçao.

The focal points for most visitors to Aruba are its beaches and resort hotels. They are a few miles north of Oranjestad and some tourists never feel a need to venture far from them. Several of the hotels have spacious gambling casinos with all the games and machines found in world-class casinos. The hotels are loaded with casual and formal restaurants and bars. Boats for sailing, water-skiing and skin-diving pick up passengers right on the beach in front of the hotels. At night there are floor shows, party games and dancing. There are some rental condos along the beaches, too, and little grocery stores and liquor stores have sprung up nearby.

A shell collector's paradise.

Bonaire: For several hundred years nothing much happened on Bonaire. It is still pretty quiet. But in the 1950s, when Bonaire was going through one of its many bleak economic periods, a few tourists ventured over to the island and discovered what experts now regard as some of the best skin-diving in the world. The island is surrounded by calm, clear waters and miles of coral reef, much of it close to shore and inhabited by as many as 1,000 species of fish. Almost all of the waters surrounding Bonaire, from the beach to a depth of 200 feet (60 meters), have been declared a government-protected marine park, supported by the World Wildlife Fund.

The landscape of Bonaire, much like that of Curaçao and Aruba, is only beautiful to desert lovers. But it is home to more than 10,000 flamingoes and more than 130 other species of birds, including the black-necked stilt, the pearly-eyed thrasher, the hooded warbler and several kinds of parrots. The northern tip of the island, 13,500 square acres, has been set aside as a nature reserve.

Even with these attractions, Bonaire is far from overrun with tourists. In the late 1980s it was welcoming about 20,000 tourists a year, compared to about 200,000 for Aruba, the leader in the field among the ABCs.

The main village of **Kralendijk**, with about 1,500 residents, consists of a few streets of Dutch colonial-style houses in pastel and earth-tones. There is a charming promenade fronting a harbor dotted with fishing boats. There is also an old fort near the post office building with a cannon dating from Napoleon's time, a handicraft center and two museums. There are several hotels on Bonaire with diving facilities and guides to the best bird-watching areas.

In 1499, Amerigo Vespucci became the first European to come across Bonaire. He and his group noted that the island seemed to be filled with trees that yielded a brilliant red dye. For the next 100 years or so, the Spanish carted off these trees. Not many are left now. The Spanish raised cattle for the skins, which they dyed with divi-divi pods, and made salt by collecting sea water in shallow ponds and letting it evaporate. One of the first things the Spanish did was to round up all the Arawak Indians on Bonaire, as well as on Curaçao and Aruba, and ship them to Spain to work as slaves in copper mines. Eventually, some of the Indians were returned to Bonaire and Aruba.

Shortly after the Dutch took over Bonaire in 1636, they expanded salt production and began raising sheep and cows to feed the

Simple dwellings in Bonaire. Following pages: pink flamingoes; blue skies, blue seas.

main colony on Curaçao. The Dutch barred white settlers from Bonaire but brought in black slaves from Africa to work what evolved into a government plantation. The last of the Indians left Bonaire in the early 19th century. After the emancipation of the slaves, it cost more to run the plantation than it could earn. So the plantation, which encompassed the whole island, was sold. Most of it went to two Europeans. They did not do a great deal with it. But the former slaves and freed men, whose descendents now make up the majority of Bonaire's population, soon found themselves homeless and impoverished.

On the southern end of the island, near glistening salt ponds that are still being worked, are some painful reminders of the brutality of slavery: several little stone houses, something like over-sized dog houses, are where the slaves slept. Their families lived a six-hour walk away. They were allowed to walk home on Saturdays, but they had to be back at the salt ponds on Sunday.

In the 1920s, many of Bonaire's men went to work in the oil refineries in Curaçao and Aruba. They sent their pay home, creating a "mail order economy" for the island. Beginning in the 1930s, taxes paid to the central government of the Netherlands Antilles by the oil companies paid for roads, electricity and an airport for Bonaire. In 1975 Bonaire got its own piece of the oil action, and a depot for storing and transferring shipments of oil from super-tankers to smaller vessels was built.

For much of its history, Bonaire has been regarded as a remote, uninviting place; ideal, in short, for a prison. In the 1600s, misbehaving Dutch soldiers and American Indians captured along the banks of the Hudson River were shipped to the island. Centuries later, at the start of World War II, several hundred Germans and a few Dutch citizens believed to be German sympathizers were picked up in Curaçao and interned in Bonaire.

According to historian Johan Hartog, they lived like princes. "They received the same food rations as the soldiers, were allowed to go for swims and could even hire themselves out against payment."

After the war, the refineries cut back on employment and hard times returned to Bonaire. In a short while, however, someone got the idea to turn the huts used by the prisoners of war into hotel rooms and a new era began in Bonaire. The **Flamingo Beach Club hotel** now stands on the grounds of the old prison camp.

TRAVEL TIPS

GETTING THERE

BY AIR

As far as accessibility goes, the islands fall pretty neatly into two groups: those that can be reached by direct flights from North America, South America and Europe, and those that cannot. The first group consists of the following islands – listed here with the cities they can be reached from, and the carriers serving each route. Itineraries change; check with a travel agent for the best current route from your city.

Accessible From:

Island	(Via Carrier)
Antigua	New York (EA, AA, BWIA, PAN AM)
	Miami (EA, BWIA, PAN AM)
	Montreal (AC)
	Toronto (AC, BWIA)
	London (BA)
Aruba	New York (AA, PANAM)
	Miami (ALM, EA, VIASA)
	Caracas (ALM, LAV, VIASA)
	Bogota (ALM, AVIANCA)
	Amsterdam (KLM)
Barbados	New York (AA, PAN AM, BWIA, EA)
	Miami (AA, PAN AM, BWIA, EA)
	Canadian Points (AC, Wardair, BWIA, EA)
	Boston (BWIA)
	Baltimore (BWIA)
	London (BWIA, Caribbean Airways, BA)
	Frankfurt (Caribbean Airways)
	Brussels (Caribbean Airways)
	Caracas (VIASA, BWIA)
	Guyana (Cubana, Guyana Airways)
Curaçao	New York (AA)
	Miami (ALM, EA)
	Venezuela (ALM, KLM) & South American (VIASA) Points
Grenada	New York (BWIA, GA)
	Miami (BWIA)
	Venezuela (LIAT)

Guadeloupe	New York (AA, EA)
	Miami (EA, AF)
	Montreal & Toronto (AC)
Martinique	New York (AA, EA)
	Miami (EA, AF)
	Montreal & Toronto (AC)
St. Kitts	New York (PAN AM, BWIA)
	Miami (PAN AM)
	Montreal & Toronto (AC)
St. Lucia	New York (BWIA, AA)
	Miami (PAN AM)
	London (BA)
St. Martin	New York (AA, PAN AM)
	Miami (EA, PAN AM)
	Dallas/Ft. Worth (AA)
	New York (BWIA, PAN AM, EA)
	Montreal & Toronto (BWIA, AC)
	Miami (BWIA, PAN AM, EA)
	London (BWIA, BA)
	Amsterdam (KLM)
	South & Central (KLM, BWIA, LAV, PAN AM)
	American Points
US Virgin Islands	New York (AA, PAN AM)
	Miami (EA, ME, PAN AM)
	Dallas/Ft. Worth (AA)

Key to Table

AA – American Airlines
AC – Air Canada
AF – Air France
ALM – ALM, Dutch Antillean Airlines
AVIANCA – AVIANCA
BA – British Airways
BWIA – BWIA, British West Indian Airways
EA – Eastern Airlines
GA – Grenada Airways
KLM – KLM, Royal Dutch Airways
LAV – LAV, Linca Aeropostal
LIAT – LIAT, Leeward Islands Air Transport
PAN AM – Pan American World Airways
VIASA – VIASA

All the islands, including those just listed, can be reached from various points in the Caribbean via numerous carriers, on a tangled spider's web of routes. A more or less complete listing of inter-island airline companies follows.

Island	Can Be Reached From
Anguilla	San Juan, Antigua, St. Martin, St. Thomas, St. Kitts, BVI.
Antigua	San Juan, Montserrat, Dominica, Anguilla, St. Barts, St. Kitts.
Aruba	San Juan, Curaçao, Bonaire, St. Martin.
Barbados	St. Vincent, Grenada, Trinidad, Tobago, San Juan, St. Martin,

	Cuba, Jamaica.
Bonaire	Aruba, Curaçao, St. Martin.
BVI	San Juan, Antigua, St. Martin, St. Thomas, St. Kitts, St. Croix, Anguilla.
Curaçao	San Juan, St. Martin, Aruba, Tobago, Bonaire, Trinidad.
Dominica	San Juan, Martinique, Barbados, Trinidad, St. Lucia, Antigua, Guadeloupe.
Grenada	Barbados, Trinidad, St. Lucia, the Grenadines.
Guadeloupe	San Juan, St. Barts, Dominica, St. Kitts, and many other islands.
Martinique	San Juan, St. Martin, Dominica,Barbados, Trinidad, St. Lucia, St. Vincent & the Grenadines, and other islands.
Montserrat	Antigua.
Saba	St. Martin.
St. Eustatius	St. Martin.
St. Barts	San Juan, St. Martin, St. Thomas, Antigua, Guadeloupe. St. Kitts and Nevis, San Juan, Barbados, St.Martin, St. Thomas, Antigua, Guadeloupe, St. Croix.
St. Lucia	Dominica, St. Vincent and the Grenadines, and other islands.
St. Martin	San Juan, Barbados, Trinidad, Martinique, St. Barts, Anguilla, BVI, St. Kitts, Curaçao, Aruba, Bonaire, St. Thomas, Tobago, Saba, St.Eustatius, St. Barts, Jamaica.
St. Vincent and the Grenadines	Barbados, Trinidad, St. Lucia, Martinique, the Grenadines Grenada and other islands.
USVI	San Juan, St. Barts, Anguilla, BVI, St. Martin, St. Kitts, and other islands.

Note: San Juan is in Puerto Rico, and can be reached from a number of international departure points. St. Thomas and St. Croix are islands in the USVI.
USVI = United States Virgin Islands
BVI = British Virgin Islands

Inter-Island carriers include: LIAT (probably the largest single carrier), ALM, IAS, Air Martinique, Air Guadeloupe, Air St. Barts, Winair, Aero Virgin Islands, Air BVI, BWIA Airbridge, Crown Air, Eastern Metro Express, Sea Jet, Virgin Islands Seaplane Shuttle, Clint Aero, Cubaba, Eastern Caribbean Airways, Vieques Airlines, Air Anguilla, Tyden Air, Air Mustique, Trinidad & Tobago Air Services and Prinair.

Schedules and itineraries do change. Once you've decided on all the places you want to visit, talk to a travel agent, tourist board, or airline company to determine the most efficient way to get to your destinations.

BY SEA

If you are the sort that fancies a lounge chair on a warm and breezy deck, the elegance of a stateroom, or maybe just a good game of shuffleboard – have no fear. A large number of cruise ships still ply the Caribbean.

The Lesser Antilles are on the itineraries of several cruise lines, though frequency of service to the different islands in the group varies widely – from hundreds of port visits each year to the United States Virgin Islands, to no stops at all at certain other islands. Itineraries change constantly. The best way to plan your trip is to first decide where you'd like to go, then contact a cruise operator or travel agent to see if there is a current itinerary that covers all or most of your destinations. Below is a list of cruise ship companies which offer Antillean service.

American Canadian Line, 461 Water St., Warren, RI 02885, Tel: (401) 245-1350; outside of Rhode Island, Tel: (800) 556-7450

Carnival Cruise Lines, 5525 NW 87 Avenue, Miami, FL 33166, Tel: (800) 327-9501

Chandris Inc., 666 5th Ave., NY, NY 10019, Tel: (212) 586-8370 or (212) 233-3003

Clipper Cruise Line, 7711 Bonhomme Ave., St. Louis, M063105; Tel: (800) 325-0010, (314) 727-2929

Commodore Cruise Line, 1015 North America Way, Miami, FL 33132, Tel: (305) 358-2622

Costa Cruises, One Biscayne Tower, Miami, FL 33131, Tel: (800) 447-6877, (305) 358-7325

Cunard Line, 555 5th Ave., NY, NY 10017, Tel: (212) 880-7500

Epirotiki Lines, 551 5th Ave., Suite 1900, NY, NY 10017, Tel: (800) 221-2470, (212) 599-1750

Fantasy Cruise, 1052 Biscayne Blvd., Miami, FL 33132, Tel: (305) 358-1588

Holland America Cruises, 300 Eliot Avenue West, Seattle, WA 98119, Tel: (206) 281-3535

Norwegian Caribbean Lines, One Biscayne Tower, Miami, FL 33131, Tel: (305) 358-6670

Ocean Cruise Lines, 1510 SE 17th Street, Ft. Lauderdale, FL 33316, Tel: (305) 764-3500

P & O Cruises, c/o Princess Cruises, 2029 Century Park East, LA, CA90067, Tel: (800) 252-0158

(California only), (800) 421 0522, (213) 553-1770; Beaufort House, St. Botolph Street, London EC3A 7DX, England, Tel: (01) 377-2551

Paquet French Cruises, 1007 North American Way, Miami, FL 33132, Tel: (800) 327-5620, (305) 374-6025

Royal Caribbean Cruise Line, 903 South America Way, Miami, FL 33132

Royal Viking Line, One Embarcadero Center, San Francisco, CA 94111, Tel: (415) 398-8000

Sea Goddess Cruises Limited, 5805 Blue Lagoon Drive, Miami, FL 33126, Tel: (305) 266-8705

Sitmar Cruises, 10100 Santa Monica Blvd., LA, CA 90067, Tel: (213) 553-1666

Sun Line Cruises, One Rockefeller Plaza, #315, NY, NY 10020, Tel: (800) 445-6400, (212) 397-6400

Windjammer Cruises, Tel: (305) 373-2090

BY CHARTER YACHT

One of the most exciting ways to explore the Caribbean is on a private yacht. There are many companies that specialize in renting yachts to Caribbean travelers. Boats are readily available both "crewed" – i.e., complete with a crew of experienced sailors – and "bareboat" – i.e., just the boat, for experienced do-it-yourself adventurers.

If the yacht-charter option interests you, get the latest copy of either the March or August issue of *Sail* magazine. Every year, *Sail*'s March issue contains an exhaustive listing of companies offering bareboat Caribbean charters. August's issue covers crewed yachts. *Sail* is available in many libraries, and back (or current) issues can also be ordered from the magazine's publisher. Contact: **Sail Publications, Inc.**, 34 Commercial Wharf, Boston, MA 02110, Tel: (617) 241-9500.

Note: If you sail in the Antilles, you will be required to follow certain rules, which vary from island to island. For example, many islands require visiting yachts to pay a harbor tax. Also, you may not anchor anywhere that may damage fragile living coral or other marine life. Familiarize yourself with the rules applying at your destination before starting out.

TRAVEL ESSENTIALS

VISAS & PASSPORTS

For travel in and around the islands mentioned here – except Trinidad and Tobago – there is no need for US or Canadian citizens to bring along their passports, though it is always the international identification of choice. US travelers must, however, have some form of proof of citizenship – a birth certificate, naturalization card, voter registration card, affidavit or even an expired passport, provided it is not outdated more than 5 years. Canadian citizens traveling without passports should have a birth certificate as proof of citizenship. Citizens of both countries should also have **some** form of photo I. D.

Citizens of countries other than the United States and Canada will generally need a passport. This restriction may be relaxed for travelers visiting a former colony of their country of origin (for example, a British citizen traveling to St. Lucia). If in doubt, check with a consulate or tourist bureau.

Visas are, as a rule, only required of citizens from East bloc countries and Cuba. In addition to proper documents, **all** travelers must have upon entering the Islands, a return or onward ticket, and adequate funds to support themselves for the duration of their stay. Also, it must be noted that **all** travelers traveling to – **or even passing through** – Trinidad and Tobago must have passports. You must have one with you even if you never leave the airport.

MONEY MATTERS

Currency: There are six major currencies officially used on the islands:

The Netherlands Antilles Florin or Guilder (NAf): Aruba, Bonaire, Curaçao, and St. Martin.
The Eastern Caribbean Dollar (EC$): Dominica, Grenada, Montserrat, St. Kitts-Nevis, St. Lucia, St. Vincent and the Grenadines, Anguilla, and Antigua and Barbuda.
The French Franc (FrF): Martinique, Guadeloupe, St.Martin, and St. Barthelemy.
The U.S. Dollar (US$): The United States and British Virgin Islands.
The Barbados Dollar (B$): Barbados.
The Trinidad and Tobago Dollar (TT$): Trinidad and Tabago.

Exchange rates fluctuate with the world market. Whatever the official currency, though, the fact is that both US dollar and pound Sterling are readily accepted throughout the Islands. In addition, major credit cards and traveler's checks find a welcome reception at most major hotels, restaurants and shops.

A note to travelers with a limited budget: If you are bringing US dollar or pound Sterling into the Lesser Antilles, check around before converting your currency. Try to get price quotes in both the local currency and the currency you are carrying. Then check the applicable exchange rate. You may find you can save some money by making purchases in whichever currency gives you greater value.

TAXES

Two easy-to-overlook taxes will be levied on you during your travels in the Lesser Antilles. The first is a **government room tax**, charged on all hotel room bills, which generally averages 5 to 10 percent of the bill's total. The second, and perhaps the most troublesome, is the **departure tax**. This fee, usually between US$5 and US$10, is payable upon departure from each of the islands. This tax can present a small problem to those who are inclined to spend all their negotiable currency on gifts etc., before leaving a vacation spot. Make sure you have a little cash on hand. The departure tax can sometimes be prepaid when you buy your plane ticket. If you should make this arrangement, retain your receipt. You will need to produce it as proof of payment.

HEALTH

Immunization: No immunizations are required of travelers to the Antilles, unless the traveler is coming from an infested or endemic area. However, it is a good idea to check with a Public Health Department or other knowledgeable source before traveling, just to make sure there are no special conditions requiring precautionary steps.

TANNING

To a traveler who is not adjusted to the tropical sun, 80-90°F may sound "just like summer temperatures back home". Don't be fooled! The sun in the tropics is much more direct than in temperate regions. When you work on a tan, a little common sense will save you much pain.

Wear a sunscreen whenever you go out, starting with a high protection factor and working your way downwards. For starters, expose yourself for only brief periods, preferably in the morning or late afternoon when the sun's rays are less intense. As your tan builds, you can increase your sunning time and decrease your protection factor – though some sort of minimal protection, such as a tanning oil, is advisable for even the most bronzed body. Finally, wear a hat, especially if you plan to do any extended hiking, walking, or playing in the midday sun.

WHAT TO WEAR

"Casual" is the word in the Antilles. Light cotton dresses, slacks, skirts, shorts and blouses for women, and slacks, shorts and comfortable open-necked shirts for men should make up the majority of your wardrobe. For evening wear, women may want to bring a dressy stole or sweater to add elegance (and a touch of warmth) to daytime wear. Men will want to bring a jacket and tie, especially if they plan to do any gambling – most casinos (and some of the fancier restaurants) require at least a jacket. For the feet, light sandals will be appropriate and comfortable on the beach and around town. A pair of sturdy walking shoes is a good idea for those planning walks or hikes on the Islands' beautiful and often mountainous interiors.

An important note: swimsuits and other beach attire are definitely not appropriate as around-town wear. When you venture from sea- or pool-side into town, cover up – a simple T-shirt and a pair of shorts should do the trick. By following this simple rule, you will show respect for the standards of many Island residents.

And while we're on the subject of beach attire – nude or topless (for women) bathing is prohibited everywhere in the Antilles except for Guadeloupe, Martinique, St. Martin, St. Barthelemy, and Bonaire. Guadeloupe, St. Martin, and Bonaire have a few designated nude beaches, and topless bathing is permitted on Guadeloupe, Martinique, and St. Barthelemy. Topless bathing is more common at beaches near hotels than on local or village beaches.

CUSTOMS

Travelers coming into the Antilles are generally allowed to bring in the following duty-free: personal effects; a carton of cigarettes or cigars, or half a pound of tobacco; one bottle of an alcoholic beverage; and a "reasonable" amount of perfume.

For US travelers returning to the United States from the Virgin Islands, there are a number of importation options. Recent changes in US law have made it possible for each individual to bring back up to US$400 worth of purchases duty-free. In addition, travelers may mail home an unlimited number of packages valued at US$50 or less, provided not more than one such package is mailed to any one person in a single day. If you exceed your US$400 limit upon returning to the States, the first US$600 worth of merchandise in excess is assessed according to a flat duty rate of 10 percent.

A final tip: US law allows the importation, duty-free, of original works of art. Because of concessions made to developing countries, jewelry made in the Antilles may qualify as original art, and thus be duty-free. If you purchase jewelry, make sure to get a certificate from the place of purchase stating that the jewelry was made in the Islands. To make sure that articles you want to bring back fall into this category, contact the **US Customs Service** for further details.

If you intend to bring a pet along with you on your trip, you must make arrangements with your destination country before you travel. Many countries do not allow foreign pets on their shores; others require quarantine periods. A tourist office, consulate or embassy should be able to provide answers to your questions regarding this matter.

The importation of firearms, including air pistols and rifles, is generally prohibited in the Caribbean.

GETTING ACQUAINTED

CLIMATE

If you dream of a South Sea isle that's warm throughout the year, with sweet breezes and an occasional shower for variety – well, dream no more. You'll find what you're looking for in the Antilles. Year round, temperatures average around 80°F throughout the region. During the "winter" – which is peak season in the Islands – nighttime lows are in the upper 60s, with daytime highs in the "summer" reaching into the 90s.

Rainfall varies widely, ranging from around 20 inches (50 cm) a year in Curaçao to up to 75 inches (190 cm) a year in Grenada. Rainfall is generally heaviest during October and November, though June is the wettest month in Trinidad and Tobago. Have no fear, though – the wet season is hardly dismal. Rain usually comes in brief showers that may delight you by providing a cool contrast to the tropical sun. The wet season is also the time of year when the Islands are greenest. It is the season of choice for many travelers. Peak season, which is during the "dry" period, is from December through April or May.

An added bonus in the Antillean climate is the trade winds, which bring regular, cooling breezes to most of the islands.

CULTURE & CUSTOMS

Courtesy: There is really nothing special to say here, except to mention that common politeness is as desirable on the Islands as it is anywhere else. "Please", "Thank you", and a respectful and friendly demeanor will go a long way toward returning the warm welcome you are likely to receive. Two more points: don't take anyone's picture without first asking permission – it is quite invasive; and don't drag up shades of colonialism and old B-grade Hollywood movies by referring to Island residents as "natives".

TIPPING

On most restaurant and hotel bills, you will find that a 10-15 percent service charge has been added by the management. If this is the case, tipping is unnecessary, although a small gratuity given directly to an attentive waitress or bellman is always appreciated. If you are unsure whether or not service has been included in your bill, feel free to ask. When service is not included, a tip in the 15-20 percent range is appropriate. Taxi drivers should be tipped within this range as well.

ELECTRICITY

Electric current in the Antilles is almost as varied as the islands themselves. A listing of the various currents follows. In order to make sense of this list, US travelers should know the following: US current is 110-120 volt/60 cycle, for most household uses. The motors in US appliances, then, will run more slowly on 50 cycle current-not an important difference for hair dryers and the like, but don't expect your electric clock to keep accurate time on 50 cycle current. As for voltage-US appliances will require converters to run on the 220-240 V which predominates in the region. Many hotels, especially larger ones, may provide these, but don't depend on it. If there is an appliance that you absolutely cannot do without, make sure you bring your own converter with you.

110-120V/60 cycle (US current): United States Virgin Islands, British Virgin Islands, Aruba, St. Martin, Trinidad and Tobago, and some Locations and hotels in Antigua.

110-130V/50 cycle: Anguilla, Bonaire, Barbados and Curaçao.
220-230V/60 cycle: St. Kitts and Nevis, Montserrat, Antigue and Barbuda, and St. Martin.

220-240V/50 cycle: Bonaire, Curaçao, Dominica, Grenada, St. Barthelemy, St. Martin, Guadeloupe, Martinique, St. Lucia, and St. Vincent and the Grenadines.

BUSINESS HOURS

The siesta, happily, is alive and well in the Caribbean. Throughout the region, shopkeepers close their operations for a couple of hours in the early afternoon, when the tropical sun is at its hottest. As a result, bussiness hours generally follow this pattern: shop open early, usually by 8 a.m., certainly by 9 a.m. Doors begin closing at noon or a little before, though in some areas, shops may stay open until 1 p.m. Business resumes about 2 hours later – 2 p.m. in most places – with stores remaining open until 6 p.m. Again, there is some variation; on a few islands, closing time may be as early as 4 p.m. On Saturday, most stores are open in the morning, and many have full afternoon hours as well. Sunday is generally a day of rest.

In Barbados, Trinidad and Tobago, shops generally **do not** close in the early afternoon, larger shops may open for a few hours.

TIME ZONES

All of the Islands covered here, **except** Trinidad and Tobago, are in the Atlantic Time Zone, where time is one hour later than Eastern Standard Time and four hours earlier than Greenwich Mean Time. When the United States goes onto Daylight Savings Time, the Islands remain on Standard Time. During this period of the year, time in the eastern part of the United States is identical to Island time.

Trinidad and Tobago are in the Eastern Time Zone – identical with the Eastern US during Standard Time, one hour later during Daylight Savings.

BANKING HOURS

Banks are dependably open mornings, Monday through Friday – from 8 a.m. or 8:30 a.m.-12 p.m. Many banks also have afternoon hours, especially on Fridays. A few banks open on Saturday mornings. If you have a banking transaction that **must** be done, plan in advance and try to schedule it on a weekday morning. Once you arrive at your destination, you can familiarize yourself with local hours. As US dollars, British pounds, credit cards and traveler's checks are widely accepted in the Islands, visitors need not worry about finding an open money exchange facility immediately upon arrival.

FESTIVALS

One of the more delightful features of Island calendars is **Carnival** – a joyous and awe-inspiring celebration of life that takes place each year, at one time or another, on all the islands.

Carnival originally developed in Catholic countries as a sort of no-holds-barred blowout before the austerities of Lent. Its true beginnings, however, must lie much further back, in pre-Christian celebrations of the return of life in the spring, after winter's dormancy. Even the later Christian Carnivals maintained an association with rebirth, in their connection with Lent and the Easter season.

In the Caribbean, Carnival also springs from the traditions of the many immigrant groups who, willingly or unwillingly, have come to the Islands

over the years. African roots are particularly important in present-day Carnivals.

Carnival is celebrated at different times on different islands, with the dates falling roughly into three groups: On Trinidad and Tobago, Dominica, St. Thomas, Aruba, Bonaire, Curaçao, St. Lucia, Martinique, Guadeloupe, St. Martin, and St. Barts, Carnival preserves an association with Easter, being celebrated (on all of these islands except St. Thomas) in the period leading up to and sometimes including Ash Wednesday. On St. Thomas, the celebration occurs after Easter. On St. Vincent, Anguilla, St. John, Barbados, Grenada, the BVI, Antigua, Saba, and St. Eustatius, Carnival takes place in June, July, or early August. In these islands, Carnival is often held in association with the "August Monday" holiday, which marks the freeing of slaves in the British islands on August 1, 1834. On St. Kitts, Montserrat, and St. Croix, Carnival takes place in December and early January, in conjunction with the Christmas season.

The festival itself consists of parades of colorfully costumed celebrants; of music from morning to night; of displays of fine dancing; of competitions for Carnival Queen and Calypso King; of food and drink, and more food and drink – in short, of every imaginable outpouring of spontaneous joy, coupled with a healthy dose of *bragodoccio* and stuff-strutting.

GETTING AROUND

BY CAR

The Islands are well stocked with auto-rental agencies. Travel by car allows great freedom and flexibility in exploring the nooks and crannies of the Islands, but there are a few things the driver should be aware of. Many of the islands are mountainous, and on all of them, roads are narrower than most US and European drivers will be familiar with. Driving thus may be a little more harrowing than at home – not for the faint-hearted! Also, in some areas yearly rainfall is quite light and this allows a film of oil to build up on road surfaces. When it does rain on these roads, they become especially slick, requiring extra caution. All in all, drivers should prepare to drive defensively and with caution, perhaps following the advice of one of the Islands' tourist agencies to "sound horn frequently!" Regulations on driver's licences vary from island to island, and will be dealt with under the individual Islands.

BY TAXI

Perhaps the most common means of transportation for visitors to the Islands is the taxi. Not only are taxis convenient and by US standards often quite inexpensive; taking a taxi also gives you access to the resources of the driver. Where else could you chat with an Island expert for the price of a cab ride? Most taxi drivers will gladly help you find things you are looking for, or that you aren't looking for but may be delighted to find! It is usually possible to find a taxi driver who is willing to give you a tour of his or her island, and in some places, drivers are specially trained to be able to do this.

Another positive feature of taxi travel for island visitors is that rates are generally fixed and published. Often, printed sheets with detailed rates are available from points of entry, drivers and tourist offices. If you plan to travel much by taxi, one of the first things you might do upon arrival is to familiarize yourself with the rates to different destinations and at different times of day, so as to be an "informed consumer".

Taxi drivers are usually friendly and extremely helpful. If you receive good service, don't forget to return the favor with a good tip, comparable to what you would pay in the US – say, 15-20 percent.

BY BUS

Most of the Islands have local bus services which many residents use to get around. There is no reason why you can't use them too. Though they are not as flexible as taxis and rental cars, buses are quite inexpensive and have the advantage of allowing travelers to get a small taste of how local residents live. Your hotel, a tourist office, or a police station should be able to supply information or schedules, and fellow riders and drivers are friendly and helpful in making sure that bewildered and camera-hung visitors get off at the right stop.

Tour buses (mini and full-sized), vans, jeeps and "communal taxis" are available on all the islands, for taking groups around to "see the sights".

INTER-ISLAND TRAVEL

As you might expect in this region of small-to-tiny islands cut off from one another by the sea, the options for getting around between islands are legion. For the traveler desiring quick transfers (and, perhaps, the novelty of a ride in a seaplane), there are at least 20 airline companies operating inter-island routes. **LIAT** is probably the largest of these, though **ALM** (Dutch Antillean Airlines) has a monopoly on flights between Aruba, Curaçao, Bonaire, and St. Martin. For a complete list of inter-island air carriers, *see* "Getting There" section.

On the sea, an armada of ferries operate regularly scheduled trips between islands, and there is even a regular run between Aruba, Curaçao, and Ven-ezuela. Some of these ferries are the familiar steel-and-smokestack variety, but there's more! The inquisitive traveler will find hydrofoils, schooners and other sailing vessels plying the waters between islands. *El Tigre*, for example, is a 60-foot catamaran making a daily run to St. Barthelemy from St. Martin. Finally, it is often possible for travelers to bargain with fishermen and other small boat owners to arrange rides out to the many small islands which lie off the major islands' shores.

WHERE TO STAY

HOTELS & GUESTHOUSES

See individual Islands for detailed listings. As far as possible, hotels are listed in ascending order of price: i.e., cheapest first, most expensive last. St. Vincent and the Grenadines hotels, however, do not follow this pattern.

Be sure to complete all mailing addresses, unless otherwise noted, with: (Name of Island), W.I.

For full details and reservations (which, by the way, are always recommended), you can contact the hotel directly, a travel agent, a Tourist Board office, or, for many hotels:

The Caribbean Hotel Association, 20 East 46th St., New York, NY 10017, Tel: (212) 682-0435

FOOD DIGEST

RESTAURANTS

See individual Island write-ups for a sampling of Island establishments. Especially in the winter season, reservations are recommended, and at some restaurants they are absolutely essential.

Our history could fill this book, but we prefer to fill glasses.

When you make a great beer, you don't have to make a great fuss.

CULTURE PLUS

MUSIC

As you travel in the Caribbean, you will constantly come into contact with the music of the Islands. Beautiful and distinctive in its own right, the music also has an underlying story that bears a happy message – that neither harsh adversity nor arbitrarily applied power can kill the spirit of music, nor plug up the sweet spring of joy.

In 1937 on Trinidad, Carnival was celebrated to the sound of rhythms pounded out on miscellaneous junk, culled from the island's wasteheaps by determined musicians banned from using traditional percussion instruments by colonial authorities.

Ingenuity and inspiration soon transformed junk into gold, as it was discovered that the tops of discarded oil drums could be "tuned" to produce a variety of ringing tones. Literally out of garbage, Trinidadians produced a new and singularly intoxicating instrument, the steel drum.

Over time, steel drums – or "pans", as they are usually called – have evolved into a standard "kit": the Ping Pong, or soprano pan; the second (alto) pan; the third (tenor) pan, which is called either a guitar pan or a cello pan, depending on its configuration; and the bass pan. Today, in Trinidad, huge orchestras made up of 40, 50, or more players compete in an all-out, island-consuming competitions every year, each band striving to be crowned champion. The bands also include accompanying percussion instruments, and the spirit of inventiveness that gave rise to steel drums in the first place is still alive and well: one instrument used in the bands, the "cutter", is nothing other than an automobile break drum, selected and tuned to play a particular pitch!

By now, steel band music has spread out from Trinidad to all the Islands, where it enjoys widespread popularity.

Another musical style of the Islands is **calypso**. Calypso is a satyric, bawdy, raunchy, irreverent song style characterized by improvisation, topicality and an imaginative use of language. Its development, like that of the steel drum, is tied to the Islands' African heritage. Years ago, during pre-Lenten Carnival periods, slaves would wander the streets, accompanying popular singers, and improvising irreverent lyrics deriding the powerful. Among other of calypso's distinctive features, the use of double-

entendres may have evolved here. Today, calypso's witty and irreverent spirit persist, as singers use their art to expose sham, pretence and injustice. Singers may be accompanied by such instruments as: *shak-shak* (maracas), guitar, cuatro and bamboo-tamboo – a large stick that is pounded on the ground. All over the Islands, at Carnival time, avidly-followed competitions are held to determine who will be crowned calypso king. Calypso singers often take wild, celebratory, elegant names, as expressive as the music they sing – for example, *The Mighty Spoiler, Attila the Hun, Lord Melody,* and *The Duke of Iron.*

MOVIES

Movie theaters are not nearly as popular as they are in the United States, but there are a few in the larger towns. Movies are usually American, but South American and European films are sometimes offered. Hotels may also rent video casettes.

NIGHTLIFE

Nightlife on the Islands ranges from relaxing over a slow dinner to frittering your money away gambling on the islands that have casinos (*see* "Casinos"). In between there are nightclubs, bars, discos and music clubs. Hotels arrange and provide much of the evening entertainment on the Islands, including music and dancing at and after dinner, and flashy floor shows and "folkloric evenings" composed of elements of the music, dance and drama native to the Caribbean. Travelers with an interest in the cultural lives of island residents may wish to venture beyond hotel walls in search of steelband, calypso and reggae music (*see* section on "Music"), and of bars and clubs frequented by locals. Discos may be found both in and outside hotels.

As with shopping, the intensity of nightlife varies substantially from island to island. The more heavily touristed islands may have several things "going" every night of the week, while the lower-keyed islands may sometimes have little more to offer than a luxuriously slow dinner to the accompaniment of recorded music, followed by a stroll along the water. In the latter category, things may pick up a little during the weekends; several establishments have discos that open only on Friday and Saturday nights. On all the islands, peak tourist season – approximately December to April – is also peak nightlife season; things get a little slower during the rest of the year.

The following is a listing of islands according to the emphasis each places on nightlife.

Light Emphasis: Montserrat, The British Virgin Islands, St. Kitts and Nevis, St. Martin, St. Barthelemy, Bonaire, St. Vincent and the Grenadines, Anguilla.

Heavy Emphasis: Aruba, Curaçao, Grenada, Martinique, Guadeloupe, St. Lucia, Antigua, The United States Virgin Islands, St. Martin, Trinidad and Tobago, Barbados.

CASINOS

If you enjoy gambling, you'll find plenty of opportunities in the Antilles. A number of the islands have several casinos, and even some of the region's more relaxed islands have a casino or two.

If you do plan to gamble, be sure to bring along a few dressy clothes. Dress code in the casinos tend to be a little more formal than that prevailing elsewhere. Men should pack a jacket and tie – although not all casinos will require them. For women, a dressy sweater or wrap to spice up daytime apparel is adequate – though, depending on your style, you may want to bring an evening dress, or some snazzy jewels or accessories.

Islands with Casinos: Antigua, St. Martin, Curaçao, St. Kitts, Aruba, Bonaire, Martinique, Guadeloupe.

Note: The legal gambling age is **18** on most islands, but on Guadeloupe and Martinique you must be **21**. Photo ID will sometimes be required for admittance, and some casinos charge an admission fee over and above what you may lose at the tables. Some casinos have slot machines.

SPORTS

WATER SPORTS

The climate and geography of the Antilles make the islands a paradise for sports enthusiasts, and the tourist trade has helped spark the development of a variety of sports facilities. Following is a list of some of the more popular sporting activities on the Islands.

SNORKELING

The abundance of marine life and clarity of the water make this a positively breathtaking activity. Equip-

ment required is minimal – a mask, a snorkel, flippers. But for travelers who don't wish to buy their own, rentals are available at many hotels on all the Islands.

SCUBA DIVING

All the Islands offer equipment rental and excursion packages, including training packages for those who have never dived before.

WINDSURFING/BOARDSAILING/BOATING

Equipment rental is available and classes are conducted on almost every island. From mini Sunfish to two-masted yachts and large motorboats, a variety of rental options are available. For those interested in the larger end of the boat spectrum: all the islands have crewed vessels for rent, and/or regularly scheduled cruises. If you wish to rent a "bareboat" yacht to sail yourself, contact your destination's tourist office before you travel, to check on availability. Waterskiing is available on most islands and equipment may be rented.

DEEP-SEA FISHING

Available on all islands. Most boats charter by the day or half day, and can accommodate several passengers. Many quote rates which include lunch, drinks, snacks, tackle, bait etc.

TENNIS

Available on all islands, to varying degrees. Courts are found primarily within the premises of hotels, but arrangements can be made to use these courts even if you are not a hotel guest. Some islands also have private clubs open to visitors, and public courts which operate on a "first come, first served" basis. The more popular islands offer instruction and equipment rental, and many hotels have resident pros to help you.

HIKING & HORSEBACK RIDING

Rainforests, mountains, waterfalls and gorgeous views await you. Many of the islands have national parks which offer prime hiking opportunities, and St. Lucia's Pitons offer experienced mountain climbers a chance to test their skills. Guides are often available to lead your excursions. For further details *see* under the individual islands.

GOLF

Golf is available on Antigua, St. Lucia, St. Martin, Grenada, Curaçao, St. Kitts and Nevis, US Virgin Islands, St. Vincent and the Grenadines, Guadeloupe, Martinique, and Montserrat. The US Virgin Islands,

Guadeloupe, and Martinique each boast an 18-hole Robert Trent Jones course. The British Virgin Islands has two small practice courses, and Aruba has what is probably one of the oddest courses in the world, with "greens" made out of oiled sand.

LANGUAGE

The multiplicity of languages in the Antilles reflects the region's checkered colonial past. Primary languages are:

English: Anguilla, Antigua and Barbuda, British Virgin Islands, Dominica, Grenada, Montserrat, St. Kitts and Nevis, St. Lucia, St. Vincent and the Grenadines, Barbados, Trinidad and Tobago, and the United States Virgin Islands.
French: Dominica, Guadeloupe, Martinique, St. Barthelemy, St. Lucia, and St. Martin.
Dutch: Aruba, Bonaire, Curaçao, and St. Martin.
Papiamento: Aruba, Bonaire, Curaçao.
Spanish: Aruba, Bonaire, Curaçao.

Some islands have more than one primary language; hence their multiple listings above.

Papiamento is the local language of Aruba, Bonaire and Curaçao. It has evolved from Spanish, Dutch, Portuguese, English, and African and native Caribbean languages.

In addition to the primary languages listed above, Chinese and French are among the languages spoken on Aruba. English (and, to a lesser extent, other European languages) is spoken in hotels and other areas of tourist concentration throughout the Islands, but don't expect everyone on every island to understand you – especially in rural areas and smaller towns. Efforts to communicate with island residents in their own languages are appreciated.

FURTHER READING

GENERAL

Andrews, Kenneth R. *The Spanish Caribbean.* New Haven: Yale University Press, 1978.

Anthony, Michael and Andrew Carr. *David Frost Introduces Trinidad & Tobago.* London: Andre Deutsch, 1975.

Botting, Douglas, and the editors of Time-Life Books. *The Pirates.* Alexandria, VA: Time-Life Books, 1978.

Collymore, Frank A. *Notes for a Glossary of Words and Phrases of Barbadian Dialect.* Bridgetown: 1955.

Cracunell, Basil E. *The West Indians.* Newton Abbot: David and Charles, 1974.

Earle, Petr. *The Treasure of the Concepcion.* New York: Viking Press, 1980.

Eggleston, George Teeple. *The Virgin Islands.* Huntington, NY: R.E. Krieger Publishing Co., 1973.

Fisher, Lawrence E. *Colonial Madness: Mental Health in the Barbadian Social Order.* New Jersey: Rutgers University Press, 1985.

Harman, Carter, and the editors of *Life. The West Indies.* New York: Time, Inc., 1963.

Hartog, J. *St. Maarten, Saba, and St. Eustatius.* 5th ed. Enlarged and translated by E.D. Fowler. Aruba: De Wit Stores, 1978.

Horowitz, Michael M. (ed.) *Peoples and Cultures of the Caribbean*: Garden City, NY: Natural History Press, 1971. An anthropological reader.

Hoyos, F.A. *Barbados: The Visitors Guide.* London: Macmillan Caribbean, 1982.

Hunte, George. *The West Indian Islands.* New York: Viking Press, 1972.

Roberts, W. Adolphe. *The Caribbean.* New York: Bobbs-Merril, 1940.

Snow, Edward Rowe. *True Tales of Pirates and Their Gold.* New York: Dodd, Mead, 1953.

Waddell, D.A.G. *The West Indies and the Guianas.* Englewood Cliffs, NJ: Prentice-Hall, 1967.

Wood, Peter, and the editors of Time-Life Books. *Caribbean Isles.* New York: Time-Life Books, 1975.

HISTORY

Andrews, Kenneth R. *The Spanish Caribbean: Trade and Plunder, 1530-1630.* New Haven: Yale University Press, 1978.

Ballou, Maturin Murray. *Equatorial America: Description of a visit to St. Thomas, Martinique,*

Barbados, and principal capitals of South America. Boston: Houghton & Mifflin Co., 1892.

Boyer, William H. *America's Virgin Islands: A history of human rights and wrongs*. Durham, NC: Carolina Academic Press, 1983.

Brereton, Bridget. *A History of Modern Trinidad 1783-1962*. London: Heinemann, 1981.

Burg, B.R. *Sodomy and the Perception of Evil: English sea rovers in the 17th century*. New York: New York University Press, 1983.

Cox, Edward L. *Free Coloreds in the Slave Societies of St. Kitts and Grenada, 1763-1833*. Knoxville: University of Tennessee Press, 1984.

de Booy, Theodor. *Archaeology of the Virgin*. New York: Museum of the American Indian Heye Foundation, 1919.

de Cardona, Nicolas. *Geographic and Hydrographic descriptions of many northern and southern lands and seas in the Indies*. Trans. and ed. by W. Michael Mathes. Los Angeles: Dowson's Book Shop, 1974.

de Grummond, Jane Lucas. *Renato Beluche, smuggler, privateer, and patriot, 1780-1860*. Baton Rouge: Louisiana State University Press, 1983.

Dookhan, Isaac. *A History of the Virgin Islands of the United States*. Epping: Caribbean University Press for the College of the Virgin Islands, 1974.

Du Terte, Jean-Baptiste. *French in St. Croix and the Virgin Islands*. Trans. and ed. by Amy Caron and Arnold R. Highfield. USVI: Bureau of Libraries, Museums, & Archaeological Services, 1978.

Dunn, Richard S. *Sugar and Slaves: The rise of the planter class in the British West Indies, 1624-1713*. Chapel Hill: University of North Carolina Press, 1972.

Evans, Luther Harris. *The Virgin Islands, from naval base to New Deal*. Westport, CT: Greenwood Press, 1975.

Fergus, Howard A. *History of Alliouagana: A short history of Montserrat*. Montserrat: University Centre, 1975.

Goslinga, Cornelius Ch. *A Short History of the Netherlands Antilles*. The Hague: M. Hijhoff, 1979.

Handler, Jerome S. *Plantation Slavery in Barbados*. Cambridge: Harvard University Press, 1976.

Honeychurch, Lennox. *The Dominica Story: A history of the island*. Barbados: Letchworth Press, 1975.

Howard, Richard A. and Elizabeth S. (eds. and transcribers). Alexander Anderson's *Geography and History of St. Vincent*. West Indies: 1983.

Hoyos, F.A. *Barbados: A History from Amerindians to Independence*. London: Macmillan Caribbean, 1978.

Jones, Anthony Mark. *The West Indian Socialist Tradition*. Port of Spain, Trinidad: Educo Press, 1974.

Jones, S.B. *Annals of Anguilla*. Belfast: Christian Journals, 1976.

Keeler, Mary Frear (ed.). *Sir Francis Drake's West Indian Voyage, 1585-1586*. London: Hakluyt Society, 1981.

Kent, David. *Barbados and America*. Arlington, Va.: CM Kent, 1980.

Knight, Derrick. *Gentlemen of Fortune: The men who made their fortunes in Britain's slave colonies*. London: F. Muller, 1978.

Laws, William. *Distinction, Death and Disgrace: Governorship of the Leeward Islands in the early 18th Century*. Kingston, Jamica: Jamaican Historical Society, 1976.

Lewis, Gordon, K. *The Growth of the Modern West Indies*. New York: Monthly Review Press, 1968.

Levy, Claude. *Emancipation, Sugar and Federalism*. Gainesville: University Press, 1980.

Marrin, Albert. *The Sea Rovers: Privates, pivateers, and buccaneers*. New York: Atheneum, 1984.

Martin, Tony. *The Pan African Connection: From Slavery to Garvey and Beyond*. Massachussets: The Majority Press, 1983.

Marx, Robert F. *Shipwrecks of the Western Hemisphere, 1492-1825*. New York: D. McKay Co., 1975.

Olsen, Fred. *On the Trail of the Arawaks*. Norman: University of Oklahoma Press, 1974.

Parry, J. H. and P.M. Sherlock. *A Short History of the West Indies*. New York: MacMillan, 1966.

Peterson, Mendel. *The Funnel of Gold*. Boston: Little, Brown and Co., 1975.

Philpott, Stuart B. *West Indian Migration: The Montserrat case*. London: Athlone Press; New York, Humanities Press, 1973.

Pope, Dudley. *The Buccaneer King: The Biography of Sir Henry Morgan, 1635-1688*. New York: Dodd, Mead, 1978.

Ramdin, Ron. *From Chattel Slave to Wage Earner*. London: Martin Brian & O'Keefe, 1982.

Sherlock, Sir Philip Manderson. *West Indian Nations: A new history*. London: MacMillan, 1973.

Smith, Bradley. *Columbus in the New World*. Garden City, NY: Doubleday, 1962.

Snow, Edward Rowe. *Pirates, Shipwrecks, and Historic Chronicals*. New York: Dodd, Mead, 1981.

Wallace, Elisabeth. *The British Caribbean from the decline of colonialism to the end of federation*. Toronto: University of Toronto Press, 1977.

Williams, Eric. *From Columbus to Castro: The History of the Caribbean 1492-1969*. New York, Harper and Row, 1971.

Wilmere, Alice (trans.). *Narrative of a voyage to the West Indies and Mexico in the years 1599-1602*. Norton Shaw (ed.). New York: B. Franklin, 1964.

Woods, Peter. *The Spanish Main*. Alexandria, VA: Time-Life Books, 1979.

NATURAL HISTORY

Adey, Walter H. Field. *Guide book to the reefs and reef communities of St. Croix , Virgin Islands.* Miami Beach, FL: Atlantic Reef Committee, University of Miami, 1977.

Burgess, Robert F. *Secret Languages of the Sea*. New York: Dodd, Mead, 1981.

Carrington, Richard. *A Biography of the Sea: The*

story of the world ocean, its animal and plant populations, and its influence on human history. New York: Basic Books, 1961.

Cousteau, Jacques. Guide to the Sea and Index. New York: World Publications, 1974.

Fernandez de Oviedo y Valdes, Gonzalo. Natural History of the West Indies. Trans. and ed. by Sterling A. Stoudemire. Chapel Hill: University of North Carolina Press, 1959.

Kaplan, Eugene H. A Field Guide to Reefs of the Caribbean and Florida, etc. Boston: Houghton Mifflin, 1982.

LaBrucherie, Roger. A Barbados Journey. Imégenes Press, 1979.

LaBrucherie, Roger. Images of Barbados. California: Imágenes Press, 1979.

Macoby, Stirling. Tropical Flowers and Plants. New York: P. Hamlyn, 1974.

Martini, Frederic. Exploring Tropical Isles and Seas: An introduction for the traveler and amateur naturalist. Englewood Cliffs, New Jersey: Prentice-Hall, 1984.

Poole, Lynn and Gray. Volcanoes in Action: Science and legend. New York: McGraw Hill, 1962.

Randall, John E. Caribbean Reef Fishes. Jersey City: T.F.H. Publications (Distrib. by Crown Publishers, New York), 1968.

Ricciati, Edward R. Killers of the Seas. New York: Walker, 1973.

Skutch, Alexander F. Nature Through Tropical Windows. Berkeley: University of California Press, 1983.

Worlds Apart: Nature in cities and islands. Garden City, NY: Doubleday, 1976.

ART & LITERATURE

Baugh, Edward. West Indian Poetry, 1900-1970: A study in cultural decolonization. Kingston, Jamaica: Savacon Publications, 1971.

Braithwaite, Edward. Sun Poem. Oxford: New York: Oxford University Press, 1982.

Brown, Lloyd W. West Indian Poetry. Boston: Twayne Publishers, 1978.

Burnett, Paula (ed.). The Penguin Book of Caribbean Verse in English. Harmondsworth: Pengiun Books, 1986.

Cummins, Willis. Calypsos, symphonies, and Incest. Toronto: Arawak Publishing House, 1974.

Dockstader, Frederick J. Indian Art in Middle America: Pre-Columbian and contemporary arts and crafts of Mexico, Central America, and the Caribbean. Greenwich CT: New York Graphic Society, 1964.

Drayton, Geoffrey. Christopher. London: Secker & Warburg, Collins, 1961.

Festival of the revolution, March 1-13. Grenada, 1980.

Freedom Has No Price: An Anthology of Poems. Bridgetown: Modern Printing and Graphics, 1980.

Figueroa, John (ed.). Caribbean Voices. Washington: R.B. Luce Co., 1973.

Fowler, Robert. Spoils of Eden. New York: Dodd Mead, 1985.

Gilkes, Michael. The West Indian Novel. Boston: Twayne, 1981.

Hill, Errol. The Trinidad Carnival: Mandate for a National Theatre. Texas: University of Texas Press, 1972.

Huckerby, Thomas. Petroglyphs in Grenada and a recently discovered petroglyph in St. Vincent. New York: Museum of the American Indian Heye Foundation, 1921.

Hughes, Michael. A Companion to West Indian Literature. London: Collins, 1979.

Huxley, Aldous. Beyond the Mexique Bay. London: Chatto and Windus, 1974.

Island Voices. Stories from the West Indies. New York: Liveright, 1970.

Jackson, Carl. East Wind in Paradise. London: New Beacon Books Ltd., 1981.

James, Louis (ed.). The Islands in between: Essays on West Indian Literature. London: Oxford University Press, 1968.

Kellman, Tony. Black Madonna Poems. Bridgetown: 1975.

Kincaid, Jamaica. Annie John. New York: Farrar, Strauss, and Giroux, 1985.

Kincaid, Jamaica. At the Bottom of the River. New York: Farrar, Strauss, and Giroux, 1983.

Krugman, Lillian D. (comp.) Little Calypsos. Far Rockaway, NY: C. van Roy Co., 1964.

Lamming, George. The Pleasure of Exile. London: Allison & Busbuy: Schocken, 1984.

Lieberman, Laurence. The Mural of Wakeful Sleep. New York: Macmillan; and London: Collier Macmillan, 1985.

Lovelace, Earl. The Dragon Can't Dance. London: Andre Deutsch, 1979.

Marshall, Trevor. Folk Songs of Barbados. Barbados: Cedar Press, 1981.

Marland, Michael (ed.). Caribbean Stories: Fifteen short stories by writers from the Caribbean. London: Longman, 1978.

Mittelholzer, Edgar. A Morning at the Office. London: Heinemann Educational Books, 1974.

Naipaul, V.S. The Mystic Masseur. Harmondsworth: Penguin Books, 1964.

Naipaul, V.S. The Suffrage of Elvira. Harmondsworth: Penguin Books, 1969.

Naipaul, V.S. A House for Mr. Biswas. Harmondsworth: Penguin Books, 1969.

Naipaul, V.S. The Mimic Men. Harmondsworth: Penguin Books, 1969.

Perry, Sylvia. Song Tales of the West Indies. Far Rockaway, NY: C. van Roy Co., 1964.

Sander, Reinhod W., with assistance from Peter K. Ayers. From Trinidad: An anthology of early West Indian writing. New York: Africana Publishing Co., 1978.

Seeger, Peter, and Kim Loy Wong. Steel Drums: How to Play Them and Make Them. New York: Oak Publications, 1964.

298

Sherlock, Philip. *West Indian Folk Tales/retold by Philip Sherlock*. New York: H.Z. Walck, 1966.

Small, Jonathan. *The Pig-Sticking Season: Jamaica Poems, 1985*. Bridgetown, 1966.

Thomas, Ned, and Derek Walcott. *Poet of the Islands*. Cardiff: Welsh Arts Council, 1980.

Toczec, Nick, Phillip Nanton, and Yann Lovelock (eds.). *Melanthika: An anthology of Pan-Caribbean writing*. Birmingham: L.W.M. Publications, 1977.

Walcott, Derek. *The Fortunate Traveller*. London: Jonathan Cape Ltd., 1983.

Walcott, Derek. *Midsummer*. New York: Farrar, Straus, Giroux, 1984.

Walcott, Derek. *Sea Grapes*. New York: Farrar, Straus, Giroux, 1976.

Walcott, Derek. *The Star-Apple Kingdom*. New York: Farrar, Straus, Giroux, 1979.

Warner, Keith. *The Trinidad Calypso*. London: Heinemann, 1982.

CONTEMPORARY POLITICS

Anderson, William Averette. *Social Movements, Violence, and Change: The May movement in Curaçao*. Columbus: Ohio State University Press, 1975.

Barry, Tom, Beth Wood, and Deb Preusch. *The Other Side of Paradise: Foreign control in the Caribbean*. New York: Grove Press, 1984.

DaBreo, D. Sinclair. *The West Indies Today: A thesis on the forces, struggles, frustrations, and peoples of the West Indies*. Barbados: Letchworth Press, 1971.

Dann, Graham. *Quality of Life in Barbados*. Macmillan Caribbean, 1984.

Elkins, W.F. *Black Power in the Caribbean: The beginnings of the modern national movement*. New York: Revisionist Press, 1977.

Gilmore, William C. *The Grenada Intervention: Analysis and documentation*. London & New York: Mansell Publications, 1984.

Goslinga, C. Ch. *Curaçao and Guzman Blanco: A case study of small-power politics in the Caribbean*. Gravehage: Nijhoff, 1975.

Guerin, Daniel. *Anarchism – From Theory to Practice*. New York: Monthly Review Press, 1976.

Guerin, Daniel. *Le Colonialisme*. Hawthorne, NY: Mouton, 1973.

Guerin, Daniel. *Fascism and Big Business*. New York: Monad, 1973.

Guerin, Daniel. *One Hundred Years of Labor in the USA*. Dover, NH: Longwood Pub. Grp., 1979.

Guerin, Daniel. *The West Indies and Their Future*. London: D. Dobson, 1961.

Naipaul, V.S. *The Loss of El Dorado*. Harmondsworth: Penguin Books, 1973.

Naipaul, V.S. *Finding the Centre*. London: Andre Deutsch, 1984.

Naipaul, V.S. *The Middle Passage: Impressions of five societies – British, French, and Dutch – in the West Indies and South America*. New York: Vintage Books, 1981.

Ngugi Wa Thiongo (James Ngugi). *Homecoming: Essays on African and Caribbean literature, culture, and politics*. London: Heineman, 1972.

O'Shaughnessy, Hugh. *Grenada: An eyewitness account of the US invasion and the Caribbean history that provoked it*. New York: Dodd, Mead, 1984.

Palmer, Ransford W. *Problems of Development in Beautiful Countries: Perspectives on the Caribbean*. Lanham, MD: North-South Publishing Co., 1984.

Payne, Anthony, Paul Sutton, and Tony Thorndale. *Grenada: Revolution and Invasion*. New York: St. Martin's Press, 1984.

Wayne, Rick. *It'll be alright in the morning*. Castries, St. Lucia: STar Pub. Co., 1977.

Williams, Eric. *Inward Hunger: The Education of a Prime Minister*. London: Andre Deutsch, 1969.

SPORTS

Clark, John R., in cooperation with the Oceanic Society. *Snorkeling: A complete guide to the underwater experience*. Englewood Cliffs, New Jersey: Prentice-Hall, 1985.

Cozier, Tony (ed.). *West Indies Cricket Annual*. Barbados: Caribbean Communications (published yearly).

James, C.L.R. *Beyond a Boundary*. New York: Pantheon Books, 1963.

Ketels, Hank and Jack McDowell. *Sports Illustrated Scuba Diving*. New York, Lippincott, 1979.

Rowlands, Peter. *The Underwater Photographer's Handbook*. New York: Van Nostrand Reinhold, 1983.

Slosky, Bill and Art Walker. *Guide to the Underwater*. New York: Sterling Publishing Co., 1966.

Sports Illustrated Magazine. *Sports Illustrated Skin Diving and Snorkeling*. Philadelphia: Lippincott, 1973.

MISCELLANEOUS

Beck, Jane C. *To windward of the Land: the occult world of Alexander Charles*. Bloomington: Indiana University Press, 1979.

Eggleston, Hazel. *St. Lucia Diary: A Caribbean memoir*. Old Greenwich, CT: Devin-Adair Co., 1977.

Hass, Hans. *Men Beneath the Sea*. New York: St. Martin's Press, 1975.

Humfrey, Michael. *Portrait of a Sea Urchin: A Caribbean Childhood*. London: Collins, 1979.

Lamming, George. *The Pleasures of Exile*. London: Allison and Busby, 1984.

Nicole, Christopher. *The Devil's Own*. New York: St. Martin's Press, 1975.

Szuk, Tad. *Dominican Diary*, New York: Delacorte Press, 1965.

Wickham, John. *World Without End: Memoirs of a time*. London: New Beacon Books, 1982.

USEFUL ADDRESSES

TOURIST INFORMATION

Following is a list of tourist offices both on and off the Islands. In addition to the individual offices listed below, there are at least three main clearing house offices, to which you can turn for any Island inquiries. If they can't help, they should know who can.

Caribbean Tourism Association, 20 East 46th St., New York, NY 10164, Tel: (212) 682-0435

Eastern Caribbean Tourist Association, 1 Collingham Gardens, London SW5 OHW, Tel: (01) 370-0925

Caribbean Tourism Association, Gutleutrabe 45/V1, D-6000 Frankfurt/Main 1, West Germany/BRD

ANGUILLA

The Department of Tourism, The Secretariat, The Valley, Anguilla, Tel: 2451, 2759, Tlx: 9313 ANGGOVT LA

• **In the United States:**

Anguilla Vacation, 6201 Leesburg Pike, Falls Church, Virginia 22044, Tel: (703) 534-8512

Tromson Monroe Advertising, 40 East 49th Street, New York, NY 10017, Tel: (212) 752-8660

Jane Condon Corp., 211 East 43rd Street, New York, NY, Tel: toll free – (800) 223-5608, regular – (212) 986-4373

• **In England:**

John Lister, Ltd., 49 Shelton Street, Covent Garden, London WC2, Tel: 01-240-6693

ANTIGUA

Antigua Department of Tourism, P.O. Box 363, St. John's, Antigua, Tel: 20029, 20480, Cable: TOURISM ANTIGUA

• **In the United States:**

Antigua Department of Tourism and Trade, 610 5th Ave., Suite 311, New York, NY 10020, Tel: (212) 541-4117

• **In Canada:**

Antigua Department of Tourism and Trade, 60 St. Clair Ave., Suite 205, Toronto, Ontario MT4 1N5, Tel: (416) 961-3085

• **In England:**

Antigua House, 15 Thayer Street, London W1, England, Tel: 01-486-7073, Tlx: 881-4503, Cable: ANTEGA LONDON W1

ARUBA

Aruba Tourist Bureau, A. Shuttestraat 2, Oranjestad, Aruba, Tel: 23777

• **In the United States:**

Aruba Tourist Bureau, 1270 Avenue of the Americas, Suite 2212, New York, NY 10020, Tel: (212) 246-3030

Aruba Tourist Bureau, 399 NE 15th St., Miami, FL 33132, Tel: toll-free – (800) 3-Aruban, regular – (305) 358-6360

• **In South America:**

Oficina de Turismo de Aruba, Edificio Centro Capriles, (Local C-29), Plaza Venezuela, Caracas, Venezuela, Tel: 781-7445

Oficina de Turismo de Aruba, Centro 93, Carrera 15 Nr. 93-60, (Local 213), Bogota, Colombia, Tel: 257-5282

BARBADOS

Bridgetown, Harbour Road, P.O. Box 242, Tel: 427-2623/4; Deep Water Harbour, Tel: 426-1716

Christ Church, Grantley Adams Int'l Airport, Tel: 428-5012/5570

• **In the United States:**

New York, 800 Second Ave. 19917, Tel: 212-986-6516

Los Angeles, 3440 Wilshire Blvd., Suite 1215 90010, Tel: 213-380-2198/9; 800-221-9831

• **In Canada:**

Toronto, Suite 1508, Box 11, 20 Queen Sreet, West M5H 3R3, Tel: 416-979-2137

Montreal, 615 Dorchester Blvd. West, Suite 960, Quebec H3B 1P5, Tel: 514-861-0085

• **In England:**

London, 6 Upper Belgrave Sreet, SW1X 8AZ, Tel: 01-235-4607

• **In West Germany:**

Frankurt, Steinweg 5, 6000 Frankfurt Au Main 1, Tel: 0611/284451

BONAIRE

Bonaire Tourist Board, Kaya Grandi, Kralendijk, Bonaire, Tel: 8322, 8649

• **In the United States:**

Bonaire Tourist Information Office, 1466 Broadway, Suite 903, New York, NY 10036, Tel: (212) 869-2004

• **In Canada:**

Bonaire Tourist Information Office, 815-A Queen Sreet East, Toronto, Ontario M4M 1H8, Tel: (416) 465-2958

• **In Venezuela:**

Mr. F. de Caso, Torre Maracaibo piso 15-E, Avda. Libertador, Caracas, Venzuela, Tel: 723-460, 723-583

THE BRITISH VIRGIN ISLANDS

BVI Tourist Board, P.O. Box 134, Road Town, Tortola, BVI, Tel: (809) 494-3134

• **In the United States:**

BVI Tourist Board, 370 Lexington Ave., Suite 412, New York, NY 10017, Tel: (212) 696-0400

BVI Information Office, 1686 Union Street, San Francisco, CA 94123, Tel: (415) 775-0344

• **In Canada:**

Jack Gouveia, 801 York Mill Road, Suite 201, Don Mills, Ontario M3B 1X7, Tel: (416) 443-1859

• **In England:**

BVI Information, 48 Albemarle Street, London W1X 4AR, England, Tel: (01) 629-6355

• **In West Germany:**

BVI Information, Lomerstrasse 28, Hamburg 70, W. Germany, Tel: (4940) 695-8846

CURAÇAO

Plaza Piar, Willemstad, Curaçao, Tel: 613-397, 611-967

• **In the United States:**

Curaçao Tourist Board, 400 Madison Ave., Suite 311, New York, NY 10017, Tel: (212) 751-8266

Curaçao Tourist Board, 330 Biscayne Blvd., Suite 806, Miami, FL 33132, Tel: (305) 374-5811

• **In Venezuela:**

Curaçao Tourist Board, Avda Francisco de Miranda, Centro Commercial Country, piso 2, Caracas, Venezuela, Tel: 713-403

• **In Argentina:**

Curaçao Tourist Board, Viamonte 1716, piso 7, Buenos Aires, Argentina, Tel: 461-160

• **In the Netherlands:**

Mr. W. Neef, Benelux, Eendrachtsweg 96-C, P.O. Box 2679, 3000 CR, Rotterdam, Tel: (010) 142-639

DOMINICA

Dominica Tourist Board, P.O. Box 73, Roseau, Commonwealth of Dominica, W.I., Tel: (809-445) 2351, 2186

• **In the United States:**

Dominica Tourist Board, P.O. Box 1061, Emhurst, NY 11373, Tel: (212) 271-9285

THE FRENCH WEST INDIES

On the individual islands (Guadeloupe, Martinique, St. Barts, St. Martin):

Office Départemental du Tourisme, B.P. 1099, 5, Square de la Banque, 97181 Pointe-a-Pitre, Guadeloupe, F.W.I., Tel: 811-560

Office Départemental du Tourisme, B.P. 520, Blvd. Alfassa (Bord de Mer), 97206 Fort-de-France Martinique, F.W.I., Tel: 637-960

Office du Tourisme, Mairie de St. Barth rue August Nyman, Gustavia, Tel: 276-008, or at airport, 276-356, Tlx: 919978 GL

St. Martin Tourist Information Bureau, Waterfront, 97150 Marigot. No telephone at present.

- In the United States:

French West Indies Tourist Board:
610 5th Ave., New York, NY 10020, Tel: (212) 757-1125;
628 5th Ave., New York, NY 10020, Tel: (212) 757-1125

9401 Wilshire Blvd., Beverly Hills, CA 90212, Tel: (213) 272-2661

645 N. Michigan Ave., Chicago, IL 60611, Tel: (312) 337-6301

103 World Trade Center, Dallas, TX 75258, Tel: (214) 742-7011

1 Halladie Plaza, Suite 250, San Francisco, CA 94102, Tel: (415) 986-4161

- In Canada:

French Government Tourist Offices:
1981 Ave. McGill College (490), Montreal, Quebec H3A 2W9, Tel: (514) 288-4264

1 Dundas St. W, Suite 2405, Toronto, Ontario M5G 1Z3, Tel: (416) 593-4717

For Press and Public Relations:
Clement-Petrocik, 14 East 60th St., New York, NY 10022, Tel: (212) 593-1895

GRENADA

Grenada Tourism Department, The Carenage, St. George's, Grenada, W.I., Tel: 2001, 2279, 2872, Tlx: 3422 MINTCA GA, Cable: "TOURISM GRENADA"

- In the United States:

Grenada Tourist Office, Suite 803, 141 East 44th Street, New York, NY 10017, Tel: (212) 687-9554

Karen Weiner Escalera Associates, 465 Park Ave., Suite 304, New York, NY 10022, Tel: (212) 838-4370

- In Canada:

Grenada Tourist Office, Suite 820, 439 University Ave., Toronto, Ontario M5G 1Y8, Tel: (416) 595-1339

- In England:

The Grenada Tourism Office, No. 1 Collingham Gardens, Earls Court, London SW5, England, Tel: (01) 370-5164, 5165

MONTSERRAT

Montserrat Tourist Board, P.O. Box 7, Plymouth, Montserrat, W.I., Tel: (809-491) 2230, Tlx: 5720 MNT GOVT. MK, Cable: Tourism

- In the United States:

Tromson Monroe Public Relations, 40 East 49th Street, New York, NY 10017, Tel: (212) 752-8660

- In England:

High Commission for Eastern Caribbean States, 10 Kensington Court, London W8 5DL, England, Tel: (01) 937-9522

ST. KITTS & NEVIS

The St. Kitts-Nevis Tourist Board, Church St., P.O. Box 132, Basseterre, St. Kitts, Tel: (809) 465-5494

- In West Germany:

STR/Stinnes Tourist Representations, Untermainanlage 5, 6000 Frankfurt/Main, F.R. of Germany/BRD, Tel: (0611) 230-304

ST. LUCIA

St. Lucia Tourist Board, P.O. Box 221, Castries, St. Lucia, W.I.

- In the United States:

St. Lucia Tourist Board, 41 East 42 Street, New York, NY 10017, Tel: (212) 867-2950

- In Canada:

St. Lucia Tourist Board, 151 Bloor St. West, Suite 425, Toronto, Ontario M5S 1S4, Tel: (416) 961-5606

ST. MARTIN, SABA & ST. EUSTATIUS

St. Martin Tourist Board, De Ruyterplein, St. Martin, W.I., Tel: 22337

- In the United States:

Mallory Factor, Sontheimer Group, 275, 7th Ave., New York, NY 10001, Tel: (212) 989-0000, 242-0000

- In Canada:

St. Martin Tourist Board, 243 Ellerslie Ave., Willowdale, Toronto, Ontario, Tel: (416) 223-3501

- In Venezuela:

St. Martin Tourist Board, Edificio EXA, Oficina 804, Avda. Libertador, Caracas, Tel: 313-832

ST. VINCENT & THE GRENADINES

Department of Tourism, St. Vincent & the Grenadines, P.O. Box 834, Kingstown, St. Vincent, W.I.

• In the United States:

Tromson Monroe Advertising, 40 East 49th Street, New York, NY 10017, Tel: (212) 752-8660

• In Canada:

Eastern Caribbean Commission, Place de Ville, Tower "B", Suite 701, 112 Kent St., Ottawa, Ontario, Tel: (613) 236-8952

TRINIDAD & TOBAGO

Trinidad, 122-124 Frederick Street (CIC Building), Port of Spain, Tel: 62-37405, 62-31932/4; Piarco Airport Tourist Bureau, Tel: 664-5196

Tobago, Tobago Tourist Bureau, Jerninghan Street, Scarborough, Tel: 639-2125/3566

• In the United States:

New York, Suite 712-14, 400 Madison Ave., New York, N.Y. 10017, Tel: (212) 838-7750/51

Miami, Suite 702, 200 Southeast First Street, Miami, Florida 33131, Tel: (305) 374-2056

• In Canada

Toronto, Aetna Centre, 145 King Street & West University Ave., Toronto, M5H 1J8, Tel: (416) 367-0390

• In England

London, 20 Lower Regent Street, London SW1Y 4PH, Tel: (01) 930-6566-7

THE UNITED STATES VIRGIN ISLANDS

Offices of the United States Virgin Islands Division of Tourism:

P.O. Box 200, Cruz Bay, St. John, USVI 00830, Tel: (809) 776-6450

P.O. Box 4538, Christiansted, St. Croix, USVI 00820, Tel: (809) 773-0495

Custom House Bldg., Strand Sreet, Frederiksted, St. Croix, USVI 00840, Tel: (809) 772-0357

P.O. Box 6400, Charlotte Amalie, St. Thomas, USVI 00801, Tel: (809) 774-8784

• In Puerto Rico:

1300 Ashford Ave., Condado, Santurce, Puerto Rico 00907, Tel: (809) 724-3816

• In the United States:

1270 Avenue of the Americas, New York, NY 10020, Tel: (212) 582-4520

3450 Wilshire Blvd., Los Angeles, CA 90010, Tel: (213) 739-0138

343 South Dearborn Street, Suite 1108, Chicago, IL 60604, Tel: (312) 461-0180

7270 NW 12th Street, Suite 620, Miami, FL 33126, Tel: (305) 591-2070

1667 K St. NW, Suite 270, Washington, D.C. 20006, Tel: (202) 293-3707

• In Canada:

234 Eglinton Ave. East, Suite 306, Toronto, Ontario M4P 1K5, Tel: (416) 488-4374

• In Denmark:

5 Trommesalen DK-164, Copenhagen V, Tel: (01) 223-379

• In England:

25 Bedford Square, London WC1B 3HG, Tel: (01) 637-8481

• In West Germany:

Freiherr Vom Stein Strasse 24-26, D-6000 Frankfurt/Main 1, Tel: (069) 725-2000

• In Italy:

170 Via Germanico, Int 11, 00192 Roma, Tel: (06) 316-401

Getting Acquainted

GEOGRAPHY

Located just east of Puerto Rico and just west of the British Virgin Islands, the United States Virgin Islands (USVI) is composed of over 50 islands large and small, with a total land area of 139 square miles (361 square km). The best known of the islands are the big three: St. Croix, St. Thomas, and St. John. At 22.7 by 7 miles (36 by 11 km), St. Croix is the largest island, and the home of historic towns Christiansted and Frederiksted. St. Thomas weighs in at 13 by 4 miles (20 by 6 km), and is home to Charlotte Amalie - the capital of the USVI and the most popular cruiseship port in the Caribbean. St. John, at 9 miles (14 km) long and 3 miles (4 km) wide, is the smallest of the three major islands, and its inhabited area is a US National Park. Cruz Bay is St. John's principal town.

ON ARRIVAL

Whether you arrive by plane, cruiseship, or ferry, you will find taxis waiting at your point of entry to take you to your hotel (or wherever else you want to go). In St. Thomas and St. Croix, rental cars may also be picked up at the airport. In St. John, cars are available in Cruz Bay.

DRIVER'S LICENSE

As things now stand, you need a valid US driver's license to drive in the USVI. If your license is from another country, and you wish to drive here, contact the Division of Tourism before you go (*see* page 300), to see what arrangements can be made.

MEDICAL FACILITIES

Excellent medical attention is available on all three islands. There are two hospitals and/or clinics on each of St. John and St. Thomas, and three on St. Croix.

HOLIDAYS

Three Kings Day
  January.
Martin Luther King Day
  Third Monday in January.

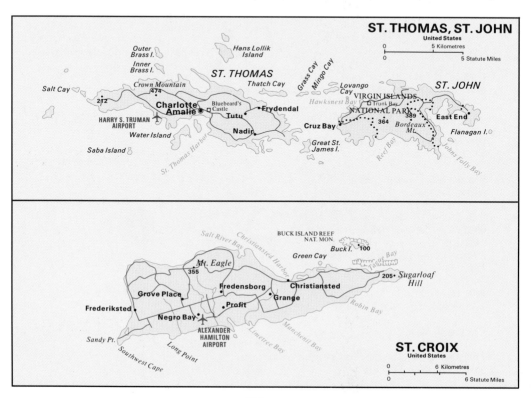

Presidents' Day
Third Monday in February.
Transfer Day
March.
Carnival
Held in April in St. Thomas.
Organic Act Day
June.
Arts Festival on St. Croix
June.
Emancipation Day
July 3.
Independence Day, and Carnival on St. John
July 4.
Supplication Day
July.
Blue Martin Tournament
August.
USVI/Puerto Rico and USVI/BVI Friendship Days
October.
Liberty Day
November.
Crucian Christmas Fiesta
Approximately December 23-January 6.

COMMUNICATIONS

Direct-dialed and operator-assisted long-distance calls may be placed from most hotel and pay phones. Some hotels may also be able to provide telex and telegraph service. However, if you have trouble making any sort of telephone or wire communication, the place to go is ITT. Offices are located at 51-A Kronprindsens in Charlotte Amalie, St. Thomas (Tel: 774-1870), and on Caravelle Arcade, Christiansted, St. Croix (Tel: 773-2525).

Post Offices can be found in the main towns of the three islands, including one at 1 Marshall Hill in Frederiksted, St. Croix, and one on Sugar Estate Road in Charlotte Amalie, St. Thomas (Tel: 774-1950).

WHERE TO STAY

Accommodations on the USVI range in price from US$30 for a double at a number of guesthouses and small hotels on St. Thomas and St. Croix, to US$205 for a double at St. Thomas's Wyndham Virgin. (Both rates quoted are exclusive of meals.) Apartments, condominiums, cottages, villas and campsites are also available, as are a number of meal plans.

ST. CROIX

Villa Morales, P.O. Box 442, Frederiksted, Tel: 772-0556

King Frederik Beach, P.O. Box 1908, Frederiksted, Tel: 772-1205

Chenay Bay, P.O. Box T, Christiansted, Tel: 773-2918

Caravelle, Cross St., Christiansted, Tel: 773-0687

Granada Del Mar, La Grande, Christiansted, Tel: 773-7472

Grapetree Bay, P.O. Box Z, Christiansted, Tel: 773-9000

Queen's Quarter, P.O. Box 770, Christiansted, Tel: 773-3784

ST. JOHN

Raintree Inn, P.O. Box 556, Tel: 776-7449

Star Villa, P.O. Box 599, Tel: 776-6704

Havens with Ambience, P.O. Box 635, Tel: 776-6322

Carla's Cottages, P.O. Box 377, Tel: 776-6133

Caneel Bay , P.O. Box 720, Tel: 776-6111

ST. THOMAS

Ramsey's Guesthouse, P.O. Box 9168, Tel: 774-6521

Mafolie, P.O. Box 1506, Tel: 774-2970

Island Beachcomber, P.O. Box 1618, Tel: 774-5250

Magens Pt., Magens Bay Road, Tel: 775-5500

Point Pleasant, Smith Bay, Tel: 775-7200

Bolongo Bay Beach, P.O. Box 7337, Tel: 775-1800

Mahogany Run, P.O. Box 7517, Tel: 775-5000

Note:
Complete St. Croix addresses with: St. Croix, USVI 00850

Complete St. John Box addresses with: Cruz Bay, St. John, USVI 00830

Complete St. Thomas Box addresses with: Charlotte Amalie, St. Thomas, USVI 00801

Complete non-Box addresses on St. John and St. Thomas with name of island and ZIP code. The USVI's Area Code is 809.

THINGS TO DO

Buck Island: A US National Monument which includes beautiful beaches, two marked underwater snorkeling trails, and scuba diving spots. Just off NE St. Croix.
    Coral World: A marine park and aquarium on St. Thomas which boasts an observation tower built underwater, where you can observe the life of a natural coral reef.
    Estate Annaberg: An abandoned sugar plantation on St. John.
    Forts: Including Fort Christian on St. Thomas and Forts Frederik and Christianvaern on St. Croix. All date from the years of Danish rule and all have been restored. Fort Christian is the oldest - completed in 1678.
    Market Square: Early mornings find fruit and vegetable vendors selling their produce at this spot in Charlotte Amalie, St. Thomas. Christiansted, St. Croix, also has an outdoor market.
    National Park: It takes up fully two-thirds of the island of St. John. Tours are readily available.
    Reichhold Center for the Arts: An outdoor theater on St. Thomas, with performances of almost every kind. Local artists are supplemented by visiting performers.

Steeple Building: In Christiansted, St. Croix. A museum which includes an exhibit of artifacts from the Arawak and Carib Indians who inhabited the islands before the European encroachment. Workings of a sugar plantation are also illustrated.
    Synagogue: In Charlotte Amalie, St. Thomas, is the second oldest in the Western Hemisphere.

FOOD DIGEST

The multinational, multi-ethnic history of the USVI, combined with its tropical location and current international reputation as a vacation spot, have contributed to a rich cuisine on the islands. Locally produced fruits and vegetables and fresh seafood provide some of the raw materials for island cooks, who produce everything from bullfoot soup (just what it sounds like) and "fungi" to French, Italian and Chinese foods.

ST. CROIX

Brady's, Christiansted. Traditional West Indian cooking.

Golden China Inn, Christiansted. Chinese food.

Oskar's, Christiansted. Continental cuisine; daily specials.

Hearts of Palm, Christiansted. Vegetarian food and salads.

La Croisée, Frederiksted. Vegetarian and natural-foods cuisine.

M & S Inn, Frederiksted. French, Continental, and West Indian.

ST. JOHN

Bamboo Inn, Cruz Bay. West Indian foods.

Meada's, Cruz Bay. Tiny and delicious West Indian restaurant. Make reservations.

The Moveable Feast, Cruz Bay. A deli.

Look out for Fish Frys while you are on St. John. Local food and music. They will be announced, or ask at Visitor's Bureau.

ST. THOMAS

Barbary Coast, Frenchtown. Italian fare.

China Gardens, Charlotte Amalie. Chinese cuisine.

Entre Nous, near Magens Bay Beach. French country cooking.

For the Birds, Scott Beach (Compass Point). Tex-Mex. Barbecued ribs.

Sinbad, Charlotte Amalie. Middle-Eastern food.

Victor's Hideaway, west of Charlotte Amalie. West Indian cuisine.

Consult the directories for current phone numbers.

Special Information

The USVI is a renowned shopping spot, and visitors will find a large variety of duty-free items to choose from.

Note: US citizens returning from the USVI have a customs exemption roughly twice that for any other island in the Caribbean. This double exemption applies to the value of gifts mailed home as well (see "Customs"). St. Thomas has a number of handicrafts outlets, and at St. Croix Leap in western St. Croix there are some excellent wood-carvers. The dance styles that have developed on the islands are particularly interesting. Performances occur often, and classes are taught on St. Croix and the other islands. In general, St. John is the more "laid back" of the islands, with St. Thomas and St. Croix offering a more cosmopolitan atmosphere. The USVI is reputedly among the finest scuba diving spots in the world.

GETTING ACQUAINTED

GEOGRAPHY

Located at the top of the Lesser Antilles, near the USVI and Anguilla and only a short hop from Puerto Rico, the British Virgin Islands is made up of over 50 islands, cays and rocks. The largest of these is Tortola, measuring some 12 miles (19 km) long and 4 miles (6 km) wide. Tortola also boasts the highest elevation in the BVI, with one peak reaching 1,780 feet (539 meters). Though most of the islands in the group are of volcanic origin, Anegada to the northeast was formed from coral, and its 28-foot (8-meter) high elevation makes it almost invisible to passengers arriving by sea. Other important isles in the group include Virgin Gorda, Peter Island, and Jost Van Dyke.

ON ARRIVAL

BVI travel information does not readily lend itself to summarization, given the numerous islands which make up the group. Suffice it to say that international air passengers can fly into either the BVI's principal airport, on Beef Island at the east end of Tortola, or into a smaller airport near Spanish Town on Virgin Gorda. Boat passengers may land at Virgin Gorda, Jost Van Dyke, or at one of two ports on Tortola: West End (at the west end!) or Roadtown, capital of the BVI, located toward the center of the island.

From these points of entry, a combination of plane, boat, and/or taxi can take you to your hotel. Not all points in the BVI are directly accessible from all others, so when you make your reservations, make sure to plan your entry into the BVI so as to provide the most direct access possible to your hotel.

DRIVER'S LICENSE

Travelers wishing to drive in the BVI should present their driver's license at the Police Station in Road Town, Tortola, or at any of the BVI's car rental agencies, for a temporary BVI license.

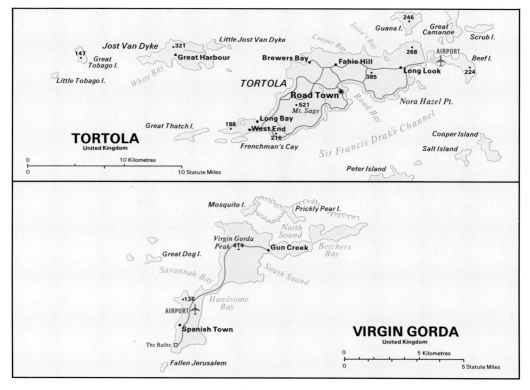

MEDICAL FACILITIES

There is a hospital at Road Town, Tortola and clinics on Tortola and Virgin Gorda. Other islands have nurses on call.

HOLIDAYS

Commonwealth Day
March 10.
Easter Festival
Virgin Gorda's Carnival. Contact Tourist Board for this year's schedule.
Easter Monday
Queen Elizabeth's Birthday
Second Saturday in June.
Territory Day
July 1.
Festival
Tortola's Carnival. First Monday, Tuesday and Wednesday in August are official holidays; festival itself lasts a week.
St. Ursula's Day
October 21.
Heir to Throne's Birthday
November 14.

COMMUNICATIONS

International phone calls may be made from most phones by working through an operator, and some hotels may be able to send telexes and telegrams. If at any time, though, you have trouble making any sort of wire transmission, the place to go is the office of the ubiquitous Cable and Wireless company. Here, you can call or wire with assurance. On Tortola, C&W's main office is on Main St. in Roadtown. The main Post Office on Tortola is also located here. If you are staying on another island, ask your hotel for details of communications procedures.

The BVI has one radio station, ZBVI, and you may be able to pick up transmissions from neighboring islands. At the present time, there is no TV on the BVI.

WHERE TO STAY

Accommodations in the BVI are legion, with most hotels falling in the "smallish" end of the spectrum – 10-40 rooms. Prices range from US$410 for a double on the two-meal-a-day Modified American Plan at Peter Island Hotel and Yacht Harbor, to $50 or less for doubles at several hotels during the summer season. Apartments and cottages are also available, and many accommodations can be rented at weekly or monthly rates. There is a partial list of BVI accommodations included below. Complete details can be obtained from the BVI Tourist Board nearest you.

Telephone prefix for the BVI is: 809-49.

TORTOLA

Way Side Inn Guest House, P.O. Box 258, Road Town, Tortola, British Virgin Islands

Tamarind Country Club Hotel, P.O. Box 509, East End, Tortola, British Virgin Islands, Tel: 52477

Moorings – Mariner Inn, c/o Ginny Cary, P.O. Box 68, Road Town, Tortola, British Virgin Islands, Tel: 42332

Prospect Reef Resort, c/o Graham Sedgwick, P.O. Box 104, Road Town, Tortola, British Virgin Islands, Tel: 43311, Tlx: 7931 PROSPECT VB

Frenchman's Cay Hotel, c/o Neil Goodwin, P.O. Box 1054, West End, Tortola, British Virgin Islands, Tel: 54844

VIRGIN GORDA

Ocean View Hotel, c/o Muriel O'Neal, P.O. Box 66 Virgin Gorda, British Virgin Islands, Tel: 55230

Olde Yard Inn, c/o Carol Kaufman, P.O. Box 26 Virgin Gorda, British Virgin Islands, Tel: 55544

Little Dix Bay Hotel, c/o Joel Jennings, P.O. Box 70, Virgin Gorda, British Virgin Islands, Tel: 55555, Tlx: 3187916, Cable: Dixbay Virgin Gorda

PETER ISLAND

Peter Island Hotel and Yacht Harbour, P.O. Box 211, Road Town, Tortola, British Virgin Islands, Tel: 42561,42562, Tlx: 7923, Cable: PETERTEL

JOST VAN DYKE

White Bay Sandcastle, c/o Billy and Lisa Hawkins, P.O. Box 9997, St. Thomas, USVI 00801, Tel: 42462

THINGS TO DO

Anegada is a good example of a coral island, rising to only 28 feet (8 meters) above sea level at its highest point. To the north and west, the island is blessed with fine beaches, and divers will enjoy the reefs and wrecks offshore.

The **Baths** on Virgin Gorda is an intriguing group of sea caves and unusual rock formations.

Amateur archaeologists and historians might like to visit the abandoned **Copper Mine**, on Virgin Gorda's southeastern tip.

Island Hopping is a delight, given the seemingly endless array of islets and cays which make up the BVI. Norman Island, with its marine caves (which a small boat can enter), and Salt Island, with its two salt evaporation ponds, are potential destinations. Boats – large and small, chartered and bareboat – are readily available in the BVI. The Tourist Board can supply complete rental information.

Mount Sage, at 1,780 feet (539 meters), offers fine hiking opportunities and excellent vistas. The mountain and its surrounding area have been declared a National Park.

FOOD DIGEST

The cuisine of the BVI includes touches of American and Continental cooking, in addition to such Caribbean creations as "fungi" and "roti". Seafood and tropical fruits and vegetables are fresh and plentiful.

GETTING ACQUAINTED

GEOGRAPHY & POPULATION

Anguilla lies at the top of the Lesser Antilles' Leeward Island chain, near the Virgin Islands and St. Martin. Dry and flat (highest elevation, 213 feet), this 16-mile (25-km) long, 4-mile (6-km) wide island bears little resemblance to an eel, but presumably that is what Christopher Columbus had in mind when he christened the island in 1493. ("Anguilla" means "eel" in Spanish.)

Present-day Anguilla is perhaps the quintessential "get away from it all" island. Its population, descended largely from Africans taken to the island as slaves of the British, numbers a mere 7,019. Most residents continue to earn their living through farming, fishing and fine boat-building, although tourism is being actively developed. Day trips to St. Martin are readily available for those who want a taste of a more cosmopolitan scene, but on Anguilla, things are quieter. The visitor won't find fevered shopping centers or flashy nightlife. Just a few friendly people, and miles and miles of beach.

ON ARRIVAL

Juliana Airport is located more or less at the center of Anguilla, a couple of miles from The Valley, the island's principal town. Passengers arriving by boat will disembark further west, at either Road Bay or Blowing Point. Taxis are available at all ports of entry.

DRIVER'S LICENSE

Upon presentation of a valid driver's license from your country of origin, you may, for US$6, purchase a temporary Anguillan driver's license, good for 3 months. The police station in The Valley and the ports of entry can all perform this service.

MEDICAL FACILITIES

There is a 24-bed hospital in The Valley, in addition to three clinics, one each in The Valley, East End, and South Hill. Limited (one dentist, two "dental auxiliaries") but qualified dental services are available. Seriously ill patients are usually transferred to St. Kitts, Puerto Rico, or Tortola, BVI.

HOLIDAYS

New Year's Day*
Large boat race.
Good Friday and Easter Monday*
Whit Monday*
Anguilla Day*
May 30. Athletic contests and major boat race.
Queen's Birthday*
Second Saturday in June.
Carnival
In Anguilla, begins on the Friday before the first Monday in August and runs for a week.
August Monday, August Thursday, and Constitution Day*
First Monday in August and following Thursday and Friday. A weeklong celebration. August Monday Regatta boat race. Big race on August Thursday as well.
Separation Day*
December 19.

Indicates National Holiday.

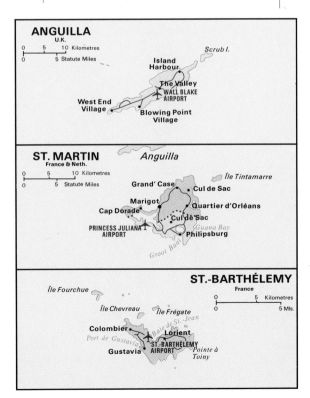

COMMUNICATIONS

International telephone calls, cables and telexes may be made from the offices of **Cable and Wireless** in The Valley. Office hours are: Weekdays, Saturdays and Holidays, 7:30 a.m.-10:30 p.m., Sundays, 10 a.m.-8 p.m. Anguilla has direct-dial services and calls may be received from other countries 24 hours. The **country code** is (809) 497.

There is a **Post Office** in The Valley (Tel: 2528), open from 8 a.m.-12 p.m. and 1 p.m.-3:30 p.m. Monday through Friday; 8 a.m.-12 p.m. Saturday. Areas outside The Valley are served by mobile postal services.

WHERE TO STAY

Hotels are scattered throughout the island. Given Anguilla's size and population, the range of accommodations available is astonishing. Guesthouse rooms go as little as US$15 a day, at the "Norman B". Feeling more extravagant? How about a villa at the "Malliouhana?" US$1,200 a month winter rates. See below for a random selection of accommodations in various price ranges. Options include apartments which rent at daily or weekly rates.

Information and mailing addresses available through Anguilla Department of Tourism. Reservations may be made through the Department as well.

Norman 'B', North Side, Tel: 2242

Fleming's, The Quarter, Tel: 2234

Inter Island, Lower South Hill, Tel: 2259

Holiday Spa, Barnes Bay, Tel: 2871, Tlx: 933

Cinnamon Reef, Little Harbour, Tel: 2707, Tlx: 9307 CINMON LA

Malliouhana, Meads Bay, Tel: 2111

THINGS TO DO

Anguilla's main attraction is its coastline, with its beaches, caves and grottos, swimming activities and abundant watersports. The curious traveler, however, may also be interested in the following:

Boat Racing, which is the island's national sport, takes place on almost every holiday. The beautiful and distinctive boats are built on Anguilla, and used for fishing as well as racing.

Fishing from one of these Anguillan boats can sometimes be arranged, either through a formal charter or through an informal arrangement made with a local fisherman. Ask the fishermen you see launching their boats from the beach. Another possibility is a fishing boat trip to one of Anguilla's tiny neighboring islands. Sombrero Island boasts a lighthouse that can be visited.

A **drive** around the island will take you through a number of small settlements, including a lobster fishing village at Island Harbor. The Wallblake House Museum, near the Valley, is a restored 17th-century plantation house.

FOOD DIGEST

SPECIAL INFORMATION

DINING

As you might expect on a boatbuilding, seagoing island, locally caught seafood is Anguilla's specialty. Conches, lobsters, whelks and tropical fish may be found, prepared in either Continental or the local Creole style. Barbeques – of fish, or of the Islands' ever popular chicken and goat – are another distinctive aspect of local cuisine.

Barbeques often take place on the beach, and the fishing visitor can often make arrangements for beach-cooking of the day's catch. Check with the Tourist Office.

A random listing of some of Anguilla's restaurants is given below.

Aquarium Bar and Restaurant, Round-a-Bout, Tel: 2720. Seafood.

Riviera Bar and Restaurant, Sandy Ground, Tel: 2833. Creole cuisine; live music on Wednesdays.

Harbour View Bar and Restaurant, South Hill, Tel: 2253. West Indian; entertainment on Fridays.

Fish Trap, Island Harbour, Tel: 4488. French cuisine; entertainment on Tuesdays and Saturdays.

Smitty's Sea Side Saloon, Island Harbour, Tel: 4300. Barbecued chicken, fish; entertainment on Saturdays.

Roy's Bar Restaurant, Crocus Bay, Tel: 2470. Fresh fruit specialties; beachfront location.

Anguilla requests that US and Canadian citizens not using passports bring proof of citizenship which includes a photograph. Conservation of water is appreciated. A monthly bulletin put out by the Department of Broadcasting serves as an informal newspaper for the island, in the absence of a local daily. There is a small library in The Valley.

Getting Acquainted

GEOGRAPHY

At the top of the Antilles, between Anguilla and St. Kitts, lies the island of St. Martin. With a reputation way out of all proportion to its size, the 37-sq mile (96-sq km) Sint. Maarten – as the Dutch refer to the island – is a popular cruise, vacation and shopping spot. The Dutch and French each control a part of St. Martin. Their 300 years of peaceful coexistence is remarkable, given the Caribbean's stormy history. To this day, there is no formal border crossing between parts of the island – only a marker and some welcoming signs. The island's geography echo its relatively peaceful history: for the most part, St. Martin is rolling and green, and Mt. Paradis (the highest point) rises to only 1,278 feet (387 meters).

Near St. Martin, and easily accessible from it, are three small but fascinating islands, Saba, St. Eustatius (known as Statia) and St. Barthelemy (St. Barts).

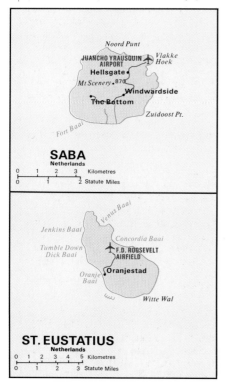

ST. BARTS

St. Barthelemy or **St. Barts** – is a 9-square mile (23-square km) French island, 15 miles (24 km) southeast of St. Martin. Settled by Norman and Breton farmers, and never integrated into the system of plantation agriculture which plagued most Caribbean islands, St. Barts is said to resemble a little chunk of northwest France set in the tropical sea. The look of the countryside, the farms, and the dress of the island all suggest rural France of some years ago. The capital town, Gustavia, is beautiful and enchanting, still bearing something of the imprint of the Swedes who controlled the island from 1784-1878. In recent years, St. Barts has become popular enough to offer a large number of hotels, many concentrated around St. Jean Bay to the north. Shoppers will also find a fairly wide range of offerings, mostly in Gustavia. Despite St. Barts popularity, however, its pace is still slow and meditative.

Note: Do **not** photograph St. Barts residents unless you have their express permission to do so. You may feel tempted by their sometimes "quaint" looking dress, but please respect their privacy.

SABA

Saba, located 28 sq miles (72 sq km) south of St. Martin, may be one of the only Caribbean islands that does not offer beautiful beaches. In fact, Saba offers no beaches at all, to speak of. There just isn't room: the highest point on this 5-sq mile (13-sq km) island is fully 3,000 feet (909 meters) tall, giving the whole island the look of a verdant cone. Although Saba was colonized at least 350 years ago, the first road on the island wasn't built until the mid-1940s, and 24-hour electric service was only instituted in 1970. Today, Saba's 1,000 inhabitants play host to some 15,000 visitors annually – a huge number compared to a few years ago, but hardly a drop in the bucket compared to the tourist traffic on other islands.

ST. ESTATIUS

St. Estatius, usually called **Statia**, is an 8-square mile (20-square km) island of great scenic and historic richness. Here it was that the US flag received its first salute from a foreign power, on November 16, 1776. At that time, Statia was one of the Caribbean's wealthiest islands, due to its location along major trade routes. Supplies to the 13 rebelling colonies often came through Statia – as did Benjamin Franklin's European mail! Statia also profited from the slave trade, and the abolition of slavery – together with changes in trade routes – ended Statia's opulence.

ON ARRIVAL

By air, visitors touch down at Juliana Airport on the Dutch side of the island. Sea passengers are likely to land at Philipsburg, the Dutch side's most important town and a popular cruise port, though some may land at Marigot or Grand Case on the French side. At all of these ports of entry, travelers may obtain cabs to transport them to their hotels.

Which side of the island you stay on may determine the type of experience you have on St. Martin. The island's French side is slower, quieter, and less populated, even though it is substantially larger than the Dutch side. Evening entertainment here might best consist of a leisurely meal. On the Dutch side, things are faster, more concentrated, more "swinging", with casinos and resort hotels abounding. The island is so small, in any case, that passing from one side to the other is no problem – but you might wish to select one or the other as your primary locale.

DRIVER'S LICENSE

Any and all valid ones are accepted.

St. Barts: Car rentals are available, but advance reservations – always a good idea – are particularly important on this little island. Also, be aware that most rental cars have **standard transmissions**.

Saba: Car rentals are not available – but there's only one road on the island anyway! Taxis and tour operators can take you where you wish to go.

St. Estatius: Rental cars are readily available on Statia. Make advance reservations.

MEDICAL FACILITIES

Hospitals in Marigot and Philipsburg. Hotels can help you hook up with English speaking doctors.

HOLIDAYS

French St. Martin's calendar resembles Guadeloupe's – with the exception, of course, of those events local to Guadeloupe. Dutch St. Martin's calendar is as follows:**Coronation and Labor Days** – April 30 and May 1; **Ascension Day; Whit Monday; St. Martin Day** – Celebrated on both sides of the island. November 11; **Kingdom Day** – December 15.

COMMUNICATIONS

On both sides of the island, overseas calls can be made from most phones, including pay phones, and most large hotels can dispatch telexes. For telegrams, French side visitors should go to the post

office where, incidentally, calls and telexes may also be made if need be. In Marigot, the Post Office is on Rue de la Liberté. In Philipsburg, telegram traffic (as well as telephone calls and telexes) goes through a central communications office in the newer Pondfill section of town, between Loodsteeg and Market Street. Dutch side hotels may also be able to send telegrams. The Philipsburg post office is on the Ruyterplein in the center of town. Before trekking to the post office for stamps though, ask at your hotel desk or, on the French side, a café tabac. Stamps are often available at these locations.

WHERE TO STAY

ST. MARTIN

Hotels on St. Martin are not cheap. During the peak winter season, the least expensive double in a major hotel on the Dutch side is about US$50 (the Caribbean Hotel). Most run between US$100-200, and the Bel Air Beach Hotel asks a minimum of US$325. During the summer season, of course, many of these rates would be substantially discounted, often 30-50 percent. On the French side the lowest priced double costs FrF 250, about US$35, at the Beausejour. Many hotels offer doubles for under US$100, although rates ranged up to US$400 at La Samanna. These rates, of course, would rise substantially in the winter.

Both sides have small guesthouses, as well as apartments, villas, etc., which can be rented at weekly or monthly rates.

• **Dutch Side**

Caribbean Hotel, P.O. Box 236, Tel: 22028
Seaview Hotel, P.O. Box 65, Tel: 22323
Great Bay Beach Hotel, P.O. Box 310, Tel: 22446
Little Bay Beach Hotel, P.O. Box 61, Tel: 22333
The Oyster Pond, P.O. Box 239, Tel: 22206
Bel Air Beach Hotel, P.O. Box 61, Tel: 23366

• **French Side**

Beausejour, Marigot 97150, Tel: 875-218
Coralita Beach Hotel, Baie Lucas 97150 , Tel: 875-181
Petite Plage, Grand Case 97150, Tel: 875-065
Le Galion, Baie de L'Embouchure 97150, Tel: 875-177
L'Habitation, Anse Marcel 97150, Tel: 875-928
La Samanna, Baie Longue 97150, Tel: 875-122

ST. BARTHELEMY

Corsaire, Gustavia 97133, Tel: 276-239
Village Saint Jean, St. Jean 97133, Tel: 276-139
Les Mouettes, Lorient 97133, Tel: 276-074
Baie Des Anges, Anse Des Flamands 97133, Tel: 276-361
St. Barth's Beach Hotel, Grand Cul de Sac 97133, Tel: 276-263
Hostellerie des Trois Forces, Vitet 97133, Tel: 276-125

SABA

Saba maintains a few small and delightful inns and guesthouses for overnight visitors.

Captain's Quarters, Tel: 2201
Carribe Guesthouse, Tel: 3259
Cranston's Antique Inn, Tel: 3203
Scout's Place, Tel: 2205

ST. ESTATIUS

Lodging is readily available on Statia. Make advance reservations.

Fairplay Villas, Tel: 2395, 2270
The Old Gin House, Tel: 2319
Hotel Gloria, Tel: 2378
La Maison sur la Plage, Tel: 2256

THINGS TO DO

ST. MARTIN

St. Martin is known primarily for its beaches, watersports, shopping, and, on the Dutch side, nightlife. Nevertheless, a drive through St. Martin's beautiful countryside, away from the large towns and resorts, can greatly enrich your stay. Some places you may want to go: **Oyster Pond** on the east coast, for its scenery; **Cul de Sac** in the north, where you can walk along St. Martin's uninhabited northern tip; **Mount Paradis**, the island's highest point, which is accessible by road; and **Cole Bay Hill**, between the airport and Philipsburg, from where you can view the neighboring islands of St. Barthelemy, Saba, and St. Eustatius.

SABA

Visitors to Saba can stroll the stone-cut steps that once formed the only paths between the islands' four villages. The steps also climb to the top of Mt. Scenery — Saba's highest point. The town of Windward-side boasts a small museum dedicated to Saba's well-known seafarers; the museum is located in a 100-year-old sea captain's cottage. In the Bottom, Saba's capital (population: 350), you'll find the Saba Artisan's Foundation, where visitors can buy locally designed and produced clothing and fabric. Another popular handicraft is Saba Lace, which has been made here for over 100 years. For scuba divers, Saba offers breathtaking tropical caves and cliffs inhabited by tropical fishes and coral. Those who prefer to remain on land can feast their eyes on the island's beautiful "gingerbread" houses.

ST. ESTATIUS

Visitors to Statia today find attractions ranging from the 350-year-old Fort Oranje, to the second oldest synagogue in the Western Hemisphere, to a museum of pre- and post-colonial artifacts and remains, housed in an historic 18th-Century house. Hikers will find a lush rainforest covering an ancient volcano, through which flits an iridescent hummingbird unique to Statia. Snorkelers and divers can swim among submerged warehouses and taverns from the old port, and visit a number of shipwrecks — some of them over 300 years old.

FOOD DIGEST

ST. MARTIN

St. Martin's restaurants reflect the various cultures which have come together on the island. On both sides, traditional French cooking and spicy West Indian cuisine are available. Sometimes the two rub off on one another, as when a familiar French recipe is prepared with very un-French tropical fruits. On the Dutch side, dining options also include such Dutch favorites as pea soup and sausages. An unexpected dining experience, though, is offered by restaurants serving *rijstaffel*, an Indonesian meal as huge and complex as a Javanese gamelan. It comes to St. Martin via the Dutch, who once colonized Indonesia.

A partial listing of restaurants on St. Martin is

included here, but there are many more to be discovered:

• **French Side**

Bistrot Nu, Marigot (No phone). Locally popular restaurant; seafood, French and Italian cooking.

Cas' Anny, Marigot, Tel: 875-338. French and Creole cooking.

La Diva, Marigot, Tel: 875-319. Italian.

Le Jardin Brésilien, Marigot, Tel: 875-488. Famous for ice-cream and desserts.

Le Santal, Nettle Bay Beach, near Marigot, Tel: 875-348. Internationally renowned as one of the best restaurants in the Caribbean, let alone St. Martin. French. Expensive.

La Rhumerie, Colombier, Tel: 875-698. Expensive Creole restaurant, well-known and popular.

Auberge Gourmande, Grand Case (No phone). Burgundian and other French fare.

Hoa Mai, Grand Case, No phone. Vietnamese cuisine.

Madame Chance, Grand Case, Tel: 875-045. French Creole; reserve early.

• **Dutch side**

Bilbquet, On Pointe Blanche near Philipsburg , (No phone). Wide ranging menu; two complete dinners offered each night. Reservations must be made in person, at least 24 hours in advance. Small place - in private home.

Callaloo, Frontstreet, Philipsburg (No phone). Locally popular bar/restaurant.

Calypso, Simpson Bay, near airport, Tel: 44233. West Indian cuisine.

Fandango Restaurant, Frontstreet, Philipsburg, Tel: 3454. "Snacky" meals, omelets, salad bar.

Le Bec Fin/La Coupole, Frontstreet, Philipsburg, Tel: 2976. French food in 18th century courtyard; bakery, open for breakfast.

Le Pavillon, Simpson Bay Village, Tel: 4254. Open-air French dining.

Paradise Cafe, Maho Village (No phone). Californian/Mexican cuisine; mesquite grill.

West Indian Tavern, Frontstreet, Philipsburg, Tel: 2965. Seafood; garden and/or sidewalk dining.

ST. BARTHELEMY

La Crémaillére, Gustavia, Tel: 276-389. Traditional French fare.

La Langouste, Gustavia, Tel: 276-640. Creole, lobster a specialty.

Le Brigantin, Gustavia, Tel: 276-028. Classy Continental dining with huge wine list.

Presqu'île, Gustavia, Tel: 276-460. Delicious Creole cooking.

Brasserie La Créole, St. Jean Bay (No phone). Open-air brasserie/cafe, serving delicious early breakfasts, in addition to lunch and dinner.

La Louisiane, St. Jean Bay (No phone). Provençal style cooking.

Topolino, St. Jean Bay (No phone). Inexpensive salad, steak, and barbecue restaurant. Italian, too.

SPECIAL INFORMATION

St. Barts, St. Eustatius, and Saba can all be reached by regular air service from St. Martin, and St. Barts is served by several catamarans and one hydrofoil, all out of Philipsburg harbor. St. Barts and St. Martin are parts of the Department of Guadeloupe; Saba, Statia, and St. Martin are each individual members of the Netherlands Antilles. Telephone communications between French and Dutch St. Martin, once a hit-or-miss proposition, have been greatly simplified. To go from French to Dutch, dial 93 plus the 4-digit St. Martin number; to go from Dutch to French, dial 06, then the 6-digit St. Martin number. Marigot is the capital of French St. Martin, but don't overlook Grand Case — especially if you are searching for a restaurant. Grand Case has many fine ones. Don't miss the delicious creations of St. Martin's many French bakeries.

Getting Acquainted

GEOGRAPHY

The two-island nation of St. Kitts and Nevis lies toward the northern end of the Leeward Island Chain, in the vicinity of St. Martin, Antigua, and Montserrat. The volcanic origin of these islands is apparent in their mountainous geography: 23-mile-long (36 km), 6½-mile-wide (10 km) St. Kitts is dominated by 3,792-foot (1,150-meter) Mt. Liamuiga, while 3,232-foot (979-meter) Nevis Peak towers over 7 by 9 mile (11 by 14 km) Nevis. Over time, the lava flows have been softened by the grasses and forests that now blanket the islands. The lava's legacy remains, however, in the fertile soil from which islanders derive much of their income, and in the black-sand beaches which ring St. Kitts.

ON ARRIVAL

St. Kitts is served by Golden Rock Airport, from which taxis are available for the 2½ mile (4 km) trip to Basseterre – the island's major town and capital of St. Kitts and Nevis. Taxis also serve the island's scattered hotels. Travelers flying to Nevis land at Newcastle airport, a 7-mile (11-km) jaunt from Nevis's principal and only town, Charlestown. Once again, taxis are on hand to bring visitors to their destinations. Visitors travelling between the islands may use the Basseterre-Charlestown ferry, a 40-minute ride which runs daily except Thursday and Sunday.

DRIVER'S LICENSE

Visitors who wish to drive must present a valid national or international license at the Traffic Department, along with a payment of EC$10. A temporary license will then be issued. Branches of the Traffic Department are located at the police stations in Basseterre (Cayon St.) and Charlestown (Island Road).

MEDICAL FACILITIES

St. Kitts has two hospitals, the Joseph N. France General Hospital in Basseterre and a small hospital in Sandy Point, towards the island's west end. The Alexandra hospital in Charlestown is Nevis's only hospital.

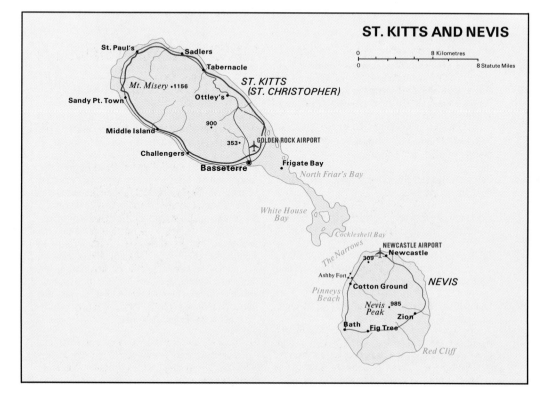

HOLIDAYS

Good Friday and Easter Monday* – Horse races on Monday.
Whit Monday*
Queen's Birthday* – Second Saturday in June.
Culturama – Late June-early August. Arts festival on Nevis.
August Monday* – First Monday in August.
Independence Day* – September 19.
Prince of Wales' Birthday* – November 14.
Carnival – Mid-December till New Year's.
Carnival Day* – Date variable; falls during Carnival.

* *Indicates National Holiday.*

COMMUNICATIONS

International telephone calls may be made from any phone 24 hours by dialing "0" and working through an Operator. Calls to St. Kitts and Nevis from foreign lands can be direct-dialed, using International Area/National code 809-465.

Telegrams and telexes go through the offices of Cable & Wireless, which are open 7 a.m.-7 p.m. on weekdays, 7 a.m.-2 p.m. and 7-8 p.m. on Saturdays, and 7-10 a.m. and 7-8 p.m. on Sundays and holidays. Offices are located at: **Cayon St.**, Basseterre, St. Kitts, Tel: 2219 and **Main Street**, Charlestown, Nevis, Tel: 5-294

Post Offices, located on Bay Road in Basseterre and Main Street in Charlestown, are open 8 a.m.-3 p.m. weekdays except Thursdays, 8-11 a.m. Thursdays.

WHERE TO STAY

Hotels in St. Kitts and Nevis are for the most part small, and many boast of having at least one employee per room. National law prohibits any hotel from being more than three floors tall, so the gleaming (and impersonal) towers that have sprouted on other islands are unknown here. A number of hotels are actually converted plantation houses and sugar mills.

Rates vary, from the US$20 double at the Windsor Guesthouse in Basseterre and the Trinity Apartments on Palmetto Point, to US$260 for a "Superior" Double in peak season at Nevis's Nisbet Plantation Inn.

St. Kitts and Nevis also offer a number of apartments, condominiums and cottages, many for rent at weekly rates. Full details on these and all accommodations may be obtained by contacting the St. Kitts-Nevis Tourist Board office nearest you.

Complete St. Kitts addresses with: St. Kitts, W.I.; Nevis addresses with: Nevis, W.I.

The direct-dial code for both islands is (809) 465.

ST. KITTS

Windsor Guesthouse, P.O. Box 122, Basseterre, Tel: 3224

Fairview Inn, P.O. Box 212, Tel 2472 or 2473, Tlx: 6811 PUBTLX SKB FAIRVIEW

Ocean Terrace Inn, P.O. Box 65, Tel: 2754, 2380, Tlx: 6821 OTI KC, Cable: OTI

Leeward Cove Condominium Hotel, P.O. Box 123, Frigate Bay, Tel: 8030, Cable: LEECOVE

The Golden Lemon, Dieppe Bay, Tel: 7260, Cable: GOLEMON

NEVIS

Austin Guesthouse, Bay Front, Charlestown, Tel: 5279

Rest Haven Inn, P.O. Box 209, Charlestown, Tel: 5208

Nisbet Plantation Inn, Newcastle, Nevis, Tel: 5325 Cable: BEACHLANDS

Cliffdwellers Hotel, Tamarind Bay, Tel: 5262

THINGS TO DO

The **Bath House** near Charlestown on Nevis is once again open to visitors as it was in the 19th century, when its hot springs were a popular haunt of European travelers.

Black Rocks, on the northern coast of St. Kitts, is a deposit of ancient lava which joins with the ocean to make for dramatic viewing.

The fort at **Brimstone Hill** offers something for history and nature buffs alike. The same high, inaccessible location, which earned it the name "The Gibraltar of the Indies" during the many French-British battles of the colonial period, now makes the fort an ideal spot for catching beautiful views. It is located on St. Kitts's southwest coast.

Alexander Hamilton was born on Nevis, and his reconstructed birthplace is now a museum. It is on Main Street in Charlestown.

Hiking is a delight on both islands, with their rain forests and mountainous terrain. A particular thrill is the hike down into the crater of an old volcano on Mt. Liamuiga in St. Kitts. Guided hikes are readily available – talk to the Tourist Office or your hotel.

Inscriptions of Carib and other American Indians are preserved at Wingfield Estates, West Farm and Pond Pasture, on St. Kitts.

The memory of the British seaman **Horatio Nelson** is kept alive on Nevis at the Lord Nelson Museum. Nelson was married to one of Nevis's own at Montpelier, a 17th-century structure which has now been restored. The couple's original marriage certificate is housed at Fig Tree Church. All three sites are in southwest Nevis.

A **Primate Research Station** at Estridge Estate in northern St. Kitts is open to the public. Its object of study: the vervet monkey, which lives on both islands.

The Basseterre **Sugar factory** is worth seeing to find out where the white stuff actually comes from. For a real eye-opener, find someone to describe to you the gruelling manual labor required to harvest sugar.

FOOD DIGEST

St. Kitts and Nevis boast restaurants specializing in West Indian, Creole, French, Indian and Chinese fare. In addition to the Caribbean's ubiquitous fresh seafood, perhaps the most distinctive feature of St. Kitts and Nevis cuisine is the abundance of fresh vegetables from the islands' volcanic soil. Tropical produce such as breadfruit joins more familiar items – eggplant, sweet potatoes, okra – on island plates. Below you will find a selection of St. Kitts and Nevis restaurants:

Bistro Creole, Cayon Street, Basseterre, St. Kitts, Tel: 4138. Creole cuisine.

Ballahoo, Bayfront, Basseterre, St. Kitts, Tel: 4047. West Indian; seafood; fruit drinks; scenic balcony.

West Indian Tavern, North Square Street, Basseterre, St. Kitts. West Indian cuisine.

Ocean Terrace Inn, Fortlands, near Basseterre, St. Kitts, Tel: 2754, 2380. Well-known for West Indian and Continental cooking

The Golden Lemon, Dieppe Bay, St. Kitts, Tel: 7260. Internationally acclaimed; Continental and West Indian; reservations required.

Cliffdwellers, Tamarind Bay, Nevis, Tel: 5262. Seafood, fresh tropical fruits.

Golden Rock Estate, Nevis, Tel: 5346. Known for its rum punch; located in early 19th-century stone building.

Longstone House Restaurant, Main St. Charlestown, Nevis, Tel: 5624. Creole and continental food; located in a late 18th-century house; known for imaginative drinks.

Nisbet Plantation Inn, Nevis, Tel: 5325. Serves lunch on beach; Sunday barbecue on beach.

SPECIAL INFORMATION

Strong currents make swimming on the Atlantic side of the islands more dangerous than swimming on the Caribbean side. St. Kitts boasts the Caribbean's only veterinary school, Ross University. St. Kitts and Nevis are known for the batik prints which their artists create. Clothes, hangings, etc. are often made from cotton grown right on the islands. Romney Manor, a restored St. Kitts manse, now houses a batik workshop; both house and shop are open to the public. There is one casino on the islands, at Frigate Bay, St. Kitts.

GETTING ACQUAINTED

GEOGRAPHY & POPULATION

Toward the top of the Antilles, surrounded by St. Barts, St. Kitts and Nevis, Montserrat, and Guadeloupe, lie Antigua and Barbuda. Together with a third island, the uninhabited Redonda, Antigua and Barbuda form an independent nation within the British Commonwealth. Antigua is relatively dry and flat, with a highest elevation of 1,360 feet (412 meters). The 62 square mile (161 square km) Barbuda is even flatter (highest elevation, 207 feet), but in contrast to Antigua, Barbuda still retains much of its forest cover. Much of the island, in fact, is given over to a game preserve. The combined population of the islands is around 75,000 with most people living on Antigua.

ON ARRIVAL

Travelers to Antigua generally enter the country (by plane) at **Antigua International Airport**, or (by boat) at the capital town of **St. John's**. Both ports of entry are in the north of the island, and at both, taxis will be available to take you to your destination.

DRIVER'S LICENSE

Would-be drivers should present their regular licenses, along with a fee of US$10 at a police station in order to be issued a local driving permit.

MEDICAL FACILITIES

There is a hospital in St. John's and one on Barbuda. In addition, there are clinics on both islands.

HOLIDAYS

Men's Tennis Week
Professional and amateur tournaments. Held in January.
Women's Tennis Week
Professional and amateur tournaments. Held in early April.

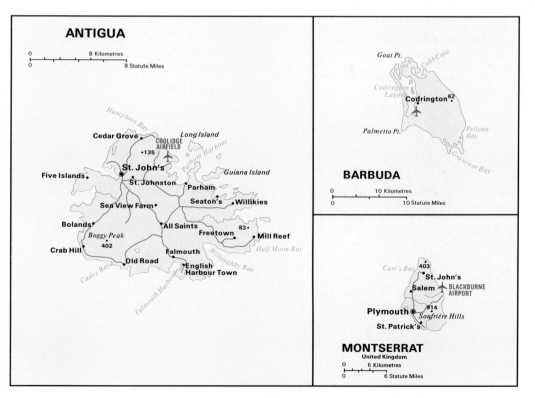

Race Week
　Week of boat races between participants from all over Caribbean. Held in late April.
Whit Monday*
Queen's Birthday*
　First Saturday in June.
Carnival
　Held during week before first Monday of August.
August Monday and Tuesday*
　First Monday and Tuesday in August.
Independence Day*
　November 1.
Independence Week Half Marathon
　Early November.
Christmas and Boxing Day*
　December 25 and 26.

* Indicates National Holiday.

COMMUNICATIONS

Local and long-distance telephone calls may be made 24 hours from most phones on the island. Calls may also be placed at **Cable and Wireless** offices. To send cables of all kinds, go to Cable and Wireless. In St. John's, the C&W office is on St. Mary Street, and there is a 24-hour office at Wireless – near Clare Hill in northern Antigua.

In St. John's, the **post office** is located on Long Street.

There is only one local **radio station** in Antigua; however, if your radio set has powerful reception, you may be able to catch signals from other islands. Some hotels have cable TV, with movies and American programs – but don't expect to find a TV in your room unless you've confirmed in advance that your hotel provides sets.

WHERE TO STAY

For the summer season, doubles at Antiguan hotels range in price from US$44 a night, exclusive of meals, at the Admiral's Inn and Falmouth Harbour Beach Apartments, to US$550 a night, including two meals per person, at the St. James Club and Casino. Many doubles are clustered in the US$50-US$90 range. For budget-minded travelers, or those contemplating an extended stay, Antigua offers a range of guesthouses, apartments, and villas, some at weekly or monthly rates.

Barbuda has one small hotel and a few guesthouses.

Complete addresses with: St. John's, Antigua, W.I. International Dialing Code: 809.

Falmouth Harbour Beach Apartments, P.O. Box 713, Tel: 463-1027/463-1534

Admiral's Inn, P.O. Box 713 , Tel: 463-1027/463-1534

Blue Heron Beach Hotel, P.O. Box 185, Tel: 463/1421, Tlx: 2164 AK

Galley Bay Surf Club, P.O. Box 305, Tel: 462-0302

Siboney Beach Club, P.O. Box 222, Tel: 462-3356/462-0806, Tlx: 2172 AK

Half Moon Bay Hotel, P.O. Box 144, Tel: 463-2101, Tlx: 2138

St. James Club and Casino, P.O. Box 63, Tel: 463-1113, Tlx: 2088 ST. JCLUB

THINGS TO DO

Archaeological sites, revealing remains of Antigua's pre-Columbian inhabitants. The best known sites are at Indian Creek and Mill Reef in the southeast.

Devil's Bridge, a natural bridge in the northeast.

Dow's Hill, with its museum of remains from the Arawak people.

Fig Tree Drive, a road which runs up from the south coast into what remains of Antigua's rainforest.

Forts, dating from the 18th century. There are at least six of them on the island.

Megaliths – ancient arrangements of stones, á la Stonehenge – on Greencastle Hill.

Nelson's Dockyard, the old British naval base, at which Horatio Nelson once served. Complete with two museums.

St. John's, where you'll find historic government buildings, handicraft and import shops, a botanic garden, a rum distillery, and an intriguing cathedral.

FOOD DIGEST

American standbys like hamburgers and steaks are available here, but why not try some local dishes, like chicken, rice, and peas, or some of Antigua's international cuisine? French, Italian and Vietnamese cooking are among the options:

L'Aventure, Dian Point, Long Bay, Tel: 32003. French and Continental.

Boston's Restaurant, Michael's Ave., St. John's, Tel: 24510. Local Antiguan cooking.

Shirley Heights Lookout, Nelson's Dockyard, Tel: 31274. Seafood; Antiguan arts and crafts shop.

Kim Sha Bar and Restaurant, Church St., St. John's, Tel: 24505. Chinese cuisine.

The Satay Hut, Barrymore Beach Apartments, Tel: 24101. Indonesian Satay; American dishes, too.

Buccaneer Cove, Dickenson Bay, Tel: 20959, 22173. Lobster a specialty; Calypso on Wednesdays, Steelband music on Saturdays, Jazz on Sundays.

SPECIAL INFORMATION

In the Caribbean, Antigua's Carnival is second in size only to Trinidad's. "Antigua Black" pineapple is reputed to be the sweetest in the world. St. John's has an open-air market, where shoppers can stock up on local food.

Getting Acquainted

Communications

GEOGRAPHY

Montserrat is located in the north-central part of the Leeward Island chain near Nevis, Antigua, and Guadeloupe. A British Crown Colony, Montserrat is known as the Emerald Isle of the Caribbean, both for its lushness and for the large numbers of Irish immigrants who flocked to its shores in the early colonial period. Montserrat's highest point, the 3,000-foot (909-meter) Chance's peak, is of a size to compare with Ireland's "bens", but the island itself is just a wee chunk, measuring 12 by 7 miles (19 by 11 km). See page 318 for the map of Montserrat. The island's population is approximately 12,500.

ON ARRIVAL

Travelers arriving by boat will disembark at the island's principle town, Plymouth. Air arrivals will touch down at Blackburne Airport, 11 miles (17 km) outside of Plymouth. At both points of entry, cabs are available to take you to any of Montserrat's five hotels, several guesthouses, or numerous apartments, condominiums and villas.

MEDICAL FACILITIES

The 68-bed Glendon Hospital is located in Plymouth and there are several dental clinics on the island as well. Severely ill patients may be taken to Barbados or Guadeloupe for treatment.

HOLIDAYS

St. Patrick's Day
An important date on this Irish-settled isle.
Whit Monday
Queen's Birthday
Second Saturday in June.
August Monday
First Monday in August.
Carnival
Runs from December 15 to January 2 here.

International calls can be made from hotel phones, or from the offices of **Cable and Wireless** on Church Road in Plymouth. Cable and Wireless is also the place to go to send telegrams and telexes. The **Post Office** is on Marine Drive in Plymouth, and is open from 8:15 a.m. to 3:55 p.m. on Mondays, Tuesdays, Thursdays and Fridays, and from 8:15 a.m. to 11:25 a.m. on Wednesdays and Saturdays.

Where to Stay

Accommodation rates in Montserrat range from US$10 a night for a double at both Humphrey's and Peter's guesthouses in Kinsale, to US$225 for a two bedroom efficiency at the Montserrat Springs Hotel during the peak winter season. When planning your trip, though, remember that the mid-April to mid-December "off-season" offers huge savings, both here and elsewhere in the Caribbean. The same Montserrat Springs suite goes for US$135 in the summer!

Apartments go from as low as US$75 a week for a summertime studio to US$350 a week for a wintertime double, at the Lime Court and Belham Valley Apartments, respectively. Villas go for as low as US$45 a night (summer), and as high as US$80 a night (winter), with weekly and monthly rates available.

Montserrat's direct-dial prefix is (809) 491.

Humphrey's Guesthouse, Kinsale, Tel: 2904, 2453

Peter's Guesthouse, Kinsale , Tel: 2628

Riley's Guesthouse, Kinsale, Tel: 2043

Wade Inn, Parliament St., Plymouth, Tel: 2881

Shamrock Villas, P.O. Box 180 , Tel: 2434

Vue Pointe, P.O. Box 65, Tel: 5210, Cable: VUEPOINTE

Coconut Hill, P.O. Box 337, Tel: 2144, 2423, Cable: COCONUTHILL

Flora Fountain, Lower Dagenham, P.O. Box 373, Plymouth, Tel: 3444, 3445, Cable: RUPCHAND

Montserrat Springs, P.O. Box 259, Tel: 2481, 2482, Cable: MONTEL

THINGS TO DO

Air Studio, located on one of Montserrat's mountain tops, has hosted recording sessions by some of the best, including Paul McCartney, Stevie Wonder, The Who, and The Police.

Galway Soufriere adds a bit o' the moon to Montserrat's otherwise verdant landscape. The rocks of this dormant volcano are encrusted with sulphur, and surrounded by hot pools and steam jets.

Hiking through Montserrat's forested mountains can bring you to, among other places, the 70-foot (21-meter) Great Alps Waterfall, and the top of Chance's Peak with its lovely views.

The Museum at Richmond, open on Wednesdays and Sundays, houses artifacts from the Carib and Arawak Indians who once inhabited the island. At the museum, ask if there are currently any archaeological digs going on which travelers may visit. The museum is housed in an old sugar mill.

Plymouth is a lovely town for walking in, and on Saturdays, the weekly public market takes place. It is both a colorful and a practical event, as the visitor will find a large selection of the island's fresh produce for sale.

FOOD DIGEST

Montserrat's own West Indian cuisine is supplemented by restaurants specializing in Indian, Italian and Continental dishes. Things to look for in particular are the profusion of fresh vegetables from the island's gardens, and the local specialty known as Goat Water, a goat stew.

SPECIAL INFORMATION

The island has one disco and two movie theaters. Boat trips around the island are available. Many of Montserrat's beaches are formed of black, volcanic sand. There are a number of underground mineral springs on the island. Tennis courts are available at Vue Pointe Hotel.

GETTING ACQUAINTED

GEOGRAPHY

South of Antigua and Montserrat and north of Dominica, towards the center of the Lesser Antilles, lies Guadeloupe. At 530 square miles (1,378 square km), the butterfly-shaped Guadeloupe is one of the Lesser Antilles' largest islands, and the 4,813-foot (1,458-meters) La Soufriere volcano ensures dramatic scenery to match the island's size. Dramatic is a word that could be applied equally well to the island's colorful population, made up of peoples of African, European, and Indian origin. These disparate groups have each contributed to Guadeloupe's present-day culture – including its cuisine, reported to be among the Caribbean's finest.

ON ARRIVAL

Seagoing passengers arrive in Guadeloupe at centrally-located Point-a-Pitre, which, along with Basse-Terre, is one of the island's two major towns. Air passengers touch down for the most part at the Rizet International Airport outside Point-a-Pitre, although some traffic passes through airfields near Basse-Terre and St. Francois – at the west and east ends of Guadeloupe, respectively. At all points of entry, taxis are available to take you to your hotel, and Point-a-Pitre and Raizet airport both have car rental agencies as well.

DRIVER'S LICENSE

Any valid license will do, but travelers wishing to drive here must have at least one year's driving experience.

MEDICAL FACILITIES

There are 5 hospitals and 23 clinics, many with English speaking doctors. Hotels and the Tourist Board can help you locate doctors for day-to-day needs.

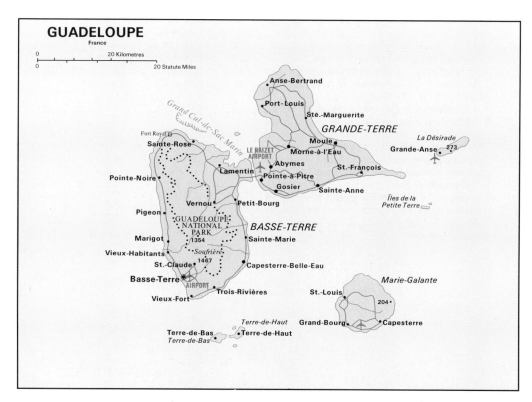

GUADELOUPE
France

0   20 Kilometres
0   20 Statute Miles

Grand Cul-de-Sac Marin

Anse-Bertrand
Port-Louis
Ste.-Marguerite
Fort Royal
Sainte-Rose
GRANDE-TERRE
Moule
La Désirade
Morne-à-l'Eau
Grande-Anse   273
LE RAIZET AIRPORT
Abymes
Lamentin
Pointe-Noire
Pointe-à-Pitre
St.-François
Gosier
Sainte-Anne
Vernou
Petit-Bourg
Îles de la Petite Terre
Pigeon
GUADELOUPE NATIONAL PARK
1354
BASSE-TERRE
Marigot
Sainte-Marie
Vieux-Habitants
Soufrière
1467
St.-Claude
Capesterre-Belle-Eau
Marie-Galante
Basse-Terre
AIRPORT
St.-Louis
Vieux-Fort
Trois-Rivières
204
Terre-de-Haut
Grand-Bourg
Capesterre
Terre-de-Bas
Terre-de-Haut
Terre-de-Bas

HOLIDAYS

Epiphany – January 6.
Carnival – Celebrated on weekends from the beginning of January all the way through Ash Wednesday.
Mi-Careme – Mid-Lent celebration.
Ascension Thursday*
Pentecost Monday*
Bastille Day* – July 14.
Schoelcher Day* – July 21. Celebrates freedom from slavery.
Cook's Festival – Occurs in August in Point-a-pitre.
Assumption Day* – August 15.
Tour de la Guadeloupe – International bicycle race in mid-August.
All Saints Day* – November 1.
Armistice Day* – November 11.
Saint Cecilia's Day – Musical festivities. November 22.
Christmas Eve – Dancing, dining, midnight Mass, carols.
Young Saints Day – Children's parade. December 28.
Reveillon de la Saint Sylvestre – New Year's Eve celebrations.

* Indicates National Holiday.

COMMUNICATIONS

Long-distance telephone calls can be made from most hotels and pay phones, and hotels can handle telex traffic. Telegrams can be sent from post offices. In Point-a-Pitre, post offices are located on Boulevard Hanne and Boulevard Legitimus; Basse-Terre's branch is on the Rue du Docteur Cabre.

WHERE TO STAY

Hotels on Guadeloupe are plentiful, with rates for doubles ranging anywhere from 180 FrF (approx. US$25) to US$195 a night. Both rates include continental breakfast, and are for the mid-April to mid-December off-season. The lower rate is available at the Canibis and Flamboyants hotels, the higher at Hamak Villas. Almost all doubles go for under US$100, and most are in the US$40-50 range. In addition to traditional large hotels, Guadeloupe offers villas, apartments, condominiums, guest-houses and bungalows, many at weekly or monthly rates.

Canibis, Gosier 97190, Tel: 841-183

Flamboyants, Gosier 97190, Tel: 841-411

Carmelita's Village Caraibe, St. Felix 97190, Tel: 840-486

Salako, Gosier 97190, Tel: 841-490

Meridien Guadeloupe, St. Francois 97118, Tel: 885-100

Auberge de la Vieille Tour, Gosier 97190, Tel: 841-204

Bouganvillee, Pointe-a-Pitre 97110, Tel: 820-756

Hamak Villas, St. Francois 97118, Tel: 885-999

THINGS TO DO

Archaeological Park: At Trois Rivieres in south-western Guadeloupe. Includes carvings and cave dwellings of the people who inhabited the island in pre-colonial days.
   Forts: Fort St. Charles and Fort Fleur D'Epée.
   Hiking: Guadeloupe has a 74,100-acre (29,640-hectare) national park surrounding La Soufriere on the western "wing" of the island. Among its attractions are waterfalls, steamy sites of volcanic activity, mountain pools to swim in, and lush, ancient rainforests. Call M. Berry at 81-4579 for information on guided trips to the park.
   Hindu Temple: East Indians migrated to the island in some numbers during the 19th century, and their religion moved with them. The temple is at Changy.
   Offshore Islands: Guadeloupe has several, reachable by regularly scheduled transport. Many have hotels for overnight stops. Of course, in addition to all of the above, a simple walk through **Point-a-Pitre** or **Basse-Terre** can be an adventure in itself.

FOOD DIGEST

Compounded of French, African, West Indian and East Indian cooking traditions, Guadeloupe's cuisine boasts specialties ranging from stewed conch to curries. Broiled dove, stuffed land crab, shellfish, and other seafood are also favorites. Tourist Office-recommended restaurants number over 100. A few are listed here:

La Reserve-Chez Jeanne, St. Félix, Tel: 841-127. Creole; inexpensive.

La Pecherie, Rue de la République, St.- Francois, Tel: 844-841. Seafood; inexpensive.

Le Barbaroc, Petit Canal, Tel: 226-271. Unusual Creole cooking; inexpensive.

Rosini, Bas du Fort, Tel: 830-781. Italian food.

Le Boucanier, Sun Village Hotel, Bas du Fort, Tel: 830-576. French cuisine.

Chez Bach Lien, Gosier Village, Tel: 841-091. Vietnamese cuisine.

Le Galion, Ecotel, Montauban, Gosier, Tel: 841-566. Restaurant of cooking school run by French chefs. Occasionally, well-known French chefs will be cooking here; call and ask.

Le Flibustier, La Colline, Fonds Thezan, Tel: 882-336. Open fire-grilled foods; located in farmhouse on hilltop.

Le Balata, Gosier, Tel: 828-529. French and Creole; French chef prepares; expensive.

Auberge de la Vieille Tour, Gosier, Tel: 841-204. Specializes in integrating local fruits, vegetables and seafood into French cooking; expensive.

SPECIAL INFORMATION

Pilots will find planes for rent in St. Francois and at the Raizet Airport. Contact the Civil Aeronautics Board at Raizet for information on obtaining a French flying license. Jacques Cousteau has called Pigeon Island, on the west coast of Guadeloupe, "one of the world's ten best" areas for scuba diving. Guadeloupe offers fine port facilities for pleasure boats, and rentals of every type and size of boat, with or without crew, are available.

GETTING ACQUAINTED

GEOGRAPHY & CLIMATE

Dominica is located smack in the middle of the gracefully curving Antillean chain, between Guadeloupe and Martinique. Measuring 15 miles (24 km) wide by 29 miles (46 km) long, Dominica is blessed with the sort of dramatic and breathtaking scenery that comes with mountainous terrain. Morne Diablotin, the island's highest peak, soars to 4,747 feet (1,438 meters), and is covered with rainforests which thrive on 150 inches (381 cm) of rain per year. On the coast however, rain averages only 40 inches (101 cm) a year, making Dominica an ideal place to sample two climates.

GOVERNMENT & ECONOMY

Since November 3, 1978, Dominica has been an independent nation with a parliamentary form of government. The President is head of state. The economy remains largely agricultural, supplemented by the manufacture of soap and oil, clothing, and agricultural products.

ON ARRIVAL

Dominica's airport is located near Marigot, on the island's northeast coast. Taxis are available there to take travelers on the long but scenic drive to Roseau, Dominica's capital, where many hotels and guesthouses are located. Other accommodations are spread throughout the island.

DRIVER'S LICENSE

For EC$20 (approx. US$7.50) you can acquire a visitor's permit which will allow you to drive on Dominica - provided, that is, that you already have a valid driver's license. Present license and payment at the Police Traffic Department in the Police Station, Bath Road, Roseau. Consult car rental companies for other Traffic Department locations.

MEDICAL FACILITIES

Main hospital at Gootwill, Roseau; other hospitals at Grand Bay and Plymouth. Clinics and Health Centers located in nearly every village.

HOLIDAYS

Carnival
Monday and Tuesday preceding Ash Wednesday.
Labor Day
May 1.
Whit Monday
August Monday
First Monday in August.
Independence Day
November 3.

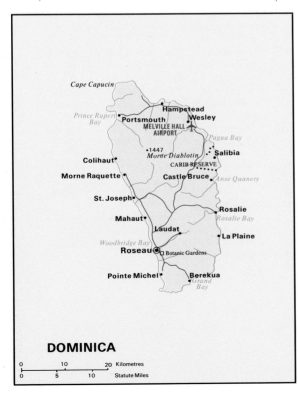

DOMINICA

COMMUNICATIONS

Currently, telephone, telegraph and telex links to overseas destinations are all best made at the offices of **Cable and Wireless**, Dominica's telecommunications company. In Roseau, the office is on Hanover Street; other towns have offices, as well. Dominica is currently planning a direct-dial system for international calls; it may be in place by the time you get there. In its absence, some hotels may be able to arrange international telephone links for you.

In Roseau, the **post office** is located on Bay Front. Other branches elsewhere. Hotels may be able to provide stamps and mailing information.

Dominica has one **radio station**, at 595 AM, and it may be possible to pick up overseas stations.

WHERE TO STAY

Accommodations on Dominica are extremely reasonable; a double room costs between US$12 (Thomas Guesthouse) to US$60 (Anchorage Hotel). Both of those prices are exclusive of meals, and as always, prices are subject to change.

A partial listing of Dominican accommodations is included below. Full details can be provided by the Dominica Tourist Board (see page 298 for addresses and telephone numbers). Options include apartments and cottages renting at weekly and monthly rates, and rooms with self-catering facilities for those who want to try their hand at preparing some of the island's lush produce and seafood.

Thomas Guesthouse, Marigot, Tel: 7264

Kent Anthony Guesthouse, Great Marlborough Street, Roseau, Tel: 2730

Emerald Pool, 1 Mile from Emerald Pool, c/o 109 Bath Road, Tel: 8095, Tlx: 8631 TONGE, Cable: POOL

Layou Valley Inn, Layou and Werner Road, P.O. Box 196, Tel: 6203, Tlx: 8628 ACTION DO, Cable: RAINFOREST

Riviere La Croix, Riviere La Croix Estate, P.O. Box 100, Tel: 1354, Cable: GETAWAY

Excelsior, P.O. Box 413, Roseau, Tel: 1501, 1502, Tlx: 8628 ACTION DO

Anchorage, Castle Comfort, P.O. Box 34, Roseau, Tel: 2638, 2639, Tlx: 8619 DO, Cable: ANCHORAGE DO

THINGS TO DO

The **Carib Indian Reservation**, located on 3,700 acres (1,480 hectares) in northeast Dominica, is home to Carib Indians whose forebears lived on Dominica when Europeans first contacted the island.

Hiking is an activity not to be missed by visitors to Dominica. The lushness of the rainforest here is almost impossible to overemphasize. Over 135 bird species are native to Dominica, including two endangered species of parrot found only here; plant species abound, with sometimes 60 different tree species appearing within a 10-acre (4-hectare) area. Pools, lakes, and waterfalls dot the interior, including the largest boiling lake outside of New Zealand. Peaks rise to almost 5,000 feet (1,515 meters).

Information and guides can be found at: **National Park Headquarters**, Dominica National Park Office, Victoria Street, Roseau, Commonwealth of Dominica, Tel: (809-445) 3106

The **Northeast Coast** offers dramatic vistas and secluded beaches.

Roseau, the capital city, offers attractions of its own, including a large Botanical Garden and a number of handicrafts outlets. Handicrafts may also be found on the Carib Reservation.

Food Digest

Specialties of Dominican cooking include the "mountain chicken" (a kind of frog), "tee-tee-ree" (cakes of tiny fish), and "crabbacks" (land crab backs stuffed with spicy crabmeat). Local produce is excellent, as are dishes made from this produce: juices, jams, sherbets, pepper sauce and guava cheese.

Dominican cooking is more varied during hunting season – September to February – than during the rest of the year.

All restaurants listed below serve creole/West Indian food with emphasis on Dominican fruits, vegetables, and seafood. Check the directory for current phone numbers.

Guyave, Cork Street, Roseau

La Robe Creole, Victoria Street, Roseau

The Orchard, Field's Lane, Roseau

Vena's, Roseau

Hannah Raffour, Roseau

Papillote, Trafalgar

Special Information

River swimming is one of the delights offered by Dominica's profusion of waterway. Vertivert grass mats and locally made soaps are two of Dominica's handicraft specialities. Also give a listen to recordings of the island's traditional "jing-ping" folk music. Divers can find delights off Dominica's coasts, including fluorescent sponges and old shipwrecks.

GETTING ACQUAINTED

GEOGRAPHY & POPULATION

Between Dominica and St. Lucia, some two-thirds of the way down the graceful curve of the Antilles, lies Martinique. Columbus called it the most beautiful country in the world, and to this day it remains lush, flowered and forested along its 50-mile (80-km) length and 22-mile (35-km) width. Volcanic in origin, Martinique's rugged terrain culminates in the 4,656-foot (1,410-meter) Mt. Pelee. Over the years, people from many parts of the world have augmented Martinique's population, but today it is still considered the most "French" of the Caribbean islands.

ON ARRIVAL

Travelers arriving in Martinique by boat will dock at or near Fort-de-France, the island's principal town. Air passengers touch down at Lamentin Airport, a few miles outside Fort-de-France. At both points of entry, taxis and rental cars are available to whisk you off to your hotel.

DRIVER'S LICENSE

If you plan to rent a car for 20 days or less, your current valid license is all you will need. If you plan to drive for a longer period, Martinique requires an International Driver's Permit. In either case, Martinique asks that visiting drivers have at least one year's driving experience.

MEDICAL FACILITIES

Martinique boasts 18 hospitals and clinics, the best of which is reported to be La Meynard. Doctors from nearly every branch of medicine practice on the island, and many of them speak English. Dental care is also available.

HOLIDAYS

Festival of Fort-de-France
A month-long arts festival which brings major international and Caribbean performers to Martinique. In July. Contact Tourist Board for this year's schedule.
Fête Nautique de Robert
Nighttime sea festival in Robert, on Atlantic coast. September.
Pro-Am Imperial St. James Golf Tournament
Mid-November.
International Guitar Festival
Concerts and master classes by internationally renowned musicians. December, Fort-de-France.

COMMUNICATIONS

Telephone calls (local and international) can be made from most phones, and the larger hotels may offer telex service. Telegrams, telexes, and phone calls can all be made from Martinique's post offices. In Fort-de-France, you'll find a Post Office on Rue de la Liberte.

Stamps are available at cafés-tabacs and most hotels, as well as at post offices.

WHERE TO STAY

Martinique's hotels are numerous, and mostly small – though there are a few 300-room resort hotels. As for price – doubles without meals may be had for anywhere from FrF 150 (approx. US$22) to US$105. The first rate is for the Chez Andre, the second for the Meridien Martinique. Both rates are valid for mid-April to mid-December off season. During this period, the majority of doubles will run between US$40 and US$60.

Some villas, apartments and homes are available for weekly and monthly rentals, and some hotels offer rooms with self-catering facilities. A partial list of Martinique's hotels is included below; complete details can be obtained from Martinique's Tourist Board. See pages 298 for addresses of offices nearest you.

Chez Andre, Anse Mitan 97229, Tel: 660-155

Eden Beach, Anse Mitan 97229, Tel: 660-119

Chez Julot, Vauclin 97280, Tel: 744-093

Leyritz Plantation, Basse-Pointe 97218, Tel: 755-392

Alamanda, Anse Mitan 97229, Tel: 660-319

Bakoua Beach, Pointe du Bout 97229, Tel: 660-202

Calalou, Anse-a-l'Ane 97229, Tel: 763-167

THINGS TO DO

Carbet, where Gauguin once lived and worked. Also the spot where Columbus landed on Martinique.

Diamond Rock, jutting 550 feet (166 meters) out of the sea. Used by the British as a military post in the early 19th century.

The **Museum** in Fort-de-France, which houses artifacts and remains from the Carib and Arawak Indians who once lived on Martinique.

La Pagerie, where the Empress Josephine was born. There is a small museum dedicated to her here.

The **Parc des Floralies**, a recently opened botanical garden, which includes representatives of many island plant species.

St. Pierre, the lava-inundated former capital of Martinique.

The **rainforest** at Morne Rouge offers lovely hiking opportunities. Hikes in Martinique's mountainous countryside yield fine views of island and sea.

FOOD DIGEST

Part of Martinique's French feeling is its celebration of good food. Lining Fort-de-France's streets, visitors can find restaurants offering fare they might expect to find only in Paris. But often, familiar French dishes are given an unfamiliar twist by the use of tropical fruits, vegetables and seafood – among them, guava, breadfruit, plantain, *cribiches* (freshwater crayfish), *oursin* (sea urchins), and *langouste* (clawless lobster). In addition to French-inspired cooking, visitors will also find plenty of spicy West-Indian specialities, including *crabes farcis* (stuffed land crabs), *blaff* (fish stew) *friscasee* of goat, and shark.

The list below contains a listing of some of

Martinique's restaurants, but as there are over 100 recommended restaurants on the island, visitors will have ample opportunity to discover their own favorite dining spot.

FORT-DE-FRANCE

L'Escalier. Creole; moderately priced.

Typic Bellevue. Creole; moderately priced.

Le Coq Hardi. Wood-fire-grilled meats.

La Grand' Voile. French fare.

Annapurna. Vegetarian cooking.

La Biguine. Creole and French.

Le Lotus D'Asie. Vietnamese.

La Baie d'Along. Oriental fare.

El Raco. Spanish.

POINTE DU BOUT

Bakoua. French and Creole.

La Marine. Cafe atmosphere; on the docks.

Le Cantonnais. Chinese food.

Chez Sidonie. Well-known for Creole cooking.

• **For fine dining in private homes (for smallish parties):**

Le Colibri. Morne des Esses.

Chez Mally Edjam. Basse-Pointe. Reserve in advance. West Indian fare in both locations.

• **For dining in rural settings:**

Plantation de Leyritz. Near Basse-Pointe.

Manoir de Beauregard. Near Ste. Anne.

Check directory for current phone numbers for all restaurants.

SPECIAL INFORMATION

Atlantic Coast swimming is quite rough – dangerous for anyone but experts, except at Cap Chevalier and Presquile de la Caravelle Nature Preserve.

GETTING ACQUAINTED

GEOGRAPHY

Toward the southern end of the Antillean chain, neatly placed between Martinique and St. Vincent, lies St. Lucia. An independent nation since 1979, this 27 by 14 mile (43 by 22 km) island supports a population of around 120,000. St. Lucia is volcanic in origin, a fact reflected in the island's rugged terrain and rich soils – and in the half-mile-high twin Pitons, among the most dramatic sights to be seen anywhere in the Caribbean.

ON ARRIVAL

International arrivals to St. Lucia touch down at the Hewanorra Airport in the far south; inter-island passengers land at Vigie Airport, in the northeast, near the capital town of Castries. At both airports, taxis are available to take you to your hotel. Most hotels are in the northeast, so Hewanorra arrivals will usually have a long (but scenic) ride ahead of them. Some hotels may provide airport/hotel transfers.

DRIVER'S LICENSE

If you wish to drive in St. Lucia, present your driver's license to a police officer at either airport, along with a US$8 fee. In return, you will receive a temporary St. Lucian license, good for 3 months. You can also make this transaction at Police Headquarters on Bridge Street, Castries.

MEDICAL FACILITIES

There is a main hospital in Castries – Victoria Hospital – and smaller hospitals in Soufriere, Dennery, and Vieux Fort. There is also a mental hospital at La Toc in Castries.

HOLIDAYS

New Year's Holiday
    January 1 and 2.
Carnival
Good Friday
May Day
La Rose Feast
    August 30.
Feast La Marguerite
    October 17.
National Day
    December 13.
Christmas and Boxing Day
    December 25 and 26.

COMMUNICATIONS

Hotels can sometimes place long distance calls and send cables for you, but the most dependable place to go for these services is an office of **Cable and Wireless**. In Castries, the office is on Bridge Street. Always ask at your hotel before trekking into town, as communications services can be expected to improve as time goes on.

The Castries **post office** is also on Bridge Street. Your hotel may be able to handle your mailings and/or sell you stamps, so ask first.

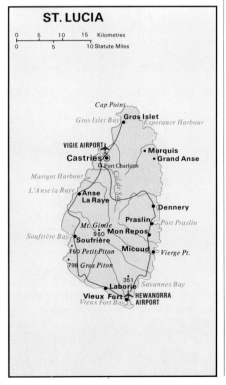

ST. LUCIA

0   5   10   15   Kilometres
0   5   10 Statute Miles

Cap Point
Gros Islet Bay Gros Islet
                Esperance Harbour
VIGIE AIRPORT
Castries   • Marquis
    Fort Charlotte • Grand Anse
Marigot Harbour
L'Anse la Raye • Anse
                La Raye
                • Dennery
        Praslin Port Praslin
Mt. Gimie • Mon Repos
    950
Soufrière Bay Soufrière
    750 Petit Piton Micoud • Vierge Pt.
    798 Gros Piton
        351
    Laborie Savannes Bay
Vieux Fort HEWANORRA
Vieux Fort Bay AIRPORT

WHERE TO STAY

Tropical Inn, Soufriere, Tel: 28240
Bayan Lodge Apartments and Guest House, Tel: 24184
Tropical Haven, Tel: 23505
Islander Hotel, Tel: 28757, 20255
Marigot Bay Resort, Tel: 24357
Cunard Hotel La Toc, Tel: 23081, 23089
Couples, Tel: 24211

THINGS TO DO

Banana Plantations near Marigot Bay and Dennery.

Several historic sites, including:
– **Pigeon Point**, former British naval station, and headquarters of Admiral Rodney.
– **Vigie Peninsula**, once used as a lookout post by the French and British.
– **Morne Fortune**, with its restored barracks, museum, and excellent views.
– **Paix Bouche**, yet another spot that claims to be Empress Josephine's birthplace.
– A new **Marine Park** for divers, complete with an explorable shipwreck. Near Vieux Fort.

A number of scenic spots, including:
– **Barre de L'Isle**, a dramatic spot inland, with 500-foot drops and stunning views.
– **Moule-a-Chique**, a high point in southern St. Lucia with views of the Atlantic and Caribbean, and of St. Vincent, 20 miles (32 km) to the south.
– **The Pitons**, twin volcanic spikes rising out of the sea in the southeast. Experienced mountain climbers can try the ascent.
– The **rainforest** in the southeast. There are trails in the forest and guides are available for hire.
– **Soufriere**, where there is a volcano you can drive into. Also mineral baths whose waters Louis XVI thought healthful, and **Diamond Falls** waterfall.

FOOD DIGEST

St. Lucian cuisine starts from a Creole base, to which are added a number of international influences. Local specialties include pumpkin soup and pumpkin soufflé, flying fish, *poile dudon* (a chicken dish), and *tablette* (a coconut sugar sweet). The following is a list of some St. Lucian restaurants.

Green Parrot, The Morne, Castries, Tel: 23399, 23167, 23168. Continental and Creole.

Le Boucan, Micoud Street, Castries, Tel: 22415. Creole; grilled foods.

San Antoine's, Morne Road, near Castries, Tel: 24660. French, Continental.

Rain, 19 Brazil Street, Castries, Tel: 23022. Creole, Continental, American.

Capone's, Reduit. Italian.

Dolittle's, Marigot Bay, Tel: 34357, 34246. Continental and West Indian.

The Still, Soufriere, Tel: 47224. Creole cuisine.

Chak Chak, Vieux-Fort, Tel: 46260. Local specialties.

SPECIAL INFORMATION

St. Lucia offers a very wide variety of tours, both of St. Lucia and of surrounding islands. Carib Touring, at 22689 or 23184, is one operator. The largest yacht marina south of St. Thomas is on St. Lucia – Rodney Bay Marina.

GETTING ACQUAINTED

GEOGRAPHY

Down at the bottom of the Antillean curve, near St. Lucia, Barbados, and Grenada, there lies an 18 by 11 mile (29 by 17 km) island, with a chain of 32 islets trailing off of it like the tail of a kite. This is St. Vincent and the Grenadines. St. Vincent itself – the large island – is mountainous, with volcanic ridges rising to over 3,000 feet (909 meters) above the sea. It is highly cultivated, with bananas, coconuts, arrowroot, nutmeg, and cocoa among its fruits. The Grenadines – varying in size from 7 square miles (18 square km) to mere dots on the ocean – have terrain both mountainous and flat, with glistening sand and clear waters to warm a beachbum's heart.

ON ARRIVAL

Travelers to St. Vincent touch down at Arnos Vale Airport, just outside the capital city of Kingstown. Taxis are available at the airport to take you to your hotel or to Kingstown proper, where boat service to the Grenadines originates. Some of the Grenadines are also served by air carriers.

DRIVER'S LICENSE

A local driver's license – required for driving in the islands – will be issued to you at the Police Station or Licensing Authority upon presentation of your regular license and EC$10 – about US$4. Both offices are in Kingstown, the former on By Street, the latter on Halifax Street.

MEDICAL FACILITIES

There are four hospitals on St. Vincent: two in Kingstown (one with a dental clinic), one in Georgetown and one in Chateaubelair. Clinics are located all over the islands.

HOLIDAYS

St. Vincent & the Grenadines Day*
   January 22.
Bequia Regatta
   Boat races and festivities on Bequia. Late March.
Whit Monday
Carnival
   10 days in late June-early July.
Caricom Day
   July 7.
Carnival Tuesday*
   Early July.
Canouan Yacht Races
   Wholesale festivities, not just boat races. Late July-Early August.
August Monday*
   First Monday in August.
Independence Day*
   October 27.
Petit St. Vincent Yacht Races
   Evening Festivities, daytime races. Late November.
Nine Mornings
   Parades and dances leading up to Christmas. December 16-24.

* Indicates National Holiday.

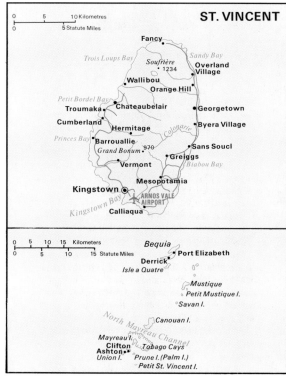

COMMUNICATIONS

The most dependable way to place long-distance calls, telegrams and telexes, is to go to an office of **Cable and Wireless**, the inter-island communications company. In Kingstown, you'll find the office on Halifax Street. There are branches elsewhere as well, but if your hotel isn't near one – ask at the desk before making your trek. It may be that your hotel can handle some of your communication needs.

The **post office** in Kingstown is also on Halifax Street. Hours are 8:30 a.m.-3 p.m., Mondays through Fridays; 8-11 a.m. Saturday morning.

WHERE TO STAY

Accommodations on St. Vincent and the Grenadines run the gamut from hotels through guesthouses and apartments. There are even two islands given over entirely to resort developments, Palm Island and Petit St. Vincent.

The following is a list of some island accommodations. Complete details, including current rates, are available from your nearest St. Vincent tourism representative – addresses on pages 299/300.

ST. VINCENT

Olives Guesthouse, Tel: 61821

Kingstown Park Guesthouse, P.O. Box 41, Tel: 61532

Sunset Shores Hotel, P.O. Box 849, Tel: 84411

Heron Hotel, P.O. Box 226, Tel: 71631

Cobblestone Inn, P.O. Box 867, Tel: 61937

The Grand Hotel and Casino, Peniston Valley, Tel: 87421

BEQUIA

Lower Bay Guest House, Bequia

Sunny Caribbee, Belmont, Bequia, Tel: 83425

Frangipani, Port Elizabeth, Bequia, Tel: 83255

Bequia Beach Club, Bequia, Tel: 83248

UNION

Sunny Grenadines, Clifton, Union Island, Tel: 88327

Anchorage Yacht Club, Clifton, Union Island, Tel: 88244

OTHER GRENADINES

Charlie's Guest House, Mustique, Tel: 84621

Canouan Beach Hotel, Canouan, Tel: 84413

Palm Island Beach Club, Prune (Palm) Island, Tel: 84804

THINGS TO DO

The **Archaeological Museum**, with its collection of stone tools and artifacts from the islands' pre-Columbian inhabitants. Located in the Botanic Garden.

The **Botanic Garden**. Dating from 1765, it is the Hemisphere's oldest, and includes – among other things – a breadfruit tree from the original plant brought from the South Pacific by Captain Bligh. In Kingstown.

Historic churches in Kingstown, including St. Georges and St. Mary's Cathedrals.

Scenic drives throughout the island. Queen's Drive above Kingstown, the road to Mesopotamia and Montreal, and the breathtaking Leeward Coast Highway are all good bets.

The **Falls of Baleine** on the northern tip of St. Vincent. These falls, which tumble from the heights above the sea, can only be reached by boat.

The **Grenadines** themselves are worth a visit, if you aren't staying on them already. Among the high points are:

– **Bequia**, with its fine harbor, the largest of the

338

Grenadines. A rugged island, and the home of famed boat builders.

– **Union Island,** the most southerly of the Grenadines. A popular yachting destination, with dramatic mountainous terrain that has suggested comparisons with Tahiti.

– **Tobago Cays,** a group of uninhabited islets with crystal clear water, coral banks, and lovely fish. Perfect for diving and snorkeling.

Hiking is a delight on St. Vincent. Seasoned trekkers may wish to make the day long trip up the La Soufriere volcano and down again. Check with your hotel or the Tourist Office before setting out, to make sure hiking conditions are good. The less athletically inclined may like to try the beautiful nature trails in the Buccament Valley.

Petroglyphs, carvings left by St. Vincent's pre-colonial peoples, may be seen at, among other places, Layou on the Southeast coast.

The St. Vincent Craftsmen's Center, located near Kingstown on the way to the airport, offers a wide range of St. Vincent's handicrafts.

FOOD DIGEST

Spicy West Indian cuisine predominates with Continental and American fare also available. A wide variety of sometimes exotic fruits and vegetables, along with fresh seafood, enrich St. Vincent's cooking. Try something unusual – barbecued goat or fresh shark, for example. Restaurants below all serve local West Indian specialties and seafood; French fare at the French Restaurant. Check directory for current numbers.

ST. VINCENT

Bonadie's Restaurant, Bedford Street, Kingstown

Juliette's, Middle Street, Kingstown

Manna Quick Snack, Halifax Street, Kingstown

The Dolphin, Villa Beach

The French Restaurant, Villa Beach

Restaurant La Mer, Indian Bay Beach

The Wheel Dining Club, Sion Beach

SPECIAL INFORMATION

St. Vincent is the world's largest producer of arrowroot – which now, believe it or not, is mostly used in computer paper. Visitors may visit the arrowroot mills at Colonaire. As with many other Caribbean islands, swimming on the windward/Atlantic coast is not recommended here. Wind-whipped waves and craggy rocks make for excellent viewing, but can endanger the swimmer. All of St. Vincent's beaches are public. If the route to a beach leads over private land, though, make sure you ask the owner before crossing. Most owners will freely grant permission. St. Vincent stamps are prized by collectors. There is a Philatelic Service in downtown Kingstown. La Soufriere's most recent eruption occurred in 1979. It is nowhere near most of the island's hotels, and closely monitored, in any case. An erupting volcano can be an awe-inspiring sight.

GETTING ACQUAINTED

GEOGRAPHY

Located about 100 miles (160 km) north of Venezuela, Grenada is the most southerly of the Windward Islands. The nation known as Grenada is actually made up of a number of islands, of which Grenada itself – measuring 21 miles by 12 miles (33 km by 19 km) – is by far the largest. Mountainous (highest elevation, 2,757 feet.) and fertile, Grenada is known as "The Isle of Spices", in honor of the nutmeg, mace and other condiments which it produces.

ON ARRIVAL

Air travelers to Grenada will touch down at Point Salines International Airport on the island's southern tip. Seagoing passengers will disembark at St.

George's, Grenada's capital and principal town. At both ports of entry, cabs are available to take passengers to the island's hotels - mostly located between the airport and St. George's, at the lovely Grande Anse Beach. Other hotels are to be found just south of the airport, at L'anse Auz Epines.

DRIVER'S LICENSE

Travelers wishing to drive in Grenada should present their valid driver's license at the Police Traffic Department for approval

MEDICAL FACILITIES

The General Hospital in St. George's is supplemented by two district hospitals: one in the island's eastern parish of St. Andrew, the other on Carriacou, the largest of Grenada's neighboring islands.

HOLIDAYS

New Year's Day*
Merrymaking and yacht races. Festivities continue January 2.
Annual Game Fishing Tournament
Late January.
Independence Day*
February 7.
Whit Monday*
Corpus Christi*
Falls in June. Religious procession.
Fisherman's Birthday Celebration
June.
Emancipation Holidays*
First Monday and Tuesday in August. Carriacou Regatta, cultural shows, and dancing.
Carnival
Falls in early August in Grenada.

* Indicates National Holiday.

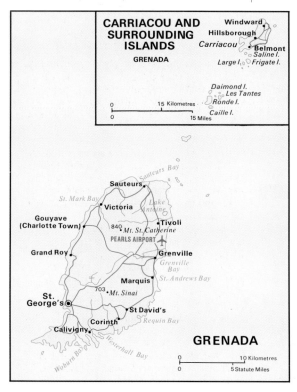

COMMUNICATIONS

Local and international calls may be made from all phones 24 hours. Telegrams and Telexes may be made through the offices of **Cable and Wireless**, at the corner of Hughes Street and the Carenage in St. George's. Hours: 7 a.m.-7 p.m., every day except Sundays and holidays, when the hours are 10 a.m.-12 p.m. Ask at your hotel, though, before making the pilgrimage to St. George's. Some may be equipped to handle wire transmissions themselves. The Post Office is located on the Carenage in St. George's, and is open for business 8 a.m.-11:45 a.m. and 1 p.m.-4 p.m., Mondays through Thursdays. On Fridays, the Post Office remains open until 5 p.m.

Grenada's state-owned **radio** operates at 525 and 990 AM. Shortwave service from Europe is available from 11:45 a.m. to 1:15 p.m. Grenada time at 15.045 KHZ. US shortwave service operates from 1:30-4:30 p.m., Grenada time, at 15.105 KHZ. There is some television on the island, and likely to be more in the near future.

WHERE TO STAY

Accommodation rates vary widely, from US$25 for an off-season double at the Apple Inn, to US$175 for a peak-season double at the Calabash. A large number of apartments and cottages is also available, at weekly and monthly rates. Below you will find a partial listing of Grenada's hotels. For a full discussion of accommodation options, contact the Grenada Tourist Office nearest you (*see* page 300). Complete P.O. Box addresses with: St. George's , Grenada

Silver Beach Cottages, Carriacou, Grenadines, Tel: 37-337 Carriacou, Tlx: 3425 GA (Attention Silver Beach), Cable: KAYAK

Cinnamon Hill and Beach Club, c/o Mr. Richard Gray, P.O. Box 292, Tel: 4301, 4302, Tlx: 3425 GA (Attention Cinhill), Cable: CINHILL

Blue Horizons Cottage Hotel, c/o Arnold D. Hopkin, P.O. Box 41, Tel: 4316, Tlx: 3425 GA (Attention Blue Horizons), Cable: Horizons

Horse Shoe Bay Hotel, P.O. Box 174, Tel: 4410, Tlx: 3425 GA or 3422 GA (Attention Horse Shoe Bay), Cable: HORSESHOE

Secret Harbour Hotel, c/o Mrs. Barbara Stevens, P.O. Box 11, Tel: 4439, 4548, 4549, Tlx: 3425 GA (Attention Secret Harbour), Cable: STECO

Calabash Hotel, c/o Mr. Charles de Gale, P.O. Box 382, Tel: 4224, 4334, Tlx: 3425 GA (Attention Calabash), Cable: CALABASH

Spice Island Inn, P.O. Box 6, Tel: 4258, 4423, Tlx: 3425 GA (Attention Spiceland), Cable: SPICELAND

THINGS TO DO

Carriacou, the largest of Grenada's "sister isles" to the north, is easily accessible by plane from Point Salines, or by boat from St. George's. Highlights include the beautiful **boats** you can see being built in the town of Windward, and the **Museum** in Hillsborough, which houses European and Amerindian Artifacts.

Hiking is a joy on Grenada, especially in the mountainous and lush Grand Etang Forest Reserve. Waterfalls, a lake, and the flora and fauna of the rainforest await you. Guides are available.

Inscriptions of the Carib Indians may be seen in the rocks near Sauteurs.

The **Grenada National Museum** in St. George's present a varied collection, including an exhibit tracing Grenada's original inhabitants from the Caribs through the Arawaks, right back to the end of the first Ice Age. Hours: 9 a.m.-3 p.m., Mondays through Fridays.

The **Spice Factories** at Grenville and Gouyave provide a fascinating glimpse of how spices get from earth to table.

St. George's is an event in itself. From the Saturday market, to the Tuesday afternoon loading of the beautiful schooners bound for Trinidad, to the historic churches which surround the city, there is much to see. Other highlights include the city's picturesque architecture and the several outlets for local arts and handicrafts – among them, the **Yellow Poui Art Gallery**, **Grencraft** and the **National Institute of Handicrafts**.

FOOD DIGEST

Grenada is known as the Isle of Spice, but it might just as well be called the Isle of Food. In addition to the 12 varieties of spice raised on the island, visitors will find 28 types of fruit, 22 kinds of fish, and a limitless number of ways to put it all together. Grenada's cuisine is West Indian with British, French and East Indian influences. Among the island's specialties are fish stew, curried chicken or lambi (conch), and Oil Down – a concoction of breadfruit, pork, coconut milk and a local green known as *callaloo*.

The listing below includes some of Grenada's best restaurants.

CREOLE/GRENADIAN CUISINE

For local Creole/Grenadian food:

• **In St. George's:**

Mama's
Quality Restaurants
Snug Corner
Pitch Pine Bar and Restaurant
Paula's

• **In Grenville:**

Bain's Sea Haven
The Drag
Wel-Fed

• **In Gouyave:**

Homestead
Kelly's Hot Spot

• **In Sauteurs:**

Big"T"
Juliet's

INTERNATIONAL CUISINE

For a more international menu:

• **In St. George's:**

The Nutmeg
Sand Pebbles
Aboo's
Cubby Hole
Restorante Italia
Rudolph's
The Crucial Factor
The Sand Pebble
The Turtle Back
The Lucky Heart
The Pastry Man
Sea Scape

• **In the Grande Anse area:**

The Apple
Ross Point Inn
La Belle Creole
Yin Wo (Chinese cuisine)

In St. George's, most restaurants are either on the waterfront Carenage, or in the shopping area along Young and Granby streets.

In L'anse aux Epines, there is an English pub-style restaurant, The Red Crab. Barbecued chicken, steaks and lobster are specialties.

Betty Mascoll's Plantation Home is just that – a home where you can go enjoy fine home-cooking. It is in Morne Fendure; those interested should call a day or more in advance to make arrangements

SPECIAL INFORMATION

Bareboat and crewed yachts are readily available, for, among other things, cruises into the Grenadines to the north. Grenadians are avid athletes. Among the sporting events of interest, you might look in on a cricket match. Played on Saturdays and Sundays from January to May. During the Carriacou Regatta, held the first weekend in August, look for the Big Drum Dancers. Their celebration of a dance and music tradition extending back to Africa is not to be missed. The word "grog" comes from Grenada. It originally stood for "grand rum of Grenada".

GETTING ACQUAINTED

GEOGRAPHY & POPULATION

One hundred miles east of the graceful Antillean curve, at about the same latitude as St. Vincent, lies the island of Barbados. When the English first arrived here, they found this small (21 by 14 mile/ 33 by 23 km) island to be uninhabited – by people, at least. Since colonization, the island's population has risen to around 260,000, but despite such density, citizens of Barbados enjoy one of the Caribbean's highest standards of living. In this case at least, a friendly economy seems to go hand in hand with friendly people and a lush landscape.

ON ARRIVAL

International flights to Barbados touch down at the Sir Grantley Adams International Airport in the south of the island, some 11 miles from the capital, Bridgetown. Cruiseship passengers disembark at Bridgetown harbor. Taxis should be in evidence at either place, or, if you make arrangements beforehand, you can have a rental car waiting for you at the airport.

DRIVER'S LICENSE

If you have an international driver's license, you're all set to drive on Barbados. If not, you can get a temporary permit for 30 Barbados dollars – provided you have a valid license from your home country. Permits can be picked up when you rent your car, or at the airport, a police station, or the Ministry of Transport and Works (Tel: 429-2191). Remember to drive on the left!

MEDICAL FACILITIES

Barbados is dotted with 8 health centers and 10 government clinics, in addition to Queen Elizabeth Hospital in St. Michael (436-6450). All provide

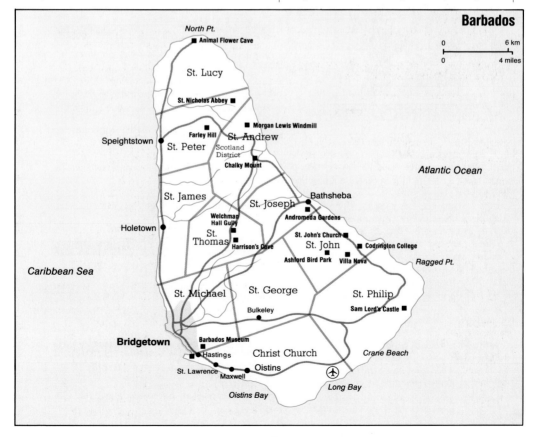

Barbados

health services free of charge.

Emergency Phone Numbers

Ambulance	426-1113
Fire	113
Police	113
Coast Guard	427-8819
Light and Power Company	436-900

HOLIDAYS

New Year's Day
Good Friday
Easter Monday
Whit Monday
May Day
Kadooment Day
First Monday in August; culmination of Crop Over Festival.
United Nations Day
First Monday in October.
Independence Day
November 30.
Christmas and Boxing Days
December 25 and 26.

COMMUNICATIONS

Local and international calls can be dialed directly from most phones on Barbados. Telegrams can be sent through many of the island's hotels, or through a post office – main branch is located in Cheapside, Bridgetown (Tel: 436-4800). All types of wire communications can be made at the offices of Barbados External Telecommunication Ltd. (Tel: 429-4852). Hours are 7 a.m. to 9 p.m. daily.

There are four radio stations on Barbados, including a cable service available in some hotels. If your hotel doesn't offer this service, you can pick up some of the station's informative programming at 790 KHZ. The other stations operate at 90.7 and 98 FM and 900 AM. One TV station – Channel 3 – operates on the island; it airs CNN news broadcasts daily.

Barbados's two daily papers are *The Advocate* and *Nation*. Useful and informative periodicals include *The Visitor*, *What's On*, *Sun Seeker* and *The Bajan* and *Bim*, a literary magazine.

WHERE TO STAY

Travelers to Barbados have a wide range of accommodations to choose from, owing to the island's popularity as a tourist spot – a popularity which, incidentally, dates back to at least the early 17th century when the English traveler Sir Henry Colt wrote that Barbados was uniquely pleasing among the islands he had seen. Modern visitors should be able to find a hotel, guesthouse, apartment, or rented room to fit any budget. There are even villas of various sizes available for daily or weekly rental. A sampling of Barbados hotels appears below.

BRIDGETOWN

Grand Beach Bay Resort, P.O. Box 639, Tel: 426-0888

CHRIST CHURCH

Asta Apartment Hotel, Palm Beach, Hastings, Tel: 427-2541

St. Lawrence Apartments, St. Lawrence Gap, Tel: 426-5070

Worthing Court Apartment Hotel, Worthing, Tel: 428-4910

Casuarina Beach Club, St. Lawrence Gap, Tel: 428-3600

Southern Palms Beach Club, St. Lawrence, Tel: 428-7171

ST. JAMES

Golden View, Sunset Crest, Tel: 432-7930

Coconut Creek Club Hotel, Tel: 432-0803

Divi St. James, Tel: 432-7842

ST. MICHAEL

Island Inn Hotel, Carrison, Tel: 436-6393

Hilton International, Needhams Point, Tel: 426-9200

ST. PETER

Tides Inn, Gibbes, Tel: 442-2403

Heywoods, Tel: 442-4900

ST. PHILIP

Crance Beach Hotel and Beach Club, Crane, Tel: 423-6220

THINGS TO DO

The **Barbados Museum and Historical Society**, a mile outside Bridgetown, is an excellent place to get your Barbadian (or, more properly, "Bajan") bearings. Exhibits cover history, geology and plant and animal life, among other things, and there is an art gallery and children's museum. Open weekdays 10 a.m.-6 p.m.; Sundays 2:30-6 p.m.

Be sure to see a game of **cricket** while you're in Barbados. Actually, it would be pretty hard not to, as the game is played almost *everywhere*. It has been called the island's national religion. The annual cricketing highlight, the Shell Shield Competition, usually takes place in January, though matches are played throughout the year.

There are a number of **art galleries** in Barbados which exhibit the work of Bajan artists. Most are in Bridgetown, though there is at least one in Christ Church and another in St. George. If you don't run into any in your wanderings, the Tourist Office should be able to help you find them.

Music, Dance and **Theatre** are plentiful on Barbados; performances occur throughout the year. Though you might find the island's major **Festivals** particularly fruitful in this regard. The Crop Over festival occurs in July and August; the Holetown Festival at the end of February; the Oistens Fish Festival on Easter Weekend; and the National Festival of the Creative Arts (NIFCA) in October and November. Check with a Tourist Office for this year's exact dates. And while we're on the subject of music...keep your eyes peeled. Maybe you'll catch sight of Mick Jagger, Rod Stewart, Sting, or any of the other internationally-known musicians who come to Barbados to relax and/or record.

Of course, the Barbadian **landscape** is a treat in itself, from the luscious beaches to the lush interior. High points include Welchman Hall Gully, a 3-quarter mile ravine covered with lavish vegetation,

and Harrison's Cave – said to be the only cavern of its kind in the Caribbean. Both are in St. Thomas parish.

FOOD DIGEST

As with many islands in the Caribbean, Barbados offers quite a variety of cuisines. Although the island was settled almost exclusively by the British – and the enslaved Africans they forced along with them – over time, other immigrant groups have added their native cookery to the melting pot. Today, travelers can sample Italian, French, Chinese and Bajan foods. The latter includes such tasties as pepperpot, a highly seasoned stew; pickled breadfruit; numerous flying fish dishes; and steamed cakes called "conkies". Try walking down Baxter's Road in Bridgetown and sample the offerings of the many roadside food stands there. Below is a selection of Bajan restaurants.

BRIDGETOWN

Queen's Park Restaurant. Local food, lunches only.

The Waterfront Cafe, The Careenage, Tel: 427-0093. English and Bajan food.

CHRIST CHURCH

The Silver Beach Hotel, Rockley, Tel: 427-1121. Home-cooked Bajan meals.

Pisces, St. Lawrence Gap, Tel: 428-658. Seafood, elegantly prepared.

Ocean View Hotel, Hastings, Tel: 427-7871. European and Bajan food; try their wonderful Sunday lunches.

ST. JAMES

La Cage Aux Folies, Paynes Bay, Tel: 432-1203. Chinese food, among other offerings.

Koko's Prospect, Tel: 424-4557. Nouvelle cuisine with a Barbadian Twist.

ST. MICHAEL

Brown Sugar, Aquatic Gap, Tel: 426-7684. Bajan lunches, continental dinners.

ST. PETER

Mullin's Beach Bar (Mama Leone's), Mullins Bay, Tel: 422-2484. Italian food; also Bajan and continental.

The Captain's Table, Heywoods Resort, Tel: 442-4900. Gourmet Continental food; seafood a specialty.

ST. PHILIP

Pavillion Restaurant, Crane Beach Hotel, Tel: 423-6220. Candlelit Bajan dinners.

SPECIAL INFORMATION

Barbados is the only place outside the US that George Washington ever visited. Bajan sunsets are sometimes rendered particularly spectacular by fine dust that drifts all the way over from the Sahara Desert. A number of supernatural occurences are said to have taken place on Barbados. See if you can find someone to tell you stories about Duppies (wandering spirits of the dead), or about the "face in the window", or the Chase family vault in Christ Church Cemetery.

GETTING ACQUAINTED

GEOGRAPHY

Seven miles off the Venezuelan coast lies the island of Trinidad, the most southerly Caribbean island and, at 1,864 square miles (4,846 square km), the largest island considered in this book. Along with Tobago, a 26 by 9 mile island (42 by 15 km), 21 miles (34 km) to the north-east, Trinidad forms an independent nation within the British Commonwealth. Lush in vegetation and oddly rectilinear in shape, Trinidad rises to its highest point at Cerra del Aripo (3,083 feet/934 meters). Tobago – which, legend has it, was Robinson Crusoe's island – is no less verdant, but decidedly smaller, rising to a high point of 1,890 feet (573 meters) in the northern hills.

ON ARRIVAL

International air arrivals land at Trinidad's Piarco Airport, where taxis are available to ferry passengers around the island. If you make arrangements before you travel, you can also have a rental car waiting for you at the airport. Seagoing passengers to either island generally debark at the principal towns, Port of Spain in Trinidad and Scarborough in Tobago – though some Tobago-bound ships anchor near Pigeon Point. Tobago is also accessible via inter-island air carriers, which touch down at Crown Point airport – approximately 5 miles (8 km) from Scarborough.

DRIVER'S LICENSE

T & T requires self-driving visitors to have an International Driver's License. To acquire one, check with your local licensing authority or, in the US, the American Automobile Association. Drivers must be 21 years old. Remember to drive on the left!

MEDICAL FACILITIES

There are at least three hospitals on Trinidad: The Mount Hope Medical Complex in Mount Hope near Port of Spain; the Port of Spain Adventist Hospital on Western Main Road, POS; and the San Fernando Medical Center, Chacon and Penitence Streets, San Fernando. Tobago and outlying parts of Trinidad are served by local Health Centers. Also, large hotels sometimes have doctors or nurses on call, or can at least recommend someone.

Emergency Phone Numbers:
Ambulance	990
Fire	990
Police	990

HOLIDAYS

New Year's Day
Carnival
  Monday and Tuesday before Ash Wednesday.
Good Friday
Easter Monday
Whit Monday
Corpus Christi
Labor Day
  June 19.
Discovery Day
  1st Monday in August.
Independence Day
  August 31.
Republic Day
  September 24.
Eid-ul-Fitre
Hosein
Divali
Christmas and Boxing Day
  December 25 and 26

COMMUNICATIONS

Local and international phone calls may be made from most phones (though you may need to go through an operator). Telegram, telex and cable traffic is handled by some hotels and post offices. If you have no luck at either place, try the Tourist Bureau on Federick Street in Port of Spain or an office of TexTel: Main Office, 1 Edward Street, Port of Spain; branch offices in San Fernando, Trinidad and Scarborough, Tobago. Wire transmissions may also be despatched at Piarco Airport.

Two newspapers, *The Trinidad Guardian* and *The Trinidad Express,* are published daily in Port of Spain, and Tobago has one – largely local – daily, the *Tobago News.* There are also a number of weekly (or semi-weekly) tabloids.

Two radio stations, Radio Trinidad and Radio 610, broadcast on the island, and some receivers may be able to pick up overseas transmissions. Two television stations – Channels 2 and 9 – are also available, and some hotels have satellite dishes to broaden their range of TV offerings.

WHERE TO STAY

Accommodations on T & T run the gamut from international hotel chains to informal camp sites. Though — to the chagrin of some and the joy of others — there are no real first-class resorts on either island, most travelers will be able to find a hotel, guesthouse, room in a private house, or camping spot to suit their needs — and budget. A random listing of accommodations on the two islands appears below.

TRINIDAD

• **In or near Port of Spain**

Success Inn Guesthouse, 4 Sarah St., Laventille, Tel: 623-5504

Fabienne's Guesthouse, 15 Belle Smythe St., Woodbrook, Tel: 622-2773

Villa Maria, 48A Perserverance Road, Haleland Park, Maraval, Tel: 629-8023

Hotel Normandie, P.O. Box 851, 20 Nook Avenue, St. Ann's, Tel: 624-1181/4

Mount St. Benedict Guest House, Tunapuna, Tel: 662-3258

Kapok Hotel, 16-18 Cotton Hill, St. Clair, Tel: 622-6441/4

Calypso Beach Resort, 103 Picton Street, New Town, POS, Tel: 622-3615/2538/4385

Hilton International Trinidad, P.O. Box 442, Tel: 624-3211/3111

• **Elsewhere in Trinidad**

Queen's Beach Hotel, Edghill Rd, Radix Village, Mayaro, Tel: 630-8583

Monica's Guesthouse, St. Ann's Rd., Mayaro, Tel: 630-8744

Royal Hotel, 46-54 Royal Rd., San Fernando, Tel: 652-3924/4881

Asa Wright Nature Centre, Arima, (c/o Caligo Centures, 405 Greenwich Ave., Greenwich, CT (1, 800-235-1216)

Farrel House Hotel, Southern Main Road, Claxton Bay, Tel: 659-2230/2271/2272

TOBAGO

Golden Thistle Hotel, Store Bay Rd., Crown Point, Tel: 639-8521

Sunstar Haven Guesthouse, Cinnamon Hill, Scarborough, Tel: 639-2376

Man-O-War Bay Cottages, Charlotteville, Tel: 639-4327

Cocriso Inn, Plymouth, Tel: 639-2961

Turtle Beach Hotel, P.O. Box 201, Plymouth, Tel: 639-2851/2

Kariwak Village, P.O. Box 27, Crown Point, Tel: 639-8545/8441/2

Arnos Vale Hotel, P.O. Box 208K, Tel: 639-2881/2

THINGS TO DO

The **Asa Wright Nature Center and Lodge** in the Northern Range's Arima Valley is an excellent place to learn about and experience Trinidad's rich and sometimes unique flora and fauna.

T & T boasts several **Museums,** including the National Museum and Art Gallery in Port of Spain and the National Fine Arts Center near Scarborough. In addition, in Port of Spain there are a number of galleries offering the work of local artists for viewing and sale. Check at the Tourist Board for further information.

Theatre and **Dance** form as much a part of the T &T cultural scene as the better-known steelband and calypso music. Port of Spain, in particular, has a number of performing groups, including a theater started by the internationally-known Trinidadian playwright, Derek Walcott. Check newspapers and at the Tourist Board for current offerings.

Steelbands need to practise as well as perform, and it is often possible to informally listen in on these sessions, for a unique musical experience. Throughout both islands, bands rehearse outdoors in empty lots known as panyards. To find them – follow your ears, ask a local resident, or inquire at the Tourist Bureau.

A mind-boggling and body-delighting array of **Festivals** is celebrated on Trinidad, in part, at least, the result of the islands' wonderful multi-ethnic population and history. In addition to the world-famous Carnival, celebrated on the Monday and Tuesday before Ash Wednesday, festivals include: Hosay (or, Hosein), originally a Muslim festival of mourning, which has become a veritable explosion of parades, music and dance; it takes place at different times. Usually, celebrations can be found between February and March in some parts of the islands; Phagwa, a Hindu New Year celebration which takes place around the time of the full moon in March; Eid-ul-Fitrr, a day feasting and almsgiving marking the Muslim New Year and the end of the Ramadan fast, usually occuring around June; and Divali, a Hindu festival of lights in honor of the goddess Lakshmi, opulently and luminously celebrated on a night in late October or November.

FOOD DIGEST

Due to the extremely diverse ethnic background of Trinidad and Tobago's population, a wide array of cuisines is available on the islands. Indian, Chinese, French and West Indian cookery have all left their marks on T & T fare, as has the ready availability of fresh seafood, fruits and vegetables. Prices tend to be on the high side, but with a little care it is possible to stay within even a very limited budget. Don't be **too** careful, though – if you rely only on hotel food or a few cautiously chosen restaurants to get you through your stay, you'll miss out on part of T & T's richness.

Following is a random sampling of T & T restaurants:

TRINIDAD

• **In Port of Spain**

Mangal's, 13 Queen's Park East, Tel: 624-4639. Indian cuisine.

House of Chan, 83-85 Picton St., Newtown, Tel: 622-1304. Chinese cuisine.

Copper Kettle Grill, 66-68 Edward Street, Tel: 625-4318. Grilled and Creole foods

Cricket Wicket, 149 Tragarete Rd., Tel: 622-1808. Pub.

The Outhouse, 82B Woodford St., Newtown, Tel: 622-5737. Creole and vegetarian cuisine; seafood.

The Hott Shoppe, Mucurapo Rd., Maraval Rd.. Roti, a kind of Indian "meal in a sandwich".

Chez Veronique, 117A Henry St., Tel: 623-8249. French cuisine.

Pot Luck, Dundonald St. Lunch.

Villa Creole, 133 Western Main Rd., St. James, Tel: 622-1518. Home-style Creole cuisine.

• **Elsewhere in Trinidad**

Soong's Great Wall, 97 Circular Rd., San Fernando, Tel: 652-2583; and 43 Coffee St., San Fernando, Tel: 652-3534. Chinese cuisine.

Farrel House, Claxton Bay, San Fernando, Tel: 657-8331

Timberline, North Coast Rd.. Tel: 638-2263

TOBAGO

Blue Crab, Main and Robinson Sts., Scarborough. Local dishes.

Old Donkey Cart, Bacolet St., Scarborough, Tel: 639-3551. Creole and international cooking; wine list.

Cocrico Inn, Plymouth, Tel: 639-2961. Tabagonian cooking.

Steak Hut, Sandy Point Beach Club, Store Bay Rd., Crown Point, Tel: 639-6533. Grilled food.

Voodoo Nest, Main and Bacolet Sts. Seafood and local specialities.

Blue Waters Inn, Speyside, Tel: 639-4341. Creole and international food.

GETTING ACQUAINTED

GEOGRAPHY & GOVERNMENT

Located 15 miles (24 km) north of Venezuela, and a good deal further west than most of the islands in the Antillean chain, Aruba is the westernmost of the Leeward group of the Netherlands Antilles – a group which also includes Curaçao and Bonaire. Aruba is 19.6 miles (31 km) long, and spans 6 miles (9 km) at its widest point. Geographically, it is fairly unusual. Where many of the other Antilles are mountainous and partially rainforest-covered, Aruba's highest elevation is 617 feet (Mount Yamanota), and its average rainfall totals a mere 20 inches (50 cm). As a result, a variety of cacti thrive on the island in addition to the remarkable *watapana* (or divi-divi), a tree whose top always grows pointing southwest, in deference to the ever present northeast trade winds. Aruba also contains a number of unusual geologic formations.

Politically, Aruba joins Curaçao, Bonaire, St. Martin, St. Eustatius, and Saba to form the Netherlands Antilles, a part of the Kingdom of the Netherlands.

ON ARRIVAL

Travelers flying into Aruba will land at the **Aeropuerto International Reina Beatrix**, approximately 4 miles (6 km) outside of Oranjestad, the island's principle city. Taxis should be available at the airport, but if you should need to call one, Aruba's **taxi dispatch office** can be reached by telephoning 22116 or 21604. Passengers arriving by ferry or cruise ship will dock in **Oranjestad**.

DRIVER'S LICENSE

Valid foreign and international licenses are acceptable, but you must be at least 21 years old to rent a car.

MEDICAL FACILITIES

In the unfortunate event that you should need medical attention during your visit to Aruba, you will be in good hands. **Horacio Oduber Hospital**, built in 1976, is modern and well-equipped. It is located near Eagle Beach, some 5 miles (8 km) to the

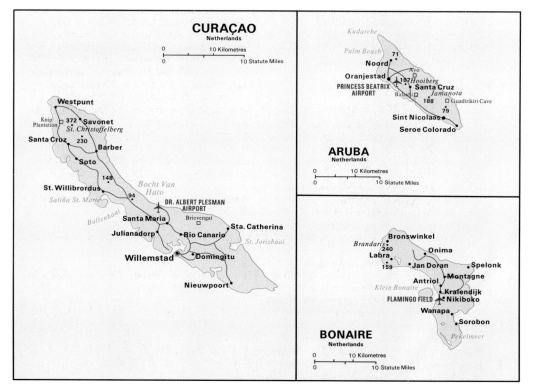

west of Oranjestad. In addition, major hotels have doctors on call if you should need one, and can assist you in making dental appointments as well.

HOLIDAYS

New Year's Day*
Fireworks; strolling groups of musicians and singers ("Dande") welcome in the new year.
Flag Day*
March 18.
Carnival
Weeks preceding Lent. Contact Tourist Bureau for details for the current year.
Whit Monday*
Watapana (Bonbini) Festival
Tuesdays, mid-April to mid-December, 6:30 p.m.-8:30 p.m. Displays of Aruban arts, crafts, music, and dance held at Fort Zoutman in Oranjestad. Food and drink, too!
Coronation (Queen's) Day and Labor Day*
April 30 and May 1.
St. John's Day
June 24. Music, dance, and "folkloric" events celebrating Aruban culture.
Deep Sea Fishing Tournament
Held in October; contact Tourist Bureau for current year's details.
St. Nicholas Day
December 15. Day of gift giving as St. Nicholas and Black Peter make the rounds of the island.
Kingdom Day*
December 15.
Christmas and Boxing Day*
December 25 and 26.

* Indicates National Holidays.

COMMUNICATIONS

Both local and international telephone calls may be placed from your hotel, or at the **Government Long Distance Telephone Office**, located in the Post Office building, off Hendrikstraat in Oranjestad. Similarly for telexes and telegrams: you can either get your hotel to send them for you, or you can dispatch them from the **Government Telegraph and Radio Office**, also in the Post Office building. Airmail letters from Aruba to the United States cost NAf 1 (approx. US$0.60); and postcards, NAf 0.60

(approx. US$0.35).

Three radio stations which visitors may like to take note of are: **Trans World Radio** (800 AM), **Radio Victoria** (960 AM), and **Radio Antilliana** (1270 AM). All three offer regularly scheduled broadcasts in English. There is one television station, **Tele-Aruba**, channel 13. It carries a number of US programs, but its hours of operation are only 6 p.m.-10:30 p.m.

WHERE TO STAY

Fanning out westward from Oranjestad, along Aruba's sheltered southwest coast, lie most of the island's principle hotels. A sampling of these hotels may be found below. For winter, rates for doubles range from US$60 a night on the **European Plan** (no meals, room only) at the Bushiri Beach hotel, to US$248 a night on the **Modified American Plan** (room, breakfast and dinner) at the Dutch Village. Winter, of course, is peak season in the Antilles, running from approximately mid-December to mid-April. Summer rates may be lower.

Accommodation options are not limited to only hotels. A variety of guesthouses, apartments, pensions, and rooms-for-rent are also available to the traveler. Most of these will offer significant savings over hotels, though facilities will be correspondingly modest. The **Aruba Tourist Bureau** can furnish information on, and arrange reservations at, these alternative lodgings. Packages can be set up which include the use of a rental car for the duration of your stay, and some accommodations are available for weekly and monthly rental. For the office of the Tourist Bureau nearest you, *see* page 297-298.

Bushiri Beach Hotel, Tel: 25216, Tlx: 5155 AHTTCNA

Atlantis Apartahotels and Villas, Tel: 24343, Tlx: 5210 ARIEL

Best Western/Talk of the Town, Tel: 23380, Tlx: 501 TOTTR

Best Western/Manchebo Beach, Tel: 23444, Tlx: 5018 TOTTR

Tamarijn Beach Hotel, Tel: 24150, Tlx: 5023 DIVIHO

Aruba Beach Club, Tel: 24595, Tlx: 5017 BCLUB

Divi Divi Beach Hotel, Tel: 23300, Tlx: 5023 DIVIHO

Dutch Village, Tel: 32300, Tlx: 5023 DIVIHO

FOOD DIGEST

Due to the island's history, dining out in Aruba is a more varied and cosmopolitan experience than you might expect. In the early part of this century, Aruba's huge oil refinery opened, bringing immigrant workers from all over the world. The refinery has since closed, but the immigrants have settled in, adding their languages, customs and cuisines to the Aruban mix. Indonesian, Chinese, French, Spanish and Italian cuisines are among those represented in Aruba's restaurants. Local specialties include a variety of seafood dishes.

An interesting feature of the restaurant scene in Oranjestad is the fleet of white trucks prowling the city, ready to fend off hunger wherever it strikes. These mobile restaurants operate into the wee hours, serving snacks and local food.

The list below includes a random selection of Aruban restaurants of various types.

Nueva Marina Pirata, Spanish Lagoon, Tel: 27372. Aruban food, seafood.

Pachi's, 19 Van Walbeexkstraat, Oranjestad, Tel: 22362. Aruban cuisine.

Mimarojurie, Bubali, Tel: 23170. Aruban food.

Cocoyoco Grill, A. Lacle Blvd., Oranjestad. Barbecued foods; moderately priced.

Oriental, 5 Zoutmanstraat, Oranjestad, Tel: 21008. Moderately priced Chinese food.

El Gaucho, 80 Wilhelminastraat, Oranjestad, Tel: 23677. Argentinian food.

Bali, Oranjestad harbor, Tel: 22131. Indonesian Rijsttafel, other Indonesian foods; located on Indonesian houseboat.

Papiamento, 7 Wilhelminastraat, Oranjestad, Tel: 24544. Continental food in old mansion.

THINGS TO DO

Of interest to the visitor is the **Artesiana Arubana**, an outlet for local artwork and crafts, some of which have been inspired by recently discovered works of the island's early inhabitants. It is located near the waterfront in Oranjestad, at 178 L.G. Smith Boulevard. Other outlets for the island's creative work can be located through the Tourist Bureau, or by calling the **Institute of Culture** at 22185.

The **Aruba Museum** is located in historic Fort Zoutman, Zoutmanstraat, Oranjestad. The museum houses a collection of artifacts and pottery left by the island's early Indian inhabitants. Hours are 7:30 a.m.-12 p.m. and 1 p.m.-4:30 p.m., Mondays through Fridays. The fort itself, in addition to its historic interest, houses the yearly Watapana festival of Aruban art, music and dance.

The **Cunucu**, or countryside in the local language Papiamento, is worth exploring both for its plant and animal life and for the colorful houses of its residents. Among the plants you'll find are the medicinal aloe, of which the island once provided 30 percent of the world's supply, and the southwest-ward-pointing divi-divi tree.

The **Bubali bird sanctuary**, located near Palm Beach on the southwest coast, is home to many of the islands' bird species, as well as migrating flocks. Sunset is a particularly fine time to visit the sanctuary.

The **Diorite boulders** at Ayo and Casibari in the north-central section of the island are geologic curiosities of still-uncertain explanation. They may be remnants of ravines dating back to the time when the island was joined to the mainland of South America.

The **caves** at Ayo, Guadirikiri (in the northeast), and elsewhere, once were home to groups of Arawak people. In many of them, the drawings, paintings, and hieroglyphs of these ancient inhabitants are still preserved.

The **gold mine ruins** at Balashi and Bushiribana – in the south-central and north-central parts of the island, respectively – mark the sites where miners once extracted ore from the earth. At Balashi, there is also an impressive stand of divi-divi trees.

Hooiberg, the dramatic conical hill in the center of the island, is another geological oddity. It is a prime example of an earth formation found only in Iceland and Aruba, known as a Hooibergite. Steps have been cut in the rock to facilitate the climb to the hill's 541-foot (163-meter) summit.

Iguanas may be found at Seroe Colorado on the southeast corner of the island, where they are protected by law.

The **natural bridge** on the north-central coast is the Caribbean's largest.

The **north coast** as a whole is dramatic and beautiful. Washed by powerful, tradewind-swept waves, it is not ideal for swimming, but is a fine place to observe the drama and majesty of the sea.

Yamanota, at 617 feet (186 meters), is the highest point on Aruba, and offers an all round view. There is an auto road to the summit.

Wilhelminastraat in Oranjestad contains some of the most historic and picturesque architecture on the island.

SPECIAL INFORMATION

For swimming and watersports, stay on the south coast of the island, which is sheltered by neighboring South America. The trade wind-whipped waves on the north side make beaches there potentially dangerous. There is bus service between Oranjestad and the hotels on Eagle and Palm beaches. The fare is presently US$0.75 each way. Check with the Tourist Bureau for schedules.

GETTING ACQUAINTED

GEOGRAPHY

Fifty miles (80 km) north of Venezuela, 30 miles (48 km) east of Curaçao, and a few hundred miles west of most of the islands discussed in this guide, you will find the isle of Bonaire. At 24 miles (38 km) long and 3 to 7 miles (4 to 11 km) wide, Bonaire, which is shaped rather like an upside-down jawbone, is the second largest island of the Leeward group of the Netherlands Antilles – a group which also includes Aruba and Curaçao. Bonaire resembles its neighboring islands in being relatively flat and dry – highest elevation, 784 feet (237 meters), average yearly rainfall, 22 inches (55 cm) – but differs from them in style and pace. While Aruba and Curaçao are synonymous with high-style, jet-set vacationing, Bonaire is slower, quieter, more easygoing and more relaxed. There's no reason to expect that to change in the near future.

ON ARRIVAL

Whether you come to Bonaire by plane or on the (fairly infrequent) Curaçao-Bonaire boat run, you will find taxis available to take you to your destination. Bonaire's largest town is Kralendijk; most accommodations are located north or south of Kralendijk along the island's west-south-west coast.

DRIVER'S LICENSE

Most valid national and international licenses are acceptable here.

MEDICAL FACILITIES

Bonaire's only hospital is on Bartolaweg in Kralendijk. There are a few private doctors and at least one dentist. The tourist board will be able to help you locate the services.

HOLIDAYS

Carnival – In or around February, in Bonaire.
Coronation Day – April 30.
Ascension Day
Dia de San Juan – St. John's Day. June 24.
Dia de San Pedro – St. Peter's Day; celebration centers in Rincon. June 28.

Bonaire Day – September 6.
Annual Sailing Regatta – Races and generally festive atmosphere. Held in mid-October.

COMMUNICATIONS

Long distance telephone calls can usually be made in your hotel or from any phone, and some hotels may be able to send your cable traffic. Or you may go to the J.A. Abraham Boulevard in Kralendijk where you will find the **Post Office** and the **Cable/Telecommunications Bureau**.

Trans-World Radio, a Protestant missionary station, is the only station that makes English language radio broadcasts. You can tune in at 800 AM. Shortwave receivers will be able to pick up several more stations, and some overseas broadcasts may reach Bonaire on standard bands. **Channel 11** is Bonaire's only television station, operating on weekday evenings.

WHERE TO STAY

Accommodations on Bonaire are few in number, but wholly sufficient, and surprisingly varied. Prices for doubles range from US$32 (a one-bedroom apartment at Coral Villas) to US$110 (a suite at the Bonaire Beach Hotel). The former is a year round price, the latter, a rate for the mid-April to mid-December off-season.

Winter brings more people and higher prices, but even then it is quite possible to find doubles for under US$50, and most cluster at around US$70-90. A variety of villas, condominiums, apartments and inns are available, in addition to more traditional hotels, and groups of visitors traveling together can enjoy substantial savings by staying in one of the larger units. Weekly and monthly rates are available at many locations.

Prefix numbers for direct dialing to Bonaire are 011 (International access code) plus 5997.

Coral Villas, Tel: 8428

Sorobon Beach Resort, Tel: 8080, Tlx: 1200 INPO

Bonaire Sunset Villas, Tel: 0033, Tlx: BTC NA

Hotel Rochaline, Tel: 8286, Tlx: 1907 UNICC

Habitat, Tel: 8290, Tlx: 1280 BONTRA

Bonaire Beach Hotel and Casino, Tel: 8448, Tlx: 1291 HOBON

THINGS TO DO

Arawak Indian inscriptions near Rincon in north-central Bonaire.

Birdwatching activities. There are the island's 126 species, including a remarkable colony of flamingos for the avid birdwatcher. The National Audubon Society gives Bonaire birdwatching a four-star rating in fall, winter and spring.

The **conch farm** at Habitat is trying to restore populations of this endangered species - which is popular on Bonaire.

The **Instituto Folklore Bonaire**, located in an old fort on Helmundweg in Kralendijk, offers a collection of historical implements and artifacts from Bonaire's past.

Several **slide shows** each week offer a sampling of Bonaire's incredible underwater beauty to those who choose not to venture to the reefs themselves. Show times: Mondays and Wednesdays at Habitat; on Wednesdays at Bonaire Scuba Center; and on Sundays at the Flamingo Beach Hotel. All shows are free, and take place in the evening.

The **Washington/Slagbaai National Park** takes up most of the hilly northwestern part of Bonaire, and is a fine place to encounter Bonaire's rich plant and animal life. Park hours are 8 a.m.-5 p.m., and there are roads, albeit rough ones, for those who prefer to drive. The park charges approximately US$2 a person.

FOOD DIGEST

Dutch, Chinese and other international cooking is available on Bonaire, but local specialties, naturally enough, focus on seafood. Pickled conch is a favorite here, although the current endangered status of the conch might make you want to think twice before eating any.

Below is a listing of some of Bonaire's restaurants.

Beefeater Restaurant, 3 Kaya Grandi, Kralendijk, Tel: 8081, 8193. Continental dishes, seafood especially.

China Garden Restaurant, Kaya Grandi, Tel: 8480. Chinese food in restored mansion

Egretta Bar and Restaurant, Lac Bay. Check the directory for the phone number. International cuisine, French wines in cactus garden; breakfast.

Hotel Rochaline, Kralendijk, Tel: 8286. Seafood, vino verde.

Zeezicht Bar and Restaurant, Kralendijk, Tel: 8434. Longtime "hangout" for local people and tourists, both. Seafood, Chinese cuisine; disco; open for breakfast.

SPECIAL INFORMATION

Bonaire's fine reefs have attracted researchers, some of whom are currently studying the mind-bogglingly intricate reef ecosystems. Two hundred and forty square meters (300 square km) of reef have been mapped all the way down to the locations of individual tubeworms! Swimming is gentler on the protected western coast of the island. Consult the Tourist Bureau before venturing into the rougher Atlantic surf.

GETTING ACQUAINTED

GEOGRAPHY

Located 35 miles (56 km) north of Venezuela and quite a bit further west than most of the islands covered in this guide, Curaçao is the central island of the Leeward group of the Netherlands Antilles - a group which also includes Aruba and Bonaire. Curaçao is 38 miles (63 km) long and between 2 and 7 miles (3 and 11 km) wide, with a dry climate (annual rainfall: 22 inches). The 1,239-foot (375-meter) Mt. Christoffel is the island's highest peak.

ON ARRIVAL

Air travelers will fly into Curaçao at Curaçao International Airport, some 6 miles (9 km) from the island's principal town, Willemstad. Ship passengers will arrive near Willemstad at Santa Anna/Schottegat Bay – the second busiest harbor in the world and home of the hemisphere's largest non-military dry dock. Taxis to take you to your hotel should be in evidence in both places, or you can call a cab at 84574 or 84575.

DRIVER'S LICENSE

Valid licenses from Geneva Convention countries are okay in Curaçao. Remember that speedometers and road-signs will be in kilometers, not miles.

MEDICAL FACILITIES

Reputedly excellent. There are two hospitals, one of them located on Roodiweg in western Willemstad. Dentists are available, and many medical personnel speak English.

HOLIDAYS

Chinese New Year – January
Carnival – Weekend preceding Lent, here.
Harvest Festival – March
Coronation Day – April 30
Ascension Day
Whit Sunday
Curaçao Flag Day – July 2.
St. Nicholas' Day – December.
Kingdom Day/Antillean Flag Day – December 15.

Note: Due to the strong and longstanding Jewish tradition in Curaçao, Jewish holidays are probably more widely recognized and celebrated here than on any other Caribbean island.

COMMUNICATIONS

International phone calls can be made from most phones on Curaçao, and some hotels may have telegraph and telex facilities. If you have any trouble making any of the above communications, however, the place to go is the **Post Office**. In Willemstad, it is located at Waaigat, near the market.

There are three **radio stations** with occasional broadcasts in English on Curaçao. They are located on the AM dial at 800 and 960, and on the FM dial at 93.9. Curaçao's sole **TV station**, channel 8, broadcasts in the evenings, and some hotels may have cable or satellite capabilities.

WHERE TO STAY

A double at one of Curaçao's hotels will cost you anywhere from US$28 (Park Hotel) to US$120 (Curaçao Concorde) during the peak winter season. Rates quoted are exclusive of meals and subject to change. Curaçao also offers a range of guesthouses and pensions, and some apartments and condos may be available for rental at weekly or monthly rates. A partial listing of Curaçao's hotels appears below; for more complete information, and help in hooking up with any of Curaçao's alternate accommodations, contact the Curaçao Tourist Board. (*See* page 298.)

Park Hotel, Tel: 81120

Hotel Holland, Tel: 81120, Tlx: 3433 COAST NA

Coral Cliff Hotel, Tel: 641610, Tlx: 3434 AGUIL NA

Curaçao Plaza Hotel, Tel: 612500, Tlx: 3324 CPHNA

Curaçao Concorde, Tel: 625000, Tlx: 1146 COCU

THINGS TO DO

Beth Haim cemetery on the west edge of the refinery outside Willemstad is one of the oldest European burial grounds in the Western Hemisphere. Tombstones from as far back as 1668.

The **Curaçao Liqueur Distillery**, where this world-famous cordial is produced, is located on the east side of Willemstad. Tours include free samples.

The **Governor's Mansion** in Willemstad was built in 1653. Still the governor's official residence.

The **Otrabanda** district of Willemstad – and the city in general – is chock-full of lovely, historic buildings, many restored to their original glory.

The **Seaquarium** offers dazzling marine life. There's even a 600-foot-long shark pool.

St. Christoffelberg National Park, at the west end of the island, is a haven for some of Curaçao's wildlife. The joy of contact with the plants and animals is augmented by the beautiful views afforded by the Park's high ground - which includes the highest point on the island.

Mikve Israel-Emmanuel synagogue in Willemstad is the Western Hemisphere's oldest Jewish congregation. A museum is adjacent.

Underwater Curaçao, on the southeast coast, includes a marked, underwater nature trail for snorkelers which concludes at a shallowly submerged 1906 wreck! Scuba diving and glass-bottom boat trips also available.

FOOD DIGEST

The diversity of Curaçao's population makes for quite a diversity of cuisines, and for the intermingling of distinct culinary traditions to form new syntheses. African, Dutch, Spanish, Portuguese, Chinese and Indonesian cooking have all made their mark here.

Local specialties include keshi-yena, a baked Edam cheese stuffed with meat and vegetables, and kapucijners, a beef, bean, and onion dish:

Belle Terrace, Avila Beach Hotel, Penstraat 130, Tel: 614-377. Scandinavian and Curaçao dishes; salad bar, in 200-year-old mansion.

Bistro Le Clochard, Otrobanda, Tel: 625-666, 625-667. Gourmet Swiss and French foods; located in 18th-century fort.

Golden Star, Socratesstraat 2, Willemstad, Tel: 54795, 54865. Creole food.

Koputrek, Caracasbaaiweg 14, Saliña, Tel: 615-384. Basic grilled foods; disco; kitchen open late.

Le Recif, Otrobanda, Tel: 623-824. Seafood; late-night dancing; floorshow.

Rijsttafel Restaurant Indonesia and Holland Club Bar, Mercuriusstraat 13, near Saliña, Tel: 612-606, 612-999. Javanese cuisine.

Trupial Inn/Sombrero Room, Trupial Inn, Tel: 78200. Curaçao specialties, including keshi yena.

SPECIAL INFORMATION

Swimming is safer on the south coast, as the north can be whipped by trade-winds driven waves and swept by odd currents. There are plenty of lovely beaches.

ART/PHOTO CREDITS

INDEX

Cathedral of St. John the Divine, 170
Catholics, 35, 128, 129, 195, 208
  festivals, 60
  church, 125
  Frair, 31
Cay Bay, 108
Cayenne, (Capital of French Guiana), 135
Cayman Islands, 192, 244
Cazabon, Michel Jean, 60
cemis, (stone idols), 29
Century Plant, (agave), 91
Cesaire Aime, 60
Chaguanas, (Trinidad's largest city), 250
Chalky Mount, 239
Challwell, 88, 89
Chamber of Commerce, 230
Change of power, 51
Charles, Eugenia, (Prime Minister), 191
Charlestown, (capital of St. Kitts-Nevis), 153, 158, 161
Charlotte Amalie, (capital of U.S. Virgin Islands), 77, 109
Charlotteville, 257
Chattel houses, 239
Cheapside, 241
Chesapeake Bay, 123
Choiseul, 210
Chomereau-Lamotte, Michele, 187
Christena ferry, 153
Christiansted, (main town), 80, 92
churches, 129, 202, 203
  Anglican, 101
  Baptist, 101
  Catholic, 98
  Methodist, 101
  Seventh Day Adventist, 102
Churches Street, 154
Church of the Immaculate, (Power of South Bend, Indiana), 161
Churchill, 52
Ciboneys, 176
Ciparis, Antoine, 203
Cipriani, (Captain), 51
Circus, The, 155
Citrine, Walter, (Sir), 49
Clay Ghaut Estate, 162
Coard, Bernard, 231
The Coconut Hill Hotel, 178
Codringtons, (a bajan plantation family), 36
Cole Bay Folk Group, 115
Cole Bay Hill, 107, 112
Cole Bay Theatre Company, 115
Colin's, (restaurant/rum shop), 239
Colonial legacy, 261
Columbier, 124, 126, 129, 130
Columbier Valley, 114
Colonialism, 52
Colonials, 167, 168
  'expatriate', 55
  habits, 40
  influence, 49
  political activites, 52
  period, (European Occupation), 29
Colonies, 73
color line, 50
Colored families, 50
Colored political class, 59
Colored women, 50

Columbus, Christopher, 27, 29, 40, 87, 90, 108, 116, 126, 136, 152, 167, 176, 183, 191, 199, 228, 245, 251
commercial capitalism, 48
commercial trade center, 36
  St. Thomas, 36
  Curaçao, 36
Concord, (hill), 116
Coney Island, 272
Congo or Kongo, 39
Conkies, 235
Coral-based island, 92
Cork Hill, (parish), 176
contemporary writers, 23
Conquistadores, 36, 40, 82, 127
Cooper Island, (BVI), 92
Copper Mine Point, 92
Coral World, 79
Corossal, (fishing village), 122, 124, 130
Cou-Cou, 235
Coup d'etat, 230
Courland, 245
Coulibistri, 193
Council On the Arts, 115
Courthouse, 109
Cove Bay, 239
Cradle of Tourism, 185
Craton, 42
Crawl, The , (beach), 92
Creole, 36, 39, 114, 125, 156, 161, 184, 185, 187, 193, 195, 208, 247, 260
  Communities, 35
  beke, 42, 50
  middle classes, 55
  blacks, 58
  whites, 58
  patois language, 40
Cromwell's Western Design War, 30
Cromwell's transported prisoner, 31
Crop-over, 60, 235, 238
Crown Colony System, 51
Crucian drink, 82
Cruz Bay, 82, 83
Cuba, 30, 60, 184
Cuban, 228
Cul de Sac, 112
culinary, 88, 114
culture, 238
cultural,
  creativity, 60
  pollution, 60
  Identity (St. Martin), 116
Cultural Center, 110
culturama, 238
Cupecoy, 112, 113
Curacao, 27, 35, 36, 60, 108, 109, 115, 136, 139, 261, 262, 263, 264, 265, 266, 267, 268, 269, 270, 271, 273, 274, 275, 276
Curacao Museum, 272
Curacao Plaza Hotel, 268
Curtin, Philip, 38
Cyril E. King, (airport runway), 77

D

Danes, 80, 92
Danish West Indies, 31, 60
Danish, 73, 82

S

T

A
B
C
E
F
G
H
I
J
a
b
c
d
e
f
g
h
i
k
l